BOUNDS OF BLACKNESS

A volume in the series

The United States in the World

Edited by Benjamin A. Coates, Emily Conroy-Krutz, Paul A. Kramer, and Judy Tzu-Chun Wu

Founding Series Editors: Mark Philip Bradley and Paul A. Kramer

A list of titles in this series is available at cornellpress.cornell.edu.

BOUNDS OF BLACKNESS

African Americans, Sudan, and the Politics of Solidarity

Christopher Tounsel

Cornell University Press
Ithaca and London

Publication of this book was made possible through the University of
Washington Department of History and the Howard and Frances Keller
Endowed Fund in History.

Copyright © 2024 by Cornell University

All rights reserved. Except for brief quotations in a review, this book, or
parts thereof, must not be reproduced in any form without permission in
writing from the publisher. For information, address Cornell University
Press, Sage House, 512 East State Street, Ithaca, New York 14850.
Visit our website at cornellpress.cornell.edu.

First published 2024 by Cornell University Press

Library of Congress Cataloging-in-Publication Data

Names: Tounsel, Christopher, 1987– author.
Title: Bounds of blackness : African Americans, Sudan, and the politics of
   solidarity / Christopher Tounsel.
Other titles: African Americans, Sudan, and the politics of solidarity
Description: Ithaca : Cornell University Press, 2024. | Series: The United
   States in the world | Includes bibliographical references and index.
Identifiers: LCCN 2023034300 (print) | LCCN 2023034301 (ebook) |
   ISBN 9781501775628 (hardcover) | ISBN 9781501775642 (epub) |
   ISBN 9781501775635 (pdf)
Subjects: LCSH: African Americans—Race identity. | African Americans—
   Relations with Africans. | African Americans—Relations with
   Muslims. | Sudan—Ethnic relations—History—20th century. |
   United States—Relations—Sudan. | Sudan—Relations—United
   States. | United States—Relations—South Sudan. | South Sudan—
   Relations—United States. | Sudan—Colonial influence. | South
   Sudan—Colonial influence.
Classification: LCC E185.625.T67 2024 (print) | LCC E185.625 (ebook) |
   DDC 327.730624—dc23/eng/20231010
LC record available at https://lccn.loc.gov/2023034300
LC ebook record available at https://lccn.loc.gov/2023034301

For Timeka and Cairo

Contents

Acknowledgments	ix
Introduction: The No-Man's-Land of the Blacks	1
1. Negro Canaan	19
2. Plain Imperialism	45
3. An Atmosphere of Good Relations	67
4. The Great Divergence	90
5. Call to Brotherhood	117
6. A Worthy Cause	143
Conclusion: Black Lives Matter in Sudan	171
Notes	183
Bibliography	217
Index	239

Acknowledgments

Timeka, you are the love of my life. Cairo, you are the best guy I know. Together, you make my life spunky, surreal, and altogether blessed. I can't believe how lucky I am to share life with you, and I commit this work to each of you.

The research for this book was made possible by general support that I have received over the course of my professional career at the University of Michigan, Macalester College, the Pennsylvania State University, and the University of Washington. A Career Enhancement Fellowship from the Woodrow Wilson National Fellowship Foundation (now Institute for Citizens & Scholars) provided me with several months of time to devote to research. Thank you, Robert Vinson, for serving as my mentor during that fellowship tenure—you took a chance on me and showered me with invaluable wisdom. Thank you, good sir.

I could not have conducted the archival research for this book without the generous patience and work of library and archival staffs in England (Durham University and Birmingham University), Italy (Father Prandina at the Comboni Mission in Rome), South Sudan (Youssef Onyalla at the South Sudan National Archive), and the United States (the Moorland-Spingarn Research Center, the Amistad Research Center, the Baker Library, the

Hoover Institution, the University of Washington Libraries' Special Collections, the Archives of Labor and Urban Affairs at Wayne State University, and the Presbyterian Historical Society).

Portions of chapter 1 appear in "'Negro Canaan': Cotton, Tuskegee, and the Anglo-Egyptian Sudan," *Journal of African American History* 105, no. 1 (Winter 2020): 28–55. Thank you, *JAAH* editors (particularly Pero Dagbovie).

The research for this book and its writing occurred amid some major professional changes. From navigating an assistant professorship to attaining tenure, changing institutions (and coasts), sojourning through the global pandemic, and living while Black in the age of Donald Trump, I could not have done it without support. Many thanks to my Penn State History and African Studies peeps, including but not limited to Alicia Decker, Michael Kulikowski, Richard Mbih, Crystal Sanders, Michelle Sikes, Ellen Stroud, and Kevin Thomas. Terrence Johnson and Derek Peterson, you will never know how much your mentorship has meant to me. I count it an honor to look up to you.

Many, many thanks to the folks at Cornell University Press for publishing this book and helping to make it the best it could be. This includes Sarah Grossman, the series editors, and the anonymous reviewers. Outside of the press, thank you, Bill Barnett, for your developmental editing.

While much of this book was conceptualized and written during my time in State College, Pennsylvania, it was completed after my family had moved across the country to the University of Washington (UW). I remain flabbergasted at the way that the UW Department of History has embraced me and welcomed me into their community. Thank you, Glennys Young, for your leadership; Lynn Thomas and Stephanie Smallwood, for your wisdom and mentorship; and everyone else in the department who have made me feel home. Outside of the history department, I extend many thanks to Danny Hoffman, Ralina Joseph, Maya Smith, Jim Wellman, and everyone in the UW African Studies Program. Thank you from the bottom of my heart.

Finally, as in all things, I thank my Lord and Savior Jesus Christ. You provided the vision, established the work of my hands, and led me up this mountain. Thank you, friend.

BOUNDS OF BLACKNESS

Introduction

The No-Man's-Land of the Blacks

On March 13, 1957, E. Frederic Morrow arrived in Khartoum, Sudan. The first African American to work in an executive capacity at the White House, Morrow arrived in that East African country as a member of Vice President Richard Nixon's delegation. In his diary entry for that date, he described the Sudanese as "a very reserved people" and noted, "[They] have enjoyed freedom for only a year . . . [and] are wearing it with dignity and a deep sense of responsibility." Beyond a brief description of the delegation's accommodations overlooking the Nile, pleasantries with local Sudanese chiefs, dinner with the Sudanese prime minister, and a travel snafu with their Tripoli-bound plane, Morrow's recordings of the Sudanese portion of his voyage are brief.[1]

Such was not the case, however, with his recollections of their stop in Ghana. "There has been much excitement in the Negro world over the birth of the new nation of Ghana," Morrow wrote on February 14, 1957. "Large private delegations are planning to go to [Prime Minister Kwame Nkrumah's] inauguration, and great pressures have been put on the White House and the State Department by prominent Negroes, asking to be named to the official delegation from the United States." Morrow put his hat in the ring, and—to his pleasant surprise—he was granted permission to travel with Nixon for the festivities. (Ghana was one of the eight countries on the vice president's African itinerary.)[2] Morrow provided a vivid description of his stop in Ghana. He noted the beautiful hotel built in Accra for the independence celebration, his experience meeting Nkrumah, the enormous stadium where a celebration was held, and the Duchess of Kent's grand entry replete with a Rolls-Royce, footmen, and outriders. In his diary entry for March 5, 1957, Morrow recorded his observations of the University College where a convocation ceremony was held and, on their departure from the college, a chance encounter with Dr. Martin Luther King Jr. and Coretta Scott King (made awkward by the fact that King had been trying to meet Nixon for several months). After visiting a village where a paramount chief danced to honor Nixon, Morrow accompanied the vice president to a reception hosted by the Speaker of the House (Parliament). That midnight, Ghana became free. "I could hear the thousands of cheering voices," Morrow wrote. "And it was a strange and stimulating feeling to lie there in the darkness and realize the significance of this moment in the history of man."[3]

Figure 0.1. E. Frederic Morrow, July 1955.
Source: US Government Printing Office.

Morrow's diary entry concerning Ghana stands in marked contrast to his accounting of Sudan. Sudan had officially augured decolonization in British sub-Saharan Africa when it became independent on January 1, 1956. Yet, writes the historian Patrick Manning, "Sudanese independence has gained little attention of the African diaspora, perhaps because it has been considered as an exception rather than the norm."[4] By contrast, the historian Kevin Gaines has noted that Ghana's 1957 independence gave momentum for freedom and self-determination for those of African descent around the world. Its independence, he further asserts, heralded the downfall of dominant racial and colonial systems established in the United States and Africa in the late nineteenth century.[5]

What racial, religious, and other historical factors might have attracted African Americans to one African nation in a way that did not manifest with another?[6] Mahmood Mamdani has noted that the trans-Atlantic slave trade racialized notions of Africa and fueled the conceptual tendency to envision the Sahara as the continent's dividing line, a "civilizational barrier," below which lay "Negro Africa," "true Africa," "real Africa."[7] Hegel's writings exemplified the emphasis on slavery's role in demarcating the separation, deeming "Africa proper" the land where slaves were captured, Northeast Africa as "the land of the Nile" (which he linked with Asia), and North Africa as "European Africa."[8] Under such delineation, the boundaries defining "true Africa" are historical and defined by the legacies of slavery and race. Writing in his 1939 *Black Folk, Then and Now*, the sociologist W. E. B. Du Bois noted that historians had generally isolated the Nile Valley from African history and that most denied any connection between the two. Du Bois countered this fallacy: "In what is known as the Anglo-Egyptian Sudan, we have pre-eminently a land of the black race from prehistoric times; and yet today . . . the Sudan is left as a sort of historical no man's land, and is regarded now as Arabian, now as Egyptian . . . and always as not worth careful investigation."[9]

The World Bank, the Office of the US Trade Representative, and the UN Human Rights Office of the High Commissioner do not list Sudan as North African, while news organizations CNN, the *Guardian*, and the Associated Press do. For those with the Hegelian propensity to detach North Africa from sub-Saharan Africa, lack of consensus regarding Sudan's regional positioning is complemented by Sudan's dual Arab and African heritage. In northern Sudan, incoming Arab traders intermarried with indigenous Sudanese to produce a genetically mixed African-Arab populace. Francis Deng has noted that the resulting racial traits mirror those of all African groups stretching across the continent from Somalia to Senegal. However, unlike most of those other countries (where people self-identify as African), Deng has suggested that northern Sudanese not only generally classify themselves as Arab; they vehemently deny African elements of their physical features. Most northern groups who claim genealogical Arab ancestry believe that, complemented by Islam, they are culturally and racially Arab. Farther south, African identity has racial and cultural connotations.[10] "Virtually all ethnic groups in the [Sudan] have their primary roots in the black African tribes," Deng writes. "Evidence of this fact is still visible in all the tribes, including those in the North who identify themselves as Arabs. Their identification with Arabism is, however, the result of a process in which races and religions were ranked, with Arabs and Muslims respected as free, superior, and a race of slave masters, while Negroes, blacks, and heathens were viewed as a legitimate target of slavery."[11]

While the history concerning the interplay of Sudan's African and Arab heritages is fascinating and relevant on its own, the way African Americans have approached the Sudan stands to shed light not only on African American engagements with Africa but with the Arab world as well. Given Sudan's mixed racial and cultural heritage, the following questions arise: What factors determined when African Americans framed Sudanese as Black, Arab, or both? How did racial solidarity and/or Pan-Africanism change as Africa transitioned from European imperialism to independence?

These questions are particularly important when considering the current Movement for Black Lives—the contemporary moniker for US-based resistance efforts against anti-Black racism that exploded in the 2010s. Anthropologist Krystal Strong has observed that Africa has been absent from the analysis and concerns of this movement. Strong contends that this absence exists even though Africa has similarly experienced an increase in popular resistance. "I make the case," she writes, "for more meaningful engagement with contemporary scholarship and struggles in Africa and other global contexts, in the interest of research and solidarity practices that have as their aim the full valuation of Black lives everywhere."[12] How have African Americans integrated Sudan and South Sudan into the Movement for Black Lives? How and/or why have those two countries been denied such integration? The answers to these questions are not only informed by the ways African Americans have historically engaged with the Nilotic Sudan. They also shed light on African American perceptions of themselves and others in the global African diaspora.

Beginning with the early twentieth century and continuing through Barack Obama's presidency, *Bounds of Blackness* explores the history of African American engagements with modern Sudan. Black Americans connected with modern Sudan through a series of literary, cultural, and diplomatic endeavors. In the process, they played a pivotal role in the construction of early independence in Sudan and South Sudan. Sudan also figured into African American conceptions of racial pride and consciousness through a sense of shared struggle. While ancient Sudan was central to the development of Afrocentrism, African American engagements with modern Sudan reveal that colonial Sudan and postcolonial Sudan are integral in the history of Pan-Africanism. (As defined by *AU Echo*, Pan-Africanism is "an ideology and movement that encouraged the solidarity of Africans worldwide, . . . [Pan-Africanism] asserts that the fates of all African peoples and countries are intertwined.")[13] But African American engagements with Sudanese ranged from supportive to antagonistic at different times.

The guiding question animating this book is how modern Sudan informed African American conceptions of Black self-definition, consciousness, and solidarity. This book frames Sudan as a signal example of how malleable transnational racial solidarity can be when sociopolitical changes occur in a single place over time. While Sudan was under England and Egypt's colonial yoke, African American newspapers often framed Sudanese as Black kin under race-based state oppression. However, after independence in 1956 and the outbreak of civil wars between the Arab-dominated northern government and Black rebels to the south, African Americans framed northern Sudanese Arabs as oppressors and southern Sudanese Blacks as oppressed. In the African American purview, Sudanese colonialism and independence presented racialized heroes and villains. This development is not only important for understanding the paradoxical relationship that African Americans have had with Sudan but also points to the capricious nature of racial solidarity and Pan-Africanism's relationship to Arabism.

If the early kingdom of Kush emerged in Nubia toward the end of the third millennium BCE, a revived Kushite kingdom reappeared several centuries later. Having conquered Egypt around 720 BCE, the Black Pharaohs established an Egyptian capital at Memphis. Henry Louis Gates Jr. has noted that African Americans have long been attracted to Nubia as the locus of power before the onset of transatlantic slavery. African American authors, particularly in the nineteenth century, looked to ancient Kush and Nubia as important to understanding their cultural predecessors. This ancient history of power gave context for those African American authors who claimed the right to possess civilization, culture, and learning (countering the narrative of slavery and humiliation).[14]

Thousands of years after the rule of the Black Pharaohs, the region formerly occupied by Nubia found itself under the weight of British imperialism. After the Anglo-Egyptians defeated the Islamic Mahdiya in 1898, Sudan entered the British empire as the Anglo-Egyptian Condominium. Bordered by Egypt to the north, the Congo to the west, Ethiopia to the east, and Uganda and Kenya in the south, the Condominium was a massive territory linking North Africa, the Horn of Africa, East Africa, and Central Africa. A diverse mix of predominantly culturally Arab and religiously Islamic populations inhabited the northern expanses of the region, while a host of Black African ethnic groups lived farther up the Nile in southern Sudan. With the locus of colonial power rooted in the northern Sudanese city of Khartoum, a sizeable socioeconomic chasm separated the North and the South. In 1956 the Condominium decolonized to become independent Sudan. In becoming sovereign, Sudan earned the distinction of becoming the first sub-Saharan nation to gain independence from Britain after World War II.[15] While African American attachments to Nubia have been traditionally strong, there is also a significant yet comparatively unknown history of Black American engagements with modern Sudan. As historian Patrick Manning has asserted, "Sudan must be seen as having an importance in the history of Africa and the Old World diaspora for the twentieth century that equals its importance since the days of Nubian kingdoms and Nilotic migrants."[16]

In the twentieth century, African Americans continued to show interest in the ancient Nile Valley. Some examples that are included in this study include the *Chicago Defender* invoking the ancient past when Sudan became independent, Langston Hughes including the aged Nile in "The Negro Speaks of Rivers," and a young Barack Obama's vision of pyramids and pharaohs when he learned about his father's Luo ancestry. Each demonstrated the persistent interest and relevance of the Nile Valley's ancient history for Black Americans during the colonial and postcolonial periods. Thus, rather than being a study that is focused on Black American engagements with modern Sudan in contrast to (or distinct from) ancient Nubia, I show that the afterlives of the ancient past percolate throughout the modern period in meaningful ways. African Americans did not approach Sudan through a zero-sum calculus, consistently choosing to either invoke the past or connect with the present. They did both at the same time, refusing to keep Africa and Africans in a noble past as contemporary developments beckoned. In doing so they showed that modern Sudan—and the continent more broadly—had (and has) immediate import for Black America and the greater African diaspora.

Several figures of varying renown figure prominently in this exploration, ranging from Booker T. Washington to Percival Prattis, Joel Augustus Rogers, Eslanda Robeson, Andrew Brimmer, Robert Kitchen, Malcolm X, Valerie McCaw, Elton Fax, Louis Farrakhan, Susan Page, and Susan Rice. During modern Sudan's complicated political history, such individuals interacted with the Sudan in varying capacities. Tuskegee Institute men participated in a colonial cotton cultivation project in Zeidab in the early twentieth century. Following World War II, editorials in Black newspapers opined on colonial Sudan's uncertain political future. As Sudan emerged onto the world stage as an independent nation, Black US foreign service members worked in the capital, Khartoum. At the turn of the twenty-first century, Nation of Islam minister Louis Farrakhan supported President Omar al-Bashir's controversial regime, and, when South Sudan became independent in 2011, an African American woman, Susan Page, became the first US ambassador to the new nation. Such individuals notwithstanding, African American organizations have also been important actors in Sudanese social, political, and diplomatic histories. These groups include the likes of the Tuskegee Institute, the Nation of Islam, the Congress of Racial Equality, the Congressional Black Caucus, and Delta Sigma Theta Sorority.

While Black Americans had a variety of experiences with and approaches to Sudan, the question of US power served as a unifying thread connecting the embroidery of African American engagements with the country and its people. How, one might ask, did Black Americans position themselves in the broader relationship between the world's most powerful nation and colonial Sudan, postcolonial Sudan, and postcolonial independent South Sudan? Often, African Americans like Andrew Brimmer and Susan Rice were official representatives of US power operating in the Sudan on official state business. In the case of Louis Farrakhan and the Nation of Islam, Black Americans used Sudan to critique US foreign policy. At all times, African Americans have been vocal about the US state's culpability in sponsoring, protecting, or otherwise supporting systemic racism. Within the context of these swirling dynamics, the reality of US power is inextricably linked to Black America's interactions with Sudan and—more generally—discussion of how the bounds of blackness are defined, distributed, and dismantled at home and abroad.

Within the ecosystem of Black internationalism and US power lives the aged colossus that is the Black press, neither mainstream nor marginal. I approach African American newspapers like the *Pittsburgh Courier*, *Chicago Defender*, and the *Final Call* as the richest sources to explore Black opinion on Sudan. Historian James H. Meriwether has noted that the Black press is possibly the most important source for understanding the gamut of African American views during the mid-twentieth century.[17] To this end, the significance of Black newspaper coverage concerning Sudan raises important questions. Why would the everyday African American reader be interested in Sudan in the first place? What guided the way Black periodicals framed Sudan at any given time? What makes certain African countries or stories marketable to African American audiences at any given point in time? *Bounds of Blackness* shows that African Americans branded Sudan in Black newspapers, other periodicals, and websites to provide a particular definition of what it meant to be Black in the diaspora and, with it, a broader story about Black struggle, pride, and consciousness. Whether stateside or abroad, in print or on the ground, during segregation or colonialism, African Americans on micro and macro levels have shown that their connections to Sudan extend beyond the ancient Nubian past and stretch into the eras of Jim Crow, African colonialism, African independence, and Black Lives Matter.

Given the recent attention given to the global auspices of the National Association for the Advancement of Colored People (NAACP), its relative absence in the first ninety years covered in this study is significant and deserves some explanation. Carol Anderson has explored that organization's role in liberating Africans and Asians as it fought American Jim Crow during the civil rights movement, while Jonathan Rosenberg has noted that its monthly publication, *The Crisis*, connected overseas developments and domestic reform.[18] While it is not my aim here to repudiate the NAACP's work or efficacy in the project of global Black liberation, *Bounds of Blackness* nevertheless shows that it did not play a significant role in the history of African American engagements with the Sudan until the turn of the twenty-first century, when the slaughter of Black Darfurians captured the world's attention. While *The Crisis* does not figure prominently in this book, other notable African American print publications do. These include newspapers like the *Chicago Defender* and the *Final Call*, magazines like *Jet*, and, more recently, the news and culture website *The Root*. In addition to such significant sources of circulating Black opinions and information concerning Sudan are those private and published memoirs written by African Americans who have traveled to Sudan since the early twentieth century. Published memoirs include those written by activist Eslanda Robeson, artist Elton C. Fax, journalist Keith Richburg, foreign service worker James Mack, and national security advisor Susan Rice.[19] Private papers are scattered across the United States and can be found at archives at Stanford University, Tulane University, Howard

University, and Harvard University. These sites contain the writings of such Sudan-associated African Americans as economist Andrew Brimmer, foreign service workers Robert W. Kitchen and Arthur McCaw, and radio host and abolitionist Joe Madison.[20] My aggregate use of these sources allows for analysis that should expand our knowledge of Black American engagements with Africa and especially those figures and organizations that have been marginalized in scholarship on the subject.

What are the bounds of blackness? Who is included and excluded? When are the bounds established, confirmed, or contested? With what consequences? Added to such whos, whats, and whens is this critical why: Why is Sudan of all places such a useful context to grapple with these questions? Sudan is the perfect place to pursue such questions because it so beautifully reflects the diversity of the Africana experience. Its geographic location—overlapping and wedged between North Africa, sub-Saharan Africa, the Horn of Africa, and the Saharan Desert—includes a kaleidoscopic array of ethnic groups and languages. It is both Arab and not, with debates about whether the country is included in Middle Eastern studies work on "the Arab world." It is an intersectional region, with Christian and Islamic histories dating back to the earliest centuries of those Abrahamic faiths but largely situated in different regions of the country. Like so many other countries in Africa and throughout the world, Sudan experienced slavery, emancipation, colonialism, postcolonialism, and the myriad joys and pains that have linked members of the Black world for generations, centuries, and millennia. Yet it is a particular place to examine the bounds of blackness because of the Nubian history and the modern state's geopolitics that have brought issues of race, religion, and culture to the fore in ways that have commanded the world's attention.

This book is informed by scholarly discussion concerning the meaning of blackness. Author Algernon Austin notes that racial categorization depends on several elements, including physical appearance, geography, ancestry, and racialized ideas of culture. The American system of racial categorization was historically assembled in response to social factors, and it continues to evolve. This categorization ignores physical appearance for many people because biology does not decide race. Austin, writes, "Whenever biology interfered with humans' desired organization of people into races, biology was readily discarded. Human beings make races, not biology."[21] Race is ultimately sociohistorical. Blackness is about definitions and significance, which change over time and space, and entails social practices and identities informed by those ideas. Over time, the implications of being Black, white, or brown have shifted dramatically and carried cultural, political, and religious import. The racial structures that shape and confine Black life change over time and place, and Black folk's understanding of who they are like and/or unlike also evolve.[22]

For African Americans, the international political landscape has played a significant role in race's sociohistorical narrative. African Americans' political position as a racially oppressed group marked their approach to foreign policy issues. Indeed, their tendency to perceive global happenings through a racial lens resulted from the domestic color line and their hatred for racial inequality.[23] For example, in his study *Mau Mau in Harlem?* Gerald Horne explores the relationship between the United States and Kenya in the context of the fight against white supremacy in both countries. British-controlled Kenya was mired in racial segregation, with separate schools, neighborhoods, and the like, as in the United States. Horne proposes the connection between those two struggles, driven partially by a similar "black-white" dynamic that distinguished it from other African conflicts happening at the time.[24] While Horne may have been focused more specifically on the US-Kenya relationship, Jonathan Rosenberg has explored why American race reform leaders were more generally enraptured by world affairs and how they integrated their understanding of international developments into their US-centered reform campaign. Movement leaders, Rosenberg contends, displayed great interest in global affairs and made their understanding of the world foundational to their message. Reformers were convinced that developments abroad could provide traction for the cause. "Although it has become a commonplace to observe that the United States has had a profound impact on the twentieth-century world," he argues, "it is worth remembering that throughout American history, the world has had a profound impact on America."[25]

Importantly for African Americans, questions concerning the bounds of blackness have extended beyond the shores of the Atlantic, percolating east of Africa and the Arab world into the Indian subcontinent. In the late nineteenth century, social reformers began to make analogies between injustices there and in Jim Crow America. Many historical actors compared struggles against American racism with movements against Indian caste oppression, effectively pairing US racism with British imperialism and all Indians with African Americans.[26] Horne has written primarily on the North American side of this equation in the period leading up to India's 1947 independence. Writing that "Negroes had been compelled to seek succor and allied globally,"

Horne echoes historian Nico Slate in contending that common opposition to racism and colonialism tended to bind Indians and Black Americans.[27] Yet this bond was not without its contradictions and limits. Slate notes that connections involved selective appropriation and at times utter misunderstanding and that many historical actors oversimplified or ignored the differences that distinguished the challenges facing South Asians and Black Americans. Furthermore, with increased African American enfranchisement, Horne states that Black Americans felt the need to distance themselves from an independent India that helped launch a Non-Aligned Movement that Washington perceived to be too cozy with the Soviets.[28] "Today," Horne writes, "the once bountiful bilateral tie has withered significantly."[29]

Further complicating this narrative of a prospective Indian–African American bond around the nexus of a shared fight against state-sponsored oppression is the manner in which they have related to one another. On this point Vijay Prashad, in his *Karma of Brown Folk*, offers a sobering critique. While acknowledging that the facts that desis (those claiming South Asian ancestry) are seen as nonwhite and don a spiritual veneer that is sometimes respected and other times undesirable, Prashad argues that when they come to America en masse "they sign a social contract with a racist polity by making a pledge to work hard but to retain a social life at some remove from U.S. society." Furthermore, he writes, the claim to a higher civilization and spirituality "allows the desis to be positioned in such a way that they are seen as superior to blacks, a social location not unattractive to a migrant in search of some accommodation in a racist polity. The tragedy of this social compact is that it perpetuates and reproduces antiblack racism."[30] Taken together, the relationship between Black Americans and Indians has been beautiful and imperfect, timely and ephemeral, mutually beneficial and, at its worst, counterproductive.

These dynamics not only provide a lens into the complex nature of subaltern solidarities but also serve as a fitting reference point to address the complexities of how the bounds of blackness factored into two other phenomena: Pan-Africanism and Afro-Arab solidarity. Black America's engagements with Sudan reveal much about African American conceptions of race, the sociohistorical nature of blackness, and the evolving nature of Black consciousness, activism, and politics. Collectively speaking, African American approaches to Sudan comprised a crucible and stage for the production and presentation of transnational blackness. Sudan has been a constituent part of Black America's global purview, and African Americans have also participated in shaping and implementing the US diplomatic relationship with

Sudan and South Sudan. Sudan's significance in the history of African American racial consciousness extends beyond the redemptive glory of ancient Nubia, stretching to the present day in hitherto unexplored ways. Notwithstanding ancient Sudan's importance in debunking racist stereotypes, the history covered here shows that Sudan fits into twentieth- and twenty-first-century Pan-Africanism in compelling ways. African American decisions to liken themselves to Sudanese or distinguish themselves from them is critical to understanding how they make sense of what makes people Black.

While *Bounds of Blackness* is primarily about how Black racial definition, meaning, and politics manifested in one diasporic relationship, the book's greatest intervention is to show the foundational role that Arabs played in this narrative. The Black-white dynamics of transatlantic slavery and European colonialism has resulted in Black diasporic solidarities that are birthed in narratives with Black oppressed and white oppressors. African American engagements with modern Sudan highlight the capacity for Black intellectuals to find, construct, and articulate racial solidarity in an oppressor-oppressed paradigm drawn along Arab-Black lines. Thus, this book is not only a microstudy of Black America's broader relationship with colonial and postcolonial Africa; it is also quite fundamentally about its connection with the Arab world. Taking those together, this book shows that it is impossible to understand the full spectrum of Black consciousness and politics in the African diaspora without an intimate engagement with the African world's affable, ambivalent, and antagonistic approaches to Arabs.

During Sudan's colonial era (1899–1956), African American newspapers framed Sudan as a Black land colonized by white (British) and Arab (Egyptian) overlords. With such framings came expressions of a racial solidarity based on shared experiences of slavery and dominance at the hands of racial Others. However, following independence and the new government's violent attempts to Arabize and Islamize the country, some African Americans articulated a north Sudanese Arab versus Black southern Sudanese binary. In this paradigm, the former solidarity expressed for the entire Sudan was now increasingly aimed at southern Sudan. Thus, Sudan provides one case in which African American solidarity with Africans came at the expense of amity with Arabs.

Yet there was an interesting twist to this equation. Some, like the Nation of Islam, supported the Arab-dominated Sudanese government by viewing it as a target of Israeli aggression. In this paradigm, some African Americans expressed support for Sudan through a racial and religious solidarity with Arabs in the larger context of the Arab-Israeli conflict. Immediately following World War II, most African American opinion leaders supported the Zionist movement and portrayed it as a model for African American self-help, African diasporic revitalization, and African independence. Over time, however, some African Americans who had supported Israel's creation began to link Zionism with colonial discourse. When the Arab-Israeli conflict reached a fever pitch in 1967, some Black radicals condemned Israel as a racist, imperialist Western proxy. Following the 1967 conflict, African American commentary displayed a pattern wherein some civil rights organizations defended Israel while groups like the Student Nonviolent Coordinating Committee condemned its position.[31]

Michael R. Fischbach's recent study on Black Power and Palestine explores the conflict's role in African American activism and its influence on the push for racial equity. Other works have investigated the civil rights movement's responses to the Israeli state, the Black Panthers in Algiers, and the Middle East's role in African American liberation politics from the Eisenhower to Nixon administrations.[32] The African American studies scholar Alex Lubin takes a longer historical approach in *Geographies of Liberation*, where he explores links between African American political thought and the Middle East in a study that goes back to the 1850s. Showing connections between the imaginings of African Americans, Arabs, and Israeli Jews, Lubin aims to extend the framework of the Black freedom struggle beyond the Atlantic world.[33] Thus, research on African American engagements with the Middle East and the Arab-Israeli conflict in particular allows for a more comprehensive understanding of African American politics, ideology, and global history.

While African Americans looked overseas, Arabs and other peoples in the Middle East looked outside of their region and worked to establish themselves as anti-colonialists and people of color with connections to Black liberation in America and Africa. For instance, the Palestinian National Liberation Movement—which called for the creation of a Palestinian state and a guerrilla war to free Palestine—expressed identification with Black American experiences and embraced Black power. However, Pan-African festivals held during the 1960–1980s brought the terms of Black-Arab solidarity to the fore in divergent ways. The First World Festival of Negro Arts (held in Dakar in 1966) celebrated Senegalese leader Leopold Senghor's idea of the unity of African and Black diasporic art and literature. However, this celebration of Black cultural achievement was paired with Arab exclusion: Senghor had established firm criteria for North African material: namely, a small number of works representing the art of North Africa's Black communities but *not* Berber or Arab art. The 1966 festival's exclusion of North Africa became a recurrent cause for critique.[34] Conversely, at the 1969 Pan-African Festival held in the North African city of Algiers, Algerian participants and officials recollected to Paraska Tolan-Szkilnik that, though Algerians may have been prejudiced against Black Africans before the festival, "they opened up and discovered their Africanness" at the event.[35] But the historian Andrew Apter notes that when Nigeria hosted the Second World Black and African Festival of Arts and Culture (FESTAC) in 1977, a divisive debate occurred over the meanings of Black cultural citizenship. Nigeria's great oil wealth motivated its inclusive vision of blackness, and Lt. General Olusegun Obasanjo maintained that North Africans should fully participate; conversely, Leopold Senghor maintained his position. "North Africa became the focus of these competing definitions of blackness," writes Apter, "[and] the struggle over North Africa in FESTAC 77 shows that the political stakes of black cultural citizenship were neither trivial or ephemeral."[36] In all these ways, non-Americans of color were reshaping the bounds of blackness as African Americans created solidarities with other people. However, the reality remains that Sudan—which joined the Arab League in 1956—has been largely absent in the field as it relates to Afro-Arab relations.

Sudan's proximity to the Arab-Israeli conflict and the Sudanese government's aims to fashion the country along Arab and Islamic lines make African American mentions of Israel and Zionism in discussions of Sudan significant. *Bounds of Blackness* shows that during the First Sudanese Civil War (1955–1972), some African Americans used anti-Israeli sentiment to express their support for the Sudanese government while others referenced Israeli assistance to southern anti-government rebels in expressions of support for them. During the late twentieth and early twenty-first centuries—when Sudan found itself in the throes of another civil war to the south and genocide west in Darfur—Louis Farrakhan and the Nation of Islam claimed that the Sudanese government was the target of an anti-Zionist plot. Thus, African American engagements with Sudan not only illustrate the tensions of Afro-Arab solidarity after decolonization but also point toward religion's capacity to strengthen or undermine racial solidarity. Taken together, Black American approaches to Sudan show how blackness operated as an imagined identity linked to evolving realities of oppression, liberation, and sociopolitical status. African American discursive framings of Sudanese as Black or Arab (or both) have changed in different moments for distinctive reasons with divergent results. In brief, the bounds of blackness have shifted over time and are continuing to shift. When African Americans proclaim "Black Lives Matter!", which lives are we invoking? Which lives are we ignoring?

Bounds of Blackness is divided into six chapters. In the early twentieth century, Booker T. Washington worked with businessman Leigh Hunt to send men with Tuskegee Institute ties to the Anglo-Egyptian Sudan. Using contemporary newspapers, the Booker T. Washington papers, and British and American archival materials, chapter 1 examines the Sudan project. The Hunt-Washington scheme is significant in the broader narrative of African American engagements with Sudan for several reasons. To begin, it was the first recorded instance of African Americans within Sudan's geographic boundaries, the first of what would be a train of several generations to do so over the next hundred years. The demographic composition of the men involved in the project—namely, their association with the historically Black Tuskegee Institute—augured the largely educated demographic of African Americans that visited the country in the decades to come. Conducted during the era of Jim Crow and its concomitant disenfranchisement, their work had an unmistakably elitist tenor. Two elements of this tendency can be found in the projects' albeit loose association with the US government (which became more pronounced in African American work in Sudan during the 1950s and 1960s) and the spirit of aid that undergirded the cotton scheme and persisted into the early twenty-first century. In these ways, the Washington-Hunt project established several elements that marked Black engagements with Sudan in the twentieth century.

Chapter 2 explores African American discourse concerning Sudan from the early 1920s until the eve of Sudanese independence (1956). More specifically, it is concerned with the ways that Black writers during this period voiced respect for and solidarity with Sudan. From interest in Sudanese ancient history to acknowledgment of Sudanese physical features similar to African Americans' own, Black Americans found the Sudanese foreign but unmistakably familial. Nowhere was this affinity more blatant than in the way that the Sudanese were described in relation to Egypt—that is, as Black people subject to potential mistreatment from a racial Other, Arabs. This expressed dichotomy delineating Arab rulers and Black subjects, Arab oppressor and Black oppressed, not only made the Sudanese more relatable in the eyes of African Americans subject themselves to state-supported racial hierarchies but also foreboded the language that African Americans would use about Sudan during that country's postcolonial civil wars, when Black, marginalized southern Sudanese waged war against northern Sudanese

Arab regimes. Thus, this period represents a discursive prologue to the rhetoric disseminated by Black writers in the latter twentieth century, language that portrayed Blacks and Arabs in an oppositional dichotomy, with blackness suffering under the weight of Arab oppression. Support for Black Sudanese went together with criticism of Egyptians specifically and/or Arabs more generally. Black racial solidarity, in this context, undermined affinity with one group of fellow nonwhites living under the auspices of white authority—namely, Egyptian Arabs under British rule.

Chapter 3 examines the work and experiences of African American foreign service workers in Sudan during the early years of independence. For both the United States and Sudan, the 1950s and 1960s were years of sweeping change. The United States was fraught with fears of nuclear holocaust, growing military action in Vietnam, and a nonviolent civil rights movement confronted by all manners of violence. Sudan was embroiled in its own quagmire: the young nation experienced a series of coups, found itself entangled in the Arab-Israeli conflict, and was nearly rent apart when southern Sudanese long confined to the margins of state power waged a long and bloody civil war against successive Khartoum-based regimes. Amid it all, African Americans like Andrew Brimmer, Valerie McCaw, and Madison Broadnax provided economic, agricultural, and cultural resources to Sudan during its early independence. The early independence years represented the most significant era of African American labor in the country since the Tuskegee project (which, coincidentally, occurred during the early colonial period). Never in the decades bookended by those two moments was the African American presence in Sudan so large. While the African American labor during the mid-twentieth century mirrored the Tuskegee project in its heavy representation of historically Black college graduates, it was distinct in the diversity of work involved and, importantly, the presence of African American women in Sudan. Finally, the diplomatic work examined in this chapter foreshadowed the work of other African American individual and organizational work later performed in Sudan under the auspices of the US government. Before considering the work of Barack Obama, Susan Rice, and Susan Page in northern and southern Sudan, one must first examine their diplomatic predecessors in the early independence period.

While chapter 3 explores the social, economic, and cultural work that African Americans performed in early independent Sudan, chapter 4 focuses on the ways African American coverage and opinion on Sudan shifted during the First Sudanese Civil War (1955–1972). Though Black newspapers had formerly framed Egypt as an Arab oppressor of Black people, writers now placed that moniker on northern Sudanese Arabs. While Black newspapers formerly voiced sympathy for colonized Sudan, amity was now increasingly directed toward southern Sudan. Thus, the early independence period witnessed the emergence of a discourse that placed Sudanese in a polarizing binary that not only classified Arabs and Blacks but also linked their oppressor-oppressed status along these racial lines. Yet this rhetoric was not adopted by all. Some writers critiqued Israel's involvement in the Sudan and, by doing so, added another layer to the issue of racial solidarity. The convergence of these issues and split opinions on Sudan portended divisive Black approaches to Sudan during the Second Sudanese Civil War.

Chapter 5 concerns Minister Louis Farrakhan and the Nation of Islam's impassioned, contrarian, and controversial support for the Sudanese government during the Second Sudanese Civil War (1983–2005). The NOI defended the Sudanese government and condemned anti-Arabism in the US mass media. As such, the Nation of Islam's approach to Sudan not only highlighted the continued salience of the Arab-Israeli conflict in Black engagements with Sudan. It also added a curious element to the role of race in this history. However, African American Christians during this time rallied behind southern Sudanese through shared Christian faith and experiences of slavery. Sudan became an ideological battlefield on which Black Muslim and Christian Americans marshaled competing racial and religious solidarities.

Chapter 6 explores how President Barack Obama's Black diplomats dealt with Sudan and the world's newest nation, South Sudan, founded in 2011. Obama was elected US senator in 2004 and then served two terms as president of the United States, and these years (2004–2017) corresponded with several major developments in Sudan: the genocide in Darfur, the end of the Second Sudanese Civil War, the achievement of South Sudanese independence, and civil war in the young nation. More than simply highlighting Obama's work with the new nation, this chapter positions two Black women—Susan Rice and Susan Page—as critical figures that shaped America's early relationship with independent South Sudan. As such, African Americans not only played an important role in establishing America's diplomatic relationship with postcolonial Sudan, but they also directed early US–South Sudan relations at the highest diplomatic level.

The conclusion reexamines the book's findings and arguments in the context of Black Lives Matter. What impact might historically Black colleges and universities have in African American relations with Africa moving forward? How might we consider the history, form, and implications of largely unexplored engagements that Black Americans have had with other African countries? How can the internet operate as an arena for Black Americans to engage the Sudanese (and others throughout the Africana world) in the spirit of Black consciousness and solidarity? The conclusion addresses these questions and offers some speculation on the future politics of transnational Black racial solidarity.

Chapter 1

Negro Canaan

During the early twentieth century, graduates of Alabama's historically Black Tuskegee Institute helped to introduce cotton culture in various parts of Africa. They advised colonial authorities in Togo, Nigeria, Morocco, and Sudan. Many Pan-Africanists, though largely critical of Booker T. Washington for appearing to acquiesce to African American subordination, shared his view that Black Americans could culturally and economically uplift Blacks in the Caribbean and Africa.[1] Washington worked with businessman Leigh S. J. Hunt to send several men with Tuskegee ties to the Anglo-Egyptian Sudan. Intended to be a multiyear cultivation project, the scheme was cut short for health reasons. (Most of the men returned to the United States due to illness concerns, and one died of malaria.) The project not only reveals assumptions and possibilities that can confirm, challenge, and expand understandings of the relationship Washington and Tuskegee had with Africa. It was also the earliest documented instance of Black Americans in Sudan.

This chapter examines the Sudan project. The scheme's planning and actualization brought several significant elements to the fore, including the terms and merits of African American emigration, Black America's role in Africa, and various class, racial, and gender politics.[2] Washington's eagerness to speak about the project's impact on Tuskegee's reputation while maintaining silence about the Sudanese people provides compelling framing with which to assess his interactions with the continent. The historian Louis Harlan noted that Washington's engagements included his special relationship with the South African government, his opposition to the Congo Free State of Belgium's King Leopold II, his role in the Liberian Commission, and his influence on African intellectuals. The African American studies scholar Michael O. West once referred to Washington as a Pan-Africanist; the Africana studies scholar Milfred Fierce noted that he was "possibly . . . the Black American individual with the most substantial record of active involvement, during this period, with Africa and Africans"; and the Nigerian historian Edward Erhagbe suggested that the Tuskegee leader operated "as one of the most important black diasporan contributors to Africa during his age."[3] Considering such assessments, Washington's silence concerning the Sudanese that his students were going to assist appears strange and invites interrogation of how he considered the importance of Tuskegee's work in Africa in relation to his views on Africans themselves. In brief, his interactions with Africa and Africans were incongruous.

Beyond the Sudan project's impact when assessing Booker T. Washington's Black internationalism, the experiment also warrants consideration within the broader contexts of Tuskegee's global operations, colonization and cotton in Africa, and the ways African Americans participated in colonial logics. In the same decade that Tuskegee's Sudan cotton scheme occurred, Washington—at the behest of the German government—invited nine Tuskegee staff, students, and graduates to develop cotton plantations in its West African colony Togoland. While the Germans wanted to secure an independent source of cotton to drive their expanding textile industry (and cease their dependence on imported American cotton), scholar Kendahl Radcliffe argues that the Tuskegeans—rather than merely serving German colonial interests—had a positive impact on the Togolese. "Tuskegeans strengthened the selling power of the Togolese by distribution of improved seeds, education in the latest agricultural and ginning techniques, and the establishment of the cotton school." Furthermore, Radcliffe contends, many Togolese gained access to new methods and understandings of how to better cope with and even benefit from Germany's presence.[4] Twenty years later and beyond Africa's shores, Americans provided technical assistance to Soviet irrigation and cotton-growing schemes in Uzbekistan (perpetuating Russia's colonial relationship with its Central Asian borderland region). In that instance Oliver Golden, himself a Tuskegee graduate, worked with a New York–based Soviet organization and recruited over a dozen Black American specialists.⁵ Golden desired "to have blacks participate in the Soviet experiment to construct a new society by helping modernize the lives of their 'colored brethren' in places such as the Soviet Socialist Republic of Uzbekistan."⁶

Against this wider backdrop, the Sudan project can shed light on Black participation in overseas colonial cotton work. African Americans—whether working under the auspices of Germans, Brits, Egyptians, or Soviets—were obviously willing to work alongside colonized populations for colonial benefits. While Tuskegee's Sudan project was arguably not as developed as the institution's activities in Togo and did not markedly shape the historical trajectory of American life, this story illustrates the reality that Black political interactions with Africa could be self-serving, with benefits being the primary reason Black Americans traveled to Africa. Unlike Golden's sense of racial kinship, neither Washington nor the Tuskegee men who traveled to the Anglo-Egyptian Sudan indicated that they saw the Sudanese as "racial brethren." Given the nature of the project's conclusion and Hunt's later assessments of Black Americans in his employ, the scheme's lasting benefits for Washington and Tuskegee were debatable.⁷

Finally, the Hunt-Washington scheme is important within the broader narrative of Black American engagements with Sudan because it marked the first recorded instance of African Americans within Sudan's geographic boundaries. Furthermore, the demographic composition of the men involved in the project—namely, their association with the historically Black Tuskegee Institute—augured the demographic of those African Americans that would visit the country in the decades to come. Conducted during Jim Crow and its concomitant disenfranchisements, their work had an elitist tenor. Two elements of this tendency can be found in the projects' loose association with the US government and the spirit of aid that undergirded the cotton scheme and persisted into the early twenty-first century. In these ways, the Washington-Hunt scheme established several elements that marked Black engagements with Sudan for the following century.

Leigh Hunt: The Man and His Plan

"Mr. Leigh Hunt is too well known a figure to our readers to need any further introduction," read the *Sudan Times* circa 1904. Employing racist language, the *Times* continued, "The Egyptian papers would have him as a giant who proposes an exodus of the American n[------] to their Canaan."⁸ Leigh Hunt was born in Indiana on August 11, 1855. In his young adulthood, Hunt traveled to Iowa and became a professor and president of the Ames Agricultural College (today's Iowa State University). During his time in Iowa he married Jennie Noble, with whom he eventually had two children. In 1886 Hunt moved to Seattle and became owner and editor of the city's first daily newspaper, the *Post-Intelligencer*. Although he became a successful entrepreneur, Hunt was hit hard during the Panic of 1893. Traveling to Korea, he established the Oriental Consolidated Mines Company and recouped his prodigious wealth. Without divesting all of his Korean mining interests, Hunt heeded his doctor's advice and traveled with his family to Egypt's "kinder climate" for health reasons. He arrived in Cairo in October 1902, and his holiday continued into 1903.[9]

While Hunt was in Egypt, the Sudanese government was encouraging private capital to develop lands along the Nile. In 1821 Muhammad Ali, the Ottoman Turkish viceroy of Egypt, sent his armies south into Sudan to conquer the region. He established a Turco-Egyptian administration in Sudan that remained in place for much of the nineteenth century. In 1881 Muhammad Ahmad, a Sudanese Islamic mystic and self-proclaimed Mahdi who would rid the country of Turco-Egyptian corruption, confronted the regime. The Mahdi's revolt spread, and in 1885 his troops defeated the Egyptian soldiers under British general Charles Gordon's command. Gordon was decapitated, and the Egyptians and British were expelled from the country. Although the Mahdi died unexpectedly, his successor the Khalifa ruled for thirteen years. The Mahdist state was beset with difficulties—two droughts in northern Sudan caused major crop losses, and each drought was succeeded by epidemics and famines. The British, who were eager to control the Nile waters, invaded with an Anglo-Egyptian army and met the Mahdists at a decisive battle at Omdurman in 1898. The battle, for the Mahdists, was catastrophic: they suffered eleven thousand dead and another sixteen thousand wounded while the British sustained fewer than two hundred fifty casualties. With the Mahdist state effectively finished, Sudan was subsequently ruled by Anglo-Egyptian administrators in a joint-rule Condominium.[10] While the Mahdist period occupies a brief chapter in the long train of Sudanese history, its impact was cataclysmic. As the former USAID administrator Andrew Natsios writes, "[The Mahdi] created an Islamic political movement rooted in a purist and puritanical interpretation of the Quran, one that sought to cleanse the country from foreign influence. This movement would make periodic reappearances through Sudanese history, with violent consequences for the Sudanese people."[11]

The ensuing Anglo-Egyptian Condominium forged in the ashes of the Mahdist regime was a dual form of colonial government. While Egyptians operated in low-level administrative and army posts, British officials wielded decision-making powers (an unsurprising dynamic, given Egypt's status as a British-occupied province and protectorate from the late nineteenth century until 1953). Sudan—the largest possession in British Africa—was run by a few hundred Brits relying on a plethora of Sudanese, Egyptian, and Syrian tax collectors, judges, and other intermediaries. Importantly, the Anglo-Egyptian colonial authorities officially abolished an economic enterprise that prospered under Mahdist rule—the slave trade. A commercial institution that dated back millennia, it was practiced along a north–south divide in the region (with slave raids occurring in southern Sudan and enslaved persons taken to Egypt and the Ottoman Empire). Slavery became an element of Islamic statecraft with the rise of the Sinnar and Darfur sultanates in the sixteenth and seventeenth centuries. Stateless non-Muslims on state peripheries—particularly in the Upper Blue Nile, Nuba Mountains, and Bahr al-Ghazal regions—were the most common source of enslaved peoples for Sinnar and Darfur. Enslaved persons were transported to places like Egypt and Arabia. During the Turco-Egyptian period and with the growth of the ivory trade, increased slave raiding occurred among Nilotic and equatorial peoples in the southern regions of the Upper Nile and Bahr al-Ghazal, as well as other locations in southern Darfur, the Ethiopian borderlands, and the Nuba Mountains. Some estimate that 20–30 percent of Sudanese were enslaved when the Mahdist state was destroyed in 1898.[12]

Two months before Hunt's arrival in Cairo, the US consul general there (John Lang) advised the assistant secretary of state that the Sudanese government was trying to develop the Condominium's agricultural resources. It was doing so, Lang continued, by encouraging capital and immigration. Hunt became aware of Lang's report, and once in Cairo hired a boat and set out to travel south. During the journey his guide spoke about the fact that the Upper Nile would become more valuable once the railroad linking the towns of Suakin and Berber was completed. Hunt began to plan a new enterprise, one that would employ African Americans while ensuring reliable labor for his hitherto nebulous plan to cultivate something in Sudan.[13]

In April 1903 Hunt wrote a letter to James S. Clarkson, whom President Theodore Roosevelt had appointed surveyor of customs for the port of New

York the previous year.¹⁴ Hunt, with paternalistic language, expressed the following:

> I can help at least a million negroes to happy [and] productive homes, and when once the South realizes that there is a safe and sure way for them to lose the black men who do all their work . . . they will conclude that the black man is not such a dangerous fellow after all . . . the poor negro is destined to be ground to atoms . . . unless something is done for him along new lines. . . . It must be done if done successfully along business lines. I think I have laid those lines.¹⁵

Hunt informed Clarkson that he was eager to discuss his plans with two individuals: Theodore Roosevelt and Booker T. Washington. The president invited Clarkson and Hunt to join him and the First Lady for a White House dinner on June 15.¹⁶ Roosevelt declared that Hunt's plan "would help mightily in solving the sad and serious problem of the negro and his present oppressed condition in the south." He listened to Hunt describe the land along the Nile and stated his hope that African Americans could go to "a country of health and richness and certain fortune if [they] desired to escape from their disenfranchised, segregated, and terrorized status in America." Hunt clarified his position, informing Roosevelt that his plan was not only humanitarian in nature "but also a great business and money-making enterprise." This pleased the president.¹⁷

Following the Civil War and amid the Reconstruction South's violence and destitution, many Black Americans supported emigration schemes with hopes of finding better prospects elsewhere. Some looked to Africa, most commonly Liberia. While figures ranging from the Americo-Liberian educator and diplomat Edward Wilmot Blyden to Frederick Douglass debated its merits, African Methodist Episcopal bishop Henry McNeal Turner was emigration's most vocal post-Reconstruction advocate. Turner and others believed that they could build a stronger Africa that would in turn demand the just treatment of Americans of African descent. With the rise of Jim Crow, the 1890s witnessed increased interest in emigration. Despite the reality of Black anti-imperialism, some African Americans believed that the race would benefit by operating as colonists in the Philippines. By 1903 the idea of Black settlement of the Philippines was so popular that President Roosevelt sent newspaper editor T. Thomas Fortune to explore the viability of mass Black emigration to the Philippines, Hawaii, and Puerto Rico. Roughly four hundred Black Americans settled on the islands during and after the Philippine-American War, and Fortune wound up supporting Black emigration to the Philippines.[18] On the other side of the world, the Gold Coast chief Alfred Sam established the Akim Trading Company in order to participate in trade, develop industry, and "encourage the emigration of the best Negro farmers and mechanics from the United States to different sections in West Africa." While the movement successfully transported Oklahoman emigrants to Africa in 1914, Black settlers who reached the Gold Coast faced difficulties with colonial officials, and many of them returned.[19] It is within the context of such contemporary Black American overseas settlement that exaggerated predictions of African American repatriation to Sudan occurred. Indeed, it was during this era when the Black press was occupied with talks of a similar plan in Hawaii and the Philippines that the Sudan scheme found its way onto its pages.[20]

However, the back-to-Africa movement had its detractors. The American Colonization Society (ACS), initially the Society for the Colonization of the Free People of Color of America, had been established in 1816 and was supported by southern whites who wanted to cement slavery by expelling free people of color from the country. Some others, however, attacked the society by arguing that colonization would remove the only people truly committed to abolition. Only twenty-five hundred African Americans settled in Africa in the forty years after the Civil War, a small number representing less than a quarter of those whom the ACS had taken to Liberia in the forty years before the war. Most African American leaders stayed committed to gaining full equality in the United States and sought to highlight progress that had been made since emancipation. Post–Civil War leaders like Booker T. Washington and W. E. B. Du Bois hoped that Black people would overcome racism over time through education and entrepreneurship.[21] None other than the venerable Frederick Douglass—described by historian James Campbell as emigration's most vocal critic—levied the following salvo in one of his final public speeches: "The native land of the American Negro is America. His bones, his muscles, his sinews, are all American. His ancestors for two hundred and seventy years have lived and labored and died, on American soil, and millions of his posterity have inherited Caucasian blood."[22]

In all these ways, conversation concerning Sudan as a potential repatriation site was part of a larger discourse concerning the benefits and pitfalls of US Black emigration. But would African Americans move en masse to Sudan? What impact, if any, would President Roosevelt's endorsement of Hunt's scheme have? Finally, would the new Anglo-Egyptian government even be amenable to the idea of Black American laborers entering the Condominium? Within this whirlwind of uncertainties, Leigh Hunt went to work.

The Politics of Post-Emancipation Labor

Having enlisted Roosevelt's support, Hunt sailed for France and planned how best to approach Evelyn Baring, the first Earl of Cromer (hereafter referred to as Cromer). Egypt's consul-general, Cromer had begun his career as an artillery officer in Corfu. He was later on the staff of Malta's governor and commander-in-chief and joined him when that officer directed the inquiry concerning Governor Eyre's suppression of agrarian unrest in Jamaica.[23]

The abolition of slavery in 1838 reduced the labor supply for Jamaica's sugar industry. Many formerly enslaved persons were unwilling to accept low plantation wages and opted instead to move to the interior and undertake small farming.[24] Thomas Holt has noted that during the late 1830s and into the 1840s the idea was pushed forward to recruit Black and white workers who would offer role models for freed Jamaicans. Released from plantation confines before new social values could take hold, freed people had apparently moved into the hills and "reverted to an African barbarism."[25] Longtime administrator Henry Taylor and his contemporaries understood the problem as "cultural regression," or the contemporary "Quashee syndrome" stereotype. According to this prejudiced paradigm, ex-slaves worked just enough to gratify immediate desires and were endowed with simple hopes that a tropical environment could satisfy. Despite the evidence, Holt continued, the "Quashee" legend arose that included elements of laziness, moral degeneration, and licentiousness. This stereotype coursed through special magistrates' reports in the 1850s.[26]

Sudan had a longer experience of slavery than its Caribbean counterpart. Sudanese slavery dated back to the Egyptian dynastic era and persisted into the early colonial period. During the Turco-Egyptian period, slave merchants of various nationalities became notorious, and many enslaved persons worked in several capacities for the regime. In the mid-nineteenth century, forty to sixty thousand people were sold in Khartoum each year. Although the trade was officially abolished in 1856, it continued until the regime's downfall. The Anglo-Egyptian conquest was made partially in the name of crushing slavery, and the 1899 Condominium Agreement abolished the slave trade once again. However, the British were hesitant to upset the country's economy and tended to ignore most of slavery's continued evidence.[27]

It is possible that Cromer's language concerning the labor situation in early twentieth-century Sudan was informed by his prior experience in Jamaica. In his "Report for the Sudan" in 1903, Cromer cited the heavy loss of life at the Battle of Omdurman and other conflicts. "Under these circumstances," he wrote, "it is certainly desirable to encourage immigration into the Soudan. In view of the large tracts of land, capable of cultivation, which are now uncultivated, there need be little fear that by the adoption of this course harm will be done to future generations of Soudanese." In his estimation, the most natural supply for more labor was Egypt, where some areas were apparently becoming congested. However, for Cromer, immigration's utility was not only linked with the diminished Sudanese labor force. There was also the question of "whether the inhabitants of the Soudan are able and willing to work," he said, a racist shot at Sudanese work ethic. While there was apparently a consensus belief among local officials that the Sudanese were not "industrious," Egyptians were by contrast "a singularly industrial race." In bigoted language that evoked sentiments concerning labor in post-emancipation Jamaica, Cromer provided the following description:

> It can be no matter for surprise that the Soudanese should be unwilling to work. Their wants are few and simple. They scarcely need any clothing. . . . Education has not yet stimulated them in any desire to improve their positions in life. . . . The slaves, for the most part, consider that the best use they can make of their newly-acquired liberty is to labour as little as possible. The lesson . . . that a man must work or starve, has not yet been brought home to the mass of the inhabitants of the Soudan.

Rather than expressing discouragement, Cromer followed, "Somewhat similar conditions existed at one time in the West Indies. It is some forty years since I was in Jamaica. . . . I used to be told that, even in the most difficult times, planters who paid fair wages and treated their men well could generally obtain labor without much difficulty." Cromer assessed that the situation in Sudan was quite similar.[28]

It was to this man that Hunt drafted a letter on his plan to send African Americans to Sudan. "In doing so," Hunt wrote, "I would . . . be promoting the best interests of our investment. I am confident the Sudan would become a place of refuge for the American negro." Hunt was keen on not having Cromer believe that he supported the removal of any African Americans from the United States; instead, enough could be moved "to serve our purpose of teaching the Sudanese how to raise cotton." Still, Hunt offered that once it was proven that Black Americans could prosper in Sudan they would have "what they [did] not . . . possess—a country to which they [could] safely migrate."[29] Aside from whatever Cromer may have thought about Hunt's designs regarding Black Americans, this much was sure: England's cotton industry was in bad shape, a reality largely rooted in its overreliance on expensive American raw cotton. America's cotton vanished from markets during the Civil War. For cotton industrialists and European statesmen, this cemented the danger of depending on the States for raw cotton. British, French, and Russian manufacturers after 1861 began to pressure their governments to get more cotton from their colonial possessions in India, North Africa, and Central Asia. In the early twentieth century, they undertook a renewed effort to grow more colonial cotton. British cotton manufacturers founded the British Cotton Growing Association in 1902, and it was this group that eventually hired Tuskegee graduates to support a cotton-growing enterprise in Sudan.[30]

Hunt and Cromer met on October 12, 1903. Cromer shared admiration for Hunt's plan and was confident, in part, in his awareness that Hunt was ready to spend thousands of dollars on an exploratory trip to the area. Cromer indicated that Hunt's investigations should be supported and that, once he had decided what he wanted, Hunt should see Sudan's governor-general, Reginald Wingate. Wingate would then negotiate with Hunt. Cromer conveyed interest in the African American element of the scheme but cautioned that the right workers would have to be selected.[31] In the same annual report in which he vilified Sudanese labor, Cromer referenced Hunt's scheme to employ Black Americans. "It is quite impossible to say beforehand how a bold experiment of this sort should answer. I see, however, no reason why it should not be tried on a small scale."[32]

Hunt's boat departed Cairo on October 29. He traveled up the Nile, going as far as southern Sudan. On his return he discussed the possibilities of cotton growing with the governor-general. In the end, both Wingate and Cromer were apparently impressed by Hunt.[33] Hunt wrote a letter from the Blue Nile on November 20 and conveyed sentiments that not only mirrored the annual report but also typified the racist hauteur of imperialism. "Believing that any and all races of men will work if properly handled and directed, I am convinced that the few surviving natives of the Soudan will in time become as good workers as they were once good fighters," he said. "When they are taught a broader and better use of money, when they are taught by example that industry pays, and when they begin to appreciate fair treatment and security of life and property, you will see a marvelous change in the lives of these shiftless, simple, lazy people." In a comment that evoked Cromer's earlier position that the right type of worker would have to be selected for the plan, Hunt made it clear that his supposed altruism was only aimed at certain African Americans: "No amount of argument could convince me that industrious, hard-working negroes would be averse to improving their condition . . . the political negro, the crap-player and the cake-walker are not the individuals I seek to influence. They naturally would remain where they are."[34]

To find "industrious, hard-working negroes," Hunt looked to Booker T. Washington and the Tuskegee Institute.

Enlisting Washington

In 1881 Booker T. Washington founded Alabama's Tuskegee Institute. Within twenty years' time, the institute boasted an all-Black faculty and staff of three hundred and had approximately fifteen hundred students. Dancing, drinking, smoking, gambling, and unregulated dating were prohibited, and Washington deemed virtues like individual responsibility, self-discipline,

Figure 1.1. Portrait of Booker T. Washington by photographer Frances Benjamin Johnston (ca. 1896).

Source: US Library of Congress Prints and Photographs division.

and cleanliness more significant than academic erudition. In the wake of the European powers' late nineteenth-century partition of Africa and the rise of the Pan-African movement, Africa's role in the Black American imagination grew. Washington involved himself in African affairs in several ways. In addition to corresponding with several Africans, he enrolled Africans at Tuskegee and supported the development of industrial education on the continent. Washington was also involved with the 1893 Chicago Congress on Africa and helped the first Pan-African Congress come to fruition in London in 1900. That year a Tuskegee faculty member and three institute graduates arrived in Germany's West African colony of Togo to work for a private German concern. The goal was to increase agricultural productivity using Tuskegee's methods.[35]

Washington believed that freedom rested on economic power. In this paradigm, people of African descent had to become part of the global capitalist economy while keeping their capacity to provide for themselves if they were to remain free. Historian Angela Zimmerman has noted that the collaboration between Tuskegee and Germany's government in Togo reflected both an emancipatory attempt to improve Black conditions on both sides of the Atlantic and an opposite effort to establish Black cotton farming in Africa that would financially benefit white economic elites in America and Europe. In the end, the German administration was led to away from the project due to the tension between their reliance on Black knowledge and their need to see people of African descent as inferior.[36]

When Hunt and Clarkson returned from Washington to New York, Clarkson, a friend of both Hunt and Washington, arranged a meeting between the two. When they met over dinner, Hunt informed Washington that he wanted skilled workers and was contemplating Tuskegee graduates for employment.[37] In a January 19, 1904, letter to Hunt, Washington expressed his opposition to Black colonization in Africa (or anywhere else). But he noted, "The opportunities which you suggest the Sudan offers are opportunities which, it seems to me, large numbers of our Negro people should take advantage of."[38]

The Media Catches Wind

While Hunt was in Khartoum, he received a letter and newspaper clippings from George Roberts, director of the US Mint. A September 27, 1903, article from the *Seattle Times* reported: "[Hunt and Washington have joined] in a colonization undertaking which promises to go a long way towards solving the negro question in this country." The paper said that Washington had informed Hunt that thousands of southern Black families "would gladly embrace the chance of going to the Sudan and making new homes." The article ended by noting that President Roosevelt, upon hearing of Hunt's plans, had become excited and pledged any help he could provide.[39] This was just one example of the newspaper coverage that the enterprise received. During the fall of 1903, several American newspapers published articles on the venture. Under the headline "American Negroes Will Remove to Africa," the African American *Trenton Evening Times* reproduced a Publishers Press wire out of Tacoma that claimed that Hunt and Washington were banding together in "wholesale colonization." The project, it said, involved "reclamation of several hundred thousand acres tributary to the river Nile in the Soudan and the cultivation of the land by negroes who are to be taken from the United States."[40] The *Worcester (MA) Daily Spy* of October 3, 1903, posited that Washington would become increasingly important on the global stage, noting that it had emerged from Paris that he would provide Hunt with educated Black men from Tuskegee to introduce skilled agricultural methods to the Sudanese. "If an experiment like this succeeds in the Sudan," the *Spy* continued, "the educated American negro may yet become the teacher of the black race of the earth, leading them back into the civilization that they possessed thousands of years ago, [putting] into their hands the power to create better lives."[41] On November 29, 1903, Hunt replied to Roberts and stated that, while he didn't mind the attention, he had issue with Roosevelt's and Washington's names being "inexcusably dragged into [a] newspaper scheme for the wholesale deportation of the American Negro." He continued, "I am here in the Sudan for selfish purposes, not as a philanthropist. It is true that I am interested in the negro, but for business and not charitable reasons."[42]

Newspaper coverage of the Sudan scheme dovetailed with another issue of the day: emigration. "There is always something in the race question," stated a writer in Topeka's African American *Plaindealer*. "If it is not in the troublesome lynching, burning and flaying so vigorously advocated . . . it leads to the other extreme of emigration." They stated that it was not their purpose discuss in detail the virtues or dangers of African emigration; rather, they aimed to present excerpts from one of Hunt's letters that had recently been published in the *St. Louis Globe-Democrat*.[43] The letter was his November 20, 1903, correspondence to Roberts. In it, Hunt embarked on a grandiose explanation of the project's potential impact and placed it in relation to other noteworthy emigrations:

> If I can demonstrate that the industrious negro's improvement is assured by moving to the Sudan, no amount of preaching, teaching and voting could stop the endless stream of immigration that would follow. The influence of the first settlement, if successful, would supply sufficient power, to set the natural law which controls the destiny of man in motion. . . . Just as the little band of Germans that settled in Germantown, Pa., is responsible for the German population of America, just as the story of John Ericsson's success drifted over . . . to influence and affect the Scandinavians, just as the tale of Tim Hooley's good fortune on the banks of the Delaware served as a beacon light to his needy and anxious friends on the Emerald Isle, so would the results of the first American community in the Sudan either brand me as an "irridescent [sic] dreamer" or give to our needy colored countrymen a new star of hope.[44]

Hunt's comparison of African American migration to Sudan with European migrations to the United States reads as duplicitous. On one hand there is the sense of national othering: African Americans—citizens of the United States—are positioned in their migratory actions with foreigners (Germans, Irish, and Scandinavians) rather than with, for example, white Americans who migrated to Oklahoma, California, and elsewhere in the West. On the other hand, Hunt's use of the phrase "our needy colored countrymen" suggests a sense of solidarity or co-citizenship with African Americans despite the racial difference. Finally, his reference to historical migrations rather than to European immigration to America occurring at the time makes one wonder whether he held them in different esteem. What is clear, however, is that Hunt believed in the long-term value that the project could have for both Sudan and Black America, a significance that rivaled other historical exoduses.

The daily Portland *Oregonian*, which also published Hunt's aforementioned letter, noted that Hunt's plan had been described as a general emigration scheme. Many emigration plans "of an impracticable character" had been presented—leading to an assumption that every Black emigration idea was similarly impracticable. But Hunt's proposal, the *Oregonian* said, "ought not to be confused with the philanthropic dreams that have had for their purpose the solving of the race problem in the United States." On the contrary: "His is a cold business proposition."[45] A number of factors may explain the *Oregonian*'s skeptical if not critical assessment of Hunt's intentions. Hunt had proven to be a successful businessman in America and Korea, and the idea that his focus on Sudan was principally driven by a desire to help Black

Americans rather than the goal of acquiring more wealth may have been silly to some. With what African American causes had he previously shown an interest, and to what meaningful effect? Was he generally interested in the work of Tuskegee, or did he simply view it as a ready-made source of agriculturalists who could help him become even wealthier with the fruits of Sudanese cotton cultivation?

The *Montgomery (AL) Advertiser* published a dispatch from Paris reporting that Washington had been "besieged" by reporters there who wanted his views on "the negro question." Washington, the *Advertiser* claimed, refuted the report that he was in Europe for the purpose of an African American emigration scheme. While he acknowledged that he had talked with Hunt about helping him with some Tuskegee men, Washington offered that based on his observations abroad he believed that "the best place for the negro" was the United States. "My belief," he said, "is based on the fact that he has there better industrial opportunities and is better off than people in the same walk of life in Europe."[46] His views on emigration notwithstanding, wild estimates circulated on the number of African Americans that would be purportedly involved in the Sudan project. The Juneau, Alaska, *Daily Record-Miner* conjectured that Washington would probably meet with Hunt in Egypt and there "perfect the plans for the colonization of the hundreds and thousands of negroes in Africa," while the *Cleveland Gazette* reported that Hunt "hoped to secure 700,000 Afro-American families for settlement in the Soudan."[47]

Such exorbitant, unfounded estimates not only spoke to the power of rumor but may have also shed light on the contemporary state of American race relations. Black American desires to move out of the South increased following the conclusion of Reconstruction (when Black people were the target of vigilante violence). African Americans lost voting rights in places where their numbers threatened white control, and the day after President Hayes withdrew federal troops from South Carolina, a Black lawyer named John Mardenborough wrote to the American Colonization Society begging the organization to send a group of seventy-five Black residents from South Carolina to Liberia. The historian Kenneth C. Barnes writes that during the late nineteenth century the back-to-Africa movement shifted from being a white man's institution to a Black grassroots movement. Barnes argues that Arkansas's African emigration movement shows not only the harsh realities for Black southerners but also their hopes for a better life. "Interest in African emigration peaked among black southerners in the 1890s," Barnes writes. "White racism reached its zenith. The [decade] saw the greatest number of lynchings in American history. As it became increasingly clear that black Americans would not get a seat at the table, Liberia posed an alternative to integration, an escape to an all-black world."[48] While the prospect of life in Sudan never possessed the potency that Liberia did among African Americans, speculation as to the number of Blacks interested in moving to Sudan—particularly in the Black *Cleveland Gazette*—could be read as encouraging the idea of Africa as an escape and "refuge from white oppression."[49]

On November 8, 1903, the *Sunday Leader* of Port Townshend, Washington, republished an account from *Collier's Weekly* concerning Hunt. "Here [Sudan], if reports be true, negro colonization in Africa takes practical shape, for the first time, with the backing of considerable capital. It has been much written and talked about. It has received the support of black as well as of white leaders of thought." Using language infused with racist stereotypes, the article noted that President Roosevelt was aware of and supported the plan and that Washington had pledged "all the field hands" Hunt desired. "There is no cotton picker like [the African American man]. But he has never been successful or happy when transplanted in large numbers, as the West Indian blacks have." To support this contention, the writer pointed to Liberia as a failed experiment in US colonization of Africa. Many of the descendants of the pioneering colonists had "unquestionably returned to the ways of savagery," the writer asserted. "The others are not the equals of their kinsmen in America."[50]

Thus, by the middle of 1904, various newspapers ensured that Leigh Hunt and his plan to send Black laborers to Sudan received a considerable amount of attention. There were wild estimates about the scope of the project and comments from Hunt about the project's potential that bordered on the absurd. Several significant questions remained unanswered. How many would actually answer the call? When would they go, and for how long? Would these workers be "successful or happy," paving the way for future streams of emigrants to travel to their "Canaan," or would the venture end in failure?

The Project Begins

Hunt developed a mixed farming operation with some cotton growing. To further develop the project, he traveled to London and formed the Sudan Experimental Plantations Syndicate in 1904. Also that year, the ambitious businessman who had reached out to Booker T. Washington for assistance set foot on Tuskegee's campus. Hunt leased a private Pullman car and traveled there with George Roberts, Roberts's wife, and another family. The group arrived in Tuskegee on May 24, two days before the institute's commencement. Washington greeted Hunt and informed him that several graduates had expressed interest in working with him in Sudan. Washington explained that he and the institute's executive council would meticulously screen these applicants and share their findings with Hunt.[51] The African American *Freeman* (Indianapolis) reported on the commencement exercises and noted that among those present was "a special party of capitalists and promoters, including Mr. Leigh Hunt, the developer of the Soudan . . . Mr. George E. Roberts, director of the United States Mint and Mrs. Roberts, Mr. Grosvenor Clarkson, son of Gen. James S. Clarkson, also Major Charles R. Douglass, son of the lamented Frederick Douglass."[52]

On June 6, the *Grey River Argus* in New Zealand published an article titled "Cotton Growing in Sudan." It reported the Reuters finding that "as a result of an important agreement which has just been signed at Cairo, between the Sudan Government and Mr Leigh Hunt . . . work has been commenced which is expected to have great influence on the development of the Sudan and on the cotton industry of the world." Hunt, the report continued, had purchased a large tract of territory located at the mouth of the Atbara River, opposite Berber Province's capital and was situated on the new railroad route intended to connect Berber and Suakin.[53] Hunt was given the only large concession on the Nile: ten thousand feddans (one feddan is slightly more than one acre: forty-two hundred square meters) at Zeidab, roughly 150 miles north of Khartoum.[54] The *Argus* continued that various preparations for construction were being made and that work had already commenced. Though Hunt already had sufficient labor for the project's immediate needs, the paper did not neglect to inform its readers, "His staff will be reinforced by expert negro planters later in the season."[55]

On June 11, the *Freeman* reported, "The [authorities] of the Tuskegee Normal and Industrial Institute have been empowered by Mr. Leigh Hunt to select a committee of three colored people to go to the Soudan . . . for the purpose of making an examination as to the conditions existing in that country and report on their return."[56] In truth, however, the three men had already been chosen. Washington had written to Hunt earlier in the month that the Executive Council had reviewed the list of interested men and agreed on Cain Triplett, Poindexter Smith, and John P. Powell. "We give their selection our heartiest endorsement. I have also talked to the men and find them in entire sympathy with your proposition."[57] Cain Washington

Triplett was a carpenter from Mashulaville, Mississippi; Poindexter Smith was a blacksmith who hailed from Winona, West Virginia; and John Perry Powell of Blakely, Georgia, was an agriculturist. Hunt offered to pay each of them $50 a month in the first year, $62.50 for the second, and $75 for the third year.[58] Washington offered his parting advice to the Sudan-bound students on December 12—advice that Louis Harlan characterized as being "amusingly similar to what one would expect from a Victorian parent, a warning against 'going native.'"[59] "A great many persons going to a warm climate," Washington wrote, "go to ruin from a moral standpoint. I hope you will keep this in mind and remember that if you yield to the temptation and lower [yourselves] in your moral character, you will do yourself, the school and the race the greatest injustice; but I feel sure you are going to stand up and be men."[60]

Washington's comments provide insight into his thinking about Africa, colonialism, and gender. To begin, his framing of Sudan as a place that could tempt the men to sacrifice their morality speaks both to his understanding of their refinement and, conversely, the comparative baseness of the people they were about to encounter. History scholar Tunde Adeleke has argued that African Americans had visions of Africa and Africans that were intrinsically saturated with Euro-American stereotypes and appropriated many of the same sentiments of social, political, and religious superiority over Africans.[61] Elsewhere in the imperial fold the British, French, and Dutch defined their civilities through understandings of sexual virtue and racial purity. Power was maintained through sexual prohibitions delineating the rulers from the ruled, the elite from the lower class, and those seen as racially virile ("white" and/or "European") from the racially weak.[62] These realities bring Washington's warnings into greater relief. From his perspective, the Sudan project was about much more than cotton; it was an opportunity for Black American men of a certain class to display their cultural and masculine superiority. Facing racism on the home front, they too could prove themselves as colonial masters. The Sudanese cotton field, therefore, would be a proving ground.

Triplett, Smith, and Powell arrived in Zeidab on January 14, 1905. Triplett wrote Washington the following day and expressed that they were pleased with a day's observation and were confident that success would come if they were careful and worked patiently. He began to teach carpentry to Sudanese youth, Smith taught them how to forge iron, and Powell showed them how to plant wheat and other crops. In addition to such labor, the Tuskegee men showed the youth how to swim and play tug-of-war (among other games) during the daily midday break. They also organized foot races and other games on Muslim holidays.[63] Powell also wrote to Washington and informed him that when he arrived he had been put in charge of a garden that covered roughly two acres. After two months of this work, he continued, he had been transferred to lead the company's farm. Leading an average crew of thirty men and boys each day, his main work there was harvesting the crop. "As there was no one here for me to converse with in English, I soon learned to speak Arabic well enough so as to transact any business with the natives."[64]

On February 3 Hunt wrote an enthusiastic letter to Washington, praising the work that the Americans had done to that point. "Your boys arrived in good health and good cheer and have taken hold in a manner which augurs well for their future," he noted. Hunt continued that if their start reflected their true character, "I congratulate you upon the kind of men Tuskegee sends out into the world. . . . I am delighted with these boys and therefore very hopeful that my experiment in blazing the way to this land of promise is going to prove beneficial to at least some of your race." Hunt also shared that the Tuskegee men had recommended L. N. Spurlock and Ocie R. Burns for the project. "I should like to have [them] come to us if they will accept the same terms as you gave me for Triplett, Smith & Powell providing you are willing to let them come. If they decide to come send them along without delay."[65] Lewis Nathaniel Spurlock and Ocie Romeo Burns were each Tuskegee-educated. Washington informed Hunt that Burns and a candidate of his own could soon join the Sudan Syndicate. In the spring of 1905, Burns and drilling expert J. Brown Twitty sailed for Africa. Twitty, who hailed from Lenexa, Kansas, was a member of Tuskegee's 1904–1905 senior class.[66]

That May, Washington sent the Tuskegee representatives—Burns, Twitty, Triplett, Smith, and Powell—a copy of the *Tuskegee Student* that included a report on their Sudan experience.[67] "I am writing this letter . . . to let you know that during Commencement season we are thinking of you, and to let you know how very much we are looking forward to your efforts in that far away land." Washington continued that Hunt thought well of their abilities and had written him, as the enclosed issue of the *Student* showed. "I wish to impress . . . that it is incumbent upon you for the sake of the institution as well as for yourselves, that you put forth every effort to make the experiment a success, if it fails it not only carries you down, but us as well, and I wish you to justify the high faith which Mr. Hunt has."[68]

On May 20, 1905, the *Freeman* published an article titled "Field for Educated Negroes: The Success of Four Tuskegee Graduates." It included Hunt's recent interview with a reporter from the *New York World*. He expressed his reluctance to talk about his bringing Black Americans to the Sudan and acknowledged the difficulty in addressing the merits of emigration as "a solution to our Negro problem." He did, however, opine, "Given favorable conditions the educated Negro can establish a home for himself in a foreign land and prosper there. Two important desiderata in such a move are congenial climate and the absence of competition with white men, especially where racial prejudice is operative." When it came time to find men to work as his plantation overseers, Hunt shared that he had asked Washington to send four Blacks who were Tuskegee-educated. "I can say that thus far there has been no cause for disappointment in the experiment. . . . They have got along well with the Soudanese laborers and the influence of the Americans on the natives has been the best." Noting that the Tuskegee men had sent for some of their colleagues (who had joined them) and that others were arranging to make the trip, Hunt stated, "All these are educated Negroes, there are no places for the others. . . . It is easy for an educated Negro who understands agriculture to make a home for himself there [Sudan], and if he is industrious to prosper."⁶⁹

One point from the interview demands particular attention: why did Hunt share with the reporter that he did not want to be seen as suggesting emigration? The answer can be found in the exchange he had had with President Roosevelt at the White House. After Roosevelt expressed his hope that US Blacks could travel to another country if they wanted to escape their status in America, Hunt responded that the scheme was both humanitarian and business-centered. The president was apparently pleased, noting that earlier philanthropic plans had failed and that each Black man in Hunt's project would be "paying for what he received and therefore be stimulated to business habits and the thrift of saving and management."⁷⁰ Thus, in seeking to distance himself from the idea that he was engaged in an emigration project, Hunt probably knew that it was politically expedient for him to broadcast a position he knew Roosevelt would support. It is also possible that Hunt, beyond wanting to stay in the president's good graces, actually agreed with Roosevelt—that African Americans should work out their salvation by the sweat of their own brows without philanthropic graces. Only a generation removed from chattel slavery, African Americans who had been so long and so violently disenfranchised should apparently be "stimulated to business habits" on their own, without the hint of assistance. It is no wonder that Booker T. Washington, the great evangelist of the gospel that Blacks should lift themselves with their own bootstraps, found a suitable partner in capitalist extraordinaire Hunt.

Despite his initial enthusiasm, all was not well when Hunt returned to Zeidab in November 1905. While the Tuskegee men were working well with the Sudanese, the project was a mess; locusts and white ants were damaging crops, and no cotton plant was planted by the end of the year. Frank Conkey, the only other white American at the site, was stricken with malaria and died. Hunt was also hit with malaria, and in 1906 each of the Tuskegee men found themselves afflicted. With mostly Egyptian labor, the Syndicate had begun to grow cotton and wheat by 1906. That year it installed its first pump at Zeidab for the purpose of cultivating cotton. Large expenses were contrasted with small yields, and Hunt was regularly absent, attending his interests elsewhere. Due to the company's financial position, Hunt's annual salary of £3,000 as managing director had to be halted in December 1906. By 1907, eight hundred feddans of wheat and cotton (each) were being irrigated.[71]

In March 1907, John Powell wrote to Washington and spoke about his work to extend the "canalization" of the plantation, his supervision of seven hundred men, and the Tuskegee alums' contributions (including the school they had provided).[72] Writing that he had taken up his own farm, Powell continued, "I think I have made a very fair crop & will make some money. It was judged that my crop was the best grown at the Syndicate." Due to the fact that their water supply was late arriving, Powell continued, they had not grown much cotton. "But with what little we have grown here I would say that this is a very good country for cotton growing & most general agricultural products. Our principal crops have been wheat, barley, clover & native corn." Triplett had apparently done well in his work and was also "teaching the native boys to speak English," Powell wrote. "He has taught many of them to read & write a little. The school[,] he operated it in his own time and expence with the cooperation of the other boys mentioned above." Powell continued that Twitty had done great work in constructing a short railroad line. "I am very sorry," he wrote, "that I have no illu[s]tration to send you of the work that Mr. Smith has done in puting up an eighty feet smoke-stack for a boiler on the banks of the Nile river. He does all the blacksmithing and machine shop work for a Thirty H Power engine & a sixty H Power engine."[73]

Of all the information Powell shared, one item presented immediate and lasting irony: "All the other boys have been in very good health with an exception of a little fever. Nothing serious or unusual."[74] On April 17—less than a month after Powell's correspondence—Twitty wrote to Washington and explained why he, Burns, and Triplett had returned to the United States.

"The African fever," he shared, "had nearly undermined our constitutions, making it imperative that we should leave immediately." A doctor, he continued, had told them that they ran "very grave risks" if they stayed longer. In addition to this medical reason, Twitty shared that Hunt was retiring from leading the company: "[He] feared to leave us out there, in the hands of strangers."[75] The following month, *Freeman* provided readers with an update on the status of the Tuskegee men. Of the five graduates who had been working in Sudan for two years, "introducing scientific farming and working at their other special trades," Twitty, Triplett, and Burns had returned to the United States. "The Company for which they worked has disposed of its interests in the Soudan, and although they were offered employment with satisfactory compensation with the new Company, yet because of the ravages of the African fever, it was thought best for them to return home." The *Freeman* continued that Poindexter Smith remained in Sudan and was in charge of the company's blacksmith and machine work. John Powell also stayed behind and was in charge of agricultural work.[76] In August 1907, Washington shared some tragic news with Twitty: Smith had succumbed to malaria.[77]

In all the correspondence between Washington and his students who went to Sudan, there is a notable absence of any language from Washington concerning the Sudanese themselves—concern about their condition, curiosity about their culture, or anything of the sort. This contrasted with his engagement with South Africa. Washington had direct though limited contact with Black South Africans, corresponded with nationalists, wrote that there was "no very great difference between the native problem there and the Negro problem in America," and proposed solutions.[78] If the "native problem" that he referenced conjured within him a sense of racial solidarity with South Africans that never materialized with the Sudanese, the racist legislation passed in contemporary South Africa would have easily explained such feeling. In the late nineteenth century, as African Americans were being exploited on sharecropped fields and excluded from voting booths, segregationist legislation was designed in South Africa to deny Africans citizenship rights while exploiting their labor in mining towns. Two years before the US Supreme Court enshrined the "separate but equal" doctrine in *Plessy v. Ferguson*, South Africa's 1894 Glen Grey Act assigned areas to segregate Africans from whites. Black South Africans were targeted with what historian Robert Vinson has termed a "segregationist onslaught" that denied them the franchise, marginalized them to low-paying employment, and offered them little judicial capacity to confront this systemic oppression.[79] While all these may explain Washington's comparatively strong connection with South Africa compared to Sudan, his silence concerning the Sudanese in his correspondence with the Sudan-related Tuskegee students is nevertheless profound.

In 1907 the company was reorganized and renamed the Sudan Plantations Syndicate, Ltd. (SPS). Hunt wound up leaving the project and sold his holdings to the renamed syndicate. According to Harlan, Tuskegeans were apparently no longer involved in the work. The Condominium government hoped to prove that long-staple cotton and grain were suitable commercial operations and opened a pump irrigation system at Taiyiba. It asked SPS to run the venture and subsequently financed a pump irrigation scheme at Barakat, with the syndicate building canals and overseeing the agricultural work. SPS was brought into a larger partnership with the government to manage the development of Gezira. A major agricultural project, it was planned before World War I and became fully operational in the 1920s. Originally a joint venture of the Condominium, SPS, and local farmers, its cotton production was a pillar of colonial Sudan's economy. The government assumed the company's role in the Gezira Scheme following Sudan's 1956 independence.[80] While it may be a stretch to state that Tuskegee agricultural aid made a significant difference to Condominium agricultural or economic development, this much is sure: the Tuskegee students, through their participation in Hunt's project, can be placed in the early genealogy of the Gezira Scheme, an effort Alden Young has labeled as "the product of an imperial imaginary."[81]

Hunt returned to the United States in 1910 and settled in Las Vegas in 1924. There he participated in real estate and, in anticipation of the Boulder Dam's completion (which he led), bought large tracts of desert property. Located southeast of Las Vegas, the dam—renamed Hoover Dam—was completed in 1936. Two years before his death in 1933, Hunt wrote about his Sudan experiment.[82] "I decided to employ some of our educated negroes who were familiar with cotton culture in America, believing they would aid me in a better contact with the natives." In an about-face from his former enthusiasm, Hunt added that the Tuskegeans proved useful, "[but] malaria killed a majority of them, when the balance lost heart and fled, hence this experiment ended in failure, and these were only some of the mistakes which a wiser man would have avoided." Hunt, by contrast, cast whites in a fairer light. "The white men in our employ, who survived malaria and lived to tell the tale, together with those who gave their lives to the project, were the real heroes of the undertaking."[83] Hunt's decision to broadcast the racial identities of his employees in this respect can be read as his prejudiced effort to argue that whites were more virile and capable than Blacks.

To be sure, the engagements Washington and his students had with Hunt were nuanced and problematic. The US historian Sven Beckert has noted that Washington and his disciples worked to obtain freedom for both Black Americans and Africans by accommodating to powerful statesmen and capitalists.[84] Hunt was quite obviously one such capitalist, and their choice to participate in Hunt's Sudan scheme can be read as complicity with an imperial, capitalistic project that benefited white interests. Where, in this particular Sudanese milieu, was the path to Black freedom? On one hand, Tuskegee men contributed to one of British Africa's best cotton-growing successes, "prov[ing] the viability of irrigated cotton cultivation in the region," and the SPS "provided the management and capital to expand operations into the Gezira plain."[85] On the other hand, the project was short-lived, a man died in the process, and others returned home ill only to be publicly denigrated by Hunt years later. While the choices that the Tuskegee men made were indeed complex, no doubt involving a mix of personal and professional interests with perceived positive and negative consequences, the negative outcomes appear straightforward. While the Tuskegee experts wanted to use science and technology to "revolutionize" Sudanese agriculture, the historian Jonathan E. Robins writes that "the Gezira project reproduced the structures of racial hierarchy, agrarian poverty, and dependency that plagued the South."[86]

"In Africa," wrote Louis Harlan, "[Washington] supported the principle if not all the practices of colonialism. . . . Washington's role and outlook were complex, but they supported the concept of the white man's burden."[87] In some respects, the Sudan project can be used as evidence to support this claim. Washington, through the participation of Tuskegee men, participated in a venture that would "uplift" an African colonial populace through agricultural training funded by a white business tycoon. These men were sent to a country that contained—at least in the minds of Hunt and Lord Cromer— "lazy" people who needed to be taught sound work ethic. Interpreted solely in this light, it is easy to read Washington as an educationalist who sent his students to a Sudanese project that would fill Hunt's coffers and support imperial interests.

However, other elements complicate this narrative. The participation of President Roosevelt, Egypt's Lord Cromer, and Sudan's Reginald Wingate injected a level of statecraft into what could have otherwise been construed as a strictly financial or philanthropic enterprise. The attention that newspapers afforded to the scheme illustrated both the sensationalized path that the story took and its status as one that garnered widespread attention. Interestingly, Hunt's insertion of emigration into the conversation regarding Sudan was not echoed by Washington or his students, reflecting perhaps that, despite Black America's plight, not all African American were buying the idea of Africa as a refuge. If anything, Washington's warning that the men not go to ruin from a moral standpoint reflected the complicated relationship that Black Americans had with the continent at the time.

While Washington articulated his willingness to assist Hunt and informed his men of the consequences of their conduct, his letters are completely silent regarding his personal views of the Sudanese. How could such silence on the very people that inhabited the country that his students were going to work in be explained from a man described by Edward Erhagbe "as one of the most important black diasporan contributors to Africa during his age"?[88] Was one's status as a Pan-African defined simply by one's willingness to support ventures on the continent? To directly correspond with Africans or comment on Africa-related issues? Whatever the reason for his silence, it is quite compelling that Washington devoted all of his language on Sudan to the white businessman Hunt and his African American pupils without a meaningful word on Sudan, its people, or its conditions. Such negligence warrants reconsideration of episodes about which Washington was more apt to comment on specific happenings on the continent, those in which he wasn't, and what those discrepancies might reveal about his approach to Africa.

In many respects, the Hunt-Washington Sudan scheme was bizarre. The plan joined an eccentric white American businessman (Hunt), the most famous African American (Washington), one of British Africa's most powerful figures (Cromer), and the president of the United States. A plan that would purportedly involve seven hundred thousand Black families ended up with a handful of Tuskegee men staying for less than five years. The project has, perhaps understandably, been relatively marginalized in coverage of Washington's (and Tuskegee's) engagements with Africa in the early twentieth century. Yet, despite these realities, the project highlights important themes that can both confirm existing knowledge of Washington and the contemporary Black public and perhaps provide some new insights. Poindexter Smith's death, the return of the students, and Hunt's subsequent denigration of the Black participation provide a fitting example of the way in which joining such capitalistic endeavors did not provide the freedom for Blacks that Washington longed for. Emigration's injection into this narrative revealed its continued salience a quarter of a century after the conclusion of Reconstruction. Washington's preeminent concern with the participating students and total documentary silence on the Sudanese calls into question his consideration a Pan-Africanist. In these ways, the Sudan scheme is a bizarre but useful topic of analysis.

Finally, the cotton scheme was the first documented instance of African Americans within Sudan's geographic boundaries. The educated backgrounds of the men involved foreshadowed the fact that many of the successive generations of Black Americans to visit the country would be similarly college-educated, whether at HBCUs or predominately white institutions. Given the paucity of African American college graduates at the time—as of 1899, only six southern HBCUs had more than twenty college students—the Tuskegee men wielded privilege that most of their Black contemporaries did not possess, thereby clothing the project with a particular exclusivity. The project's loose association with the US government became more pronounced in the 1950s and 1960s, when several African Americans worked in US foreign service capacities in Khartoum during the early period of Sudanese independence. The spirit of aid that undergirded the cotton scheme persisted into the early twenty-first century. One example of the posture of aid that endured came in the person of Andrew Brimmer, who—in addition to becoming the longest-serving member of Tuskegee's board of trustees—would serve as a member of the Federal Reserve's Central Banking mission to Khartoum and help to establish a central bank in the country.[89] In these ways, the cotton scheme examined in this chapter foreshadowed significant elements that marked Black engagements with Sudan for the twentieth and early twenty-first centuries.

Roughly thirty years after Twitty, Triplett and Burns returned from Sudan, Italy invaded neighboring Ethiopia. Ethiopia's fight to maintain its sovereignty fueled African American internationalism and engagement with modern Africa, and in the ensuing years the community became fervently anticolonial. Some early twentieth-century African American intellectuals, including W. E. B. DuBois, sought to redeem African history.[90] In the period bookended by Italy's invasion of Ethiopia and Sudan's 1956 independence, Black writers shined a spotlight on Sudan's ancient glory and contemporary colonial status under Anglo-Egyptian rule. Sudan, in this paradigm, was not just a far-off place where Tuskegee men could cultivate cotton. It was also a place where readers of Black newspapers could develop a sense of racial pride and solidarity. While Booker T. Washington may have been silent concerning the Sudanese people, Horace R. Cayton and others would not.

Chapter 2

Plain Imperialism

Horace R. Cayton Jr. was born in Seattle in 1903 to a distinguished family. His mother, writer Susie Revels Cayton, was the daughter of Hiram R. Revels (the first African American US senator), while his father, the elder Horace, rose from slavery to attain a college education and become a newspaper publisher. The Cayton household lived in a wealthy white neighborhood and employed a full-time Japanese servant. Horace's father was politically active and associated with national Black leaders, and in 1909 none other than Booker T. Washington stayed at their home. Young Horace, who recalled Washington's visit in his autobiography *Long Old Road*, attended the University of Washington and graduated in 1931. Though he worked toward his PhD in sociology and attended graduate school at the University of Chicago, Cayton's involvement in the Black struggle in Chicago preempted his training, and he never acquired the doctorate. He served as special assistant to the secretary of the interior, taught economics at Fisk University, and directed Chicago's Parkway Community House. It was while Cayton was serving in this capacity that he and St. Clair Drake published their formative 1945 study of Black life and culture in Chicago, *The Black Metropolis*.[1]

In addition to the aforementioned labors, Cayton also wrote for the African American *Pittsburgh Courier* newspaper for approximately thirty years.[2]

He made a striking claim in its October 27, 1951, edition. "Fifteen million American Negroes may not know it," Cayton wrote, "but they have a vital hereditary stake in the highly explosive efforts of the Arab League and Egypt to unite the entire Moslem world, including . . . the Anglo-Egyptian Sudan. The first slaves brought to the U.S. in 1620 came from that same Anglo-Egyptian Sudan."[3] Cayton noted that while the Arab League's first objective was to unite all Arabs, its second aim was the larger goal of linking the Muslim world. In his view, this held "much significance to American Negroes": "it was from this storm center of the present Middle East controversy, that the forefathers of the American Negro were brought to this country by Dutch slave traders in 1620 and sold at Jamestown, Va."[4] Given the fact that over 80 percent of those exported into transatlantic slavery came from West Central Africa, the Bight of Benin, the Bight of Biafra, or the Gold Coast, Cayton's claim that African Americans were descended from Sudan—located on the other side of the continent—may immediately appear bizarre.[5] Any claim, furthermore, that positioned the Nilotic Sudan as a significant source for American-bound enslaved persons would be empirically false. Nevertheless, his claim showed history's ever-present centrality to links that African Americans made with Sudan. Whether it was in reference to ancient Nilotic kingdoms or Cayton's claims about transatlantic slavery, such connections were intrinsically historical.

Contemporary political intrigues on the Nile also drew African American attention to Sudan. Under the Anglo-Egyptian Treaty of 1899, Great Britain had recognized Egypt's legal claim to Sudan but administered the country on behalf of Egypt's king. Over time the British more firmly established their power, and in 1924 they expelled Egyptian officials and troops from Sudan after an Egyptian nationalist assassinated the British governor-general. The British did not reference Egypt's fictive sovereignty over Sudan until 1936, when they negotiated a new treaty of military cooperation with Egypt. While this action affirmed Egypt's claims to the country, it did not lessen Britain's practical authority in Sudan. World War II inspired African and Arab nationalists to seek independence, and the British—in part to prevent a union between Egypt and Sudan that would potentially threaten their control of the Suez Canal—supported Sudanese hopes for independence.[6] Thus, one European colonizer (Britain) was eager to support the independence of its sub-Saharan African colony (Sudan) to prevent it from joining its co-colonizing North African partner (Egypt). It was a byzantine situation.

Regardless of the invalidity of Cayton's claim, his October 1951 thoughts in the *Pittsburgh Courier* are significant. To begin, there was the medium in which his views were conveyed. Black newspapers boomed in the 1930s–1950s. From 1933 to 1940 their circulation more than doubled to 1.27 million readers (and, since each issue had multiple readers, this figure was an underestimation), and in 1954 the Black press's circulation eclipsed two million.[7] Within this newspaper ecosystem the *Courier*, where Cayton's thoughts were published, was arguably "the nation's leading black newspaper."[8] In addition, the focus and timing of his piece reflected the broader reality that Black Americans remained interested in Sudan long after the Hunt-Washington scheme. Finally, there is Cayton's multitiered argument that African Americans were related to Sudanese and had a stake in that African people's affairs. Such a claim stood in stark contrast to former house guest Booker T. Washington, who was altogether silent on the Sudanese during the Tuskegee-Hunt project on the Nile five decades earlier.

This chapter explores Black American discourse concerning Sudan from the early 1920s until the eve of Sudanese independence (1956), a period when Black writers voiced respect for and solidarity with Sudan and showed interest in its ancient history. The Sudanese were foreign but unmistakably familial in the African American paradigm, in part due to similar physical features. Perhaps nowhere was this affinity made more clear than in the way the Sudanese were described in relation to Egypt: that is, as Black people subject to potential mistreatment from Arabs. This expressed dichotomy delineating Arab rulers and Black subjects made the Sudanese more relatable in the eyes of Black Americans subject to state-supported racial hierarchies, and it foretold language that African Americans would use about Sudan during its postcolonial civil wars, when Black, marginalized southern Sudanese waged war against northern Sudanese Arab regimes. Thus, this period represents a discursive prologue to the rhetoric disseminated by Black writers in the latter twentieth century. Black racial solidarity undermined affinity with Egyptian Arabs, another nonwhite populace living under white rule.

Rising Black Internationalism

During the interwar years, Black nationalism and internationalism owed a great debt to a Sudanese intellectual and his more luminous counterpart, Marcus Garvey. Born in 1866 to an Egyptian family of Sudanese descent, Dusé Mohamed Ali was a member of the organizing committee for the First Universal Races Congress held in London in 1911. He became a renowned Pan-Africanist after the congress and began publishing a journal titled *African*

Times and Orient Review (*ATOR*) the following year. While its run only lasted a few years, it is notable for publishing the literary debut of Marcus Garvey, founder of the Universal Negro Improvement Association (UNIA). Begun in 1914, the UNIA boasted a membership of approximately two million by 1919 (when *ATOR* ceased publication). Ali worked as foreign affairs correspondent for Garvey's *Negro World*, served for a time as the UNIA's foreign secretary, and died in 1945.[9] While Garvey has largely overshadowed Ali in history, the Sudanese journalist nevertheless played a central role in early twentieth-century Black internationalism and Garvey's career.

Garvey believed that African Americans should create their own alternative to mainstream society. Encouraging his followers to join in a struggle for Africa's redemption, Garvey did not stop at condemning racism and encouraging economic independence; rather, he sought the return of African Americans to their ancestral continent and the emigration of Blacks to and from the Caribbean. An international phenomenon, Garveyite groups stretched from Florida to Seattle, Senegal to South Africa. Importantly, women—including UNIA cofounder Amy Ashwood, UNIA national organizer Maymie De Mena, and Pan-Africanist feminist Amy Jacques Garvey—were active in the 1920s Garveyite movement. While Marcus Garvey himself had a masculinist vision of Black liberation and believed that Black men would lead the fight to improve the lot for those throughout the diaspora, historian Keshia Blain notes that women like Amy Jacques Garvey, Maymie De Mena, and Henrietta Vinton Davis challenged male supremacy and tried to change the organization's patriarchal leadership structure. In seeking Black American repatriation to Africa, Garvey's return plan failed after lengthy talks with Liberia. Garveyism—numbering four hundred million members—declined, no doubt accelerated by his 1925 imprisonment and following deportation. Despite its decline, Garveyism continued to inspire future generations.[10]

The following decade, African American consciousness of Africa was stimulated by epochal events that occurred in Ethiopia. In October 1935, an Italian army of 120,000 invaded Ethiopia. The army wrought havoc on that country's countryside, bombed villages, and spread poison gas by air. The Italians occupied the capital city of Addis Ababa in May 1936, and the following month Haile Selassie fled into exile in Europe. Following an unsuccessful attempt on the life of Italian viceroy Rodolfo Graziani in February 1937, scores of Ethiopians were killed in revenge. Guerrilla resistance continued during the five-year occupation, and many women who had been raped by Italian soldiers joined Ethiopia's resistance movement. By May 1941, Addis Ababa had been retaken, and Selassie reestablished his throne.[11]

Ethiopia's defense of its sovereignty galvanized African American internationalism and engagement with the ancestral continent. When African Americans opposed US neutrality in the Italo-Ethiopian War, it was not Black America's first twentieth-century effort to influence an American foreign policy decision toward Africa or the Caribbean. The first occurred with the 1915 US occupation of Haiti. However, the historian Michael Krenn has noted that it was not until the 1930s and the Ethiopian invasion by Italy that a growing number of Black Americans started to liken their own civil rights struggle with the broader, international battle that people of color waged against colonialism and racial discrimination.[12]

Importantly, Black women played a significant role in drawing attention to Italy's predations. On June 22, 1935, twenty-four-year-old Eloise Robinson—donning a shirt that read "Hands Off Ethiopia"—walked up to the Italian consulate in Chicago, chained herself to a street-post, and staged a dramatic protest. A little over three months later, on October 4 (the day after the invasion had commenced), a crowd of one hundred female students at Hunter College picketed in front of the Italian consulate on New York's Upper East Side.[13] Following the invasion, Amy Ashwood Garvey delivered a speech in support of Ethiopia in London's Trafalgar Square. Garvey, who worked with the International African Service Bureau (a revolutionary Black organization that advocated for racial equality, anticolonialism, and self-determination), boldly declared, "We will not tolerate the invasion of Abyssinia.... You said you brought us from Africa to Christianize us, but the only Christianity you gave us was three hundred years of enslavement."[14] Such episodes not only highlight the diversity of forms that Black solidarity with Africa could take outside the pages of Black newspapers, they also point to the reality that any examination of Black engagements with twentieth-century Africa demands a serious accounting of Black women's formative role in this history.[15]

The same stands true concerning Sudan with, among others, the first Black American woman to make a documented appearance in the Anglo-Egyptian Condominium: Eslanda Goode Robeson. Born in 1896 in Washington, DC, Eslanda Goode attended the University of Illinois but ultimately earned her degree in chemistry from Columbia University. She became the first African American to work at New York City's Presbyterian Hospital and in 1921 married renowned singer, actor, and activist Paul Robeson. Her first book—a biography of her husband—was published in 1930, and in 1934 she began graduate study in anthropology at the London School of Economics and University College, London. She aimed to learn more about African history and culture. "I wanted to go to Africa," she wrote in her formative *African Journey*. "It began when I was quite small. Africa was the place we Negroes came from originally. Lots of Americans, when they could afford it, went back to see their 'old country.'"[16] In 1936 she traveled with eight-year-old son Pauli through South Africa, Basutoland, Uganda, Kenya, Tanzania, Egypt, and Sudan. In a lecture she later delivered at First Methodist Church in Hartford, Connecticut, Robeson recalled that she and Pauli had come up with a game that they often played called "Matching People." When they would meet a new set of Africans, they would try to tell each other which ones they could match. "Always in groups," she recounted, "we would find several people who so closely resembled Negro friends whom we knew . . . that they could easily have passed for immediate relatives. So many of our new African friends looked so much like our old American Negro friends, that we felt very much at home among them."[17] In her August 19, 1936, journal entry, Robeson recounted their visit to Wadi Halfa, Sudan. "The Africans hereabouts are extraordinarily handsome," she wrote. "They belong to the Shilluk Tribe and are about seven feet tall. . . . Their skin is bronze-black, well oiled and beautifully kept . . . Pauli just can't get over their height. 'They are taller than Daddy, but they are not as broad,' he said. 'Nobody can be as everything as Daddy.'"[18]

By 1937 an African American former YMCA missionary named Max Yergan had persuaded Paul Robeson, five other prominent Black Americans, an African, and five white liberals to join him in organizing an International Committee on Africa (ICA). The ICA was founded for several purposes, not limited to but including educating the public about Africa, petition, and protest. Paul and Eslanda Robeson were the earliest and most enthusiastic supporters of Yergan's idea for the committee, and, though Eslanda's role was initially small, it grew when the committee transformed into the Council on African Affairs (CAA) in 1941. Operating until 1955, the Black-led CAA aimed to educate the public about Africa and promote its liberation.[19]

The 1930s–1950s were cataclysmic decades in the history of Black America's relationship with Africa. While Italy's invasion of Ethiopia launched extraordinary interest in that region of the Horn of Africa, African Americans would not ignore Sudan, Ethiopia's western neighbor. Just as African Americans may have found solidarity with Ethiopia through a shared sense of suffering from violent white statecraft, the post–World War II period showed that some Black writers expressed kinship and solidarity with the Sudanese. No empty or romantic musings, these sentiments were infused with political meaning and consequence.

Egypt, Sudan, and African American Opinion

In 1938—three years after Italy's invasion of Ethiopia commenced—Sudanese nationalist elites organized the Graduates' General Congress. Representing Sudan's intelligentsia, the northern Sudanese educated class that formed the congress did so with the intention of presenting a united front to the Condominium government. The British, for their part, wanted the educated class as an ally. The congress, however, was soon divided between those who wanted union with Egypt and those who wanted an independent Sudan. In time, rival Sudanese nationalist groups were organized as political parties: the Ashigga Party emerged in 1943 and favored union with Egypt under the Egyptian crown; the Umma Party emerged in 1945 and called for complete Sudanese independence. Northern Sudanese activists applied the Atlantic Charter—the Anglo-American agreement affirming the right of nations to self-government and self-determination within their boundaries—to the Sudan. While the Condominium government rejected this attempt, the activists' actions put self-government and self-determination on the postwar agenda.[20]

Egypt's cabinet explained that the country would not accept any settlement that did not support unity of the Nile Valley and the immediate withdrawal of British troops. Egypt's government went so far as to ask the infant United Nations Security Council for "the total and immediate evacuation of British troops from Egypt including the Sudan and to terminate the . . . administration in the Sudan," but the UN did not provide a ruling.[21] Egyptian prime minister Nokrashy Pasha, speaking before the Chamber of Deputies in December 1946, posited, "[A] very natural link . . . binds together the two parts of the Nile Valley, ties of language, kinship and interest in olden and recent times, ties which cannot be assailed or severed and which everyone in Egypt maintains."[22] Egyptian sentiments notwithstanding, in June 1948 Sudanese governor-general Sir Robert Howe announced the Executive Council and Legislative Assembly ordinance. The partially elected Legislative Assembly was responsible for proposing laws. Discussions occurred in the Assembly concerning self-government, self-determination, and a federal constitution for the Sudan. In April 1952 the Assembly enacted the Self-Government Statute, which provided for an all-Sudanese council of ministers that would be responsible to an elected parliament. Just three months later, the Egyptian monarchy was overthrown, and the new government recognized Sudan's right to self-determination and self-government. The British government approved the Self-Government Statute in October, and self-determination and self-government were achieved when the Anglo-Egyptian Agreement was signed on February 12, 1953. The agreement stated that the Condominium would be terminated within three years, after which point a referendum would be held deciding between independence or union with Egypt. On December 19, 1955, the House of Representatives approved a resolution declaring Sudan's independence. Sudan unanimously declared its independence two weeks later, on January 1, 1956.[23]

Much of the political intrigue in Egypt and Sudan occurred concomitantly with the rise of Black American internationalism and the boom of Black newspapers. These realities converged on the pages of these papers. Ranging from short blurbs to longer editorials, this coverage not only provides African American views of Egypt and Sudan but also broader understandings of race, colonialism, and northeast African history. While Black newspaper coverage on the Britain-Egypt-Sudan situation was not monolithic, the overarching sentiment was decidedly pro-Sudanese. The architecture of this position comprised three distinct yet interlocking elements: recognition of Sudanese Blackness, Egyptian Arabness, and Egyptian mistreatment and colonialism of the Sudanese. Taken together, solidarity with the Sudanese was articulated through the grammar of race, a double-edged sword that resulted in amity for the Black Sudanese and antagonism for Egyptians Arabs. Support for one nonwhite people (Arabs) was sacrificed at the altar of solidarity with another (Black Africans). This oppositional duality set a precedent for Black American discourse pitting northern Sudanese Arabs against southern Sudanese Blacks during the postcolonial era.

Acknowledging Sudanese Blackness

One of the foundational elements of African American newspaper coverage of Sudan was its focus on the literal blackness of the Sudanese. J. A. Rogers was one writer responsible for such descriptions. Born in September 1883, Joel Augustus Rogers hailed from Jamaica before relocating to Chicago in his early twenties. A writer, historian, journalist, and publisher, Rogers was an acquaintance of Marcus Garvey, wrote for the UNIA weekly *Negro World*, and lectured to local UNIA chapters, and researched Africa's global history. In the 1930s Rogers conducted research in Egypt and Sudan, and he traveled at the behest of *Pittsburgh Courier* editor Robert L. Vann to cover the Italo-Ethiopian War.[24] In 1931 the African American *Philadelphia Tribune* published

Rogers's following observation: "I have seen Jews in Abyssinia, the Sudan, and North Africa so dark and with hair and features so Negro-like that in America they would be thrust a mile deep in the Jim Crow car, if such a thing were possible."[25] Over fifteen years later, Rogers doubled down on his earlier observations regarding the phenotypical similitude. "In the Sudan," he wrote in a 1947 *Pittsburgh Courier* piece, "say at Khartoum, Omdurman and Atbara, both the Arabs and non-Arabs would at once be called Negro in America. They were more Negroid than the people in any American Negro district."[26]

Percival Prattis joined Rogers in his comparisons of Sudanese to African Americans. Born in 1895 in Philadelphia, Prattis had studied at Hampton Institute and was stationed in France during World War I. Honorably discharged in 1919, he began editing the *Michigan State News* (Grand Rapids) but moved to Chicago in 1921 to become city editor of the African American *Chicago Defender*. In 1936 Prattis moved to Pittsburgh to take a position with the *Pittsburgh Courier*, which by the mid-1920s had become America's leading Black paper. Named city editor, Prattis also worked as a reporter and was sent on assignment to the Middle East.[27] Prattis's opinion about the similarities between Black Americans and Sudanese were unambiguously conveyed in his piece "Sudanese Are the People in Egypt Who Are Most Like American Negroes," which appeared in the *Courier* on August 6, 1949. "They seem most like my own people in physical appearance and general attitude," Prattis wrote. He clarified his opinion further: "I would exclude the mulatto portion of the American Negro population. The Sudanese I saw were brown or dark brown, rather uniformly. Few were what you would call black." Continuing that the Sudanese had "features . . . like those of American Negroes, though perhaps a bit finer," Prattis noted that their noses were "less bulbous," their lips "generally thinner," and their hair "short but of a rather fine grade." Prattis then proceeded to list a handful of prominent African Americans whose features would have apparently proved his point. "If Paul Robeson, Jackie Robinson, Marian Anderson, Jesse Owens or Larry Doby were seen walking along the street in Cairo, they would be regarded as Sudanese."[28]

Six years later, Prattis reiterated his opinion on Sudanese–African American resemblances by claiming, "There is perhaps no other group in Africa which more nearly resembles the American Negro than the Sudanese."[29] Unlike Robeson and Rogers—but like Horace Cayton—Prattis expressed a genealogical connection linking Sudanese with African Americans. "The Sudanese," he wrote, "of whom perhaps some American Negroes are kin, have contributed generously to the culture of mankind." But how, exactly, were the two peoples related? Slavery provided Prattis's answer. "From 1600 to 1870," he claimed, "thousands of slaves were taken from the Sudanese 'Slave Coast.' Some of these . . . were brought, as slaves, to America. It is not only to Nigeria, Liberia, and that region that the American Negro must look to find his racial kinfolk. He must also look to the Anglo-Egyptian Sudan."[30]

Whether or not Black Americans and Sudanese were linked by a shared history of slavery, the two peoples were connected by present-day marginalization. He pointed his readers to the plight of the Sudanese in Egypt on multiple occasions. "The Sudanese are very numerous in urban Egyptian communities. But . . . they are found principally in menial, domestic and unskilled occupations. They seem to be stratified on a lower level of Egyptian life." Yet this reality was contrasted with another: "Everybody praises these Sudanese for their industry, their native intelligence, their politeness, their kindness and their honesty."[31] Prattis followed these sentiments with another statement in October 1951: "Almost everybody admits that the Sudanese are the finest human beings you meet in Egypt. The Egyptian ruling class classifies them as Egyptians, but it doesn't treat them as such. Sudanese are second-class citizens in Egypt. They do all the dirty work."[32] The following month, in an editorial aptly titled "American Negroes Should Be Concerned about What Is Happening in Egypt," Prattis likened the experience of Sudanese in Egypt with that of Blacks in the United States: "The Sudanese in Egypt are regarded as a servant class and are largely restricted to menial types of service. In the large hotels in Cairo, the Sudanese are employed almost exactly as are Negroes in Southern hotels in the United States. The clerks and cashiers are whites, Egyptians and other nationalities. The bell boys and bell captains and porters are Sudanese."[33]

Against the backdrop of Sudanese discrimination at the hands of Egyptians, African American writers characterized the Sudanese as Black, while Egyptians, conversely, were Arab. But what in fact did "Arab" mean? How was it understood in Egypt and Sudan? Finally, how did African Americans looking to the shores of the Nile interpret those two nationalities through the lens of Arabness?

Shifting Meanings of "Egyptian" and "Sudanese"

Egyptian identity in the early twentieth century dovetailed with Arabness, whiteness, and emerging ideas of the Third World. To begin, Egypt is the most populous Arab country, with nearly one in four of all the world's Arabs being Egyptian. The country's Arab heritage dates back to the seventh century and the Arab conquest of Egypt in 639–642 CE. However, Arab national consciousness among the general Egyptian populace is not documented in the nineteenth century, and when the Arab nationalist movement arose in opposition to Turkish hegemony (ending the 1916 Great Arab Revolt), the Greater Syrian Arabs took the lead in the fight for Arab unity for the following twenty years. Nevertheless, during the 1920s, Egyptian solidarity with neighboring Arab peoples began to rise, and Cairo became a focus of intellectual life and popular culture in the Arab region. The country's growing interdependence with eastern Arab countries as a result of the Middle East Supply Centre during World War II, the 1945 formation of the Arab League (headquartered in Cairo), and the ever-boiling Palestinian situation amplified Egypt's identity as an Arab state. Egypt's leadership position in the Arab League became increasingly significant when Gamal Abdel Nasser came to power.[34]

A 1952 coup brought the Egyptian Nasser and his army officers to power, ending over twenty centuries of foreign dynastic rule. The country became the Arab Republic of Egypt. In standing up to the former colonial powers and pursuing the dream of pan-Arab unity, Nasser became the Arab world's de facto leader. Egypt's foreign policy from 1955 to 1967 was partially grounded in Third-Worldism. Nasser attended the 1955 Afro-Asian Conference in Bandung, which established the roots of the Non-Aligned Movement through a Yugoslavian, Indian, and Egyptian partnership; he opposed the British-designated Baghdad Pact military alliance and tried to replace it with an indigenous Cairo-led security order; and he announced a Soviet-inspired arms deal with Czechoslovakia that ushered in Egypt's two-decades-long link with the Soviet bloc. Egyptian nationalism during the 1950s and 1960s was replaced by a state policy of Pan-Arabism, a political movement that called for Arab unity, combated the old colonial powers of Britain and France, and—from the 1970s on—was anti-imperialist (particularly against US intervention in the region).[35]

South of Egypt, "Arab" in the Sudanese context can only reasonably be described as a hybrid concept. Degrees of Africanization spread the farther south one goes, and historically southern slaves brought northward experienced Arabization, or *ta'rib*. *Ta'rib* commenced with the entry of Arab Muslim nomads in the early Islamic period and involved the gradual percolation of Arab identity and Arabic language among peoples in northern Sudan. Arabization quickened after the fall of Nubia's Christian kingdoms in the fourteenth century and reached consolidation with Islamic culture after north-central Sudan's Funj sultanate rose in the sixteenth century. Arabization did not, however, result in a cultural monolith. Today peoples like the Daju, Fur, and Nubians are deeply Arab and Muslim but speak their own non–Afro-Asiatic languages rather than Arabic, and there are Arabic speakers who are not adherents of Islam and instead identify as Christian or Jewish. Still, until decolonization in the mid-1950s, learning Arabic as a first language often led to the acquisition of Arab identity as families forged pedigrees to claim lineage from noble, Arabian-origin male descendants.[36]

British policies favored a small elite from these northern Sudanese "Arab" communities after the Anglo-Egyptian conquest, and members of this cadre eventually crafted an idea of a self-consciously Sudanese Arabic national identity. In the process—and somewhat counterintuitively, from a racial standpoint—the term "Sudanese" (*sudani*), which derived from an Arabic word for blackness, was adapted.[37] In the 1930s a new Arab nationalist politics emerged, creating a genealogy stretching far into Islamic Arab history. According to the historian Amir Idris, "It suggested a primordial and essential identity shared by all those who lived in the north regardless of their particular historical experiences." Importantly, he adds, race and descent became important in determining Sudanese nationalism's course. "Being an Arab," Idris contends, "became a criterion for citizenship and leadership in Sudanese nationalism."[38] By the 1950s, some Sudanese nationalists sought to quickly spread the Arabic language throughout a linguistically diverse land. Southern Sudan began to witness the implementation of the Arabist vision. Although vernaculars (local ethnic languages) were used in all village and primary schools, while English was employed at the intermediate and higher levels, Arabic was introduced as a main subject in the Ater Intermediate school, the Rumbek Secondary government school, and Juba Training Centre in 1949.[39] It could be said that these measures were the fruit of an Arab ideology articulated by the Graduates' Congress to the Condominium Government back in 1939. "Education should be orientated towards the Arab and Islamic, but not African, culture, because the Sudan had much in common with the Arabic countries of Islamic Orient . . . [they argued that education in the South could not be improved by a subsidized missionary system] but [only] through the opening of government schools, similar to those in the North, and where the Arabic language would provide the lingua franca."[40]

This emphasis on Arabism did not go unopposed. Recognizing the growing power and influence of the northern elite, Adam Adam—a medical practitioner in Khartoum who came from a Darfurian slave family—founded Kutla as-Suda (the Black Bloc) in 1938. He argued that all Blacks, being "the only true Sudanese," should unite at a time when Arabized townspeople used the term "Sudani" as a slightly derogatory term to describe un-Arabized Black men. Attracting people from the Nuba and Fur people—there were then not many people from southern Sudan in Khartoum—Adam hoped that the movement could develop into a political party. Resolutions were passed demanding that their rights be recognized and that power never be handed to Arabs. However, the Ashiqqa and the Umma Parties, which each objected to the Black Bloc, accused it of racism. The British were compelled to concede to Ashiqqa and Umma pressure and refused the bloc the right to be licensed as a political party.[41] In a striking display of how racial identities were marshaled in the Sudanese political sphere, this attempt at Black inclusion was stifled in the face of accusations of bigotry, and none other than the British overlords were there to enshrine the exclusion.

While the history of Arab identity in Egypt and the Sudan stretched back for a thousand years, American conceptualizations of Arabness in the early twentieth century were far newer and less politically significant than in those two countries. However, such understandings were not devoid of meaning. In nineteenth-century American discourse, "Arab" was often used figuratively and could—and did—convey a transitional point between Black and white, primitive and civilized, foreign and native. As one illuminating example, literate Black enslaved persons on the plantation were at one time described as Arab.[42] Anti-Asian legislation began while the first Syrian immigrants arrived in significant numbers to the United States, and Syrian immigrants wanted to communicate that they were not from Asia in order to avoid anti-Asia legislation and immigration restrictions. Jim Crow persuaded early Syrian newcomers that they had to contest their Asiatic racial designations and legally prove their "whiteness."[43] Arab immigrants in the early twentieth century pursued whiteness and petitioned the government to grant them this designation. The government obliged; important judicial decisions in 1915 and 1944 solidified Arabs' legal definition under the law as white.[44] Against the backdrop of Jim Crow and legal US classifications of Arabs as white, African American newspapers presented the Egyptian-Sudanese relationship as one not only between colonizer and colonized but also—in a dynamic all Black readers could understand—between light-skinned rulers and Black ruled. The racialized nature of such coverage resulted in a decidedly pro-Sudanese position in Black newspapers and consequently expressions of anti-Arab prejudice.

In the early twentieth century, Egypt figured into African American discussions of race in curious ways. Importantly, it was the ancient Nile Valley civilization that was invoked. In 1922 British archaeologist Howard Carter famously discovered the tomb of the ancient Egyptian boy-king Tutankhamen.[45] In a forum held around 1922 at Denver's Grace Community Church, W. E. B. Du Bois discussed how the recent excavations represented a civilization that was older than the white race. "As a matter of fact," he declared, "it can be proven by history that King Tut-Ankh-Amen himself was part negro. History also records that Egyptian civilization came from the southern part of Africa, the land of the negro, and not from the north by way of Asia."[46] Years later, in *The World and Africa*, the famed sociologist pushed against British historian Arnold Toynbee's characterization of Egyptian civilization as "white" and noted that the science of Egyptology had blossomed concomitantly with the apex of King Cotton and American Black enslavement. "We may then without further ado ignore this verdict of history, widespread as it is, and treat Egyptian history as an integral part of African history."[47] J. A. Rogers joined Du Bois in shining a light on ancient Egypt's Black heritage, writing that Cheops, "a Negro," built the Great Pyramid of Giza and that several Ethiopian "or unmixed Negro" individuals ruled ancient Egypt.[48]

Some went beyond pointing to ancient Egypt's Black heritage and went so far as to claim that African Americans were descended from ancient Egypt. Black writers in the nineteenth century like Samuel Ringgold Ward and William Wells Brown claimed African American links to the architects of ancient Egypt, and by the mid-nineteenth century northern educated Black Americans and abolitionists generally believed that Black Americans were descendants of ancient Egyptians. In his 1854 commencement address at Western Reserve College, Frederick Douglass cited Herodotus in his argument for the link between ancient Egyptians and African Americans. And later, during the 1920s Harlem Renaissance, many prominent Black intellectuals took interest in contemporary Africa.[49] If African Americans may have had a history of linking themselves with ancient Egyptians, those like Percival Prattis were not invested in making the same claim of connection with the modern Egyptian populace. If ancient Egypt represented a glorious heritage to which they could point to debunk racist stereotypes, modern Egypt appeared to represent something altogether dissimilar.

Prattis acknowledged that because Egyptians were alleged to be "African people of color," Black Americans would be inclined to them (as people trying to wrest themselves from British military oversight). He opined that Egyptians should be free to run their own country regardless of their racial identity. But he asserted, "If American Negroes are to shed any tears over the plight of the Egyptians, they should not do so on the basis of any so-called blood relationship which they believe they have with the modern rulers of Egypt. That simply does not exist." Prattis explained that the country's ruling class had been more or less white or European "since the Greeks landed in the fourth century before Christ." Farouk, Egypt's king at the time of Prattis's writing (1951), was in Prattis's estimation "a Turk, not an Egyptian Arab or Negro." "The dominant political and social classes are white, mulatto, or bronze-colored. These people do not associate themselves culturally with the browns and the blacks."[50] His position on the racial makeup of Egypt's leadership followed comments made by George Padmore in the *Chicago Defender* four years earlier. Padmore said that Sudanese resented the "[Egyptian landlords and capitalists] who form[ed] the Pasha class." These were "not real Egyptians but [rather] descendants of the former Turkish rulers," and Sudanese resented their efforts "to turn the Sudan into an Egyptian colony."[51] George F. McCray, writing in the *Atlanta Daily World*, noted that the Sudanese were quick to challenge Egyptian nationalist extremists' claim that they should control Sudan based on common racial (as well as religious and cultural) ties. "They [the Sudanese] point out that though the Northern third of the country and as far south as Khartoun [*sic*] the population in varying degrees is . . . racially mixed with Arab, Negro and Egyptian." McCray continued, "[The southern third of Sudan is] peopled by almost 3,000,000 pure African Negroes. Nuers, Shilluks, Dinkas, who are in no way related to the Egyptians. Between the blacks of the south and the mixed Arab-Negro groups of the north are several million very dark, wooly headed peoples who are racially Negro."[52]

Prattis acknowledged Egyptians' color diversity. "What I would call the native Egyptian is of all colors," he wrote, "from black to white, with features that are more Caucasian or Semitic than Negroid and with, generally, wavy black hair." Just as he likened Sudanese to the likes of Paul Robeson and Larry Doby, Prattis similarly compared Egyptians to certain notable African Americans. "Eyre Saitch, the tennis player, was an Egyptian type. But so are Charles Drew, of blood plasma fame, and Lena Horne and Billy Eckstine and Effa Manley and John P. Davis and Adam Powell."[53] However, when Black newspapers discussed Sudan's political future (and, more specifically, whether it would be independent or under Egyptian authority), writers highlighted the blackness of the Sudanese and Egypt's supposed status outside the bounds of blackness. "There is a color line," wrote *Courier* correspondent Hugh Weston with reference to Egypt. "The color line is very thin—not sharp as in America—but just the same, there is a color line."[54]

Arab Difference, Arab Dominance

In the late 1940s and early 1950s, African American periodicals articulated the prospect of Egyptian rule over Sudan through the grammar of dominance. "Egyptian Arabs want the Sudan reunited with Egypt," Weston wrote in 1946. "This leads many people to feel that Egyptian Arabs might completely dominate the Sudanese, and exploit them with far less tenderness than their present English masters, while perhaps allowing a certain freedom to the Arab gangs that deal in the slave trade."[55] George Schuyler, writing the following year in the *Pittsburgh Courier*, posited that the Egyptians had "imperialist ambitions," while the British wanted to remain in Sudan "as co-partners in the fleecing of the . . . black natives."[56] In 1947 the *Chicago Defender* noted, "The tan colored Egyptians, who . . . regard themselves as Caucasian feel that they have a vested right in the country of the Sudanese whose inhabitants are African blacks."[57]

In June 1947 W. E. B. Du Bois referred to Abdul Rahman Mohammed Ahmed el Mahdi's call for Sudanese independence and made repeated references to his famous father, the Mahdi:

> To-day . . . there appears in England the son of the black Mahdi of the nineteenth century. What does he ask? He demands that in the treaty by which Great Britain recognizes the independence of Egypt, that this recognition shall not include the Sudan as belonging to Egypt . . . the son of the Mahdi declared that . . . the Land of the blacks had never been conquered by the Pharaohs of Egypt, the Kings of Assyria . . . or even the great Saladin. Only after the final overthrow of the Mahdi and the Khalifa, did the Sudanese submit to unwilling rule under the English and Egyptians, who still call the Sudanese, slaves.[58]

Born three weeks after his famous father's death, Abdul Rahman Mohammed Ahmed el Mahdi had lived in poverty, was subjected to police supervision, and—before the First World War—struggled to support his large family. However, with Britain's war against the Ottomans, the government feared the rise of Sudanese fanaticism and conciliated with the Mahdists. Mahdi was encouraged to contact the Ansar (his father's followers) and use personal influence to win support for the government. While the government adopted indirect rule in part to curb his growing appeal, it still hoped to use him to counter any Sudanese nationalist sentiment that allied with Egypt (Mahdism's old foe). By the 1920s Mahdi was an important Sudanese leader, and his Omdurman house became a meeting place for politically minded government officials.[59] In early 1947 the *Chicago Defender* noted that "Egyptian-Arab domination of black-skinned Sudanese" loomed in the background of the recent breakdown of treaty negotiations between the British and Egyptians, as well as Mahdi's preference for "British rule over Egyptian-Arab domination." The *Defender* included his recollection that "Egyptians still call his people Abed (slaves) in memory of the times when Sudanese . . . were sold in slave marts of Alexandria and Cairo."[60]

In late 1947 the *Defender* provided readers with a glimpse of what the Sudanese leader thought about Black Americans in an interview with George Padmore. In his exchange with Padmore, Mahdi—whom Padmore described as "distinctly Negroid in appearance"—expressed solidarity with

Figure 2.1. Abd al-Rahman al-Mahdi (1885–1959).

the African American community. "We are proud of the colored people in America," shared the Sudanese leader. "They are an inspiration to Africans at home. Despite the great disadvantages they suffer politically and racially, no other community of peoples of African descent can present the same amount of positive and constructive achievement as our brothers in America."[61] Perhaps Mahdi, cognizant of the fact that his words would be transmitted to an African American readership, seized the opportunity to rally support by complimenting that community. Conversely, he may have been expressing authentic sentiments about his "brothers in America" and had no intention to gain any political advantage. Whatever his intentions, his exchange with Padmore in *Defender* was a rare but important moment that highlighted the fact that as African Americans were looking to the Nile, at least one Sudanese—and Abdul Rahman el Mahdi, no less—was conscious of African Americans. Black American engagements with Sudan were not one-sided but, rather, mutual. The following decades would continue to show this.

Percival Prattis offered the most remarkable commentaries on the possibility of Egypt controlling Sudan. The first example appeared in the *Pittsburgh Courier* on October 27, 1951. In his article "Egyptian Grab for Sudan Is Plain Imperialism of the White Ruling Class," Prattis argued that Egypt's fight for freedom was not the struggle of a Black people but rather of "a white ruling class" that wanted to be free of British interference. "This white ruling class," he contended, "would not mind being a partner with the British in the exploitation of Egypt's browns and blacks, and other browns and blacks, if it could be an equal partner." Prattis, again employing the language of race for his readers, made the provocative decision to compare Egypt's intentions for Sudan with apartheid South Africa's vision for South West Africa (Namibia): "The Egyptian grab for the Sudan is plain imperialism. The white ruling class of Egypt wishes to extend its dominion in Africa at the expense of the Negroid Sudanese. That effort is similar to South Africa's determination to add Southwest Africa to its territory. . . . There is not too much difference, so far as black Africans are concerned, between the ruling class Egyptian mentality and that of the rulers of South Africa."[62]

South African occupation of Namibia began in 1915, when the South African army conquered the German colonists there during the First World War. Namibia became a League of Nations trust territory in 1919. Though Britain received the official mandate to rule, the British transferred the responsibility to its dominion of South Africa. Following World War II the League's trust was given to its successor, the United Nations, but the South African government refused to honor the terms of the trust and prepare Namibia for independence. The government instead treated Namibia as an additional South African province and—with the country settled heavily by white people—applied apartheid's legislation to indigenous Namibians.[63]

Prattis's article accomplished several things. First, it underscored his argument to his readers that Egypt had imperialistic desires for Sudan. Second, it cast light on the racial division separating Egypt from Sudan. By stating that there wasn't much difference between Egypt's ruling class and that of South Africa ("as far as black Africans are concerned"), he reinforced the notion that Egypt and Sudan were racially distinct. Finally, though the apartheid regime at the time of his writing was still in its infancy (the National Party was being elected to power in 1948), the very mention of South Africa would have already conjured an understanding of racial discrimination in the minds of some *Courier* readers. Dating back to the nineteenth century, Black activists in the United States and South Africa engaged in political dialogue that informed their fights against such discrimination. Black Americans were mesmerized by African efforts to confront apartheid after the National Party's election, inspiring several activists to action.[64] Prattis's decision to reference South Africa would have made the situation in Northeast Africa more palatable to his audience, sullied Egypt's reputation, and made the Sudanese more sympathetic figures.

In November 1951—a month after making his Egypt–South Africa comparison—Prattis doubled down on his portrayal of the racially defined oppression Sudanese could face with Egyptian rule. In his piece titled "American Negroes Should Be Concerned about What Is Happening in Egypt," he declared, "[If Sudan were added to Egypt] the six million Sudanese would become second-grade people in the new Egyptian empire and the Sudan would be exploited for the benefit of the upper-strata of white and brown Egyptians. . . . The Egyptians might be worse than the British." In an important discursive move, Prattis not only offered his opinion on what America's position towards potential Egyptian rule over Sudan should be but also encouraged Black America to take action. "The United States should oppose this Egyptian grab of the Sudan. Negroes should tell their Senators and the State Department (Mr. Acheson) that they don't want their country in on such a deal."[65] Prattis's admonition to his readers to contact their senators can be viewed in light of the fact that four years earlier he had become the first African American journalist to be granted membership in the Senate and House press galleries.[66]

If Egyptians were framed as Arab overlords, African American writers conversely painted the Sudanese in a glowing light. Hugh Weston noted, "Sudanese are universally regarded as being persons with many fine qualities, among them loyalty courage and honor. Although there was considerable question about the Arab role in the war, no one has questioned the role of the Sudanese. . . . The Sudanese inflicted grave losses on Italy's haughty forces that expected to make the Sudan an easy colonial conquest."[67] Prattis offered that Sudanese appeared to be "such a good, sturdy and competent people that it seems a pity they must be grabbed at by outsiders."[68] Virtues aside, Black newspapers pointed attention to what the Sudanese wanted: freedom from both the British and Egyptians. George Schuyler noted that the Sudanese "craved" freedom from both parties; Prattis similarly wrote that the Sudanese wanted independence from both and that they would simply be exchanging "one exploiter for another" if the Egyptians replaced the British; and the *Courier*, reporting that "the natives of the Anglo-Egyptian Sudan [were] demanding their freedom from England and Egypt," stated, "Eventually this black nation must be free, so why not now?"[69]

The period bookended by the end of World War I (1918) and Sudanese independence (1956) was dynamic on several fronts. Sudan—the Anglo-Egyptian possession where the bizarre and ill-fated Hunt-Washington cotton project occurred—started the period as the Anglo-Egyptian Condominium and ended it in independence. Egypt, one of its colonial overlords, itself became independent from Britain but desired to maintain hegemony over its Sudanic neighbor. While Ethiopia began and ended this period as a sovereign state, it endured a harrowing Italian occupation in between. Half the world away from the United States, the Italian invasion ignited African American internationalism and anticolonialism and—importantly—invited that community to fix its eyes on the ancestral continent. Each of these developments converged to result in a partisan, multilayered Black American discourse concerning Sudan during those cataclysmic years. While Booker T. Washington may have been silent on the Sudanese in the early twentieth century, Black writers addressing millions of Black readers of Black newspapers were not.

African American writers during this period voiced unabashed respect for Sudan and solidarity with Sudanese. While such sentiments ranged from recognitions of similar phenotypes to claims that African Americans were linked to Sudan through slavery, perhaps nowhere was Black American affinity more manifest than in the way that African American newspapers described Sudanese in relation to Egypt—that is, as a Black people subject to potential subjection from Arabs. This articulated dichotomy delineating Arabs rulers from Black ruled made the Sudanese more relatable to Black Americans subjected to systematic racism but also portended words African Americans would use about Sudan during its postcolonial era, when Black southern Sudanese would wage war against northern Sudanese Arab regimes.

Black American newspaper engagement with Sudan was racialized before its independence and the racially fraught postcolonial civil wars that injected "Arab" and "Black" with even stronger meaning. The Black press was foundational in fostering African Americans' relationship to Sudan. Just as Black papers had covered the Hunt-Washington scheme in the early twentieth century, they continued to shine a spotlight on Sudan for Black readers through both World Wars right up to and through independence. Black anticolonialism was not limited to criticism of white imperialists. The case of Egypt shows that it could target an African country as well. Prattis, for all his pejorative language concerning the Egyptians, advocated for Egyptian independence and claimed that it should play an important role in the Near East. "But," he continued, "it can't play its proper role if it only seeks a change for freedom in order to get a strangle hold on somebody else."[70]

Finally, Black newspaper attention to the Sudanese as fellow Black people is critical when interrogating the terms of African American racial solidarity with African peoples. While this is certainly evident with Egypt during the period under study in this chapter, the same matter applies to the ways African Americans made meaning of Ghana's 1957 independence moment. While that nation is commonly misunderstood as the country that ushered in postwar African independence, it was in fact Sudan (which did so in 1956). However, it was Ghana that enthralled African Americans. This fascination, writes the historian James Campbell, was rooted in Ghana's location on the same coast where millions were transported into transatlantic slavery and augmented by the appeal of Ghanaian prime minister Kwame Nkrumah, who had spent time in the United States.[71] The *New York Amsterdam News* noted a "common bond between American Negroes and Ghana" and added, "There is more than meets the eye behind the birth of the new nation of Ghana. . . . To the millions of colored people around the world Ghana represents the first robin of spring after a long cold and dark winter." This "first robin" reference, the historian James H. Meriwether rightly suggests, signaled that Ghanaian nationhood held more significance than independence in Asia or North Africa. Ghana's independence was—apparently—the first Black African nation to throw off the colonial chains.[72]

But what about Sudan, Ghana's counterpart on the other side of the continent? Patrick Manning asserts that Sudanese independence garnered little attention from the African diaspora because it was perhaps deemed an exceptional case, while Meriwether posits that few African Americans at the time linked Sudanese independence to "Black Africa."[73] However, the African American newspaper coverage presented here clearly shows that Black Americans understood Sudan to be "Black" by the time it became independent in 1956, a year before Ghana. Something—whether West Africa's connection with US slavery, Nkrumah, or other elements—distinguished Ghana from Sudan in the Black American imaginary. An attempt to explain this discrepancy may shed light on the ways that African Americans across space and time have decided what makes someone or something Black. Simply put, the implications of seeing Ghana as the first sub-Saharan African state to become independent after World War II are problematic for several reasons. It would presume that blackness, globally speaking, is preeminently one with intimate connections to the Atlantic world, transatlantic slavery, and a dynamic that most readily features white Europeans and Americans as the harbingers of oppression. According to such logic, Sudan—with its geographic distance from the Atlantic, long-running history of non-European slaveholding, and legacy of Arabs exploiting Blacks—would rest outside such bounds of blackness. Excluded, its monumental achievement would be marginalized by the very African world that could have been galvanized months before Ghana's liberation moment. It is a counterintuitive, self-limiting calculus.

As Sudan went from colony to independent country, the United States established diplomatic relations with the new nation.[74] In perhaps their most significant appearance in Sudan since the Tuskegee project, African Americans entered the country and labored in the service of the US government. The next chapter begins with African American reaction to Sudanese independence, explores the observations and contributions made by Black Americans in Sudan during the late 1950s and 1960s, and examines changing representations of Sudan in Black newspapers as the young nation devolved into civil war.

Chapter 3

An Atmosphere of Good Relations

Louis Martin was born in Shelbyville, Tennessee. A graduate of the University of Michigan, Martin began his journalistic career at the *Chicago Defender*. By the time of his 1997 death, the *Washington Post* had crowned him as "the godfather of black politics."[1] In the January 14, 1956, *Defender* Martin wrote, "A news dispatch on New Year's Day took me back some 20 years to a class room at Ann Arbor where the distinguished Prof. Arthur Lyon Cross sought valiantly to teach us English history. The news dispatch was datelined Khartoum . . . the historic spot around which Prof. Cross . . . recounted the exploits of the British General Gordon." The dispatch Martin referenced reported that a new tricolor flag would be hoisted over the new nation of Sudan. Martin said that this news was especially meaningful "to those who sat at the feet of little Artie": "I am sure that he never dreamed that the day would come in our life time when the 'blacks of the Sudan' would form a nation and raise their own flag over Khartoum." Nearly sixty years after the Battle of Omdurman had placed Sudan under the Union Jack's shadow, the day of jubilee had finally come. "The old world is dying and a new one is being born," Martin said. "The British empire as Prof. Cross knew it has gone."[2]

While it may be known that Black Americans in the 1950s and 1960s paid attention to Kwame Nkrumah's Ghana, Patrice Lumumba's Congo, and racist apartheid South Africa, it is a curious yet hitherto unexplored reality that Sudan was a physical crossroads for Black Americans in the same period.[3] Black Muslim leader Malcolm X, congressman Charles Diggs, activist Shirley Graham Du Bois, and artist Elton Fax represent just a portion of those African Americans who made their way to Sudan between 1955 and the early 1970s.[4] As diverse as this lot was, one particular cadre of African American travelers to Sudan made the most enduring impact: Black US service personnel.

The 1950s and 1960s were years of sweeping change for the United States and Sudan. America was fraught with fears of Cold War nuclear holocaust, growing military action in Vietnam, and a nonviolent civil rights movement confronted by all manners of violence. Thousands of miles and an ocean away, Sudan was also embroiled. The young nation experienced multiple coups, found itself entangled in the Arab-Israeli conflict, and was nearly rent apart when southern Sudanese on the margins of state power waged civil war against successive Khartoum-based regimes. As the United States and Sudan faced existential internal crises, African Americans took center stage in establishing and maintaining diplomatic relations between the two nations. From Andrew Brimmer to Arthur McCaw, Valerie McCaw to Madison Broadnax, Black Americans were instrumental in providing economic, agricultural, and cultural resources to Sudan during its early independence. As such, it is impossible to properly chronicle or understand US-Sudan relations and the development of early postcolonial Sudan without exploring African Americans' role.

This chapter fits in the genealogy of African American engagements with Sudan in several ways. Sudan's early postcolonial era was the most significant period of African American labor in the country since the Tuskegee project fifty years earlier (which, coincidentally, occurred during the infancy of the colonial period). While African American work in Sudan mirrored the Tuskegee project in its heavy representation of historically Black college graduates, it was distinguished by its diversity and, importantly, by the presence of Black women. Finally, Black American diplomatic work during these years foreshadowed other Black labor performed in Sudan under the auspices of the US government in the late twentieth and early twenty-first centuries. Before considering the subsequent Sudanese work by Black Americans at the highest levels of the US foreign policy system—all the way up to President Barack Obama—it is first necessary to examine their comparatively lesser-known but no less important predecessors.

Early US-Sudan Relations

Upon Sudan's 1956 independence, Sudanese-American relations got off to a healthy start—that is, until Sudan embraced nonalignment. The United States did not look favorably on Sudan's relationship with Egypt when it turned to the Soviet bloc in 1955, and Sudan in turn resented US support for Israel and perceived the States as the new colonial power. However, when Sudan asked for technical and economic assistance in 1957, the United States—which looked to slow Soviet influence in the region—responded favorably. US aid from the late 1950s to 1967 measured $103 million and went mainly to education, transport, and agriculture.[5] The US Agency for International Development (USAID) not only supported the University of Khartoum and secondary schools but also assisted in road construction that improved Sudan's major export, cotton. In addition, the US Information Agency created a library that, in the words of one official, was "new and much needed . . . with books and films of the best and most up-to-date scientific, economic, historic, and mathematical information in the world."[6]

Just two years into independence, Sudan experienced a shock to its political system when General Ibrahim Abboud led a coup in 1958. The overthrow that ended Sudan's first democratic era is believed to have had tacit support from the United States and Britain; each were concerned about the precarious southern Sudanese situation and Khartoum's leftist politics. As southern Sudanese who had previously been relegated to the margins of Condominium statecraft feared domination from northern Sudanese, it is pertinent to underscore the British role in encouraging Sudan's North-South division.[7] The British, who conceptualized the North as "Middle-eastern and Arabicized" and the South as African and "Negroid," had divided and administered the Sudan along these regional lines.[8] According to Muddathir 'Abd al-Rahim, the Condominium's "Southern Policy" attempted to administratively eliminate "all traces of Muslim-Arabic culture in the South and the substitution of tribal customs, Christianity, and the English language, with the ultimate objective of giving the three Southern provinces a character and outlook different from that of the country as a whole."[9] After 1946 North and South were reconstituted as a single unit, and in the 1950s the British-led Condominium government sought to unify the mainly missionary southern school system with the government-run northern school system. "Thus," writes scholar Iris Seri-Hersch, "we are dealing with a situation in which Sudan was hastily reunited in a context of British imperial dismantlement."[10] The South did not experience major socioeconomic developments during

Figure 3.1. Map of Sudan, 1956.
Source: Drawn by Bill Nelson.

the early independence years, and the Southern Union Party demanded federation. Other demands included the insistence that Christianity be an official religion along with Islam (the predominant religion of the North) and that English be the official language along with Arabic. Southerners were concerned about the nationalist vision shared by northern parties in which southerners would be assimilated into a Sudanese identity through Islam and Arabic.[11]

Following the 1958 coup, Sudan warmed its relations with Gamal Abdel Nasser's Soviet-allied Egyptian government. From the 1960s onward the expanding South Sudanese civil war (which exploded into a full-scale conflict in 1963), the conflict's specter of regional disintegration, and concern over Arab nationalist policies each influenced US relations with Sudan. Meanwhile the West was leery of the Muslim Brotherhood, who wanted an Islamic republic.[12] Sudan's second civilian government took power after a 1964 coup unseated Abboud's regime. Prime Minister al-Sirr al-Khalifa (1964–1967) was succeeded by Sadiq al-Mahdi (1967–1969). Sudan's warm relations with the Soviet Union continued, and when the country—an Arab League member—sided with Arab nations and accused the United States of complicity with Israel, Sudan declared war on Israel in 1967 and severed its diplomatic relationship with the United States.[13] In 1969 Colonel Jaafar Nimeiri led yet another coup, unseating Muhammad Ahmad Mahjub's democratically elected government, after which US-Sudan relations did not change. Nimeiri supported Nasser's pan-Arabism and established close relations with the Soviet Union. However, a shift occurred when Nimeiri suspected Soviet involvement in a 1971 communist attempt against his government. Sudanese-Soviet relations broke down, and Nimeiri aligned Sudan with the United States. Washington embraced this rapprochement, giving $18 million to rehabilitate southern Sudan and resettle refugees (the long civil war ended in 1972, resulting in a degree of southern autonomy). Nimeiri's shift to the United States notwithstanding, a 1973 Palestinian terrorist attack in Khartoum resulted in the deaths of the US ambassador, his deputy, and the Belgian charge d'affairs. This violence severely undermined relations with Washington.[14]

In the early 1950s a small number of Black people worked in the State Department, and some magazine articles discussed the limited opportunities for African Americans in the department. In an interview with Black American ambassador Terence Todman, diplomatic historian Michael Krenn noted that several State Department documents from the 1940s to the 1960s discussed where the department "could or could not send black Americans to serve because of the country's practices and so forth." The department, Krenn noted to Todman, "seemed very tense about . . . sending black Americans to Arabic nations."[15]

While Presidents John F. Kennedy and Lyndon Johnson pursued the matter of Black employment in foreign service work, only small inroads were made in the mostly white State Department and Foreign Service.[16] Such lack of progress was evident in the African American representation in American posts abroad. In May 1966, the deputy under secretary of state for administration (William J. Crockett) wrote a memorandum to Joseph Palmer II, the assistant secretary of state for African Affairs. The memo was titled "Urgent Need to Increase Minority Group Representation at African Posts." In it, Crockett shared that Bill Hall of USAID had recently passed along impressions from visits he had made to four African nations, including Sudan. Hall's critique was categorically blunt: "None of the foreign affairs agencies had adequate minority representation on its staffs. AID and USIA are better than State, but all are completely inadequate. We need to consider how we can improve this situation." Crockett said that Hall's views were buttressed by a report Palmer had sent to African American congressman Adam Clayton Powell Jr. the previous December regarding Black Americans assigned to African posts. Twenty-six of forty AF (Bureau of African Affairs, Department of State) posts where Americans were assigned lacked any Black officers, and of the four posts Hall had personally visited there were two Black officers in Congo, one in Nigeria, two in Ethiopia, and none in Sudan.[17]

Despite the dire lack of representation of Black Americans in US foreign service at the time, African Americans found themselves at the epicenter of US-Sudan diplomatic relations. The narrative of their contributions begins with economist Andrew Brimmer.

Economical and Educational Work

Andrew Felton Brimmer Jr. was born on September 13, 1926, in Newellton, Louisiana. The son of a sharecropper, Brimmer picked cotton and attended segregated schools. Brimmer moved to the state of Washington after graduating from high school, lived with an older sister, and worked in a navy yard as an electrician's helper. Drafted into the army in 1945, Brimmer attained the rank of staff sergeant and entered the University of Washington upon completing his duties. He graduated with a bachelor's degree in economics in 1950. Discovered by Secretary of Urban Development Robert Weaver, Brimmer was awarded a John Hay Fellowship to complete his master's degree, which he obtained in 1951. His interest in foreign economics resulted in a Fulbright Fellowship to India, where he did postgraduate work at the Delhi School of Economics and the University of Bombay. Brimmer enrolled at Harvard in 1952, married the following year, and completed his doctorate in 1957 with a concentration in monetary economics and economic development.[18]

From 1955 to 1958, Brimmer worked as an economist at New York City's Federal Reserve Bank. It was during this time that he worked on a Federal Reserve Central Banking mission to Khartoum to explore the feasibility of a central bank in Sudan.[19] The Sudanese government had requested the mission through the State Department, and the Federal Reserve System's board of governors organized the project. Brimmer was joined by Oliver Wheeler (vice president of San Francisco's Federal Reserve Bank) and Alan Holmes, who also worked with the New York Fed. The mission arrived in Khartoum on December 7, 1956, and Brimmer stayed there for roughly three months, departing on March 10, 1957. The mission was tasked "to advise the government of the functions and organization of a Central Bank for the Sudan which would best fit the economic and institutional setup of this country and to frame accordingly a draft charter of the Central Bank." The Sudanese Ministry of Finance provided working facilities and arranged for interviews with government officials, commercial bankers, and members of the business community.[20]

The Sudanese banking system before independence was essentially colonial banking; commercial banks were part of foreign institutions, and no local currency or central bank existed. Within this colonial milieu, the expatriate banks that largely comprised the Condominium's banking and credit system aimed to serve the needs of export and import trade and accept deposits for foreign and Sudanese firms. Following independence, the Sudan Currency Board was established to issue the new national currency, and the Bank of Sudan Act was passed in 1959. In 1960 the Central Bank of Sudan's became one of Africa's first working central banking institutions. The bank took charge of foreign exchange and currency matters like regulating the issuance of coins and notes, developing a sound credit and banking system, and advising the government on banking and financing. The formation of the Central Bank was part of a larger transformation in government structure that by the mid-1960s was structured around a formidable Ministry of Finance and new organizations like the bank, planning agencies, statistical bureaus, and agricultural banks. The Sudanese state, through its capacity to tax and control credit, aimed to create a unified national market.[21] Brimmer's advisory role concerning the formation of a central bank placed the sharecropper's son at the center of the process that laid the economic foundation for Sudan's postcolonial state.[22] He went on to become the assistant secretary of commerce for economic affairs and was serving in that role when President Johnson named the sharecropper's son to the Federal Reserve Board in 1966. Brimmer, the board's first Black member, became its international monetary policy expert.[23]

Brimmer was not the only African American to work in Sudanese economic affairs. Robert Kitchen and Madison Broadnax followed in his stead. Kitchen was a Brunswick, Georgia, native and 1943 graduate of Morehouse College. He earned an MS from Columbia University, taught at Atlanta University and the Hampton Institute, and became an associate professor of business administration at West Virginia State College (all historically Black institutions). Kitchen's association with US economic assistance programs in newly developing countries began in 1952 through his work with the International Cooperation Administration (ICA) mission in Liberia. He worked there as a staff assistant, officer, and acting director. Back in Washington, DC, Kitchen led the ICA's Pakistan desk.[24]

In November 1957—eight months after Brimmer's farewell—Kitchen led a survey team to Sudan to explore the prospects of a US assistance program. As a direct result of the visit, the Sudanese and American governments signed a bilateral agreement in Khartoum on March 31, 1958. The agreement provided a framework for US economic and technical assistance to Sudan in agriculture, vocational education, road development, and communication. A US economic mission would be sent to Khartoum to create an ICA operations office there.[25] *Jet* magazine reported that Kitchen, then thirty-six years old, had been appointed to lead the mission:

> Robert W. Kitchen, Jr., was named to head a 12-man U.S. aid mission to the two-year-old country of Sudan in what State Dept. officials call one of the most important and strategic projects in Africa. Top aide to Dr. John W. Davis, who headed a Point IV mission to Liberia six years ago, Kitchen will supervise a study of the economic needs for the new African nation and will recommend self-help projects which could run well into the millions. The assignment is considered "highly delicate" since it is the first such U.S. aid group to be assigned to the Sudan, whose leaders in the past have turned down U.S. financial help. Senate confirmation is required for the post, which has diplomatic status.[26]

Kitchen was appointed a Class I officer in the US Operations Mission to Sudan and counsellor of embassy, and the US Senate confirmed him in July 1958. Martha Kitchen, Robert's wife, accompanied him to Sudan.[27]

François M. Dickman, who worked as a foreign service officer in Sudan, described Kitchen as "highly intelligent and motivated." Dickman recalled Kitchen's return to Khartoum after the agreement was signed to lead the USAID mission. "Soon, we had a large number of AID technicians whose numbers completely dwarfed the embassy's. However, the large AID mission resulted in the embassy receiving a Marine guard detail.... The embassy in Khartoum had changed from being a very small one to a very large one."[28] On April 26, 1958, Kitchen wrote a letter from Khartoum to friend and former colleague John Warren Davis, long-time president of West Virginia State University. While he described his new responsibility as "awe-inspiring," he noted that uncertainties in the political scene had postponed his swearing-in four times. He said that they would need "six absolutely top-rate trade and industry instructors within the next four months, with particular interest in the areas of building construction, automotive engineering, arts and handicraft and machine shop." If Davis knew of any strong candidates, Kitchen continued, he should please let Kitchen know. "I have offered the Chief Extension job here to Madison Broadnax and hope that it will be possible to have him as the only outsider on our staff by mid-June."[29]

Sudan represented Broadnax's first assignment with the USAID. Broadnax, a former professor of agriculture at West Virginia State College, joined the ICA in Sudan in 1958 and served there until 1962 (though he would return in 1972). "I knew," stated Broadnax years later, "that my position was to go and assist the government of the Sudan in establishing the National Agricultural Extension Service.... I had to design it and sell it to the Sudanese, which wasn't much of a problem really. But I had some barriers to overcome." Broadnax arrived in Sudan just before the 1958 coup.[30] When the government provided its first extension workers, Broadnax was given six graduates from the College of Agriculture. In addition to being college graduates, these individuals had received postsecondary education at Khartoum's Shambat Institute of Agriculture, where junior officers were trained beyond high school. The Ministry of Agriculture decided that they wanted to initiate the program in southern Sudan.[31]

The selection of the Shambat-trained agriculturalists shines a light on the broader context of development and empire in which Broadnax operated. A colonial institution, the College of Agriculture began operating in the city of Shambat in 1938. The first six students were given a three-year professional course in agricultural sciences and agricultural engineering, as well as tours "to familiarise the students with the peasant farmer and with the traditional method[s] and social life in rural areas."[32] The first students graduated in 1942, and all entered positions in the Sudanese Department of Agriculture. In 1945 the College of Agriculture was incorporated into Gordon College, an institution providing direct access to jobs in colonial government (and, importantly, often at the highest level available to northern

Sudanese). In 1954 the Ministry of Agriculture established the Shambat Institute of Agriculture.[33] It is evident, then, that US cooperation with the Shambat Institute was both a form of nation-building agricultural assistance and, in another sense, a direct continuation of a colonial enterprise. The figure of Broadnax highlights one African American's positionality working for the success of an early postcolonial African state while also being a Black neocolonialist in the golden age of African nationalism.

Broadnax later recalled, "When the government asked to introduce the program in the south, it turned out it was the best thing that could ever happen." An agricultural adviser joined Broadnax at Maridi (in Western Equatoria, now a state in South Sudan). This adviser had a senior counterpart assigned there who was one of the six people Broadnax had been assigned, as well as three junior agricultural officers from the Shambat Institute. "There we built offices; we built houses, and we had a horticulture advisor to come on board shortly after that." Broadnax suggested a 250-acre farm where every crop that could be cultivated in the South could be grown. "We could bring the chiefs in to give them training. Then we had satellite village farms. That's where these junior officers were. They brought people into those satellite village farms." In his view, the demonstration farms "revolutionized" farming through the Maridi area. Crop variety changed to those that were brought to the demonstration farm. "[They brought] open pollinated seeds so they could save the seeds," Broadnax reported. "They would take these varieties back and try them." Though the typical southern farm was small, the work—in Broadnax's estimation—was significant. "We improved the crops they were growing—vegetable crops. And eventually, we put in . . . small tropical tree crops as a cash enterprise, including coffee and pineapple." They placed one of the Shambat extension officers in charge. "[By the time the program was closed] we had increased the farmers' income in that locality by five percent, which was a great achievement at that time."[34]

"In the northern provinces," said Broadnax, "we used the farms that the government had already established and we improved them." When they made a reconnaissance survey of the farmers in the province of Gezira—which contained a two-million-acre farm for cotton—they found that some of their practices did not yield maximum returns. "We organized the extension program around food crops," he shared. "We were bringing farmers into Shambat for field days and show[ed] them a variety of vegetable crops and practices. In El-Obeid . . . we organized a demonstration in a village about

60 miles from there. We set up demonstration farms there too." They also brought seeds from the United States. "[The US Department of Agriculture] backstopped us on selecting seed varieties that they thought would do well, and I must admit we didn't fail on any. We had extension advisers posted in the capital, who taught cultural practices conducive to the region."[35] In addition to his aforementioned labors, Broadnax taught a course in extension "to the Shambat Institute people" and taught elementary agriculture for a week to boys and girls at the Tang school in the province of Bahr el Ghazal. When asked to review his accomplishments during his tenure, Broadnax responded, "We trained 83 Sudanese in agriculture.... We sent them to the United States for short and long-term training. They came back and worked in the Ministry of Agriculture until opportunities came for better jobs, salary wise. They wanted to build houses and that sort of thing."[36]

In summation, Madison Broadnax may have been among the most consequential individuals on Kitchen's staff during his tenure in Sudan. When it came to supporting Sudan's agricultural production during the early independence period, American assistance was significant. In addition to USAID's role in helping to launch Sudan's nationwide extension service, USAID assistance included agricultural research and crop development, livestock and poultry development, farm machinery training, pest control, agricultural economics, and rural water development. However, the civil war disrupted indigenous production systems in southern Sudan.[37] One country report from 1983 said that agricultural development was "frustrated by the absence of ... infrastructure, technologies, extension, [and] supply of inputs." "Emphasis on developing this important sector should be the core of the development assistance for this region, as it is in fact central to USAID concerns in the area [the South]."[38] Such realities should not obscure the significance of Broadnax's labor. Done upon Kitchen's invitation, it illustrates the multidimensional work of African Americans (and HBCU graduates) in the execution of US assistance to newly independent Sudan. Broadnax's experiences provide insight into what such labor looked like in rural Sudan, such as that done by his Tuskegee predecessors, geographically distant from Sudan's epicenter of economic and political power in urban Khartoum. Yet they also point to the mitigating effect that political unrest (and a civil war, no less) could have on the long-term impact of such assistance work. How deleterious was the war on Broadnax's labor? How would history have remembered the impact and legacy of US aid during the early independence period in the absence of such serious shocks to Sudan's political, economic, and social milieus? Such questions address the importance of not relying exclusively on statistical indicators in assessing the impact of African American foreign service work.

A couple of days before Christmas 1958, Kitchen mentioned to Davis, "[Sudan] could use sewing kits, carpentry kits, and a host of other packages which the American people have contributed to other rapidly emerging countries in recent years." Kitchen, in the same letter, acknowledged that after an unbelievably fast nine months, he and his cohort were "rapidly approaching" the end of their tour.[39] In May he would remark to Davis, "[We are] swamped here in trying to stay on the tracks. The personnel situation has been horrible but stands to improve quite considerably over the next few weeks." He added that he would be in the United States at some point in July and August for a month. "[We] are beginning to think in terms of being home next spring [1960] for leave and possibly transfer to Washington."[40] Two months later, Kitchen informed Davis that he would be in the States in August and that health concerns were partially responsible for his forthcoming return: "I have had repeated nervous difficulty which the local doctors claim resemble cerebral hemorrhages . . . [and] the tour is up next April. However, there is some thought being given to going back to Washington working on problems of the Soviet economic war." His wife, Martha, he shared, had also not been well: "Her condition is a factor to be considered also."[41] The September 3, 1959, *Jet* reported that Sudan mission chief Kitchen would be returning to the United States shortly for a new position with the ICA. In three fiscal years, Sudan's USAID mission—the largest USAID mission and program in tropical Africa—had involved allocation, planning, and execution of projects that exceeded $100 million in expenditures. Kitchen, who had led the massive effort, would reportedly be considered for Sudan's ambassadorship but never occupied the position. In November 1963 Kitchen became the first Black director of the USAID International Training Division.[42]

Robert Kitchen's stint in Sudan was remarkable for what it revealed and, in comparison, what it left wanting. Preceded by coverage in *Jet* magazine, the publicity given to Kitchen's path to the Sudan reflected the Black press's investment in highlighting African American activity in US diplomacy generally and in postcolonial Africa particularly. Unlike Brimmer—a graduate of two predominantly white institutions—Kitchen had an HBCU pedigree that linked him with Tuskegee predecessors a half-century earlier who had traveled to the Condominium as part of Leigh Hunt's cotton project. While Kitchen may not have toiled in Sudanese agricultural fields, his time in Sudan represents an evolution in the type of African American aid work in Sudan and the continued presence of HBCU-affiliated figures involved in such work (including his bringing fellow HBCU alum Broadnax to the country). Given postcolonial Sudan's long record of war and otherwise poor human rights record, Kitchen's administration of the first major USAID program in Africa—the US mission to Sudan—positions him at the origins of US aid to independent Sudan (the United States, as of early 2023, was Sudan's largest international humanitarian aid donor).[43] Yet, such elements notwithstanding, Kitchen's correspondence—like Booker T. Washington before him—is silent regarding the Sudanese themselves. What did he think about the people? Did he identify with or perceive the Sudanese racially, politically, or otherwise? Those examining the archival record in search of such insights will leave unsatisfied. It would be irresponsible to conclude that such silence must mean that Kitchen did not see the Sudanese as racial kin. However, we lack primary evidence that he worked in Sudan with a concerted sense of racial consciousness and/or solidarity with the Sudanese. One is left to wonder how Kitchen reconciled his work in Sudan with the social and political forces of his time and the contemporaneous contexts of the rising US civil rights movement and African nationalism.

Broadnax's work in agricultural education was complemented by advances made by other African Americans in Sudanese education during the early independence era. In July 1961, F. A. Williams—dean of North Carolina A&T's University's Graduate School—left for an ICA assignment in Sudan. He was tasked with serving as an economics professor at the University of Khartoum for the year and did so with a State Department grant under the Smith-Mundt Educational Exchange Program. While Williams returned to the United States for three months the following summer, he reportedly returned to Sudan for the beginning of the first semester of the 1962–1963 year.[44] Gordon L. Bradshaw, former press room instructor at Hampton Institute, was appointed for a two-year tour of duty with USAID in Sudan. Bradshaw was then serving as printing instructor at Ferris Institute in Big Rapids, Michigan. A report published by Virginia-based Black newspaper *New Journal and Guide* noted that Bradshaw would "advise and train Sudanese education officials in printing techniques and produce printed materials for instructional use." The paper added, "He will be accompanied by his wife on the trip to Africa."[45]

African Americans also contributed to Sudanese dentistry education, the *New York Amsterdam News* reported on February 3, 1962: "[An abundant number of students around Khartoum] were given a 'Come Ahead' this week because two farsighted Harlem businessmen donated a complete office of dental equipment for their use in the course of their dental studies, at the University of Khartoum." The men at the center of this were dentist and Howard alumnus W. Kenneth Williams and Roosevelt Zanders, described as "probably richest chauffer in the world" and "the close friend of celebrities, diplomats. actors and heads of state." Williams and Zanders, who had traveled the world together, reportedly had witnessed firsthand the extreme need for technical equipment in schools abroad and students' eagerness to study dentistry. The donated dental chair, which Williams had once used, was said to have had a storied history: luminaries including Fats Waller, Duke Ellington, Ethel Waters, Dina Washington, the Peters Sisters, Countee Cullen, A. Philip Randolph, and Jackie Robinson had used it.[46]

Valaria McCaw distinguished herself as a teacher for blind Sudanese. Born in Texas in March 1912, she later became a member of Delta Sigma Theta Sorority, and she married Arthur McCaw in 1931. Arthur's government positions took him around the world, and Valaria used her talents and art teaching degree to train artists in Korea and design materials for demonstrations there. In time, Arthur's work took him to Sudan.[47] Following a visit to Khartoum's Nour Institute for the Blind, Valaria started a ceramics class so that its students could "see beauty through the use of their fingers." She received help from the headmaster, Khartoum Technical Institute's art department, and Khartoum Ophthalmological Hospital's chief surgeon. In addition to leading regular classes at the Nour Institute, she trained a Sudanese woman to carry on the program with twenty-eight students. Nour students, despite their blindness, could reportedly make cups, Sudanese coffee pots and bowls, and sculpture heads by using their faces as models for accurate proportions. "It was most rewarding," Valaria recounted. The class of twenty-eight ranged from ages ten to twenty-two and included one girl. The Lions Club of Sudan sponsored the school, the Ministry of Education provided the building for the activity, and "the American Women's group in Khartoum provided materials for the project."[48] Arthur McCaw said, in a statement published in the *Pittsburgh Courier* on March 26, 1966, "Valaria has been an asset and a compliment to me in my career."[49]

From Brimmer's work on Sudan's Central Bank to McCaw's work with blind students, African Americans provided unique contributions to the Sudanese economy, agriculture, and education during its early independence era. Their activities provide insight into the shifting nature of Black American engagements with Sudan. For a few decades, US newspapers had covered the country but not African Americans' experience in it. The labors of Valaria McCaw and others show ways that the new relationship between the United States and postcolonial Sudan was actualized on the ground. Yet the African American presence in Sudan in the 1950s and 1960s was not limited to the service described in this section. On the contrary, it was in areas of art, other culture, and society that Black American engagements made their strongest impacts.

Social and Cultural Contributions

During the early days of the Cold War, global condemnation of US race relations hindered US foreign policy objectives. As a result, the State Department sent prosperous Black Americans on overseas goodwill tours to highlight that community as prominent figures in the African diaspora rather than the victims of systemic racism that they, of course, also were. The US State Department, in its aim to secure the loyalty of Ghana and other African countries, sponsored an African tour for Wilbur de Paris's New Orleans (and all-Black) jazz band. He became popular with Sudanese jazz fans.[50] In June 1958, John Warren Davis sent Robert Kitchen a copy of a letter that he had just received from Dr. Randolph Edmonds of Tallahassee. Edmonds wanted to present a group of his drama students in Sudan. "May I respectfully ask you," queried Davis, "to pass this request of Dr. Edmonds to the proper officials of your staff and/or of the Government of the Sudan for consideration and action."[51] While it is unclear from Kitchen's papers at Howard University's Moorland-Spingarn Research Center whether or not he did as Davis requested, a few months later the *New York Amsterdam News* reported that Florida A&M University's Playmakers Guild had departed New York for a two-month tour of Africa that would include a stop in Sudan, among other nations. The *Amsterdam News* noted that the tour, arranged by the King Travel Organization, would be in cooperation with the President's Special International Program for Cultural Presentations (a program ultimately administered by the State Department). Ten student actors made the trip with Dr. Edmonds, head of the university's Speech and Drama Department. The students were slated to present four plays: Robinson Jeffers's *Medea*, Thornton Wilder's *The Happy Journey*, Paul Green's *Fixin's*, and George Kelly's *The Flattering World*.[52]

In March 1966, the De Paur Chorus visited Sudan as part of the State Department's cultural exchange program. New Jersey–born Leonard de Paur was an orchestra and chorus conductor who served as director of community relations for New York's Lincoln Center for the Performing Arts, worked as a consultant for cultural development in Tunisia, and received an honorary doctorate from Morehouse College, among other accomplishments in his long career. In 1966 his chorus visited several African countries, and their time in Khartoum included stops at the University of Khartoum, Omdurman's enormous outdoor stadium, and a public garden in the city. "The university presentation was well attended," one observer later remembered, "and enthusiastically received by the Sudanese intellectuals. The chorus' stadium appearance did not fare as well because the broadcasting station's public address system was not synchronized. A large segment of the audience could not hear the chorus clearly."[53]

The De Paur Chorus stop in Sudan occurred during James Mack's tenure as a cultural affairs officer in Sudan. James Mack was born in Edwards, Mississippi, on June 4, 1916. After his father was offered a job as a messenger in the Department of Agriculture, the Mack family moved north to Washington, DC. Mack later recounted a day when his mother and father locked all of the doors and windows and lowered the shades and curtains. "We had never locked the doors," he remembered. "My father said many Ku Klux Klansmen were coming up G Street from Union Station. Some men were marching with their faces masked and wearing long white sheets." His father said that they were in Washington for a Klan convention.[54] Decades later—in April 1963—Mack received a letter from the US Information Agency informing him that he had received a five-year appointment to the limited officer corps. After six months of French-language training, there was an urgent need for a cultural officer in Khartoum, and he was placed in the position.[55] In Mack's first overseas assignment as a US diplomatic representative, he and his wife Marjorie arrived in Khartoum in May 1964 and stayed in Sudan for three years. Mack noted, "Some have cultural shock seeing people in long white *jallabias* reminiscent of the Ku Klux Klan's attire." But the reality was far from this. "The Sudanese surprise you by being courteous, friendly, and efficient, speaking Arabic and English," Mack noted.[56]

The United States offered specialists to African governments through its educational and cultural exchange programs. Mack, as cultural attaché in Sudan, led the cultural exchange program on behalf of the State Department. As fate would have it, Mack's first effort in this regard occurred just two weeks before the conclusion of the 1964 October Revolution that removed General Abboud from power. Ethiopian king Haile Selassie had invited Howard University professor of history William Leo Hansberry to visit Addis Ababa to receive the Haile Selassie Award for his research on

African history and culture. Majorie Mack's mother knew the Hansberrys and asked if Mack would stop to see them in Sudan. The professor said that he would be delighted to be their guest in Khartoum. He arrived in Khartoum on Friday, October 16, 1964. Friday was the weekly Islamic holy day (and all government offices consequently closed), but James Mack recalled, "We were fortunate enough to make phone calls on Thursday to invite Sudanese officials and members of the American Embassy country team." While some embassy officials were apparently unsure as to whether Sudanese would attend a reception on such short notice—senior government officials preferred at least a week's advance notice before accepting an embassy invitation—they did indeed attend. "Professor Hansberry's visit was a special occasion and they accepted," Mack later recalled.[57] He received a phone call the morning after the reception requesting an interview with Hansberry, and two Sudanese reporters subsequently conducted a two-hour interview at the Mack household. At the end of the exchange, one of the reporters said that Hansberry was "very knowledgeable about the history of the Sudan, especially the Nubians." A full Arabic account of the interview appeared the next day, and Mack forwarded the report to Hansberry (with an English synopsis). "The professor was impressed and pleased with his visit to the Sudan, and so was I," Mack would remark in his autobiography.[58]

Notwithstanding the visits made by the De Paur Chorus and the Hansberrys, Langston Hughes's May 1966 stop in Khartoum was perhaps the most significant Sudanese visit by an African American during Mack's assignment. Mack was familiar with the famed author's early success as a poet, dating back to Hughes's days at Wardman Park Hotel in Washington, DC. On May 1, 1966, the Khartoum-based *Morning News* newspaper reported, "Langston Hughes, distinguished American Negro poet and author, is visiting the Sudan from April 28 to May 4."[59] The article said that Hughes's visit would be made in cooperation with the University of Khartoum, School of Extra-Mural Studies, and the US State Department's cultural program. After noting that he would give a public lecture at the University of Khartoum titled "American Negro Fiction," the *News* remarked, "[Hughes] has long been one of the most effective spokesmen for the American Negro and has kept in touch with many young Negro poets and writers throughout the years."[60]

When Hughes arrived in Khartoum, just before midnight, Mack greeted him and took him to his hotel (the Sudan Hotel, facing the Blue Nile). "The one important factor for Hughes' visit to Khartoum," Mack would write, "was [that] the Sudanese inherited the Arabs' love of poetry. They love to write poetry but receive greater satisfaction from the written words. Thus this visit could not have been more suitable for Langston Hughes." Mack enlisted the support of Ishag el Mahdi and Ahmed Abdul Halim, director of the University of Khartoum's School of Extra-Mural Studies. While they planned Hughes's itinerary together, Halim scheduled Hughes for talks and readings at the university's lecture hall and a tea party at the student union. Before his university lecture, Hughes met Vice-Chancellor Nezeer El Defalla, a poetry enthusiast.[61]

"The lecture that night," remembered Mack, "was stimulating and the lecture hall filled to capacity, including many professors, civil servants, students, and diplomats. Langston gave a short talk about the Harlem Renaissance movement in New York City and the growing influence of Negroes in the arts in America. Then he read a few of his poems, including 'The Negro Speaks of Rivers.'"[62] The poem, which Hughes had written in 1921, traces a continuous stream of Black history from the Nile River and the Congo to the Mississippi:[63]

> I've known rivers:
> I've known rivers ancient as the world and older than the flow of human blood in human veins.
>
> My soul has grown deep like the rivers.
>
> I bathed in the Euphrates when dawns were young.
> I built my hut near the Congo and it lulled me to sleep.
> I looked upon the Nile and raised the pyramids above it.
> I heard the singing of the Mississippi when Abe Lincoln went down to New Orleans, and I've seen its muddy bosom turn all golden in the sunset.
>
> I've known rivers:
> Ancient, dusky rivers.
>
> My soul has grown deep like the rivers.[64]

Mack recalled that Hughes's lecture was well-received and that the audience included members of the Muslim Brotherhood and Sudan Communist Party.[65] This was no small feat. "The Islamists have expressed public distaste and hatred of communism," Mack noted. Just two years after Hughes's visit, Islamic sectarian political parties in Sudan passed a bill depriving eleven communist MPs of their parliamentary seats on the basis of their perceived atheism.[66] "Fortunately," wrote Mack when referring to their collective attendance at Hughes's lecture, "they all had one thing in common, their love of poetry. After the lecture, selected persons received autographed copies of Hughes' book, *The Best of Simple*." The following evening, Halim invited some of Khartoum's most renowned poets to attend a tea party. "The Sudanese, with their Islamic teachings, were especially interested in hearing Hughes' poetry. . . . The poets were honored to have a such a distinguished American poet visit their country." After tea, some Sudanese recited poems in Arabic and English. Hughes was apparently pleased to listen to poetry "with such rhythm and phrasing." While the evening was supposed to conclude with him reading some of his poems, the Sudanese poets would not allow the festivities to end without some of them reciting his material from memory. "I cannot remember having a nicer Sudanese-American evening," Mack would recall, "and Langston was the vehicle for it all."[67]

Ishag el Mahdi was apparently so pleased with the party's outcome that he made a special effort to have another, more elaborate bash the next evening. Hughes was an honored guest, and among those present at that dinner were President Ismail al-Azhari, Prime Minister Sadiq el Mahdi, and the University of Khartoum's vice-chancellor Nezeer El Defalla; the ministers of foreign affairs, interior, and information; the US ambassador; University of Khartoum professors; and Mack, the cultural affairs officer. While it was "most unusual" for the president and prime minister to attend the same event (unless it was a state affair), Mack wrote, "Ishag was able to persuade all to come. A huge cow, instead of a lamb, was cooked, and a variety of cakes were served. Langston Hughes, an American, had been paid the supreme honor by the Sudanese people. . . . The next day Langston left the hotel for the airport."[68] Hughes would be dead in a year, passing away on May 22, 1967.[69]

If Langston Hughes was arguably the most prominent Black American to set foot in Sudan during this period, the most significant visit by a group of African Americans was that made by the women of Delta Sigma Theta Sorority. Founded by twenty-two Howard University students on January 13, 1913, the organization—in the words of historian Paula Giddings—"has shaped and been shaped by its members—many of whom rank among the most important figures in American history." Its first public event involved marching down Pennsylvania Avenue in Washington, DC, in the momentous women's suffrage demonstration leading up to Woodrow Wilson's inauguration.[70] Headquartered in Washington, the Deltas counted thirty-two thousand college-educated women in its ranks by 1962. In January 1962 the *New York Amsterdam News* reported that the sorority had recently announced a plan to tour Africa that summer. Senegal, Guinea, Liberia, Ghana, Nigeria, Kenya, Ethiopia, Egypt, and Sudan would be included as stops on the trek.

The tour aimed to provide the organization with primary knowledge concerning problems facing the continent. Later that spring, national president Dr. Jeanne L. Noble announced that the tour would commence July 26 and include eight African countries (Guinea was apparently removed from the itinerary). The African tour was planned in lieu of an annual convention and highlighted the sorority's Golden Anniversary.[71] "Members of the sorority who elect to make the tour," reported the *Pittsburgh Courier*, "will study the dynamic social, economic and cultural forces which are revolutionizing the long-dormant continent. In many places they will be met by fellow members who are now working in Africa in key positions."[72]

On July 18, 1962, travel entrepreneur Freddye Henderson wrote to Arthur McCaw. Arthur—himself a member of a Black fraternal organization, Kappa Alpha Psi—had begun his stint as chief end-use officer for USAID in Khartoum earlier that year. As noted, his wife, Valaria, was a Delta. "We are very pleased that you and Mrs. McCaw would like to entertain the members of Delta Sigma Theta Sorority Tour when they come to Khartoum. Delta, too, is pleased to have so distinguished a Soror in Khartoum, and would be pleased and honored to share their time with you and Mrs. McCaw." Henderson informed McCaw that the Deltas would arrive in Khartoum the morning of August 7 from Lagos, Nigeria, and remain for a day.[73] The State Department sent an airgram to each of the locations on the trip concerning the "Tour of 45 members of Delta Sigma Theta Sorority to Africa and Europe." Dr. Noble, whom the airgram described as "a very able young women, well known to the Department," would lead the tour with Anna Harvin Grant (professor at Grambling College) and Charlayne Hunter (the University of Georgia's first Black student). The traveling group would be composed of college students and older women, freedom riders and conservatives, women from large Eastern cities and small Southern towns.

> For many of the women this is their first trip abroad and their first face-to-face contact with Africans. They will be interested in observing women's organizations and activities in the countries they visit, as well as the secondary educational needs of the African nations, with a view to evaluating future project proposals. The women will also be interested in locating an African woman leader in the field of volunteer organizations to bring to the United States next year.

The airgram said that State Department officials had met with the sorority's executive director about the trip and supplied informational material and a reading list on the continent. For their part, the Deltas hoped that country briefings could be arranged by the respective posts.[74]

On August 7, 1962, the McCaws honored the visiting Deltas at their Khartoum home. In addition to the Deltas, other guests included Mrs. Gerri Majors of *Jet* and *Ebony* magazines; Ambassador William Rountree and his wife; the USAID mission director; and Sudanese government officials, educators, and press representatives. Valaria introduced Dr. Noble to the gathering, and the sorority president spoke of Delta's interest in Africa's emerging nations and women's welfare in these countries. Noble introduced Dr. Grant, who presented each member of the traveling sisterhood and shared their individual accomplishments. "The Americans present," wrote Arthur McCaw, "were all agreed that the Deltas had succeeded in creating an atmosphere of good relations between the U.S. and the Sudanese that had never been reached before." The following day, Wednesday, August 8, Valaria and Fresno State's Mildred Edgar took the visitors on a tour of historic locations in Khartoum and Omdurman. The Delta contingent departed Sudan for Nairobi the next morning.[75]

Arthur McCaw, at Gerri Majors's request, provided the aforementioned summary of events to Robert Johnson of Johnson Publishing Company, which he addressed "for your personal attention for *Jet*." McCaw lauded the Deltas to Johnson, noting that the impact they were having on African countries was "tremendous": "The fact that they are paying their own way [and] that they represent an organization of 32,000 American College Women, strikes the African mind as incredible [*sic*] and brings much admiration for them and our country. The good they are doing in public relations for the U.S. is immeasurable." McCaw then congratulated Johnson on his "great publications," saying, "I have for a long time admired and boosted the Negro Press."[76] *Jet* published photographs from the visit in its September 6, 1962 issue.[77]

A month after *Jet* featured the Delta's Sudan visit, President Noble sent a letter to Arthur McCaw expressing gratitude for material that his office had sent concerning the trip. "I certainly want to take this opportunity," wrote Noble, "to thank you and Soror McCaw for your gracious hospitality. From the moment you met us at the airport, to the final evening both of you were most gracious. And, that party was just wonderful." Acknowledging that there were other people that she should thank for their work on facilitating a good trip, Noble requested that McCaw forward specific names he felt were important.[78] In their 1963 Christmas message, Val and Arthur McCaw said that the visit was the "highlight of the year." "[The Delta women's impact in] advanc[ing] the interest of womenhood in this Moslem country was something to behold. People who had been here for a long time called the party we gave in our home for them and 200 Sudanese the most effective affair that has been held to advance U.S. Sudanese relations."[79]

While the visits of Langton Hughes and the Delta Sigma Theta sisters represented major moments of the African American presence in Sudan, their visits were not reported to a broader audience in the white American press. This negligence in reportage does not, however, diminish the significance of those two trips in the history of Black engagements with Sudan. Mention of the Delta Sigma Theta stop in Sudan in venues like *Jet* and the *Chicago Defender* show that even if such diasporic moments were ignored by the white US mass media, they did not escape the purview of the Black media—an industry with voluminous sweep.[80] That the only source we have concerning Hughes's visit comes from the memoir of James Mack—the African American cultural affairs officer who facilitated the poet's visit to Khartoum—speaks both to the significance that the visit had for him personally and the fact one should not conflate impact with publicity (fewer readers, no doubt, have read his memoir than have read the *New York Times*). Thus, while Hughes's Sudan trip may not directly relate to how Sudan informed Black American understandings of Black definition, consciousness, and solidarity, it is nevertheless worth including in this study as proof of Sudan's appearance in the late life of one of Black America's greatest writers and of the richness of all documentation—official or otherwise—produced by Black US foreign service workers in memorializing such diasporic moments.

Sudanese independence and the establishment of relations with the United States resulted in the greatest presence of African Americans in the country to date. Black foreign service workers played more than a marginal role in the nascent years of US-Sudan relations. From Andrew Brimmer's examination of the prospects of a Sudanese central bank, Madison Broadnax's work in agricultural training in northern and southern Sudan, and James Mack's facilitating opportunities for Sudanese to engage with Langston Hughes to Valaria McCaw's education of young blind people in Sudan, African Americans provided vital economic, educational, agricultural, and cultural resources to Sudan at a time when both the United States and Sudan were embroiled. This reality is not only important for understanding African Americans' role in US-Africa relations during decolonization but also fits into the genealogy of Black American engagements with Sudan in significant ways.

The period explored in this chapter was not only the most significant era of African American labor in the country since the Tuskegee project, it was also, in many respects, a continuation of the kind of aid work that those men had done decades earlier. The Tuskegee project and foreign service work explored in this chapter were two cases in which African Americans traveled to Sudan for the purposes of helping the Sudanese (rather than receiving assistance from them). Though separated by half a century of time and colonialism, the neocolonial labor in the second mirrored that of the first. Another link connecting those two moments was the role played by graduates of historically Black colleges. Those Black Americans who embarked to Sudan were a particularly classed and race-conscious cadre. However, an important distinguishing factor between the early twentieth century and the 1960s was the presence of Black American women in the country in the latter. Finally, if the Black American diplomatic work examined here in some ways evoked the earlier Tuskegee project, it also foreshadowed the work of other Black individual and organizational work performed in Sudan under the auspices of the US government in the late twentieth and early twenty-first centuries. Taken together, this period shows an important transition from what were primarily Black American media engagements with Sudan to more interpersonal interactions with Sudanese. While the following chapter shows that African American writers continued to keep Sudan under the gaze of Black newspaper reporters, more African Americans traveled to the "Land of the Blacks" than ever before.

While Black newspapers in the preceding decades were full of depictions of "Black" Sudanese and "Arab" Egyptians, the First Sudanese Civil War—waged between northern "Arabs" and southern "Blacks"—brought racial differences in Sudan to the fore. Against this violent and racially charged backdrop, Black Americans in Sudan observed and recorded their racial perceptions of northern and southern Sudanese. Did they consider Sudanese "Black" in the way that Black newspapers had previously portrayed Sudanese? How did their depictions of Sudanese align or conflict with Black newspaper coverage of the war? Finally, how did the war generally impact Black America's relationship with Sudan? As the following chapter shows, the First Sudanese Civil War not only set in motion decades of division along racial and religious lines in that country; it also stoked the same divisions in Black America's relationship with Sudan.

Chapter 4

The Great Divergence

January 1, 1957, marked the first anniversary of Sudanese nationhood, and a young African American economist named Andrew Brimmer attended an independence celebration there. The festivities made quite an impression on Brimmer, who was stationed in Sudan as a member of a US Federal Reserve Bank mission. He deemed it "undoubtedly one of the most amazing celebrations I shall ever witness!" and reported that three thousand people may have attended, consisting entirely of diplomatic corps and high-ranking Sudanese ("and people like us"). In his correspondence he described the event's setting (a palace that reminded him of the White House), strolling with others to partake of tea and cake, and the prime minister shaking hands with senior members of the US diplomatic corps. "It was at this gathering," Brimmer noted, "that I saw a genuine Shilluck [Shilluk]! He was magnificent—tall, slender, straight as a lance. He was as black as coal, with very [fine] features and enough scar-tissue to satisfy Evan.Pritchards [anthropologist Edward Evans-Pritchard] 100 times over!! But—he had a suit on!!"[1] A couple of months later, Brimmer recorded another man's appearance. At a cocktail party he met Benjamin Lwoki, a member of parliament from Equatoria and leader of the Southern Liberal Party. Brimmer wrote that Lwoki was a Bari. "Aside from his great height, the most impressive thing about him is that he is coal black with pure white teeth and red lips!!"[2]

Brimmer's exclamations concerning Lwoki and the unnamed Shilluk exhibit the curiosity that white people had conveyed regarding Africans long before his arrival to Sudan. Although he was in Sudan on official government business and acknowledged that his mission consumed most of his time, Brimmer also invested time in learning about the land and the people. "Regarding the people," he wrote days after his encounter with the Shilluk, "I—perhaps especially—have found them extremely interesting." While the Shilluk's Blackness enthralled him, Brimmer followed with a comment that suggested that not all Sudanese he had encountered were Black. "Here I must ask with John Gunther: 'What *is* a Sudanese?' In answers I saw [that] a Sudanese is an 'Arabized' [Hamite]-Negro—or perhaps a pure Negro or a pure Hamite—or a Syrian or a Greek [underlined in original] an Egyptian or a Scot!! I have had much fun in this regard."[3]

Brimmer's difficulty in categorizing the Sudanese occurred during a period when the meanings of blackness were shifting in his own American context. In the 1950s "Negro" was the predominant moniker, widely used by Black organizations and accepted by Black and white media alike. However, the term came under attack as the civil rights movement made progress in the late 1950s and early 1960s. African Americans not only changed how they saw themselves but also changed their expectations of how others would see them. "Negro" was critiqued as an appellation that white people had imposed on Black people and conveyed pejorative meanings of complacency and subservience. "Black" was encouraged in its place, with the belief that it promoted racial pride, power, militancy, and rejection of the status quo. Yet, as the civil rights movement won protective legislation like the 1965 Voting Rights Act, national rights were connected with the image of what Randolph Hohle has described as "good black citizenship"—namely, a racially nonthreatening, idealized representation of the good American.[4] Thus, blackness was being reshaped in the United States even as African Americans like Brimmer discussed the nuances of Sudanese identity.

As Sudan's future weighed in the balance following the Second World War, some writers in Black American newspapers went beyond directing attention to Egypt's status as Sudan's colonizer by framing the two countries as occupying opposite sides in a racial binary. In this framework, Arab Egypt ruled Black Sudan, a picture of racial mastery that would have appealed to an African American readership familiar with the experience of domination under a racial and racist state. However, the onset of civil war after Sudanese independence and the racialized nature of that conflict helped stoke a remarkable shift. The Khartoum-based Sudanese government sponsored Arabization in southern Sudan in the 1950s and 1960s, and, as social and political tensions between northern and southerners increased, portrayals of northern Sudanese as Arab and southern Sudanese as Black swelled.[5] Though Sudan had hitherto been framed as Black in contrast to Arab Egypt, writers now moved this racial binary south and fashioned it to fit an exclusively Sudanese mold. As a result, Egypt was no longer the face of historical and contemporary Arab dominance of Black peoples in Sudan. Within the context of the civil war, African American writers now demonized northern Sudanese Arabs as oppressors and Black southern Sudanese as the oppressed.

This chapter focuses primarily on the ways African American coverage and opinion on Sudan shifted during the First Sudanese Civil War (1955–1972). Whereas Egypt formerly occupied the role of an Arab oppressor of Black people, writers now placed that ignominious moniker upon Northern Sudanese Arabs. Although African American amity was increasingly directed toward southern Sudan and the Arab-identified North seen in opposition, this rhetoric was not wholesale. Some writers critiqued Israel's involvement in the Sudan and thus added another layer to the issue of racial solidarity. What did it mean to support Black people fighting Arabs in Sudan if other Arabs in the Middle East were struggling for liberation from white Israel? In this way, discussion of events in Sudan dovetailed with African American engagements with the Arab-Israeli conflict.

Thus, the First Sudanese Civil War provided a stage in the evolution of Black American approaches to Sudanese as raced people. In a testament to the centrality of racially marked oppression to African American conceptions of blackness, those identified as marginalized and oppressed in early postcolonial Sudan were Black, while those purportedly responsible for the oppression—northern Sudanese formerly deemed Black in the colonial period—were not Black to some African American commentators. It was a bittersweet calculus in which an oppressed racial minority in America reached out to one in Africa but did so with a paired attempt to discursively exclude other African people from blackness. In showing the fickle nature of kinship, it marked a dangerous precedent.

Black America and African Liberation

In order to understand the full context of African American approaches to the First Sudanese Civil War, it is necessary to appreciate the context of Black America's relationship to Africa as it transitioned from colonialism to independence. From the late 1930s to the mid-1970s, several African American groups worked to support African causes. Such organizations included the Council on African Affairs, the American Negro Leadership Conference on Africa (ANLCA), and the Congressional Black Caucus. Several prominent African American individuals demonstrated interest in and commitment to Africa, including Martin Luther King Jr., Dorothy Height, Adam Clayton Powell Jr., and A. Philip Randolph. Notwithstanding such organizational leaders, identification with Africa could be found among people through dress, adoption of African names, and contribution to African causes. Perhaps no contemporary African issue stoked the Black American imagination more than South African apartheid. Rising Black Nationalism and televised scenes of violence against Black South African protests encouraged a sense of shared oppression. When anti-apartheid activists joined anti-Jim Crow demonstrators, the African American foreign policy lobby shifted its gears from assisting Africans outside of the US to removing white racist regimes the world over.[6]

The specific focus on white oppression was best evinced through two of the more prominent organizations of the era: the American Committee on Africa (ACOA) and the ANLCA. Founded in 1953, the ACOA was a multiracial, anticommunist, and Pan-Africanist organization birthed from a partnership of the Fellowship of Reconciliation and the Congress of Racial Equality. In its first twenty years, the ACOA focused on anti-apartheid struggles and Gold Coast decolonization.[7] George Houser, who began his tenure as the ACOA's executive director in 1955, two decades later acknowledged that the organization had long been related primarily to "the struggle for freedom" and had never tried to serve as an international civil liberties organization to protest breaches of citizens' rights in independent Africa. While he noted that there had been issues that had "tempted the organization to shift focus" and that some ACOA supporters had "pressed for such change," Houser stated that the organization had not developed a program related to the southern Sudanese conflict against the Sudanese government. "If ACOA had wanted to pursue a policy in support of economic development projects, or of refugee aid, or scholarship assistance," Houser wrote, "It would have had to seek large foundation grants and government subsidies. It would have had to de-emphasize policies and actions critical of government positions supportive of white minority regimes and continued Portuguese colonial domination in southern Africa."[8] However consciously or unwittingly, such prioritization of white-ruled states in Southern Africa over Sudan ranked one kind of kind of racial oppression over another.

The ACOA was not alone in taking this position. In the early 1960s, Black American leaders created the American Negro Leadership Conference on Africa to bring African problems into mainstream America's awareness. The ANCLA was sponsored by entities that included the NAACP, CORE, the Urban League, and Southern Christian Leadership Conference.[9] Regarding the ANCLA conference in November 1962 at Columbia University, executive director Theodore Brown said years later, "We passed many resolutions on vital issues in Africa like the Congo problem and the problem of Southern Africa in terms of [apartheid] in the Union of South Africa, and the Rhodesian situation. . . . Back in 1962, there were still many territories that were not sovereign[,] and the question of the colonial holding powers was still widely prevalent in that area."[10] The organization did not meet again until 1964, when it recommitted itself to pressuring the US government to act in support of African independence.[11] Yet, like the ACOA, the ANCLA ignored the Sudanese civil war and the suffering of southern Sudanese.

What might explain the uneven African American attention to different parts of Africa at the time? James Meriwether has noted that imaginings of singular Africa were undermined by the reality of leftist revolutionaries, authoritarian leaders, democratic hopefuls, coups, and civil wars. As a result, African Americans focused more on those countries struggling for national liberation than on those that had already become independent. This prioritization allowed Black Americans to continue forging transatlantic links and sustain broader internal unity in the United States as the civil rights movement splintered in the 1960s. In this paradigm, those who disagreed on the American struggle or problems in independent Africa could still unite against injustices that continued with white minority rule on the continent.[12]

It is against the backdrop of Black American focus on those parts of Africa still struggling under white-minority rule that African American newspaper coverage of Sudan can be more fully understood. While the ACOA and ANCLA may have neglected to address the Sudan crisis, periodicals like the *Chicago Defender* and *New York Amsterdam News* did. Black press coverage overwhelmingly approached the events unfolding in Sudan using a racial framework that was not Black and white as in South Africa but instead Black and Arab. This showed the governing influence of race on Black America's gaze on Africa but also the fact that the gaze saw something other than white and Black spaces. In no small way, Arabs came to occupy the role of racial oppressor in African American reporting and commentary on Sudan, and this mirrored the way white Portuguese and Afrikaners were framed in

Southern Africa. Recognition of this dynamic is necessary for a comprehensive understanding of the bounds of Afro-Arab solidarity.

Blacks, Arabs, and Slavery

During the early years of Sudanese independence, African American newspapers recognized Sudan's Black and Arab identities in non-conflictual ways. On January 7, 1956—six days after Sudan became sovereign—the *Pittsburgh Courier* described the country as having "nine million black people spiritually and politically aligned by RELIGION and color with the Moslem world of Asia and North Africa."[13] "Sudan means black," wrote the *Chicago Defender*. "Here black people are rising again after several thousand years and they are building a new civilization, where they helped light the torch of history in the ancient past."[14] Such recognition of Sudan's blackness was coupled by similar acknowledgments of its Arab composition. "In its one million square miles," said Norfolk's *New Journal and Guide*, "are between six and eight million Arabs living in the northern areas, and about four million native black tribes in the south."[15] In an enormous testament to its Arab heritage, Sudan joined the Arab League in 1956 and, in doing so, became that organization's third African member (after Egypt and Libya).[16] "As may have been expected," wrote Marguerite Cartwright in the *Pittsburgh Courier*, "[Sudan] joined the originally British-conceived Arab League. . . . Previou[s]ly, the Sudanese were quite insulated from Arab politics, but they are Arabs, and when they joined the Arab League, they were doing what comes naturally."[17] Despite such recognition of Sudan's Black and Arab heritage, African American newspapers increasingly framed Sudan in racial and religious opposition in the years following General Abboud's 1958 coup. Importantly, this was often conveyed through references to Sudan's history of slavery.

The history of Sudanese slavery stretched to ancient times, when enslaved persons were sacrificed or used by Sudanese kings when exchanging goods. In the eighteenth century, the Islamic Baggara people capitalized on the rise of the Darfur sultanate and supplied it with enslaved people. While the trade was mainly local until the nineteenth century, it was at that point that the Muslim world's growing demand for enslaved persons increased the trade. When Muhammed Ali, the Ottoman ruler of Egypt, conquered Sudan in the early 1820s, one of his motives for doing so was to conscript enslaved persons into his army and for use as inexpensive labor in his modernization project. Following the conquest, his Turco-Egyptian government conducted slave raids in Nubia, the Upper Blue Nile, and southern Sudan. When the Upper Nile basin was opened, southern Sudanese were vulnerable to diverse private Turk, Arab, European, and Sudanese entrepreneurs. One slave route percolated from Bahr el Ghazal (in modern northwestern South Sudan) to El Obeid (in Kordofan, in northern Sudan) and Khartoum north along the Nile to Egypt. Some historians have reported that 20–30 percent of the population was enslaved at the time of the British reconquest of Sudan (1898).[18]

In the late nineteenth century, several African American newspapers painted the Mahdi and his movement as harbingers of slavery and enemies of Christianity. In 1883 the *New York Globe* reprinted from the *London News*: "The presence of English officers . . . in the distant provinces of the Sudan will undoubtedly aid the extinction of the curse [slavery]. Let the Mahdi be disposed of . . . a new moral teaching firmly and sternly inculcated will shed a new light through these dark lands."[19] Reporting weeks before the fall of Khartoum, the *African Repository* stated that a lamentable element of the Mahdi's progress was "the impetus [that would] be given to the atrocious slave trade." "His minions will bring down their slave caravans of boys and girls to be sold in Mecca to the Mohammedan pilgrims who religiously believe in the divine origin of slavery."[20] Black newspapers continued to deprecate the Mahdiya in the early twentieth century. Weeks after the Battle of Omdurman, the *Colored American* reported, "A fanatical religious power that threatened to overrun Africa is crushed forever. Mahdism is dead. . . . For thirteen years the power [the Mahdi] founded ruled the Soudan despotically and cruelly."[21] Two years later the *Wisconsin Weekly Advocate* reprinted a piece from the *New York News* that included a scathing critique of the Mahdi: "He lacked many of the essential qualifications of a great leader, for, in addition to being a hopeless voluptuary, he was devoid of a possible policy, and was, in addition, the creature of the most degraded slave dealers."[22]

When General Herbert Kitchener was appointed the first governor-general of the Anglo-Egyptian Sudan in 1899, he instructed his provincial governors to proceed with caution when it came to slavery. "Slavery is not recognized in the Sudan," he wrote, "but as long as service is willingly rendered by servants to masters it is unnecessary to interfere in the conditions existing between them." He added that he would leave it to their discretion to employ the best means of gradually eliminating the propensity to rely on enslaved labor.[23] However, Steven Serels has noted that Anglo-Egyptian officials were complicit in maintaining slavery and the slave trade following the Mahdist War. In the early twentieth century, policies established by top

Anglo-Egyptian officials allowed Sudanese cultivators to increase the number of enslaved workers in northern Nilotic Sudan by an estimated eighty thousand men. However, the Condominium government faced slavery scandals in 1924 that drew the ire of the Anti-Slavery Society and questions from the British Parliament and the League of Nations. Even though the Sudanese government decreed the complete right to freedom for all Sudanese in May 1925, some incidents of the trade appeared thereafter.[24]

J. A. Rogers's "Rambling Ruminations: Slavery Still Exists" appeared in the *New York Amsterdam News* in July 1930. Rogers cited information provided by Joseph Kessel, a French aviator and explorer that French newspaper *Le Matin* had dispatched to examine the slave trade in Sudan and Abyssinia. "The great slave-port," wrote Kessel (quoted by Rogers), "is Port Sudan, which flies the British flag. . . . Thus the fine zeal that England shows on this subject and the reproaches that she makes against her neighbors (France and Italy) concerning the slave trade can also be applied to her even more, since slavery still exists in the Sudan."[25] Two years later, in an editorial that appeared in the *Philadelphia Tribune*, Rogers forwarded information on a report that "Abyssinian bandits" had been raiding Sudan for slaves. The report found that one attack had resulted in the deaths of twenty-seven men and the kidnapping of twenty-seven women and fifty-five children. Rogers wrote that the enslaved Sudanese were "for the Arabian trade and . . . bootlegged across the Red Sea."[26] Rogers was not the only figure to draw attention to modern Sudanese slavery. In January 1930, the *Pittsburgh Courier* published a piece on African slave trafficking more broadly. "Slave traffic is still rampant in many places like the Sudan, Abyssinia and Arabia," it noted. "In the White Nile Province, in the Sudan, the British authorities recently learned that a woman named Sitt Anna . . . was one of the principal parties engaged in the slave traffic with Abyssinia. She was . . . imprisoned. An inquiry made in the same province resulted in the liberation of 500 slaves."[27]

While slavery in Sudan never completely disappeared during the colonial period, the British successfully eliminated the domestic trade. But, while the supply and demand for free labor following the conclusion of World War II "had reduced the most egregious abuses of slavery," the historian Robert O. Collins notes, the continued shortage of labor revived domestic slavery.[28] Matters of scale notwithstanding, the African American press was clearly privy to and condemned the injurious practice of slavery in Sudan. Whether reading Black newspapers during the late nineteenth century Mahdiya or the Depression-era Condominium, readers would have been exposed to the idea that Sudan was a place where Black people were being enslaved. One might imagine the sense of pain and horror wrought in some readers who had a particularly intimate connection with slavery less than a century removed from American emancipation. Such reportage and commentary concerning Sudanese slavery provide a backdrop for the ways that writers in the Black press injected the history of slavery into reports of conflict in contemporary postcolonial Sudan.

In August 1955, southern Sudanese rebels mutinied against northern Sudanese soldiers at Torit. Though order was eventually restored, the event commonly marks the beginning of the seventeen-year war between the Sudanese government and southern rebels. A month after the Torit mutiny, the *Atlanta Daily World* published an article that invoked the history of Sudanese slavery. The writer framed the conflict as one between southern Sudanese "pagan blacks" and northern Muslim Arabs ("who will probably be rulers when the territory achieves its independence"). While the antebellum United States was divided between a free North and enslaving South, the writer noted, "Unlike the American situation, it is the Northerners in Sudan who are guilty of a slave trading. Recently South Sudan explained that it sent three aged men to a conference in the North because 'if we sent our young men those Arab northerners would kidnap them and sell them into slavery.'" "This feeling," the writer explained, "is what led to the bloody revolt several weeks ago."[29] In 1959 George Schuyler added a racial binary that the *Atlanta Daily World* had not. "There is another complex situation in the Sudan where the dominant people are the Moslems who regard the southern Sudanese . . . as inferior, and always have," Schuyler wrote. "They regularly roamed southern Sudan for slaves until the Anglo-Egyptian condominium stopped it. The uprising of the Mahdi in the Sudan in [1882] was due largely to the interference with the Negro slave trade which enriched the coffers of the Sudanese slavers."[30] By portraying Sudanese Muslims as dominant people who formerly roamed the South for slaves and still regarded southerners as inferior, Schuyler injected race into the picture by asserting that interference in a particularly "Negro" slave trade sparked the famous Mahdi rebellion. In this reading, the dominance of contemporary Muslims in Sudan was not only rooted in past slavery; it was also—in his words—racial slavery perpetrated by a religious group.

The discussion of northern Sudanese as slavers—while including some historical truth—is also problematic in its tendency to exoticize and essentialize an entire group of people. Unlike Schuyler's portrayal, the Mahdi rebellion had different causes and was conducted in a particular Islamic register. In showcasing the suffering of one group, another group is categorically pathologized in the absence of nuanced inspection that accounts for heterogeneity of attitudes toward and participation in the slave trade. This dynamic, while not altogether identical to the more modern context, nevertheless mirrors Western portrayals of Arabs and Muslims during the War on Terror in the early twenty-first century, with its depictions of violent, deranged, bloodthirsty extremists eager to inflict fear and terror on peaceful, civilized, non-Arab and non-Muslim peoples. As Nigerian writer Chimamanda Adichie once offered, "The single story creates stereotypes. And the problem with stereotypes is not that they are untrue, but that they are incomplete. They make one story become the only story."[31] If the history of Sudanese slavery is told—and it must be shared—then those northern Sudanese experiences untethered to or opposed to slavery (or both) must be told as well. An oversimplified depiction of northern Sudanese as slavers and southerners as enslaved does a disservice to members of each group. It is morally imperative to discover and disseminate the diversity of peoples' truths.

Riots in Sudan in 1964 provided an opportunity for another newspaper to invoke historical slavery in its reporting of contemporary developments. That year, student disturbances at the University of Khartoum led to the ouster of General Ibrahim Abboud's regime. These protests were followed by mass demonstrations led by the nation's professional elite against the government, demonstrations supported by trade unions and Communist and Umma Parties. This popular uprising became known as the October Revolution.[32] Two months later, a crowd of southern residents in Khartoum gathered to welcome Clement Mboro back from his visit to the South. Mboro was the minister of the interior and the first southerner ever appointed to a senior cabinet position. When his return flight was delayed, rumors spread that he had been assassinated. Southerners were enraged and violently tore through the city, killing Arabs. Southerners seeking shelter from vengeful northerners took refuge in buildings run by the American Presbyterian Mission. While the military was called to restore the peace, one hundred people ultimately died. Minister Mboro was very much alive and died of natural causes forty-two years later.[33]

That month, December 1964, the *Chicago Defender* published several portrayals of Arab-Black clashes in Sudan. One was a UPI report that was published on December 8. "Negroes and Arabs battled through the streets of Khartoum in new outbreaks of racial rioting," it said. Invoking the familiar refrain of historical slavery, the report stated, "[The fighting underlined the traditional racial hatred between Arabs and Negroes stemming from the days of slavery when Arab traders raided Africa for slaves. Despite the modern-day claims of fraternity and brotherhood between Arab and African nations, racism remains." It regionalized the racial division by noting that "Negroes" mainly populated the South while the North was "dominated by Arab Moslems who . . . [had] controlled the government."[34] The following day, December 9, the *Defender* published another UPI report that detailed the rioting that began when Mboro returned to Khartoum. Arab-Black antagonism was again put on full display through the lens of slavery. Noting "a century of smouldering hatred between Negroes and Arabs," the article stated, "Steel-helmeted police arrested Negroes and set up barriers to separate them from stone-throwing Arabs. . . . The seeds of the trouble were sewn [*sic*] 100 years ago in the Arab slave trade among the Negro peoples of the Southern Sudan."[35] The next day, December 10, an article in the *Defender* posited that the rioting in Khartoum was "symptomatic of a trend throughout black Africa to curb the power of the Arab constituents in politics": "Africans with retentive memory do not nurture too good a feeling toward the Arabs who are remembered for their perfidious traffic in black slaves."[36]

Black readers of African American newspapers from the late 1950s to mid-1960s were presented with antagonistic, oppositional framings of Sudanese Arabs and Blacks. Importantly, this racial divide was often expressed through the language of slavery, a relatable, accessible dynamic inviting Black readers to understand the Sudanese situation and have compassion for southern Sudanese more fully. While this chapter will later show that such portrayals would continue through the end of the 1960s, some African Americans with direct experience in Sudan refused such divisive characterizations. Instead, they noted the ambiguous nature of race in Sudan and the physical resemblance that those in northern Sudan had with Blacks in America. Their statements illustrated the gap between the politicized and polarizing way race in Sudan was depicted in African American newspapers and what Black Americans perceived firsthand.

Recognizing Racial Ambiguity

The *Chicago Defender* printed two pieces in December 1964 challenging the Sudanese Arab-Black binary that had been disseminated. One was a Negro Press International report that cited newspaper headlines that read "Negroes and Arabs Clash in Sudan," "10 Dead, Scores Hurt in Arab-Negro

Race Riots," "Negroes Attacking Arabs," and "Arabs Counter-Attacking the Negro Area in Khartoum." The article recognized that friction existed between Northern and southern Sudanese but argued that the recent violence in Khartoum was rooted in nonracial social factors like politics and religion. Furthermore, it contended, many Sudanese remembered that the British had created an artificial disdain between North and South in its divide-and-rule strategy. "[Given Sudan's pervasive racial mixing], it would be an anthropological monstrosity to attempt to speak of Arab-Negro race riots in Khartoum. It would be closer to the truth . . . to speak of friction and clashes between Arab-speaking and Moslem northern Sudanese and Sudanic-speaking and non Moslem southern Sudanese." While the article acknowledged that foreign correspondents were qualified to do their jobs, it continued that some of their dispatches from Sudan betrayed their weak anthropological and historical knowledge. Noting that "Sudan" literally means "Land of the Blacks," it stated, "All present-day Sudanese are not wholly black any more than most American Negroes are not black. The Sudanese . . . are a fusion of Arab, Negro, Nubian and Egyptian blood. . . . Centuries of this miscegenation left their mark heavier in the northern than in the southern part of the Sudan."[37]

Two days later the *Defender* published an editorial by Chatwood Hall that doubled down on the danger of placing Sudanese into Black and Arab binaries. "Chatwood Hall" was a pen name used by Homer Smith, a syndicated columnist and author. As "Chatwood Hall" he served as Russian foreign correspondent for the Associated Negro Press, and he later moved to Ethiopia, where he served as senior editor for Ethiopia's Ministry of Information. Smith returned to the United States in 1962, and the Johnson Publishing Company published his memoir *Black Man in Red Russia* two years later.[38] In his December 1964 *Defender* piece, "Hall" expressed befuddlement at an American correspondent—one he presumed to be white—who wrote of "the festering squabble between the Arab north and the Negroid south," "Negroid Southerners," and "Arab Northerners." The Black journalist, who had thrice visited Sudan, wrote that anyone who had been there should have known that modern northern Sudan was part of ancient Nubia. "The indigenous people of this region, the Nubians, are among the blackest people in all Africa and in the world. The President . . . Ibrahim Abboud, is a very dark brown man who would be just another Negro anywhere in America. And he is a Sudanese 'Northerner.'" While "Hall" acknowledged that there had long been an infusion of Arab blood in some of the region's people, anyone who tried to equate one's language and faith to race had to be "a shallow thinker indeed: all American Negroes speak English, but they are not Anglo-Saxons." In what may have been his effort to disentangle his audience's understanding of Sudanese as Arabs, "Hall" echoed some of his precedents by likening Sudanese to African Americans: "If most of the Sudanese, with their rivers of Negro blood, were dumped into America, they would be but an addition to America's Negro population."[39]

Two other African American visitors to Sudan echoed Homer Smith in his comparison of Sudanese to Black Americans: Christine Wilson and Elton C. Fax. Wilson, a pre-engineering major at Eastern Michigan University, received a scholarship from the Sudanese government to study at the University of Khartoum. "I believe that it was here," Wilson later said, "among these warm and very generous people that I secretly began to accept Islam." After spending nearly two years in Khartoum, Wilson joined the Nation of Islam in 1967 and received her Muslim name, Bayyinah Sharrieff, that December. Her experiences and observations in Sudan were reproduced in *Muhammad Speaks*, the Nation of Islam newspaper that boasted a weekly circulation that may have exceeded over one hundred thousand.[40]

Sharrieff opined that the Sudanese she encountered resembled Blacks in the States and said that this perception was generated soon after she arrived at the university. She recounted that one of the assistant registrars drove her from the airport to the university's girls' hostel when she came to Khartoum. They arrived at the hostel at about 8:30 p.m., and the assistant registrar carried her luggage inside the gate.[41] Sharrieff described entering the dorm for the first time "among her own people" and finding, much to her chagrin, that the housemother was a white English woman. The housemother called for an elderly Black woman named Sit-Ruth, who introduced Sharrieff to some of the women. "I was so happy when I saw them," she said, "for many of them looked like the black girls one would see here in America. Their hair varied in degrees of curliness as does [that of] the so-called American Negroes. . . . I told them that there were millions in America who looked like them. They were fascinated."[42] On another other occasion she remarked that "the Sudanese range in color from very dark to very light, as do the so-called American Negro."[43]

Notwithstanding the observations provided by the likes of Brimmer, Sharrieff, and Hall, no African American visitor to Sudan provided more extensive observations concerning Sudanese racial identity that Elton Fax. Born in Baltimore in 1909, Fax had begun his career as an artist in 1931 after graduating from Syracuse University's College of Fine Arts. A world traveler, Fax lived in Mexico in the 1950s, traveled to South America and the

Caribbean for the US State Department's Educational Exchange Program, and visited Africa several times. The State Department's Educational and Cultural Division arranged his trips to Uganda, Ethiopia, Tanzania, and northern Sudan. In his 1974 book *Through Black Eyes: Journeys of a Black Artist to East Africa and Russia*, Fax provides a detailed summary of his experiences in Sudan.[44]

In March 1964 the Sudanese *Morning News* published word of Fax's then-forthcoming African tour. Under the headline "Negro American [sic] Artist to Visit Sudan," the article noted that Fax would visit several cities and "give 'chalk talks'[—]a combination of drawing, story-telling and teaching in schools and community centers."[45] In *Through Black Eyes* Fax remembered that he hadn't been in the country twenty-hours before having an encounter with a public affairs officer (PAO) that brought understandings of race in Sudan to the fore. The PAO informed Fax, "[Sudanese Arabs] hate the Negroes who live in the southern part of this country. The Arabs are determined to dominate the Negroes, who are rather backward." "Of course," the officer continued, "it must be admitted that the Arabs are far more intelligent and therefore more ambitious. Still, things are in a bad state inasmuch as Arab cruelty to Negroes is colossal. So with this racial trouble here we have made no arrangements for you to travel south." The PAO informed Fax that they had arranged for him to visit the Technical Institute's Art Department and then the Sudanese Cultural Center's women's bazaar.[46] Fax remembered that while he had to respect the PAO's position, he could not completely believe what he had told him.

> I had been looking intently at the people of Khartoum from the moment I had arrived. Most of them were black. There were varying shades of brown among them and hair textures ranged from straight to kinky. . . . Few resembled my artist's concept of Arabs, "swarthy skin, fairly sharp features, piercing grey or brown eyes, and straight or curly hair." . . . The vast majority I had seen so far, at the airport, on the streets, in the hotel, looked more like blood relatives of mine. To the best of my knowledge, few of *them* are likely to be mistaken by any well-traveled white American for Arabs.[47]

Fax's account of how the PAO distinguished between Arabs and Blacks is supported by documentary evidence illustrating the US government's understanding of Sudan. In a 1957 national security report concerning US policy regarding sub-Saharan Africa, Sudan was listed along with Ethiopia and the Somalilands as having "sizeable Negro minorities." However, the report continued, "[Those countries] tend in their political, cultural and economic outlooks to be oriented much more towards North Africa and the Middle East . . . than they are toward tropical Africa. Thus the Moslem populations of Sudan and the Somali area look primarily towards their co-religionists in the other Arab states." For the purposes of US doctrine, Sudan was officially recognized as being part of the Middle East.[48] From an American foreign policy perspective, Sudan was a constituent member of the Arab and Middle Eastern world. But what, then, of those Sudanese who identified neither as Arab nor Middle Eastern?

US State Department officials' understandings of Sudan included thoughts regarding religion. A year after the aforementioned national security report was sent, Julius C. Holmes, the special assistant to Secretary of State John Foster Dulles, wrote to him and shared that Sudan was Muslim "excepting the pagan South."[49] However conscious or unwittingly, by his use of the term "pagan" to describe southern Sudan, Holmes harkened to Western, timeworn, colonial-era missionary lingo to describe people in that region.[50] It appears that the term continued to be deployed in official US foreign policy documentation describing southern Sudanese, as over a decade later—when Fax was in Sudan—he went through material that Washington had issued him and found the briefing sheet on the country. He read and reread one paragraph stating that the country was composed of nine million mostly Arab-speaking Muslims in the North and three and a half million "largely pagan" people in the South. "So *that* was it," Fax wrote later in his memoirs. "They were a mixture of Arab and black African and they were loosely referred to as 'Arabs' because of their ethnic mixture and Arabic tongue. There was no reference whatever in the official memo to 'Negroes.'" He concluded that the officer's use of "Negro" "obviously stemmed from his [the PAO's] *personal* interpretation of what it implied to *him* [italics Fax's]."[51]

Fax was introduced to Ahmed Omar, a local assistant and liaison attached to the US Information Service (USIS) in Khartoum. Omar's work included the transportation of visitors like Fax to locations in town.[52] One morning Omar was scheduled to pick Fax up and take him to Khartoum's women's bazaar. As he waited to be picked up, Fax saw men in clean, white robes and women in long, white attire passing along in the streets. "I continued to look carefully into the faces of the men," he would recall. "Most of them were black and subtler shades of dark brown, with features ranging from rounded and flat [to] near aquiline. The same people walking in Harlem or Watts or along Chicago's southside would, except for their gleaming white clothing, attract little attention."[53] After meeting with a Black US embassy officer and some other African Americans stationed in Khartoum, Fax and the others laughed over the PAO's Arab-Negro explanation. After marveling in his autobiography about the State Department briefing sheet, Fax stated that in hindsight he sensed something in white officials' mindsets and actions that reflected US interests as much as their own biases. He felt that the US government did not think highly of the Sudanese government when it came to the interests it represented to the United States on the continent.[54] "Therefore," Fax opined, "the questions of who and what was good and bad—of who was a 'cruel Arab' and who a 'downtrodden Negro,' were not wholly . . . tied to the admittedly twisted American concepts of race and color."[55]

Notwithstanding US statecraft and its problematic interpretations of Sudan's diverse racial demographics, Fax had entered the country at a time when Sudanese were presenting themselves to the world in calculated ways. In April 1955, newly independent African and African states participated in the historic the Afro-Asian Conference in Bandung, Indonesia. Aimed at promoting cultural and economic cooperation and standing together in the face of imperialism, the Bandung summit was attended by delegates from twenty-nine countries. Sudan—mere months from becoming independent—joined Ghana, Libya, Liberia, Ethiopia, and Egypt as the African representatives. By implicitly condemning Western and Soviet interventionism as the Cold War raged, the conference helped establish the Non-Aligned Movement and is seen as having been the vanguard of South-South cooperation.[56] Sudan's participation in this multiracial gathering was coupled by internal reckoning with its own cultural diversity. With independence the following year, Sudan's multiculturalism was brought to the fore with election campaigns featuring non-Arab ethnic groups and a parliamentary influx of non-Arabized intellectuals ("especially those," according to writer M. Jalāl Hāshim, "of jet-black colour who were very aware that they could only be accommodated in a multi-cultural, not mono-cultural, Sudan"). This helped to fuel the emergence of Afro-Arabist cultural and political discourse.[57] National scholars spurred pioneering studies examining Sudan's African identity (particularly in the middle part of the country), and, as the 1960s dawned, intellectuals realized that Arabism alone would be an insufficient descriptor for Sudanese identity.[58]

Yet such recognition was countered by Sudanese government efforts to fashion itself as an Arab state. Egypt's Gamal Abdel Nasser, the champion of Pan-Arabism, visited Sudan in November 1960 to commemorate the second anniversary of Abboud's 1958 coup. Nasser's trip included a journey south to Juba and Nimule.⁵⁹ Sudan's pro-Arab stance was reciprocated by several nations that offered military support to Khartoum to aid its war effort against the southern rebels. In August 1965 Kuwaiti finance minister Jabir al-Ahmad al-Jabir described the southern Sudanese independence movement as "imperialist and Zionist" while announcing a Kuwaiti loan of approximately £5 million to help its "sisterly Arab country" preserve "the unity of its territory."⁶⁰ The Arab League Summit of August 1967, held in Khartoum, represented the height of Sudanese Arabism during the civil war. The summit addressed several matters but is known chiefly for its resolution on future Arab-Israeli relations. Arab countries would unite to force Israel's withdrawal from the Occupied Territories, insist on Palestinian rights, and declare that no negotiations with Israel would be made. Sudan's choice for the summit's setting was considered a victory for Prime Minister Muhammad Mahgoub, who desired a role in settling Arab disputes.⁶¹ Egypt, Libya, and Syria talked with Sudan about the possibility of forming a federation, and the fruits of the agreement included Egyptian and Libyan support in the form of troops on the ground. Such pledges of Arab support illustrated that Sudan's membership in the Arab League and other efforts to ally itself with the Arab world were yielding tangible results. More importantly, Jabir's quote showed one way the war was viewed not just domestically but also regionally as one with important ramifications for all Arabs. In May 1969, Col. Jafaar Nimeiri took power in a coup modeled after Egypt's 1952 revolution that had brought Nasser to power (Nimeiri termed his coalition the Committee of Free Officers, the term used by Nasser). The new Sudanese leader embraced the same pan-Arab ideology, and in 1970 Nimeiri and Libya's Muammar Gaddafi presented themselves as Nasser's heirs.⁶²

An obvious dissonance existed between Sudan's cultural diversity on the ground and the way the Sudanese government aligned itself with Arab politics. Still, while US foreign policy portrayals of Sudan and Sudanese as "Arab" existed in the same ecosystem as the Sudanese government's own Arab-aligned efforts, it cannot justify the dichotomous stereotyping that Elton Fax perceived concerning Sudanese (that they were "good, downtrodden Negroes" or "cruel Arabs"). While in Sudan, this Black American artist found himself at the nexus of dueling forces. His travels were funded by an American state still emerging from its racially divisive civil rights movement, and he was navigating a culturally diverse Sudan whose government had done much in the previous decade to align itself with Arabness in symbolic and violent ways. It was, as in other instances of African American engagements with Sudan, an often bizarre situation to behold. Back home, this strange dynamic also played out in African American newspapers. Despite testimonies by Fax and other Black Americans in Sudan concerning the physical similitude of Sudanese to African Americans, Black newspapers continued to cast the civil war in racialized terms.

African American newspapers disseminated a decidedly pro-Black, pro-southern position. In July 1966 the *Pittsburgh Courier* reported that the American Friends Service Committee was sending clothes and other supplies to Sudanese refugees in Congo. "Fleeing from alleged persecution by the Arab majority . . . [southern] Sudanese have arrived in neighboring countries in large numbers. . . . The condition of the refugees, according to reports received at the Service Committee, is grave."[63] The *New York Amsterdam News* published an anonymous op-ed that asserted, "Arabs are engaged in a silent war against black Africans while we remain silent. Newspapers all over the world have reported massacres of black[s] in Sudan, secret slavery in Arabia, and Egyptian pilots bombing Biafra. The *New York Times* reported that blacks are reported to be in concentration camps in Sudan. I hope that the *Amsterdam News* will alert the Afro-American community as to the true conditions of our brothers."[64] Familial solidarity, for this writer, was apparently limited to a particular group of Sudanese—those who were Black.

In December 1971, southern Sudanese students held a conference at New York City's International House and appealed "to the Black people of the world to support in whatever way possible the struggle of the Southern Sudanese people for freedom and national cultural identity." Before the conference, Black African students and African Americans demonstrated in front of Sudan's mission to the United Nations and in front of the UN. Black groups joining the UN protest included the Federation of Pan-African Nationalist Organizations, the African Nationalist Activist Movements, Our Families Protection Association, and members of the Congress on Racial Equality (CORE). The *New York Amsterdam News* reported that the African American groups joined the conference as they began to formally cooperate with the southern Sudanese "to pursue the 'liberation' sought by the non-Muslims in 16 years of war with Arab-dominated Sudan government." Roy Innis, CORE's executive director, gave closing remarks at the conference and pledged his organization's assistance in publicizing the southern plight "under Arab Northern Sudanese rule." Innis also stated that CORE would include southern Sudan in its support of liberation movements on the continent: "Their demands to be freed from the 'dehumanizing' effect of 'Arab domination' are legitimate."[65]

The physical observations made by Chatwood Hall, Bayyinah Sharrieff, and Elton Fax in their recollections of Sudanese appearance was not in accord with the polarizing way Sudanese were often portrayed in African American newspapers. If many of the Sudanese they encountered resembled African Americans who wouldn't have considered themselves Arab, then why were Sudanese—and particularly those described as violent and oppressive—framed as Arab in Black newspapers? Operating within a broader US media and political context, African American newspapers and their coverage of Sudan not only reflected continued Black American interest in the country but also the increasingly pervasive racial characterizations of Sudanese in the popular US imagination. In its only full-length article published on Sudan in the 1960s, *Time* magazine divided Sudanese between eight million northerners who were "Arabic and Nubian in origin, and Moslem to a man" and four million southerners who were "black Africans." Importantly, this description was made in the context of the article's focus on the caustic treatment facing Christian missionaries in the country.[66] Lawrence Fellows of the *New York Times* referred to southern Sudan's "black, Africa-oriented tribes" fighting "savagely against their Arab-oriented Government in the north"; the *Washington Post* published C. C. Miniclier's report that the Sudanese army was "battling Christian and pagan blacks who seek a separate identity from the Islamic, Arabic-speaking, usually lighter-skinned peoples from Northern Sudan"; and the *Los Angeles Times* referred to the rebels as "small, guerrilla forces of Negroes who demand independence from the Arab north and claim to speak for Sudan's minority of 6.5 million blacks in the Moslem-dominated nation."[67] Thus, it was quite evident that propensity to describe northern and southern Sudanese in racial and religious binaries was not the domain solely of contemporary Black writers.

While Africans Americans may not have been alone in racializing Sudanese as "Arab" or "Black" during this period, the way this behavior related to Black America's approach to the concurrent Arab-Israel conflict is revealing. By shining a light on how the bounds of blackness were reconciled with one Arab group outside of Africa, this engagement overlapped with African American approaches to the Sudan in remarkable ways.

Sudan and the Arab-Israeli Conflict

Following the end of World War II and Germany's genocide of six million Jews, some within the Jewish community demanded their own country.

On November 29, 1947, the UN General Assembly adopted Resolution 181, dividing Britain's former Palestinian mandate into Jewish and Arab states in May 1948. With this action, Jewish people were given a large area of Palestine: a region they considered their traditional home but that was inhabited by Arabs who already lived there. Neighboring, predominantly Muslim countries believed that the move was unfair and did not accept the new Israeli state. Immediately after the state of Israel's independence was announced on May 14, 1948, several Arab states invaded land in the former Palestinian mandate. This action sparked the Arab-Israeli War of 1948. In 1948–1949, approximately 750,000 Palestinian Arabs—more than half their total population—were expelled or fled. Israel and the Arab states did not reach an armistice until February 1949. While Israel gained some territory that Palestinian Arabs had been granted under the UN resolution, Egypt retained the Gaza Strip, while Jordan controlled the West Bank. These armistice lines held until 1967.[68]

In 1956 Israel joined Britain and France in attacking Egypt. The young nation did so in order to reverse Egypt's nationalization of the Suez Canal (and reopen it to Israeli shipping) and end armed Palestinian incursions from Sinai. While US- and Soviet-led international pressure forced Israeli forces to retreat to the armistice lines, the region soon became an area where the Americans and Soviets were competing for influence. In the spring of 1967, the Soviets falsely informed Syria that Israeli forces were massing in northern Israel to attack them (there was no such mobilization). In May 1967, Egyptian troops—responding to Syria's request for help—entered the Sinai Peninsula and eventually proclaimed a blockade of Israel's port of Eilat. Israel launched a decisive attack on Egyptian and Syrian forces on June 5, 1967, and attacked Jordan's military. In the subsequent Six-Day War, Israel established itself as the region's dominant military power. However, following the war, the UN Security Council adopted Resolution 242 calling for Israel's withdrawal from lands taken in the war. Nevertheless, Israeli troops—who occupied Gaza and the West Bank during the war—remained there for years, and Jewish settlements were set up in East Jerusalem, the West Bank, Gaza, Golan Heights, and Sinai with government approval.[69]

In 1954, as the Anglo-Egyptian Sudan was progressing toward independence, Sudanese leaders initiated ties with Israel through British intermediaries. When the 1958 coup d'état brought Ibrahim Abboud to power, Khartoum's secret ties with Israel were severed. In 1967 Sudan joined nine other Arab states in cutting diplomatic ties with Germany after it had exchanged ambassadors with Israel, and with the Six-Day War came more showings of Arab support. Sudan cut diplomatic ties with the Britain and the United States (restored in 1968 and 1972, respectively) and sent military personnel to support Egypt's efforts.[70]

A Sudanese brigade was positioned on the Suez Canal until 1972. It benefited Israel for a significant portion of Sudanese armed forces to be focused on the South, with Mossad head Zvi Zamir believing that Sudan's threat against Israel at the canal and the Red Sea would be minimized by a more powerful force in the South. It was also believed that the Sudanese army's distraction by a southern war could necessitate a partial diversion of the Egyptian army to northern Sudan. Israelis under former paratroop officer David Ben-Uziel trained a southern military force, arranged for weapons and supplies to be dropped, and oversaw a goodwill effort in the form of a medical team and field hospital. Israeli assistance extended to propaganda. From 1969 to 1970 Yossi Alpher was in charge of producing and distributing anti-Khartoum propaganda. In Tel Aviv Alpher created pamphlets and a type of bush newspaper.[71]

After the 1967 conflict, Israel took center stage in African American newspaper editorials commenting on Sudan. While some referenced Israel when pointing to Arab oppression, others framed Israel as oppressive. In this way, pro-southern and pro-northern Sudanese positions in African American newspapers were expressed through the lens of the Arab-Israeli conflict.

Sudan, Israel, and African American Opinion

Due to the similarities between anti-Jewish antisemitism and anti-Black racism in the West, Jewish and African diasporic politics have often overlapped. Black American radicals like W. E. B. Du Bois supported the creation of the Jewish state, and Percival Prattis—who had advocated for Sudanese independence—traveled to Israel in 1954 and wrote favorably about the country. Over time, however, some African Americans who had supported Israel's creation began to link Zionism with colonial discourse. Some Black American leaders and commentators praised political initiatives from the Arab world, like Algeria's liberation struggle against France, and Nasser's pan-Arab nationalism. During the summer of 1967, when the Arab-Israeli conflict reached a fever pitch, some Black radicals condemned Israel as a violent, racist, and imperialist Western proxy. Black moderates, including Martin Luther King Jr., rebuked such critics and doubled down on their devotion to the Jewish state. Following the 1967 conflict, Black American commentary followed a pattern wherein some civil rights organizations (like the National Urban League) defended Israel while others (like the Student Nonviolent Coordinating Committee) condemned Israel's position.[72]

Whitney Young Jr. was not among those African Americans with a particular allegiance to the Arab world. Born in Kentucky in 1921, Young was appointed to lead the National Urban League in 1961 and was one of the principal leaders of the 1963 March on Washington for Jobs and Freedom.[73] In his 1968 op-ed "To Be Equal," Young used Sudan to illustrate the Arab oppression of Blacks:

> I have never been able to understand the love affair between some Black nationalist spokesmen and the Arab world. Arabs were enslaving Black people long before Americans imported slaves. A UN report said that slavery existed in Arab countries right up until a few years ago. . . . In the Sudan . . . Arab northerners are waging civil war against Black southerners. For the past ten years, arms supplied by Arab countries have been used in this war to massacre many thousands of Black Sudanese who want their independence.[74]

Two years later, the *Philadelphia Tribune* referenced Israeli assistance to southern Sudanese within the context of a racial struggle. Israeli-made weapons, the report said, were "reaching the black rebels in the southern Sudan, who for years have been fighting the Arab regime in Khartoum."[75]

The *New York Amsterdam News* published several pieces that articulated pro-Israeli, anti-Arab Sudanese sentiments. In her 1970 editorial titled "Sudan," New York City's Veronica Johnson explained that she had recently read an article from a London paper that made her wonder: "Where is the New Left censure of Arabs killing Blacks?" The article Johnson had read concerned "Sudan, host to the Arab War Council against Israel." She continued that Sudan was responsible for the killing of half a million of its Blacks "without a word of protest from American black militants and their white fellow-travelers of the 'New Left,' who have been taking up the Arab cause." Johnson stated that "Sudanese Negroes" seeking self-determination and independence were fighting their "Arab overlords." After stating that two million had fled into exile and half a million had been "butchered by the Arab regime," Johnson asked why these events had not been publicized in the American press and whether the *News* editor was aware of these developments.[76] That same day—March 14, 1970—the *News* published S. Norman Grouse's editorial "Arabs, Jews, Us." Grouse began by stating that some

Blacks zealously proclaimed support for democracy and socialism. "Some like Eldridge Claever [sic]," wrote the New York City native, "preach the destruction of Israel as an enemy of exploited, oppressed Arabs, linked with the blacks of the world. Ignored is the clear evidence of the murder of tens of thousands of blacks by the Arabs of Sudan." Grouse later mentioned that Israel had sent thousands of medical and technical experts to help "colored nations in Africa and Asia."[77]

Additional editorials appeared in the *News* that pointed to Israel's assistance in the context of Arabs oppressing Blacks. Stephen Appell of Jackson Heights, New York, wrote, "It is the Arabs who historically engaged in the black slave trade; who have only recently slaughtered Blacks in the Sudan. . . . Israel, to the contrary, has always lent friendship and assistance to the Black African states."[78] Richard Levinson, in his editorial of October 3, 1970, deployed familiar rhetoric by invoking the history of Arab slavery in contrast to Israel's comparative benevolence (through its aid to southern Sudan). "Arab history shows who the slave traders in East Africa were; they were Arabs. Today, Blacks living in the southern Sudan are fighting for self determination against an Arab regime. Israel . . . is helping to supply Blacks with guns while the Arabs slaughter these people in village raids, much like those conducted against civilians living in villages in Israel."[79]

While some writers positioned Israel as a nation fighting to liberate oppressed Black southern Sudanese, others cast Israel in a negative light. James R. Lawson, president of the United African Nationalist Movement, was among this number. Lawson asked, "[How do those] who pretend to be of African extraction advocate war machines to a predominantly white nation (Israel) to destroy their own kind?" He said that many Arabs were Black and African, adding, "It is ironical, and tragic, that a group of 'Negroes' would take this course against their own kind. Nine of these Arab countries are in Africa." He listed Sudan among his examples.[80] In the *Black Scholar*, Harold S. Rogers wrote that the British *Sunday Times* had noted that Israel was arming and training the Anyanya separatist movement in southern Sudan.[81] Rogers explained that Israeli leaders considered Africa as part of the "second ring" of countries around it (after the "first ring" of Arab states). "Israel," he continued, "tries to bribe and neutralize the attitudes of the 'second ring' of countries towards its brutal aggression against the peace loving Arab countries. . . . Israel's ideological advance in African countries often takes on the form of exploiting old colonial racist myths, of 'Black Africans' vs. 'White Africans,' and of Arabs as being great slave traders. Hence the Zionist hope to split African countries on the question of race." Later in the article, Rogers described Israel's role in Africa as being one of overthrowing progressive governments and training local armed forces. He framed Israel's African missions as "centers of subversion and espionage against the African states" and listed examples of its military role on the continent "and the part she plays in subversion."[82]

The most pointed indictment of Israel's participation in the Sudanese war appeared in the newsletter of the Pan-Africanist Student Organization for Black Unity (SOBU), based in Greensboro, North Carolina, at North Carolina A&T, founded in 1969. SOBU activists—some of whom had been members of the Student Nonviolent Coordinating Committee—encouraged Black American students to connect politically and cultural with Africa.[83] On May 1, 1971, the article "Race War in the Sudan: Big White Lie" appeared in the SOBU newsletter. Produced by the Pacific News Service, the article contended that the Sudanese war mirrored Nigeria's civil war. This time it was Sudan's government that faced attempted regional secession (from the Azania Liberation Front, a southern political organization formed in 1965) and genocidal accusations from religious and social organizations.[84] The article contended that white mercenaries who had fought in the Congolese and Nigerian civil wars were in Sudan and that "the motive for Western support for the [southern Sudanese] secession [was] the same—divide and weaken one of Africa's largest nations." There was, however, an "interesting" difference. What was that preeminent difference? "The direct involvement of Israel."[85]

The writer noted that since the Azania Liberation Front's creation a decade earlier, the organization had become more dependent on Israel's political, economic, and military support. "[ALF leaders] are known to be receiving military training in Israel[,] and Israeli agents recently staged a [successful] military coup in Uganda." Aside from giving Israel control over Nile headwaters that were critical to Egypt, the article stated, Israel viewed the Ugandan coup as essential to ensuring the continuous flow of supplies and advisers to Sudan's rebels. In addition to acknowledging Israel's purported role in East African affairs, the writer shined a light on the Western media's role in framing the Sudanese conflict as one with antagonistic racial and religious elements. The writer argued that Israel had a part to play in this:

> The news media in most western countries (particularly in the U.S.), have taken great pains to depict the struggle in the Sudan as one of Black Christian southerners seeking independence from cruel and oppressive Arab-Moslem northerners. The fact that most Sudanese, be they Arab-Moslem

or Christian[,] are both Black somehow gets lost in the propaganda. The Israelis, however, using their vast network of Jewish organizations in the U.S. have brainwashed a number of Blacks in this country into being sympathetic to the cause of the Azana [sic] Liberation Front. Foremost among those parroting Israel's propaganda line are such "traditional negro leaders" [who] have been long time supporters of Jewish causes and head civil rights organizations which are heavily dependent [financially] on . . . Jewish liberals.

The writer argued that the struggle to divide and weaken Sudan was another example of America and its allies working to stymie African progress. "It is one more reason why African unity is of the utmost importance to African people around the world. Unless Africa unites, the Western powers will continue to pick off African nations one by one until our people are again with complete slavery and degradation."[86]

With Israel framed in some cases as supporting Black fighters against Arabs and at other times as oppressors, Black American recognition of Israeli assistance to the southern Sudanese became an opportunity to discuss Israel's role in the world and African America's relationship to Arabs. Yet, despite dissidence concerning Israel's role in Sudan specifically, Black American newspapers in the waning years of the war still conveyed a general support for southern Sudan.

Importantly, one editorial from Sudan's *Al Sahafa* newspaper illustrated that Sudanese were willing to reference Israel in their expressions of solidarity with Black America. A daily newspaper published in Arabic, the paper was one of several established to promote an agenda that aligned with government needs. Though the August 1970 press law turned all publishing over to a public corporation, the private *Al Sahafa* was continued and had an estimated circulation of 25,000 by 1972.[87] In late July 1967 the paper discussed Black America in its editorial, stating that the Sudanese people and its press supported African Americans in their struggle against racial discrimination. As the Sudanese English-language *Morning News* explained, "Sudanese support was expressed unconditionally before the recent Israeli aggression against the Arab countries and in service of justice and human rights and dignity, [an *Al Sahafa*] editorial pointed out." In a revealing statement, the *Al Sahafa* editorial—according to the *Morning News*—said that the Sudanese acted despite Dr. King's "support of Israel for its last hostility against the Arabs." The editorial purportedly concluded: "The Arab will never fail to support the cause of freedom and justice in any part of the world and at all times for the simple reason that they hate tyranny and hostility."[88]

In its creative display of discursive solidarity, *Al Sahafa* devoted space to articulate Sudanese (and Arab) solidarity with African Americans while distancing itself from the pro-Israeli view of the US civil rights movement's most prominent figure. Furthermore, its reference to apartheid extended the bonds of solidarity beyond the borders of Sudan and the United States to those struggling under the weight of state-sponsored racial oppression in South Africa. Yet, in what could only be described as an elephant in the room, southern Sudanese were waging a struggle for liberation against the Sudanese state that was fraught with racial dimensions and received Israeli assistance. If African American expressions of solidarity with Sudan during this period showed serious contradictions, perhaps the same was true for those Sudanese looking west of the Sahara and Atlantic to contemporary America.

The early years of Sudanese independence were a dynamic period in the history of Black America's relationship with the country. On one level, it witnessed the most significant presence of African Americans in Sudan in the twentieth century. Individuals like Andrew Brimmer, Madison Broadnax, and Valerie McCaw performed labor that not only laid the foundation for early US-Sudan relations but also contributed to the development of postcolonial Sudan's economy and agriculture. The early independence period also witnessed a remarkable shift in the racial language Black writers used when describing the tumultuous events unfolding in Sudan at the time.

Before independence (1956), when it was unclear whether Sudan would become sovereign or ruled by Britain or Egypt, some writers in Black American newspapers framed colonizing Egypt and colonized Sudan in a racial binary wherein Arab Egypt ruled Black Sudan. However, after Sudan became independent, the racialized nature of civil war stoked a remarkable shift. As social and political tensions between northern and southern Sudanese increased, portrayals of northerners as "Arab" and southern Sudanese as "Black" or "Negro" swelled. While Sudan had hitherto been framed as Black in contrast to Arab Egypt, writers now transferred this racial binary south and fashioned it to fit an exclusively Sudanese mold. In a moment that highlighted the fickle nature of diasporic solidarity, African American writers now cast northern Sudanese Arabs as oppressors and Black southern Sudanese as the oppressed. In this vein, the beauty reflected in Black America's capacity to reach out to an oppressed group on the other side of the world was contrasted by its willingness to discursively exclude a formerly included people from the bounds of blackness. From a Black American perspective, it appeared that one (in this case, northern Sudanese) could lose their proverbial Black card if they decided to oppress other Black people (southern Sudanese). African Americans so used to the unjust experience of marginalization and exclusion now showed themselves, in this stage of its history with the Sudan, as racial gatekeepers at a moment when white supremacy still reigned. It was regrettable.

Though Black newspapers generally published material that cast southern Sudanese in a sympathetic light, such sentiment was not always on display. Some infused Israel—then in conflict with Egypt and other Arab states—into their reporting on Sudan. In critiquing Israel's involvement in Sudan, some writers added another layer to the issue of Black American racial solidarity meant in the context of the Sudanese civil war and drew the Arab-Israeli conflict into this equation. The convergence of these issues and divided African American views concerning Sudanese matters would be expressed decades later during the Second Sudanese Civil War (1983–2005).

The following chapter is situated during that conflict, when southern Sudanese rebels once again took up arms against the Sudanese state. Just as African Americans covered, commented on, and traveled to Sudan during the first conflict, Black Americans did the same during the second war. In an interesting twist, one prominent group of African Americans would support the Sudanese government even as millions of Sudanese Blacks suffered under its weight: the Nation of Islam. Sudan became a stage for African American Christians and Muslims to wage a crusade.

Chapter 5

Call to Brotherhood

Louis Eugene Walcott was born on May 11, 1933, in Bronx, New York. The Walcott family eventually moved to Boston's Roxbury neighborhood and belonged to St. Cyprian's Episcopal Church. Louis studied music at Winston-Salem Teachers College but dropped out after three years to pursue a music career. In 1953 he married Betsey Ross, and from their union four sons and five daughters were born. In 1955 Walcott joined the Nation of Islam (NOI), the Black American organization founded on components of orthodox Islam and Black nationalism. He, like many others, was attracted to the NOI's Black empowerment message. Walcott eventually emerged as Minister Louis X of Boston's Temple. Louis became rivals with one Malcolm X, perhaps the Nation of Islam's most famous face after (or alongside) leader Elijah Muhammad. He condemned the Harlemite minister in 1964, and, when Malcolm broke with the NOI after differences with Muhammad, Walcott took Malcolm's place as minister of Harlem's Temple No. 7. Louis also replaced Malcolm as the Nation's national spokesman and in the late 1960s took the name Louis Abdul Farrakhan. Though many believed that Elijah Muhammad was preparing Farrakhan to succeed him, he instead appointed son Wallace Deen Muhammad. Angered, Farrakhan started a splinter group in 1978, a competing Nation of Islam that preserved Elijah Muhammad's teachings.[1]

On October 15, 1995, Farrakhan was one of the main speakers at the Million Man March, a gathering of an estimated 800,000 African American men and women in Washington, DC. Farrakhan helped to promote the event as an African American national holiday and envisioned it as an arena for generating more participation among young Black males in their communities.[2] Soon after the Million Man March brought Farrakhan closer to the political mainstream, he found himself on Sudanese soil. In early 1996 he embarked on a nineteen-country tour. Farrakhan sparked criticism for his anti-American statements during the trip and visits to countries that the US considered to be the equivalent of enemies. One such state was Sudan. On February 8, 1996, Farrakhan visited Khartoum. He met with President Omar Al-Bashir and informed him that Western attacks and sanctions imposed on Sudan would cease if his country adhered to God's word.[3]

Just eleven years after the First Sudanese Civil War ended, a new war broke out. The Second Sudanese Civil War began in 1983 and was rooted in repeated violations of the Addis Ababa Agreement (the 1972 treaty that had promised the South some political autonomy), economic marginalization of the peripheries, and forced government Islamization. The war was fought primarily between various Khartoum regimes and the Sudan People's Liberation Movement (SPLM), led by John Garang. Government violence was expressed through Islamic calls for an anti-southern jihad and accusations of an international conspiracy to unseat the Islamic state. The regime's jihad was mostly waged against noncombatants: undefended villages were attacked, huts and crops burned, and civilians indiscriminately killed. Women and children were abducted. SPLM leader Garang envisioned a country in which adherents of all faiths would have a stake in defining the nation. The Comprehensive Peace Agreement ended the war in 2005.[4]

African Americans kept a keen eye on Sudan, as they had done throughout the century. Black people debated the Sudanese government's perceived acquiescence in a Black slave trade and—importantly—Farrakhan's expressed support for the government.[5] The Nation's transnational Muslim solidarity with "Muslim/Arab" Sudan and its government offered a narrative that was similar and oppositional to the contemporaneous Judeo-Christian account. The NOI's historical and contemporary support for pan-Islamist and Pan-Africanist unity has generally concentrated on US racism and imperialism as a way to define its political identity and alliances.[6] While recent work has focused on African American Christian activism in and concerning war-torn Sudan, scholarship has not seriously examined the Nation of Islam's approach to Sudan during the late twentieth and early twenty-first centuries.[7] What was the form of the Nation's support for the Sudanese government? How did this support compare with earlier African American expressions of solidarity with Sudan? What import should be assigned to the NOI's Sudan-related rhetoric in the broader narrative of Black American engagement with that country if the language is both aberrant and abhorrent?

This chapter concerns the Nation of Islam's approach to Sudan during the Second Sudanese Civil War (1983–2005) and on through 2008, when Barack Obama was elected president of the United States. Sudan during these years experienced the agonies of war, slavery, and genocide. Within this sordid context, Minister Louis Farrakhan and the Nation of Islam provided impassioned, contrarian, and controversial support for the Sudanese government. The Nation based its support for Sudan on its accusations of a Zionist conspiracy and condemnation of what it portrayed as an anti-Arab US mass media. As such, the Nation's strategy highlighted the continued salience of the Arab-Israeli conflict in Black engagement with Sudan and added a curious element to race's role in this history. Arabs—so long referenced by African American writers as the race of enslaving oppressors—and Arabness were now marshaled by Farrakhan and others as the instrument with which to defend Sudanese from what were perceived to be racist, unjust attacks. More than merely an occasion to claim pan-Islamic unity, the Nation's rhetorical approach to Sudan was an important moment in Black America's relationship with the Arab world. During the Second Sudanese Civil War, Farrakhan and his NOI's attempts to defend the Sudanese government were expressed at the expense of Black lives oppressed by the Bashir regime. The Nation of Islam loosened the cords of blackness and shared enslavement that had long drawn Black Americans to the banks of the Nile. A sense of international Black kinship was sacrificed at the altar of Islamic solidarity.

Finally, this chapter closely interrogates the Nation of Islam's official communications medium, the *Final Call*. Launched by Louis Farrakhan in 1979, the newspaper continued the tradition of *Muhammad Speaks*, the widely circulating newspaper founded by Malcolm X and others. Today the *Final Call* digital edition exists as the newspaper's online companion.[8] By showing how the *Final Call* was a central space where Black Muslim and non-Muslim readers could read about Sudan, I continue the book's broader argument about the centrality of African American print culture in the long history of Black America's engagement with the country.

African Americans, Islam, and Sudan before Farrakhan

Historian Dawn-Marie Gibson has traced America's Muslim community to those African Muslims who arrived on slave ships. From the sixteenth through the nineteenth centuries—the tragic era of the transatlantic slave trade—Muslims from North and West Africa arrived in the Americas. Though Muslim enslaved persons tried fervently to preserve their religious heritage, from the nineteenth century American slaves faced violent efforts to stamp out any vestige of Islamic and traditional African faiths they may have had. However, many African Americans began to identify with Islam in the early twentieth century. This phenomenon was particularly true among Black people in some of the northeastern states and was even more apparent for those who had recently escaped the southern United States, which was then mired in Jim Crow racism.[9]

One man's efforts contributed to Islam's rise in the United States, and his focus on American-born Blacks in Sunni Muslim organizations transformed American and African religious history. This figure was Sudanese-born Satti Majid Muhammad al-Qadi Suwar al-Dhahab (or Satti Majid, for short). Satti Majid was born in Sudan's Old Dongola province in 1883. A member of a well-known family of religious judges and clerics, Majid studied Islam under local sheikhs. A self-described missionary, Majid entered the United States around 1908 and stayed until 1929. He worked primarily in New York City, Buffalo, Pittsburgh, and Detroit. Majid paid particular attention to African Americans, and throughout his ministry he pointed to what he perceived were violations of Black American rights. Islam, from Majid's perspective, was a religious and moral system that would curb American injustice. In articulating his message that Islam was a great option for African Americans, Majid was concerned with conveying Islam's universality, addressed misconceptions, and explained the religion's egalitarian concerns. In the greatest testament to the efficacy of Majid's message, he is said to have converted over forty thousand Black Americans to Islam.[10]

Majid was disturbed by the teachings of one Noble Drew Ali. Born Timothy Drew in North Carolina, Ali created the Moorish Science Temple (MST) in 1913. He saw Black Americans as Asiatic and descended from biblical Moabites and the Islamic Moorish Empire. Being Moors, African Americans—in his cosmology—are religiously Muslim. However, Islam was recast so that only a handful of practices and idioms were ostensibly Islamic.[11] Satti Majid was so troubled by Ali's teachings that he traveled on behalf of American Muslims to Cairo in 1929 to discuss the Moorish Science

Temple with scholars at Al-Azhar University. They speedily issued a fatwa, or ruling, on the MST's "errors." Though Majid wanted to return to the States as an official missionary representing Al-Azhar, the institution declined, and he never returned.[12] A year after Majid's departure, W. D. Fard Muhammad founded the Nation of Islam in Detroit. The NOI turned popular racial assumptions on their head by demonizing Europeans. Rather than blackness representing the epitome of evil or worthlessness, the organization instead taught that it embodied positive virtues like cleanliness and self-confidence. Blacks were divine; whites were devils. Fard labeled his doctrine Islam and tried to convert Black people, claiming that the religion would liberate them from white dominance. Fard mysteriously disappeared in 1934. By the end of the 1940s the Nation believed that he was God incarnate and claimed that his successor, the Honorable Elijah Muhammad, was God's messenger.[13]

The Nation of Islam became increasingly popular in the late 1950s and early 1960s, years when the American civil rights movement was intensifying. The 1955 arrest of Rosa Parks spurred the Montgomery Bus Boycott that catapulted Dr. Martin Luther King Jr. into prominence; federal troops were sent to Little Rock, Arkansas, in 1957 to enforce school desegregation; student sit-ins forced desegregation in public facilities in 1960–1961; and in 1963 approximately 250,000 people gathered in the March on Washington. African Americans struggled for integration, equality, and economic improvement. Nigerian professor E. U. Essien-Udom noted in his 1962 study *Black Nationalism* that there was growing feeling among Blacks in northern US cities "for re-identification with Africa": "In the last few years a significant number of groups have cropped up among Negroes representing the interest of those who seek a re-identification. Such interest should be expected in view of the wind of change blowing across Africa." Yet NOI leader Muhammad did not seem to completely grasp this re-identification, Essien-Udom said.[14]

As synonymous as Elijah Muhammad may have been with the Nation of Islam, his prominence was soon rivaled by Malcolm X. Born Malcolm Little in 1925, he was arrested in 1946 for burglary and began serving a ten-year sentence. While in prison he became exposed to the Nation's teachings and submitted to its discipline and guidance. Upon his release in 1952 he was renamed Malcolm X and speedily rose in the Nation's ranks. Outside of his interest in Black America, Malcolm's primary political interest was in Africa. In 1954 he compared the situation in Vietnam with the Mau Mau rebellion in Kenya, and in 1959—while serving as Elijah Muhammad's ambassador—he toured Egypt, Nigeria, Ghana, and Sudan. Malcolm was hosted in Sudan by

Malik Badri, a Sudanese student he had corresponded with before his arrival. Badri noted that Malcolm X was already versed in Sudanese history before his arrival in Khartoum. Near the Mahdi's tomb in Omdurman, Malcolm mentioned that he was particularly "fond of the Mahdi and his revolution, as a revolution at that time between the blacks and the whites, and the way that he had defeated the British in a number of battles." Malcolm, furthermore, was "very proud" of the Sudanese Mahdi "as a hero of the blacks—not as a Sunni Muslim," scholar Robin D. G. Kelley writes.[15] While in Mecca, Malcolm X connected with Sudanese political officials and spiritual guides. Sheikh Hassoun was one of the men he encountered there. Born in 1898 to a prominent family in Sudan, Sheikh Hassoun had been lecturing in the Grand Mosque and preaching in Masjid al-Haram for some time before meeting the famous Harlemite. Hassoun eventually became Malcolm's spiritual adviser and mufti of New York's Muslim Mosque, Incorporated. Following Malcolm's February 1965 assassination, Hassoun washed his body with sacred oil and wrapped him in white shrouds.[16]

That decade, another American Muslim organization emerged. Blending Islam and Black Nationalism, the Ansarullah was led by the controversial Imam Isa. Born Dwight York, Isa became interested in northern Sudanese Nubians and traveled to Sudan. He paid homage to the Mahdi's tomb in Omdurman, met with members of his family, and visited Aba Island. On his return to America, York claimed descent from the Mahdi. The Sudanese Mahdi was supposed to have said, "I'll have a descendant who will rise in the West, that my name will be heard there." Isa claimed that Al-Hadi al-Mahdi, who was killed in 1969, had come to the United States a long time ago, married an African American woman, and returned to Sudan. Isa claimed that he was a product of that marriage and was consequently the Mahdi's grandson. He gave himself the name Al-Hajj al-Imam Isa Abd Allah Muhammad al-Hadi al-Mahdi. His followers believed that he was the lamb that would suffer the sins of his people (the 144,000), and Ansarullah recruitment of that multitude was seen as a precondition for the millennium.[17] In the 1970s and 1980s, the Ansarullah community ("Ansaaru Allah") adhered to Islamic beliefs and adopted Muslim social patterns. The group positioned Sudan as Islam's true epicenter and Arabic, the Koran, the true Sunna, and Islam to be Nubian.[18]

While some may read Imam Isa as a curious or even bizarre individual, his significance in the history of African American engagement with Sudan is perhaps most discernible when read against the grain of previous Black invocations of Sudanese history. Though Horace Cayton argued that the first enslaved people brought to the United States came from Sudan, Imam Isa made a personal genealogical link to the Sudanese Mahdi. Though Malcolm X envisioned the Mahdi as a racial exemplar rather than a Sunni Muslim, Imam Isa's followers believed that he—supposedly the Mahdi's grandson—possessed eschatological significance. Thus, in his claims to literal familial relationship to the Mahdi and the religious significance that this may have imparted upon him, the figure of Imam Isa represents a singular union of African American invocation of Sudanese history and religion. An atypical person that stands out from the multitude of other African American men and women covered in this study, Imam Isa reflects one element of the diverse invocations of modern Sudanese history and engagements with it.

Imam Isa's 1970s-era pamphlets and newsletters did not provide much commentary on contemporary Sudan.[19] This negligence, however, was not only not indicative of the entire African American Muslim community, it was also amplified by the reality that epochal events were unfolding in Sudan at the time.

The Second Sudanese Civil War

The Second Sudanese Civil War ignited in 1983. President Jafaar Nimeiri, who had been in power since 1969, had become increasingly annoyed by southern autonomy, and most of the officer corps had been opposed to the integration of former Anyanya rebels into the Sudan People's Armed Forces. In May 1983 a military unit at Bor (in southern Sudan) refused an Armored Division company's attempt to disarm the 105th Battalion. The garrison escaped on their way to Ethiopia to rendezvous with senior southern commanding officer John Garang, effectively beginning the war. In addition to these military origins, southern Sudanese resistance was also sparked by the Sudanese government's new policy of forced Islamization. President Nimeiri, who in 1977 had created a committee to Islamize Sudanese laws, began a nuanced program of literalist Islamization in Sudan in September 1983. That month he decreed that sharia would be state law, and judicial applications included amputations to punish theft and whippings for alcohol offenses. Specific interpretations of Islamic law were imposed on Muslims and non-Muslims alike. Colonel Garang would lead the rebel Sudan People's Liberation Movement/Army (SPLM/A) for the entirety of the war, which dragged on for the next two decades.[20]

The war years witnessed a series of political shocks and human sufferings. In 1983–1984 alone, famine took the lives of an estimated two hundred thousand people in northern Sudan. After a popular uprising unseated Nimeiri from power in 1985, the Sudanese military governed the country for a year before Sadiq al-Mahdi—the Mahdi's great-grandson—was elected prime minister in 1986. In the late 1980s another famine—this time in the South—killed an estimated quarter of a million people. In 1989 Brig. Gen. Omar al-Bashir overthrew the young al-Mahdi government and established an Islamist state. That same year, the UN established Operation Lifeline Sudan to provide access for humanitarian relief operations.[21]

Sudan's Islamist government encouraged slavery during the war. Reports of slaves captured in the aftermath of the 1988 al-Da'in (Darfur) massacre came to the attention of international human rights groups, and reports of slavery continued after the 1989 coup that brought Bashir to power. Government-organized militias sold hundreds of thousands of people from southern Sudan and the Nuba Mountains into slavery. Some women and girls were kept as concubines, and many were subject to rape. Others were sent north, where they worked on farms.[22] According to the US State Department and several human rights groups, slavery not only existed but thrived during the war. According to the human rights groups, the government allowed militias to keep what they had pillaged rather than paying them directly.[23] "It's war booty," said Jemera Rone, a field representative for Human Rights Watch/Africa, in the *New York Times* in March 1996. "They're given free license by the government. They're not prosecuted. In fact, the government denies that it is taking place."[24] While calculations on the number of enslaved vary, estimates range from tens of thousands to upwards of one hundred thousand.[25]

The 1990s, like the war's previous decade, were tumultuous to say the least. Amid the war against the Khartoum regime, Dinka and Nuer peoples waged their own conflict that caused massive casualties before the Sudan People's Liberation (SPLA) could establish hegemony. The first half of the decade saw the Sudanese government declare a jihad, a series of military operations, and the UN Security Council ultimately sanctioning the Khartoum government in 1995. By the late 1990s President Bashir was locked in a power struggle, and, in a move smacking of authoritarianism he dissolved the national assembly and declared a state of emergency. In July 2002 the Sudanese government and the SPLM/A signed an agreement in Kenya that included a framework of principles—including southern self-determination—as a foundation for negotiating a peace. Following pressure from the US government and a coalition of American religious groups, the Sudanese government signed a peace deal with the southern rebels in 2004. In 2005 the Comprehensive Peace Agreement was signed, ending the sordid war. More than two million died, and another four million southern Sudanese were displaced. Longtime leader John Garang—president of the southern Sudanese government and first vice president of the Government of National Unity—would not live out the year, losing his life in a helicopter crash.[26]

While a fierce conflict was waged on Sudan's soil, other belligerents waged a different war with different munitions. What transpired was a holy war between African American Christians and Muslims, contesting the terms of solidarity with the Sudanese in unprecedented fashion.

Black Christian Solidarity and Southern Sudan

During the Second Sudanese Civil War, US political campaigns for southern Sudan were dominated by religious opposition (Muslim vs. Christian) and racial opposition (Arab vs. Black African). American human rights groups like Christian Solidarity International (CSI) and the American Anti-Slavery Group (AASG) framed the war with narratives of modern slavery and connected Southern trauma to the travails of American Christian, Black, and Jewish minorities.[27]

CSI's John Eibner played a critical role in pushing for African American mobilization. In 1992 Eibner—at the invitation of the New Sudan Council of Churches—traveled to southern Sudan to investigate slave raids and other abuses. Encouraged by local leaders, he began a series of publicized slave redemption efforts in 1995 and made a whopping thirty-five trips to Sudan between 1995 and 2003. He records redeeming over eighty thousand enslaved persons on these trips. The CSI marshaled African American history, allowing the organization to craft familiar polarization that appealed to the US public. Anthropologist Amal Fadlalla writes that the white versus Black dynamic in the US context mapped onto the Arab versus Black Sudanese framework, and the language of the eighteenth- and nineteenth-century abolitionist movement was used to fight twentieth-century slavery in southern Sudan on religious and humanitarian terms.[28] Several African American leaders and pastors joined Eibner on his sojourns to Sudan, and the CSI went so far as using the term "underground railroad" in referencing its mission.[29] By the middle of 2000, in the waning months of Bill Clinton's presidency, a group of Black clergy from around the country felt moved enough to address a pointed letter to Congressional Black Caucus chairman

James Clyburn. After calling out President Clinton and other world leaders for remaining silent on the issue of Sudanese enslaved people, the letter made a plea that linked contemporary Sudan with historical US slavery: "We, African-American pastors from around the nation, write to ask the Congressional Black Caucus to come to the front of this battle. As the descendants of African slaves, we must not rest until those now held in bondage are freed."[30]

One Black clergyman who just so happened to have founded the Congressional Black Caucus did his part to bring attention to the issue. Rev. Walter Fauntroy—a longtime pastor of New Bethel Baptist Church in Washington, DC, as well as former DC congressman—was embedded among Black church networks and leaders. After radio talk show host Joe Madison's initial CSI-facilitated trip to the Sudan (where he participated in a mass slave emancipation), he recruited his friend Fauntroy to join him on a second trip to southern Sudan in the spring of 2001. The two men helped to galvanize Black churches and took the issue to the Urban League, Congressional Black Caucus, and the NAACP. Following Fauntroy's Sudan trip, two African American clerics from Boston—Gloria White-Hammond and her husband and co-pastor Ray Hammond—went on a slave redemption trip with John Eibner to southern Sudan in the summer of 2001. Enthralled by the stories of women redeemed from slavery, White-Hammond was compelled to form My Sister's Keeper, a humanitarian organization designed to help Sudanese women rebuild their loves. She took additional trips to Sudan that were covered by the likes of the *Boston Globe* and NBC's *Today Show*, making her a major figure in the Sudan campaign. Rev. Al Sharpton, who himself was flown to Sudan by CSI, pledged to spread the word about Sudanese slavery, and the organization's efforts to connect Frederick Douglass's story with that of Josephine Bakhita—a Darfurian Sudanese woman who was born in the nineteenth century, experienced slavery, and became a Catholic nun following her emancipation—attracted African American Catholic attention. Black Christians were not alone in this abolitionist movement. The camp included conservative Republican senators Jesse Helms of North Carolina and Sam Brownback of Kansas, the latter of whom joined African American congressman Donald Payne on a trip to southern Sudan in 1998.[31] "As well as being a black radical issue," writes Richard Crockett, "slavery in southern Sudan and the persecution of the Christian churches also became a key issue for Republican-voting white Christian evangelists."[32]

For those African Americans who aligned themselves with southern Sudanese, the reality of slavery bound them together in a way that few—if any—other shared experiences could. Because blackness in the American context was the singular feature defining who could and could not be enslaved, an argument can be made that a history of enslavement is one of the defining elements that is needed for African Americans to endear ourselves to Black people beyond American shores. In this paradigm, a shared history of enslavement is perhaps even necessary for the deepest level of solidarity to be possible. But the idealization of southern Sudan was problematic. The CSI linked Frederick Douglass to Josephine Bakhita, and her narrative attracted the African American Catholic community. Fadlalla writes that Bakhita's experience of slavery, conversion, and liberation through Christian faith showed "how affective violence is narrated to celebrate ideas of humanity, rescue, and salvation." "This narration," Fadlalla continues, "also highlights the feminized vulnerability of the Southern Sudanese and links their struggle to that of Jewish and Christian blacks in the United States."[33] Any presentation of southern Sudanese as vulnerable, helpless people in need of Western intervention reeks of the kind of infantilizing language of benighted, helpless Black Africans that forms the bedrock of neocolonialism. African American Christian usage of such language would complicate the question of racial solidarity to the extent that it would effectively be a discursive camaraderie predicated on Black American superiority over Black South Sudanese.

While African American Christians certainly had their eyes on Sudanese happenings, they were not the only Black American religious group deeply invested in the Sudan at the time. Black Muslims stood on the other side of the aisle and showed a differed side of solidarity.

In 1994 Charles Jacobs organized the Boston-based American Anti-Slavery Group. Jacobs, who is Jewish, was among the first to publicize the reality of slavery in Sudan and the West African nation of Mauritania to the American public. He, along with a Mauritanian Muslim named Mohammed Athie, broke the story of a modern slave trade in those two countries in the *New York Times*. The AASG faxed materials to Black newspapers in its attempt to kindle support for abolition, and it was largely through the AASG that Samuel Cotton, an African American, acquired his knowledge of slavery's history in Africa and the contemporary situation. Cotton was a student at Columbia University and part-time journalist for the weekly *City Sun*, New York's second-largest Black paper. In 1995, after much research, Cotton wrote a series of articles on contemporary slavery in Sudan and Mauritania.[34]

NOI spokesman and international representative Akbar Muhammad took the defense, contending that Cotton had succumbed to a Jacobs-led Jewish plot against the Muslim world. Muhammad swore that neither slavery nor trafficking of enslaved persons existed in the modern Arab world.[35] In an NOI press release dated March 24, 1995, he noted: "Mr. Samuel Cotton . . . said that the President of Africa's largest country, the Sudan, has six to eight slaves in his home in Khartoum. . . . Cotton's quotes and most of the information called 'research' was obtained directly from the Anti-Slavery Group based in Washington, D.C., via Dr. Charles Jacobs. Dr. Jacobs has been using the pain of a Black Mauritanian to justify his attack on Islam." Muhammad, in the press release, said that an invitation had been offered to members of the Black press—including Cotton—to visit Sudan.[36] Cotton stated that he could not accept the invitation: "What could I possibly learn while traveling under the auspices of the very [Sudanese] government that my sources alleged was guilty of gross human rights violations and of winking at the practice of slavery?" He realized that Muhammad's principal aim was to protect Islam and encourage its continued advance among African Americans.[37] After issuing the press release, Muhammad claimed that Cotton and the *City Sun* were being used as puppets in a "Zionist plot" to assail Islam and slow its growth in the United States. This "plot," in Muhammad's estimation, was not limited to an anti-Muslim agenda. Rather, it also aimed to divide the Black community over the slavery issue and discourage those engaged in business from investing in Africa.[38] Muhammad termed Jacobs a "Jewish consultant" and described his press releases as "using the old FBI trick of planting stories."[39]

While any antisemitic attack on the figure of Charles Jacobs would be fundamentally reprehensible, the notion that he criticized the Sudanese government on Islamophobic grounds is justifiable. To begin, Jacobs frequently deployed anti-Muslim and anti-Arab rhetoric. His political investments in his abolitionist work were linked to a commitment to the most conservative arm of the American pro-Israel movement and, according to Melani McAlister, "would evolve into an activist agenda on the dangers of 'Islamic extremism' that eventually pitted him against most of the liberal and progressive Jewish community in Boston." After founding the AASG, Jacobs began working with another organization he had founded—the David Project—to produce a film that framed Columbia University's Middle East Institute as hostile to Jews and anti-Israel.[40] Jan Rakowsky, reporting for the Jewish newspaper *Forward*, wrote that after its founding the David Project "quickly developed a national reputation for hounding Muslims that it perceives to be a threat to the Jewish community."[41] David Project executive director Phillip Brodsky admits that the organization's approach was "combative" before it was moderated in 2015.[42]

It is unfair to ascribe Jacob's personal views to Samuel Cotton. However, it is important to consider the progeny of his knowledge concerning slavery in Sudan and, with it, the larger infrastructures of knowledge production and media circulation informing the history of African American engagement with the country. While the veracity of slavery in Sudan during the Second Civil War has been proven, it is fair to consider how Jacob's views (and those of others) may have influenced reportage of the subject and consequently helped shaped Black American knowledge and opinions. While I am not likening Jacobs to the following entities, it would be foolish to think that Black newspaper editors and contributors, diplomats, and other figures who wrote about Sudan and/or journeyed through the country did so through lenses completely untouched by their class, racial, gender, and other perspectives and biases. Given the fact that Cotton was one of the most influential Black Americans bringing Sudanese matters to light, the complexities of one of his sources—Jacobs—warrants mention.

On November 6, 2004, Akbar Muhammad—still the NOI's international representative—pivoted again to anti-Zionism on a panel concerning Sudan. During the discussion, Muhammad, who acknowledged that he had traveled to Sudan three times, claimed that there was a war against Islam taking place and that part of that effort was to break up Africa. Propaganda was involved, he said. "And what pains me is we allow our enemies, especially the Zionists, to give us agendas." He cited the example of Sudanese slavery, which had apparently been "given" to Black people as an agenda. What, then, was the target of this supposedly Zionist agenda? "They used this false issue of Arabs enslaving Black people as a way to attack and discredit the Honorable Minister Louis Farrakhan," Akbar claimed. He further argued that Zionists wanted Blacks to oppose Sudan and were concerned about Islam's influence among the descendants of American slavery.[43] Muhammad did not stop at claiming that the matter of Sudanese slavery was a false Zionist plot. Rather, he used the panel discussion to claim that the Zionists had given Black people a new agenda. Muhammad challenged those present to examine the reasons for the continued "propaganda program" against Sudan and argued that the plan was to break up that country. "There are large deposits of oil, which are yet untapped. There is uranium, gold and the most important resource . . . the vast reserves of water that flow under the sands in the Sudan. They want to control those resources."[44]

Farrakhan also denounced critics of the Sudanese government as tools of Zionist or State Department conspiracies and insisted that reports of Sudanese slavery were an Israeli-CIA anti-Arab smear campaign.[45] In July 1996 he openly queried, "[Is Sudan being condemned] because this Islamic government is trying to build an Islamic nation?" He continued that he should and would condemn slavery but would not allow himself to be used as a Western pawn in a political game to destabilize Sudan's Islamic government. The *Final Call* noted that Farrakhan had visited Sudan in recent years and met with SPLA leader John Garang. "Not once," the article stated, "did Mr. Garang mention slavery as an issue of conflict with the government of the north."[46] Years later, Farrakhan appeared on James Mtume's *Open Line* radio show on New York City's 98.7 KISS FM, joined by Akbar Muhammad. During the discussion, the Garang meeting came up. After reiterating the fact that slavery was never mentioned in that conversation, Farrakhan shared that Rebecca Garang (John Garang's wife) broke down and cried after he had mentioned the word "justice." Rebecca, said Farrakhan, said that he was the only person who came and talked about justice. The injustice, he shared, was racism. "The Arabs," he stated, "had mixed their blood with the Africans that live in the North. They are Arab-ized and Islamic; and the same racist poison that has poisoned the bloodstream of Islam has made the Arab North feel superior to the Christian Animist-African South in the Sudan." Farrakhan continued that southern Sudan was Black: "Racism exists there like the enemy has done to us: When you are lighter, you think you are better than your Black Brother or Sister."[47]

NOI antipathy was not only directed toward Jews; it was also directed toward sources of information concerning Sudan. Farrakhan and other NOI members often disputed the veracity of Sudanese slavery on the grounds that the sources had an anti-Arab agenda. This shows the racial elements of NOI solidarity with Sudan and contrasts with those Black writers who, at earlier moments of the twentieth century, highlighted the history of Arab slavery in Sudan. If those earlier statements were made to conjure sympathy for and solidarity with Black Sudanese, the decision made by Farrakhan and others to defend the Sudanese government on the grounds that there was an unjust anti-Arab agenda at play is striking. The meaning of Arabness had different functions for different Black Americans at different moments in Sudan's history.

In March 1996, the Black-oriented National Newspaper Publishers Association presented Minister Farrakhan with an award. At a press conference held in Washington, DC, Farrakhan answered questions about his African tour that had made a stop in Sudan. He was on his way out of the press conference when someone shouted a question to him concerning Sudanese slavery.

He pointed at the inquirer and issued a challenge: "If slavery exists, why don't you go as a member of the press?" Farrakhan added, "If you find it [slavery in Sudan], then you come back and tell the American people what you have found. But don't let the State Department be your official source" (one State Department report showed that 400 Black Sudanese had been sold in Libya).[48] Two *Baltimore Sun* reporters—one Black and one white (Gregory Kane and Gilbert A. Lewthwaite, respectively), took up the challenge and went to Sudan. They found a slave market, purchased two half-brothers in a rural market for $500 each, and returned them to their families in a Dinka village. Human rights organization Christian Solidarity International assisted the reporters who wrote a major investigative series for the *Baltimore Sun* in June 1996 concerning the sale of African children by Arab slave traders in southern Sudan. Farrakhan repeatedly refused the *Sun*'s interview requests.[49]

On July 17, 1996, the *Final Call* published an interview with Farrakhan. In it he referred to articles published by the *Sun* that documented how Kane and Lewthwaite had illegally traveled to Sudan and purchased two enslaved youth. Now a month after the *Sun*'s reporting on slavery in Sudan, Farrakhan condemned all forms of slavery but nevertheless wanted reports of its reality in Sudan "verified" by an interfaith team of Muslim and Christian journalists and leaders. "The Baltimore Sun is not a news source I should accept as gospel," said Farrakhan in the interview. The *Sun* said that he cited the Koran to underscore his position: "When an unrighteous man brings you news, look carefully into it lest you harm a person in ignorance, then be sorry for what you did." Farrakhan, in addition to questioning the *Sun*'s validity, wondered in the *Final Call* how long slavery had existed in Sudan if it was indeed present. He noted that when Amnesty International pronounced a list of indictments against Sudan in 1985 (including political imprisonment, torture, and the death penalty), they mentioned nothing concerning slavery.[50]

"Muslims need our own news service and Africa needs our own news service," declared Farrakhan in a Q&A with Sudanese media in January 1998. "[These are necessary] so we can counter the managed news of *Reuters*, *BBC*, *Associated Press* and all of them who color the news for their purposes. We need to have an independent news media that will allow us to free our people from the lies and distortions that are promoted by the Western media."[51] Minister Akbar Muhammad blamed the media for what he perceived as their intentional efforts to cast the Darfur crisis in an Arab versus Black dichotomy. During his joint radio interview with Farrakhan, Muhammad stated, "Whenever we look at the world and talk about a government, they show a picture." He continued by saying that if you talked about Iraq during

Saddam Hussein's reign, the media showed an image of the Iraqi leader, and the same went for Syria and its president, Hafez al-Assad. "They have talked about the Sudan, but if I asked an audience across this country what the president of the Sudan looks like, most people do not know." Muhammad noted that Bashir had just traveled to Iran but that little information was printed depicting him with the Iranian leader. This, he argued, was because Bashir was Black: "as Black as me or [even] Blacker" ("So he does not fit the script of 'the Arab who is killing Africans'"). Muhammad recalled being in a room and a man asking for Arab tribal leaders to stand up. Those who stood up were Black. When the man proceeded to ask African tribal leaders to stand, those who did were also Black. "So we looked at each other because the picture in America is that these White Arabs are killing Africans. The Brother said clearly what makes them Arabs is that they only speak Arabic. . . . What makes them Africans is they speak an African language and Arabic." Muhammad asserted that the language framing Sudanese Arabs enslaving Africans was "very clever" and something that the media pushed to spur "natural hatred of Blacks for Arabs so that Arabs look like the real culprits."[52]

The grandest refutation of the Arab versus Black narrative given before the Nation of Islam did not come from Farrakhan but from the Sudanese president himself. On February 23, 2007, President Omar al-Bashir granted an exclusive video interview to workshop attendees at the NOI's Saviours' Day convention at Detroit's Cobo Center. The Nation's chief of staff had extended the invitation to the Sudanese leader. The conversation was simulcast on Sudanese state-run television and reported by Askia Muhammad in the *Final Call*. Speaking before NOI members and reporters, Bashir said he was using his speech—which, according to Muhammad, may have been the first interactive video conference between an African head of state and a Black American group—to invite the media and American public to learn the truth about Sudan.[53] Bashir injected race into his speech—"Talk of Arabs killing Blacks is a lie," he said. Adding that Sudan's government was "a government of Blacks, with all different ethnic backgrounds," he conflated Sudanese, African, and racial identities: "We're all Africans. We're all Black." Muhammad, reporting on the speech in the *Final Call*, prefaced his coverage by describing Bashir as a "brown-skinned president who would be considered 'Black' in the U.S." Muhammad reported that "[Bashir] called 'false' charges that his 'White, Arab' government enslaved some of its 'Black,' African countrymen, and even engaged in . . . 'ethnic cleansing' in order to rob and dominate the country's Black population in the southern regions of the country. Those charges were proven to be hoaxes by investigative reports."[54]

Figure 5.1. Omar Hassan Ahmad al-Bashir, the president of Sudan, listens to a speech during the opening of the twentieth session of the New Partnership for Africa's Development in Addis Ababa, Ethiopia, January 31, 2009.

Source: US Navy photo by Mass Communication Specialist 2nd Class Jesse B. Awalt.

Askia Muhammad's decision to describe President Bashir as someone his *Final Call* readers might consider Black like them calls to mind earlier decisions by Percival Prattis to comment about the physical similitude between Sudanese and Black Americans in the *Pittsburgh Courier* decades earlier, when Sudan's postcolonial future was in question. It also invokes the way that George Padmore described nationalist leader Abdel Rahman el Mahdi in the 1940s. Just as Prattis and Padmore had done over fifty years earlier, Muhammad now attempted to make a Sudanese figure more relatable to his African American audience by drawing attention to his skin color. What made this latest discursive move such an enlightening—if not bizarre—point of contrast with those earlier counterparts is that Bashir was leading a regime that was complicit in the enslavement of Black south Sudanese and the alleged genocide of Darfurians. Muhammad's decision to highlight Bashir's physical resemblance to Black Americans, while perhaps productive in refuting common binaries between Black and Arab Sudanese, reads as an affirmation of racial solidarity with a man who was leading the slaughter of other Black people. In this light, Muhammad's comment was at once self-serving and self-defeating.

"I can appreciate the Nation of Islam's need to promote black pride," said African American columnist Clarence Page in 1995, "especially when it means profits for the Nation of Islam. But, if black pride means anything it means caring about black people, even when their oppressors don't happen to be white."⁵⁵ Cotton, writing in his book *Silent Terror*, noted that the silence of those in the Islamic world (and particularly Black Muslims in Africa and the United States) on the issue of slavery in the Arab world was "disturbing."⁵⁶ Randall Robinson, president of the TransAfrica Forum (an African American social justice advocacy organization), was quoted in the *New York Times* stating that he wasn't sure whether Americans knew much about slavery in Sudan: "If more people had known, they would have been shocked and disappointed with his [Farrakhan's] statements of support for Sudan." Black newspapers, radio stations, and television programs like PBS's *Tony Brown's Journal* publicized the Nation's support of a regime accused of condoning slavery.⁵⁷

Two of the most notable responses to Farrakhan and the Nation came not from African Americans but—fittingly—from Sudanese themselves. The first came from Sabit Abbe Alley. As a toddler, Alley was forced to flee with his family to Uganda during the First Sudanese Civil War. Following the peace agreement that ended that conflict, Alley returned to Sudan and studied at the University of Khartoum. He joined the civil service in the South after graduating in 1977 and worked in the regional parliament, governor's office, and tourism department. Bashir's 1989 coup halted his career. Alley, who criticized the regime, fled to Kenya and later to the United States. While in exile, he served as an associate representative for the Sudan People's Liberation Movement. Working in that capacity, he engaged with UN officials, US politicians, nongovernmental organizations, and churches about the southern Sudanese struggle.⁵⁸

Alley's article "Genocide and Slavery in the Sudan" appeared in the June 6–11, 1996, edition of the Brooklyn-based *City Sun*. In it, Alley mentioned that Farrakhan had spoken over radio station WLIB and addressed a rally at a Brooklyn church on the Sudan catastrophe. On both occasions, the minister refuted reports of Arab Sudanese enslaving Sudanese Africans. "According to brother Farrakhan, the claims of genocide and slavery in the Sudan are mere fabrications and propaganda by the Western world and media to disgrace Islam and at the same time tarnish the 'good' image of the Islamic Republic of the Sudan." Farrakhan, according to Alley, also argued that the United States and European and African countries were plotting to stop Sudanese authorities from establishing a model Islamic state and exporting Islamic fundamentalism abroad. "Members of the Southern Sudanese Community in America in particular and their friends were stunned and outraged by these statements," Alley said. "They found it hard to believe that a man of Farrakhan's standing and intelligence could stoop so low as to flirt with Arab slavers and deny the existence of an industry (slavery) which has grown tremendously over the years and has become common knowledge the world over."[59]

Alley took direct aim at Farrakhan by claiming that his defense of the Sudanese government's war and slave apparatus was because he had a personal stake in the matter. "He is on Khartoum's payroll. . . . The arguments about Western propaganda and the defense of Islam are merely rationalizations and cover-ups. What true Muslim would defend an Islamic government whose pronounced policy is the extermination and enslavement of its citizens, including Muslims[?]"[60] After concluding that Farrakhan seemed to be playing a critical role in oppressing people in southern Sudan, the Nuba Mountains, and the Ingessina Hills, Alley suggested that no one should be surprised because it was known that the minister loathed southern Sudanese. For evidence to support his claim, Alley pointed to comments Farrakhan made at his February 1996 Saviours' Day address and subsequent speeches "where the Minister graphically described the people of South Sudan as being very, very, very, very . . . very dark with kinky hair, as compared to the brown (white!) Northern Arabs, who, according to Farrakhan, looked exactly like him! He used the adverb *very* 15 times to emphasize his color prejudice against the Southern Sudanese."[61] Just as Askia Muhammad likened President Bashir to American Blacks, Farrakhan's decision to distinguish northern and southern Sudanese according to skin color (and identifying with the former) recalls Percival Prattis's mid-century comparison of Sudanese to Black Americans. In that context, however, Prattis did so while distinguishing Sudanese from historical Arab oppressors. Farrakhan, in contrast, was now likening himself (physically) to northern Sudanese now accused of enslaving Black southerners. "It is indeed ironical," Alley argued, "that a supposedly black man of slave descent should hate his kith and kin and actively participate in programs aimed at their eradication from the face of the earth. . . . Minister Louis Farrakhan should realize that despite his support for the Arab and Islamic fundamentalist government of the Sudan, the black African people of the Sudan will not disappear from the face of the earth."[62]

The "kith and kin" line was taken up by another Sudanese figure. Born in Sudan in 1938, Bona Malwal studied journalism at Indiana University (where he graduated in 1963) and later economics, journalism, and international relations at Columbia University. During the First Sudanese Civil War, Malwal served in a variety of capacities. He worked as an information officer for Sudan's Ministry of Culture and Information, edited the English-language *Vigilant* newspaper in Khartoum, and was elected to Parliament representing Northern Gogrial in April 1968. In 1975 he was appointed a full cabinet member, becoming the first southern Sudanese appointed minister of culture and information. In the early 1980s, Malwal—by then a critic of the regime—was imprisoned with other leading southern politicians for his opposition to the government's southern Sudan policies. Upon his release he went into exile in the UK and later the United States. Returning to Sudan after the 1985 fall of Nimeiri's regime, his newspapers (*Vigilant* and *Sudan Times*) reported on violence against intellectuals in the South and dissension in the government. In July 1989 he again went into exile in London, where he founded the *Sudan Democratic Gazette*. Malwal would later be involved in negotiations for the Chukudum Agreement, in which the Umma Party and SPLM/A pledged themselves for the South's right of self-determination.[63]

On August 21, 1999, Malwal delivered the annual Bayard Rustin Lecture at the A. Philip Randolph Institute's National Education Conference. Founded by labor activists and civil rights leaders A. Philip Randolph and Bayard Rustin in 1965, the APRI was created "to continue the struggle for social, political, and economic justice for all working Americans."[64] "Your distinguished gathering being largely an African American audience," Malwal said, "most of you will wonder why I should be so overwhelmed. After all, I am one of you and should feel at home, which I do." He continued, "Only in very rare moments like this one, when you honour me as you are doing . . . do my people know they have kith and kin in America who have not forgotten them." Malwal acknowledged that APRI president Norman Hill had eloquently spoken in an address titled "Slaughter and Slavery in Sudan" and said that the candor of Hill's message had emboldened him to be candid about one particular aspect of his people's suffering: "the attitude of a small section of the African American community, and of some very few Black leaders, to the enslavement and genocide being perpetrated by the government of Sudan against my people." Noting that Hill had mentioned Farrakhan in his address, Malwal continued that he would confine his comments on the matter to Minister Farrakhan because of his denial that he had seen any slavery in Sudan. "[This] has caused not just considerable damage to the cause of the enslaved people of Sudan," he said. Returning to the familial paradigm, he continued, "Coming from a blood brother . . . it is both humiliating and demoralising to the Black people of Sudan." While Malwal described Farrakhan as a close friend of many Arab and Islamic leaders, he positioned him as being particularly close to the Sudanese government. "We do not begrudge that friendship," he continued. "[As an African American Muslim leader] we would expect him to use his friendship with the regime in Khartoum to plead the just cause of the Black people of Sudan, as he does the cause of the African American Muslims." Malwal contended that if that had been the case, Black Sudanese might have benefited from the minister's relationship with their enemies as a mediator. However, denying their suffering to protect their enemies was "a betrayal of one's own" and an encouragement to Sudan's government to continue its anti-Black genocide.[65]

After informing his audience that it was impossible for Farrakhan to have been mistaken about who was mistreating whom in Sudan, Malwal stated:

> Some of you may remember the joke Mr Farrakhan made about those of us in Southern Sudan on an American television show when he got back home, five times referring to us as "Black, Black, Black!" He then went on to say, "As for the people of Northern Sudan, they are just like you and me!" Mr Farrakhan chose to put some colour distance between himself and us—with his fair skin closer to that of the Arab—in preparation for the public somersault he was about to perform in defence of the enslavers of my people.

"We had known all along that Mr Farrakhan represents a sector of the African American community" he said, "but not the entire lot." Malwal then contrasted his listeners with the NOI leader. "We have always believed that you [the audience] . . . would be for us if you knew the truth, the facts of our suffering." He declared his hope that from that day forward, the southern Sudanese cause—and particularly their struggle for racial equality, right to live in dignity, and the end of slavery and genocide—would have "many strong advocates" among them. "As you return home . . . we hope you will rally the African American people to join the struggle to free the Black people of Sudan."[66]

In brief, Black responses to the NOI rhetoric about Sudan were marked by several important observations. Clarence Page and Samuel Cotton were able to acknowledge that the words of Farrakhan and other Black Muslims carried significant weight. While the racism and denial that permeated such rhetoric may have separated them from the likes of the NAACP or Congressional Black Caucus, it did not hollow the significance of their standing. Yet it was the very recognition of the influence that Farrakhan and Black

Muslims wielded that disappointed some Black observers. If harnessed the right way, opined Cotton, the NOI could have played a remarkable abolitionary role not only in Sudan but in Mauritania as well. Notwithstanding the words of Cotton, Page, and Randall Robinson, perhaps the most enlightening Black responses to Farrakhan and the Nation came from Sudanese figures Sabit Alley and Bona Malwal. Their use of the "kith and kin" phrase to argue for Sudan's relationship to Black America is captivating due to comments made decades earlier about Black Americans being descendent from Sudanese slaves. It is also ironic, given NOI attempts to liken northern Sudanese—so often framed as Arabs who enslaved Black Sudanese—to African Americans. It seemed that African Americans like Farrakhan could phenotypically self-identify with the very Sudanese accused of oppressing Black Africans. The politics of African American solidarity with Sudan at the turn of the century was in many ways more difficult to crack than ever before.

Genocide in Darfur

Sudanese slavery was coupled with genocide in Darfur, in western Sudan. The First Darfur Rebellion began between the Fur tribe and government-allied Arab tribes in 1987. While the conflict ended two years later with a negotiated peace agreement, peace did not last long. The Second Darfur Rebellion began in 1995, this time between the Masalit tribe and Khartoum-allied Arabs. Though that rebellion ended in 1999, the Third Darfur Rebellion began in 2003. This time, an alliance of Fur, Masalit, and Zaghawa peoples allied together and fought against the government and its allies among Arab tribes in northern Darfur. The Sudanese army launched a brutal counterinsurgency campaign to quash the rebellion. Three hundred thousand people died, 1.8 million were displaced, and nearly three thousand villages destroyed. The N'djamena Humanitarian Ceasefire Agreement between the Sudanese government and Darfur rebel movements was signed in 2004. That year, a UN commission of inquiry was created to explore the question of Darfurian genocide. International leaders and aid agencies accused the Bashir-led government of supporting the Janjaweed, a militia accused of atrocious acts like burning villages and slaughtering civilians. In 2009 the International Criminal Court (ICC) charged Bashir for crimes in the region, and ICC prosecutors issued an arrest warrant for him on charges of crimes against humanity, war crimes, and genocide.[67]

While Akbar Muhammad's aim in drawing attention to Sudan may have been antisemitic, oil's role in US-Sudanese relations could not be ignored. The State Department—despite legislation restricting trade with Sudan due to terrorist activities—allowed two American companies to negotiate oil contracts with Khartoum in early 1997. Minister Farrakhan himself pointed to oil as an integral American interest in Sudan. In April 2006, five members of Congress were arrested during a protest outside the Sudanese embassy that aimed to draw attention to the genocide in Darfur. Rep. Tom Lantos, a Holocaust survivor, was among those arrested.[68] "When you see Senator Tom Lantos leading the march on the Sudanese Embassy and [fellow Holocaust survivor] Eli Wiesel, these are Zionists," Farrakhan claimed in comments published in *Final Call*. "Why are they leading the march? . . . It is that there is oil in the West [western Sudan]."[69]

In addition to pointing to oil's possible influence on America's focus on Sudan, Farrakhan referenced Palestine to interrogate the intentions of those who sought to shine a light on Sudan but ignore other violent contexts. During Farrakhan's radio appearance in which he mentioned Senator Lantos and Elie Wiesel, he made the following accusation: "Do you really think that they have compassion for what is going on in Darfur? Human suffering is human suffering. Don't tell me you have compassion for the Blacks who are suffering in Darfur when you have Palestinians suffering under your nose and you do not care anything about that."[70] He noted that at first 180,000 dead were reported in Darfur, then 400,000 and another two million displaced. He added, however, that 3.5 million had died in the Democratic Republic of Congo without any talk. In addition, children in northern Uganda were fleeing kidnappers and being made to fight against the government. Yet, like the Congo case, Farrakhan mentioned, there was no talk. Why, then, was there talk about Sudan? "The Sudan has been on the agenda for regime change," he opined, "because the country housed Palestinian Resistance Fighters and Osama bin Laden, and put him out. But the Sudan is an Islamic regime that is against the State of Israel."[71]

To be sure, Sudan's relationship to Israel since the conclusion of the First Civil War could not always be described as oppositional. Sudanese President Jafaar Nimeiri (1969–1985) was the only Arab leader to endorse the Camp David Accords, not just out of loyalty to Egyptian leader Anwar Sadat but also, according to Andrew Natsios, because he may have feared Israeli interference in Sudan's affairs (as had happened in the First Civil War). After Sadat was assassinated in retaliation for his peace agreement with Israel, Nimeiri was the lone Arab head of state to attend the Egyptian leader's funeral. In addition to these actions, Nimeiri helped evacuate the Beta Israel Jewish community from Sudan and enabled their relocation to Israel. However, all links ended with Bashir's 1989 coup. His government was not only initially hostile toward Israel and the United States but also preferred to align with Iran and extremist groups. Hassan al-Turabi, leader of Sudan's Muslim Brotherhood, invited Osama bin Laden, Hamas, and several extremist leaders to operate in Sudan. However, following a nasty split with Turabi in late 1999, Bashir terminated relations with Iran and realigned with Qatar, the United Arab Emirates, and Saudi Arabia. Sudanese foreign minister Ibrahim Ghandour stated that Sudan wasn't opposed to exploring the possibility of normalizing relations with Israel, a strategy many saw as the best means of getting Sudan removed from the US list of state sponsors of terrorism.[72]

Farrakhan, speaking at Chicago's Mosque Maryam in April 2007, again referenced Palestine in his attempt to question the altruism of those concerned with goings-on in Darfur. "These people who claim to desire to help the suffering people of Darfur don't desire to stop the suffering of the Palestinian people that live in the West Bank and Gaza Strip. America wants to set up a secular government in the Sudan and overthrow the Islamist regime." His remarks were published in the *Final Call*.[73] Farrakhan was joined in his assertions by William Reed, president and CEO of Black Press International. Writing as a guest columnist in the *Final Call* in January 2008, Reed asserted that anyone who claimed that genocide was occurring in Darfur and didn't acknowledge that the same or worse were taking place in Occupied Palestine, Uganda, the Central African Republic, or the Democratic Republic of Congo was "engaged in deception about the subject."[74]

Thus, it is evident that NOI messaging concerning Sudan was infused with anti-Israeli, anti-Zionist, and generally antisemitic messaging. Minister Farrakhan and others linked such language with denials of Sudanese slavery, oil, and the racial nature of the Darfur crisis. The comments concerning Israel and Palestine are part of the same genealogy of anti-Israel statements made in the context of the First Sudanese Civil War. This reality speaks to the enduring proximity that the Arab-Israeli conflict had for some Black American observers—Muslim and non-Muslim—of Sudanese politics and social life, and how it became a ready instrument to express endearment for Sudan. As such, the views expressed by the NOI in this section show that Black solidarity with the Sudanese (whether northern or southern) often came with antipathy for some other group.

On May 15, 2007, the *Final Call* published Jehron Muhammad's report on a Black delegation that had returned from Darfur. The report not only featured further critique of the supposed Arab-Black dichotomy in Sudan but also levied additional salvos at media coverage more broadly. "The truth concerning the atrocities and fighting in Sudan's Darfur region," Muhammad wrote, "is more complex than the U.S. media would have you believe." He noted that the Black press delegation—led by Abdul Akbar Muhammad, president of the Youth for Africa Foundation—wanted to get a clear understanding of what was happening in Darfur. During their nine-day visit the delegation met with and questioned President Bashir about the role of the African Union and UN peacekeeping forces in Darfur. The delegation comprised thirty-two people representing such media outlets as the *Tom Joyner Morning Show*, Black Entertainment Television, TV One, New York's 98.7 KISS-FM, and *Final Call*. "What they're saying," said delegation leader Muhammad, "is there are some Arabs killing Black Africans trying to exterminate them, raping their women, killing their children, pushing Black Africans off their land. But if there is another side to it then we should report it." The delegation reportedly interacted with government officials, residents of internally displaced persons camps, and typical Sudanese citizens and, during these exchanges, asked why Sudanese called themselves Arabs. Muhammad reported that many said that they identified as Arab because Arabic was their first language, and that if an African language was their mother tongue, then interviewees described themselves as African or referred to their tribe. Many Sudanese apparently answered with "Do I look like an Arab?"[75]

From Satti Majid to Malcolm X to Imam Isa, Sudan was a part of twentieth-century African American Islam in compelling ways long before the Second Sudanese Civil War's first shots were fired (in 1983), the first person was enslaved in that conflict, or the first whispers of genocide emerged from Darfur. Notwithstanding the actions of those men, Black American Islam's most significant engagement with Sudan occurred during the cataclysmic events of the late twentieth and early twenty-first centuries. Such engagements were led by Minister Louis Farrakhan and the Nation of Islam. Their positions, words, and actions shed light on the terms of racial and religious solidarity, the continued centrality of print media, and Sudan's place as an arena where Black America's relationship with Israel and Jews was contested.

Toward the end of his memoir, Samuel Cotton writes that he had met with leaders from Black orthodox Muslim organizations who appeared both sympathetic and cautious in their approach to slavery in the Arab world. "They have perhaps been more concerned about the image of Islam to be of any assistance or support to the anti-slavery movement. Torn between loyalty to Islam and their perception of themselves as black people, they have placed their religion above the liberation of their fellow man. As a result, they too have shown no interest in helping to eliminate this plague upon the homeland of their ancestors."[76]

NOI accusations of a Zionist conspiracy and condemnations of an anti-Arab agenda were the two foundations on which the Nation's defense of Sudan were built. Their actions not only highlight the continued salience of the Arab-Israeli conflict in Black engagements with Sudan but also throw a wrench into the role of race in this history. Though African American writers had largely linked Arabness with Sudan's enslaving oppressors, Farrakhan and other Nation members now marshaled that racial identity in their defense of the Sudanese government. While this resulted in yet another instance of Afro-Arab solidarity (coming after anti-Israeli sentiments expressed during the First Civil War), NOI efforts to defend the Sudanese government were done at the expense of those oppressed Black people suffering under the Bashir regime.

Diving deeply into the substance of their commentary, one finds a calculated—and clearly problematic—strategy at play. The Nation was arguably the only American organization of its size (Black or white) to support the Sudanese government. When it sought to dismiss the credibility of slavery and genocide claims by pointing to an anti-Arab agenda, there was in fact anti-Arab demonization in the United States after the events of September 11, 2001. By pointing to physical similarities between African Americans and northern Sudanese, Farrakhan merely repeated what Percival Prattis had said decades earlier when, in the pages of the *Pittsburgh Courier*, he made the Sudanese more familial to his African American readership. Thus, it is of no small consequence that the Nation of Islam—one of Black America's largest, most prominent organizations—took a pro-Sudanese position even when its government was guilty of the most heinous crimes. The Nation's position in this regard may not be morally defensible, but it does show how determined and complicated African American sentiments toward Sudan could be.

Chapter 6

A Worthy Cause

Barack Hussein Obama was born on August 4, 1961, in Honolulu, Hawaii. While his father, Barack Hussein Obama Sr. was from Kenya, his mother Stanley Ann Dunham was from Kansas. They divorced when their boy was two years old, and he was raised with help from his mother's parents. Having left Hawaii in 1963, he only knew his father through stories from his mother and grandparents. One day, however, everything changed when he learned that that his father was coming to see him. His mother sensed his nervousness leading up to his dad's arrival and tried to assure her son that the reunion would be smooth. She explained that she had kept contact with him when they were in Indonesia and that his dad knew all about him. Because his father had been in a car accident, this reunion trip also had a convalescent purpose.[1]

As his father—like his mom—had remarried, Barack now had six siblings in Kenya. Though his mother provided him with information about that East African country, he later recounted that he didn't remember much of it. However, she successfully kindled his interest when she told him that his father's tribe, the Luo, were a Nilotic people who had migrated to Kenya from their ancestral home on the banks of the Nile. "This seemed promising," Barack remembered. "Gramps still kept a painting he had once done, a replica of lean, bronze Egyptians on a golden chariot drawn by alabaster steeds. I had visions of ancient Egypt, the great kingdoms I had read about, pyramids and pharaohs, Nefertiti and Cleopatra." One Saturday he went to the public library and—with a librarian's assistance—found a book on East Africa. Unfortunately, the book failed to mention pyramids. "In fact," he recalled, "the Luos merited only a short paragraph. *Nilote*, it turned out, described a number of nomadic tribes that had originated in the Sudan along the White Nile, far south of the Egyptian empires. The Luo raised cattle and lived in mud huts and ate corn meal and yams and something called millet. Their traditional costume was a leather thong across the crotch." He left the book on the table and left the library.[2]

Barack eventually graduated from Columbia University in 1983, relocated to Chicago, and continued his education at Harvard Law School. Elected the first African American president of the *Harvard Law Review*, he married Michelle Robinson in 1992. His career in electoral politics began in 1996 when he was voted to the Illinois Senate. His keynote address at the 2004 Democratic National Convention catapulted him to new heights of popularity. Obama was elected to the US Senate that year, and in 2008 he defeated Hillary Clinton to win the Democratic nomination for president. In the general election, Obama defeated Arizona senator John McCain to become the first African American president.[3]

Sudan—so far from Obama's focus as a young boy—played a major role in his rise to the White House and his two terms as president. He spoke at Save Darfur: Rally to Stop Genocide, held at the National Mall in 2006 and later demanded an end to the genocide during his first presidential campaign. President Obama referenced Sudan during his first speech before the UN General Assembly and mentioned the new nation of South Sudan in his speech accepting the 2012 Democratic nomination.[4] In March 2015, when the first family traveled to Selma, Alabama, the president referenced Sudanese from the Edmund Pettus Bridge. "We're the immigrants who stowed away on ships to reach these shores, the huddled masses yearning to breathe free—Holocaust survivors, Soviet defectors, the Lost Boys of Sudan."[5]

This chapter explores how the Black diplomats of President Barack Obama's administration engaged with Sudan and South Sudan. Obama was elected senator in 2004 and departed the White House in 2017, and these years corresponded with convulsions in Sudan. These included the genocide in Darfur, the end of the Second Sudanese Civil War, the independence referendum that resulted in South Sudan's 2011 creation, and the onset of civil war within that young nation. More than simply highlighting Obama's work with the new nation, this chapter highlights two Black women—Susan Rice and Susan Page—as critical figures who shaped the early US relationship with South Sudan. Rice served as the US ambassador to the UN and national security advisor in the Obama administration, while Page served as the first US ambassador to South Sudan.[6] African Americans played an important role in establishing US-Sudan relations sixty years earlier, but they played an even more foundational role in early US-South Sudan relations. It is impossible to discuss the US diplomatic relationships with Sudan and South Sudan without a serious accounting of African American contributions.

Yet the Black representation at the heart of the US relationship with the Sudans was not coupled with an explicitly Black political ethic. Speeches, policies, and all manners of their public and private Sudan-related dialogue were virtually devoid of any reference to Sudanese as Black, Arab, or otherwise. In brief, diplomatic and political engagement was done outside of racial solidarity. The Obama administration's approach to Sudan showed that foreign policy conducted by Black people did not, by default, mean a Black foreign policy—one done out of a sense of racial kinship, common experiences of race-based oppression, or another racial paradigm. As such, it provides a point of comparison with Booker T. Washington's correspondence regarding his Sudan project over a century earlier: insofar as Washington made no mention at all of the Sudanese, the Obama administration made no reference to Sudanese as raced people or any indication of racial solidarity with them. This phenomenon illuminates the historian Ibrahim Sundiata's larger observation concerning African Americans in US foreign policy during his administration: "The contradictions between the bonds of ethnic solidarity and the demands of American foreign policy will persist. Barack Obama presents a grand paradox—the accession of a 'son of Africa' to the American presidency may well sound the death knell of traditional Pan-Africanism."[7] But while the Obama administration's silence on race when it came to Sudan and South Sudan may have represented a lost opportunity to galvanize African American attention on the region, some individuals outside the sphere of government did seize the moment. In doing so, they kept a storied legacy alive.

The United States, Sudan, and Senator Obama

In January 2005 the Sudanese government and SPLM/A signed the Comprehensive Peace Agreement (CPA). In addition to ending the long Second

Civil War, national multiparty elections were required by 2009, and by January 2011 the South would decide in a referendum on the matter of secession. Though SPLM/A leader John Garang became president of the Southern Sudanese government (and first vice president of Khartoum's National Unity government), he died in a helicopter crash later that year (2005). Salva Kiir, Southern Sudanese vice president, became the interim South Sudan government's new president.[8] The CPA, signed just before President George W. Bush's second inauguration, was considered a victory for US diplomacy. According to Herman J. Cohen—former secretary of defense for the Clinton administration—Bush could take pride in the fact that he had achieved his primary political objective of ending the oppression of English-speaking southern Sudanese Christians by the Arabic-speaking government. "He had merited the trust invested in him by the evangelical base of the Republican Party in the Bible belt states."[9] Due to the massive killing in Darfur, the Bush administration labeled the Sudanese government guilty of genocide within the Geneva Convention's definition. In May 2007 Bush imposed new economic penalties on Sudan: these blocked the assets of those Sudanese implicated in the violence and sanctioned government-owned or -controlled companies. It is worth noting that under President Bush, Black Americans held the government's highest positions in shaping foreign policy. Jendayi Frazer served as Bush's assistant secretary of state for African Affairs from 2005 until President Obama entered office, and Bush appointed two African American secretaries of state in succession (Colin Powell and Condoleezza Rice).[10]

Preceding this foreign policy work by African Americans in the Bush administration was the labor of one Susan Rice. A graduate of Stanford University and Oxford University, Rice served as special assistant to President Clinton and senior director for African Affairs at the National Security Council from 1993 to 1997. She subsequently served as US assistant secretary of state for African affairs from 1997 to 2001. While Clinton's choice of the relatively inexperienced and young Rice for that position did not fit the typical profile, it did with respect to race (as a post typically held by African Americans). In the absence of an established record, race became more salient for Black Americans and Africans responding to her selection and appointment as assistant secretary of state for Africa. Rice successfully encouraged the Clinton administration to impose sweeping sanctions on Sudan, barring any American or corporation from doing business in the country. Rice left the State Department upon Bush's arrival in the White House, and for the next few years she was a senior fellow at the Brookings Institution. In that

Figure 6.1. Susan Rice, national security advisor for Barack Obama from 2013 to 2017. Source: Chuck Kennedy, White House Photo Office.

capacity, she conducted research and published extensively on matters that included US foreign policy, transnational security threats, and weak states.[11]

In time, Rice would play a formative role in the Obama administration's relationship with South Sudan. Before that, however, Sudan occupied a central place in Obama's rise to the presidency during his years as a US senator.

As a member of the Senate Foreign Relations Committee from 2005 to 2008, Obama was at the forefront of the effort to end the genocide in Darfur. On April 30, 2006, he spoke at Save Darfur: Rally to Stop Genocide. Held on the National Mall before the US Capitol, the event aimed to raise awareness of the genocide and apply public pressure on the Bush administration to act. Thousands of protesters attended the rally, along with politicians and celebrities carrying signs demanding that the administration to take greater steps to end the slaughter. Kweisi Mfume (former NAACP president and CEO), Joe Madison, and Rev. Al Sharpton were among those who attended the rally along with Senator Obama.¹² "Today," Obama shared, "we know what is right and what is wrong. The slaughter of innocents is wrong. Two million people driven from their homes is wrong. Women gang raped while gathering firewood is wrong. Silence, acquiescence, paralysis in the face of genocide is wrong."¹³ "If we care, the world will care," he said. "If we act, then the world will follow."¹⁴ The NAACP's *Crisis* reported that Obama was a major voice at the rally, and *Jet* reported that he and actor George Clooney had attended a news conference at Washington DC's National Press Club to draw awareness to the situation in Darfur. "The notion that we are going to stand by in the face of this is unacceptable," Obama shared.¹⁵

As the summer of 2006 waned, Obama embarked on a two-week fact-finding tour of Africa. He stopped in Chad—which borders Sudan to the west—to highlight the worsening situation in Darfur. Fighting had resumed between government forces and Darfur rebels despite a May peace agreement. The senator visited refugees from Darfur at a camp in eastern Chad

Figure 6.2. Senator Barack Obama (D-IL).
Source: US Senate.

and called for the United States to take the lead in getting peacekeepers to Darfur. "I think what struck me was how anxious and eager the people in the camps are to get the U.N. protective force on the ground," Obama said at the time. "I think there's a sense that without that U.N. protective force, they will never be able to go back home. And they continue to feel vulnerable because the border is so porous." While his trip coincided with a UN Security Council resolution calling for a 20,000-strong peacekeeping force to Darfur to replace the African Union troops struggling to keep the peace, the resolution stipulated that the Sudanese government would have to give the UN its blessing. It did not.[16] Senator Obama worked with Sen. Sam Brownback (R-KS) to pass the Darfur Peace and Accountability Act. Passed by the Senate on September 21, 2006, the act conveyed Congress's sense that the horrors in Darfur constituted genocide and that US and international involvement was needed in that region. Among other measures, the act directed President Bush to block the assets of anyone complicit or responsible for the genocide and to and deny them visas. It also expressed Congress's sense that President Bush should sanction anyone who impeded the peace process and authorized him to help reinforce an expanded African Union Mission in Sudan.[17]

When Obama announced that he was running for president, he stated that his first priority was ending the Iraq War.[18] Sudan also figured into his platform. His campaign website said: "[I am] deeply concerned by reports that the Bush Administration is negotiating a normalization of relations with the Government of Sudan. . . . This reckless and cynical initiative would reward a regime in Khartoum that has a record of failing to live up to its commitments."[19] In May 2008 candidate Obama joined in a statement demanding that the genocide in Darfur be ended and the Comprehensive Peace Agreement completely implemented.[20] During his campaign Obama called the Darfur crisis "a collective stain on our national and human conscience" and said that on the first day of his administration he would prioritize ending the tragedy. He promised to appoint a special envoy concerning Darfur and to implement the CPA.[21]

Perhaps the most compelling Sudan-related moment during his campaign occurred at a San Francisco fund-raiser where two men—Dave Eggers and Valentino Achak Deng—presented Obama with a signed copy of their book *What Is the What*. Eggers was a best-selling author, and Deng was a Lost Boy. (The term "Lost Boys of Sudan" was given to some Sudanese refugees who resettled in Canada, Australia, and the United States.) *What Is the What* chronicles Deng's life from the time he was separated from his family, including years in Ethiopian and Kenyan refugee camps and encounters with

Western culture beginning in Atlanta.[22] "We had a brief talk about what has happening in Sudan," Eggers remembered later. "Some of the book takes place in a part of the continent [Obama] knows quite a lot about." Eggers later learned through a call from *Politico* that Obama had read his book. "It's surreal. There's no brain I respect more than Obama's. To have occupied his time for a few hours . . . it's a profound honor." Obama reportedly enjoyed the book so much that he eventually urged his White House aides to read it.[23]

Sudan played a central role in Barack Obama's foreign policy agenda. Although the US senator from Illinois and Democratic presidential candidate never set foot in the country, he met with Sudanese refugees during his trip to Chad, advocated for an end to the violence in Darfur, and supported the implementation of the Comprehensive Peace Agreement. Later, during his first term in the White House, Obama's engagement with Sudan would assume greater importance. Two Black women helped him steer the US relationship with Sudan and what soon became the world's newest nation, South Sudan.

Sudan Policy in Obama's First Term

Following his historic election, President Obama nominated Susan Rice to become ambassador to the United Nations. Rice had served on his presidential campaign staff, and her ability to provide foreign policy advice to the campaign built on her previous experience as assistant secretary of state for Africa under Clinton. In her tenure as ambassador to the UN (which ended in 2013), Rice played an integral role in formulating the White House's approach to Sudan and the all-important southern Sudanese independence referendum.[24]

In March 2009 President Obama appointed retired major general Scott Gration as his special envoy to Sudan. While Rice says that she got along fine with Gration, major policy differences on Sudan emerged between the two. He favored a more accommodating approach to the Sudanese government, publicly cast doubt on the continuance of genocide in Darfur, and recommended that the US ease sanctions and lift Sudan's designation as a state sponsor of terrorism. "As the administration conducted its first review of Sudan policy," Rice records, "I argued strenuously at the Principals' table [Principals Committee of the National Security Council] that we should not give rewards to Sudan without concrete, irreversible changes in their policies and actions." As the Sudan policy review continued, Rice sensed that Secretary of State Hillary Clinton might be leaning toward an accommodationist position (leaving Rice, consequently, more isolated as an advocate for a conditional approach). After perceiving that some in the White House may have been mischaracterizing her positions to President Obama, Rice says, "I took what was for me the rare step of invoking my privilege as a principal and member of the cabinet to write a memo directly to the president outlining my concerns about the direction of the policy review and explaining my recommended approach."[25]

In July 2009 Obama made his first speech before the UN General Assembly as president. In addition to pressing the UN to reassert itself as a leading force in addressing the most urgent issues, Obama also looked to distance his administration from the Bush administration's unilateral policies. He specifically referenced Sudan: "We will strengthen our support for effective peacekeeping while energizing our efforts to prevent conflicts before they take hold. We will pursue a lasting peace in Sudan through support for the people of Darfur and the implementation of the comprehensive peace agreement so that we secure the peace that the Sudanese people deserve."[26] When the Sudan policy review concluded three months later and Obama had rendered his decision, Susan Rice was content with the outcome: Khartoum wouldn't receive any major benefits unless their actions on southern Sudan and Darfur changed significantly and permanently. In addition, they agreed to a list of penalties that would be inflicted should Sudan's behavior continue or regress.[27]

In the summer of 2010, Obama summoned his Sudan team to the Oval Office. According to Denis McDonough—who at the time was the chief of staff for the National Security Council (NSC)—the president stated that he would not allow a return to violence between northern and southern Sudan. Rice remembers that as the referendum approached there were several causes of concern. Though six years had elapsed since the CPA had been signed (2005), thorny issues between North and South hadn't been resolved. Electoral arrangements were behind schedule, and fears grew that the Sudanese government would not fulfill its pledge to allow the vote to occur. When UN secretary-general Ban Ki-Moon proposed a foreign-minister-level meeting on the edges of the annual gathering of world leaders at the General Assembly's September 2010 opening, Rice recommended that President Obama attend. She believed that his presence could transform the meeting into a significant summit a little over three months before the referendum. The president did attend. He insisted that the CPA be completely implemented, that the referendum be held safely and on time, and warned of more pressure and isolation for those who violated their commitments. However, Obama also offered better relations between the United States and Sudan, more trade and investment connections, and an exchange of ambassadors if Sudan kept its commitments (including assured accountability for war crimes in Darfur). Rice contends that his intervention and the prospects of improved relations with the United States probably compelled Sudan to allow the vote to go on.[28] "At this moment," Obama said, "the fate of millions of people hangs in the balance . . . what happens in Sudan matters to all of sub-Saharan Africa, and it matters to the world."[29]

Two weeks after the September UN meeting, Rice led a Security Council delegation to Khartoum, Darfur, and southern Sudan. During the southern Sudanese portion of the trip, they pressured SPLM leaders to ready themselves to govern in service of their constituents "rather than in the insular, corrupt fashion to which they had already grown accustomed." According to Rice, the delegation's meetings in Khartoum allowed them to reiterate the need to allow the upcoming referendum to proceed without interference.[30] President Obama sent diplomat Princeton Lyman to Juba to help facilitate negotiations on unresolved matters leading up to the vote, and throughout the autumn of 2010 the NSC's McDonough led nightly meetings of Sudan policy makers. While the group discussed what incentives to offer the Sudanese government in exchange for allowing the South to secede, they determined that they could not force the parties to concur on anything except the referendum. In December 2010, mere weeks before the epochal vote, Voice of America reported that Obama had spoken by phone with southern Sudanese leader Salva Kiir to express support for the referendum.[31]

The referendum occurred over a week beginning on January 9, 2011.[32] The African American news and culture website *The Root* posted Zachariah Mamphilly's report on the historic occasion. Mamphilly, an assistant professor of political science and Africana studies at Vassar College, provided a poetic description. "They have returned to this part of Africa traveling via every type of transport or simply on foot. After decades in exile in foreign lands or displaced internally from their own homelands, Southern Sudanese have begun to claim their own future." Mamphilly noted that the returnees' stories were familiar, with tales of destroyed lives, lost relatives, and unspeakable pain. However, he continued, a sense of optimism now mixed with anxiety. Noting that rarity of one's chance to see the birth of a new country, he said that he was reminded of scenes of Black South Africans lining up in 1994 to vote. "But even after 10 years of visiting and writing about

Sudan, it is hard as an outsider to convey the powerful emotions that this long-suffering population is experiencing. All I know is that at this moment, at this place on earth, something special is happening."[33]

Five hundred international monitors reported no interference or intimidation from either the northern or southern governments. The North, to be sure, had a special incentive to refrain from interfering: the Obama administration had offered the Bashir regime a plan to normalize US-Sudan relations (including removing economic sanctions, establishing full diplomatic recognition, and taking Sudan off the list of terrorist-sponsoring countries). In the end, 98.8 percent of voters opted for southern independence.[34] On January 16, President Obama released a statement on the referendum. He began by congratulating the Sudanese people and government on the conclusion of the vote. "The sight of so many Sudanese casting their votes in a peaceful and orderly fashion was an inspiration to the world and a tribute to the determination of the people and leaders of south Sudan to forge a better future." He also commended the Referendum Commission, Referendum Board, domestic and international observers, the UN Mission in Sudan, "and most of all, the voters, who turned out in high numbers and high spirits to take their turn at the ballot box." The American people wanted Sudan to have a bright future, he said, and the United States would continue to help the parties amid the obstacles and opportunities ahead.[35] Nine days later, Obama incorporated the referendum results into his State of the Union address. Speaking before Congress and millions of television viewers, he stated, "In south Sudan—with our assistance—the people were finally able to vote for independence after years of war. . . . One man who lost four of his brothers at war summed up the scene around him: 'This was a battlefield for most of my life,' he said. 'Now we want to be free.'" The audience applauded.[36]

On July 9, 2011, South Sudan became an independent nation. President Obama released a statement declaring that the United States formal recognized South Sudan as a sovereign state. "After so much struggle by the people of South Sudan," he stated, "the United States of America welcomes the birth of a new nation." Among other assertions, he declared that the CPA had to be fully implemented and that the safety of all Sudanese had to be protected. Acknowledging the southern Sudanese who had struggled and the part that Sudan's African neighbors and the African Union had played in making independence possible, Obama also noted, "Many Americans have been deeply moved by the aspirations of the Sudanese people, and support for South Sudan extends across different races, regions, and political persuasions in the United States." It is noteworthy that in Obama's entire statement, the only individual that he identified by name—Sudanese, South Sudanese, or otherwise—was Martin Luther King Jr. The president quoted the civil rights leader's words concerning Ghanaian independence: "I knew about all of the struggles, and all of the pain, and all of the agony that these people had gone through for this moment."[37]

President Obama's decision to reference and quote Dr. King in the official White House statement recognizing South Sudan's independence is arguably the most revealing moment in Black America's engagement with Sudan. It uniquely braids Black America's political and social histories with the culmination of South Sudan's long liberation struggle. While some may read Obama's reference to King as artificial or romantic, the significance of his mention is amplified by a curious story concerning King and the First Sudanese Civil War. The King Center's Digital Archive contains an undated letter from King to a "Mr. Taban." In it, King lamented, "[You] had to leave Sudan in the face of the atrocities which were being perpetrated upon your people and flee to Kenya in order to continue your education. It is a deplorable situation and I anguish over the suffering which the Sudanese are having to indulge." Though King noted that neither he nor the Southern

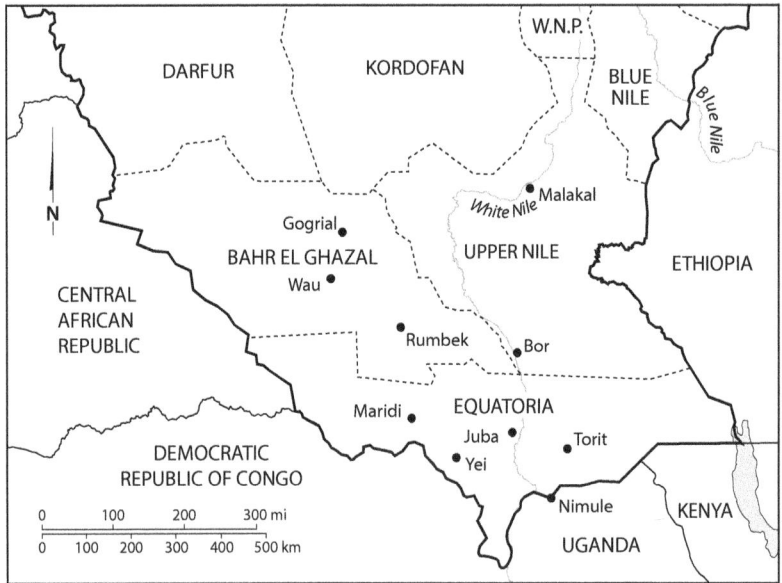

Figure 6.3. Map of South Sudan, 2011.
Source: Drawn by Bill Nelson.

Christian Leadership Conference had resources to assist Taban, he directed him to other potential funding sources and expressed hope that Sudan would eventually be liberated and Taban able to return to his native land.[38] Written during the civil right movement, the letter is an important—if virtually unknown—bond connecting the southern Sudanese liberation struggle with Black America's fight for social equality.

President Obama's connection of southern Sudanese independence with Dr. King was followed by Ashley Makar's similar rhetorical move in Alabama's *Huntsville Times*. Makar, the daughter of a Coptic-American immigrant to the United States, hailed from Birmingham and was a writer, editor, and Yale Divinity School graduate student. In her editorial published a week after the independence celebration, Makar said that Dr. King's "Free at last!" dream was alive in Juba. "The Sudan People's Liberation Movement, Mandela's African National Congress, King's Southern Christian Leadership Conference and the antebellum abolitionist movement were all struggles against a nexus of oppression: racial discrimination, labor exploitation and systemic impoverishment." She added, however, that, though Blacks were no longer second-class citizens in those countries, they were not completely free, as the legacies of Jim Crow, apartheid, and Sudan's civil wars continued to do harm. Noting that King himself framed the 1963 March on Washington as a beginning and not an end, Makar ended by saying that the struggle of Sudanese youths continued. "Meanwhile, [such youths the world over] are learning their new national anthem, their own way of singing 'Free at last.'"[39]

While Zachariah Mamphilly had not used his reference to the 1994 elections in South Africa as an occasion to frame the southern Sudanese referendum through a racial lens, Makar invoked South Africa in her effort to situate Sudan in a global framework of racial oppression and liberation. On one hand, the fact that high school students from Birmingham and Johannesburg were about to launch Birmingham's first commemoration of Nelson Mandela International Day provided a convenient moment for Makar to stitch the United States, South Africa, and South Sudan together. On the other hand, it is significant that Makar invited mainstream readers in Alabama to include Sudan among examples of systemic racism that would have been well known to them. By claiming that Sudan warranted inclusion in the same heritage as Jim Crow America and apartheid South Africa, Makar's piece could be read as a not-so-subtle argument that the bounds of Black oppression had to be expanded. South Sudanese independence, while categorically different from those other historical examples, nevertheless belonged in the same narrative and genealogy of global Black liberation, even if the oppressive government was not white.

Early Independence (2011–2013)

"As Southern Sudanese undertake the hard work of building their new country," declared President Obama in his independence statement, "the United States pledges our partnership as they seek the security, development and responsive governance that can fulfill their aspirations and respect their human rights."[40] An African American woman played a formative role in this process. On October 18, 2011, Susan D. Page was confirmed as the first US ambassador to South Sudan. A graduate of the University of Michigan and Harvard Law School, Page had joined the State Department in 1991 and worked in the Office of the Legal Advisor for Politico-Military Affairs. She traveled to southern Sudan for the first time in 2003. Page served as the legal adviser to the Intergovernmental Authority on Development (IGAD) Secretariat for Peace in Sudan and helped to negotiate and draft the peace agreement that ended the Second Civil war. She later served as the director of the Rule of Law and Prison Advisory Unit for the UN's Sudan Mission, providing legal and constitutional advice to the UN's special representative of the secretary general to Sudan on the CPA's implementation.[41] Page remembered the mood when she arrived in South Sudan as US ambassador. "It was exciting. It was hopeful. I think everyone believed that they would be able to overcome so many of the problems that other new states had suffered from just because they had fought so long and so hard."[42]

When asked years later what her role was as the first US ambassador to South Sudan, Page noted that there were several objectives. These included ensuring that the relationship between Sudan and South Sudan was healthy, that South Sudan was ruled peacefully, and that there would be economic development. In the six months following independence, the US government pledged $370.8 million in aid to the new nation.[43] "South Sudan started off with so much less than even the nations in Africa that gained independence some 50-plus years ago," Page later recalled. "They had no paved roads. They had antiquated buildings that existed maybe from the time of the Anglo-Egyptian Condominium. They had to start everything from scratch."[44] She noted that after the CPA was signed in 2005 it took several months to institute a capital in Juba. "There was almost no infrastructure; there were not any paved roads; dilapidated buildings that were literally falling apart

Figure 6.4. Inauguration of the US embassy in Juba, South Sudan, July 9, 2011. Left to right: Johnnie Carson, US assistant secretary of state for the Bureau of African Affairs; Colin Powell, former US secretary of state; Susan R. Rice, US permanent representative to the United Nations; and US ambassador R. Barrie Walkley.

Source: Jenn Warren, United States Agency for International Development.

because of the war." To drive home her point that southern Sudan had to start from nothing, Page said, "We are not talking about just ordering some new furniture—they didn't have pens, papers, and stationery, let alone computers, electricity, and running water, vehicles, roads." She asserted that while she didn't feel that she had a nation-building role, she felt compelled to try to encourage the new country in their nation-building journey and using their resources to try to help the citizenry.[45]

In the wake of independence, South Sudan ended up with three-quarters of Sudan's oil, a resource that Sudan's elite had once dominated. President Obama added oil-exporting South Sudan to the Generalized System of Preferences (GSP) US trade program for developing countries. The president's decision to add South Sudan to the GSP allowed it to ship oil (and thousands of other goods) to the States without paying US import duties once the president's action took full effect. US trade representative Ron Kirk urged South Sudan to use the program to continue necessary economic reforms. On the security front, President Obama added South Sudan to the list of nations that were eligible to purchase weapons from the United States.[46]

Figure 6.5. US Department of State portrait of Susan D. Page, US ambassador to South Sudan (circa 2011).

Source: US Department of State.

Ambassador Page and the US government attempted to address several issues during the first two years of independence. The Americans had programs supporting a highway police unit, assisting police to aid capital roadways and improve their capacity. "There are still a lot of problems and crime; however, we are determined and committed to identifying direct violations." While Page noted that there were some military units that they could not assist, they concentrated on education and security programs where they could. An Access to Justice program helped people through the Judicial Review Initiative, while another program educated people on the South Sudan Constitution, the constitutional review process, and national elections negotiations. "We have to monitor the ongoing political process. . . . It is not just a mission statement, but includes a resolution for the establishment of political parties in Southern Sudan on a Constitution that is eternally based on democratic documents, . . . something I never expected."[47]

Despite South Sudan's long-awaited freedom, by late April 2012 the new nation found itself inching closer to war with its longtime belligerent to the north, Sudan. The two countries disputed the demarcation of their border and the sharing of oil revenues, and fighting put a virtual halt to the oil production so crucial to both of their economies. Under South Sudan's control, the oil-rich region of Heglig—one of Sudan's primary sources of income—was basically destroyed, and, while the southern army stated that Sudanese planes had hit the oil processing facility, Sudan posited that it was southern sabotage. At one point Sudanese president Bashir suggested that the time for talking had passed and that only fighting remained. President Obama stated that conflict was not inevitable and asked Bashir and Kiir to resume negotiations.[48] "We know what needs to happen," Obama said in a videotaped message to Sudanese and South Sudanese. "The government of Sudan must stop its military actions, including aerial bombardments."[49]

That fall, Sudan and South Sudan struck deals to secure their border and increase trade. While this opened the door for the resumption of oil exports, it did not end other conflicts that remained after the secession. It would, however, prevent the fighting that had exploded along the border earlier in the year.[50] In a statement released on September 27, 2012, President Obama welcomed the settlement and commended the work of the African Union's High-Level Implementation Panel for its role in guiding the deal. "The leaders of Sudan and South Sudan have chosen to take another important step on the path away from conflict toward a future in which their citizens can live in dignity, security, and prosperity. The United States is committed to working with both countries as they implement these agreements and as they seek to resolve those issues that remain outstanding."[51]

Two months later, Obama defeated Republican challenger Mitt Romney to secure another four years in the White House. While his administration had spent the first term helping to place South Sudan on a firm footing, it would spend its second term doing what it could to keep it from tearing apart.

South Sudanese Civil War

On June 5, 2013, President Obama appointed Susan Rice as the new national security advisor. In his announcement, Obama said, "[Rice] understands that there is no substitute for American leadership . . . she is passionate and pragmatic, but mindful that we have to exercise our power wisely."[52] Rice's passion and pragmatism would be sorely tested by events in South Sudan over the next three years. "In 2013," Susan Rice writes in her book *Tough*

Love, "South Sudanese president Salva Kiir and his then-vice president, Riek Machar, were the Grinches who stole Christmas."[53]

In early 2013, Vice President Machar began to express criticism of Kiir's leadership and handling of the economy. Machar announced his intention to challenge Kiir for the presidency in the forthcoming election set to be held in two years. In June, President Kiir dismissed Finance Minister Kosti Manibe and Cabinet Affairs Minister Deng Alor over a multimillion-dollar financial scandal. The following month he fired the entire cabinet, the cabinet's deputies, and—perhaps most notably—Machar himself in a power struggle within the SPLM. While the situation remained comparatively calm in the ensuing months, a conflagration exploded in December when forces loyal to Machar clashed with those friendly to Kiir. While Kiir accused Machar of having attempted a coup, others claimed that presidential guards of Kiir's Dinka ethnicity attempted to disarm guards who were Nuer (Marchar's ethnicity). With old tensions and violence between the two ethnicities, the fight devolved into a maelstrom. Targeted killings in the capital city of Juba sparked revenge attacks and similar horrors. Generals mutinied and seized the capital of Jonglei (the country's largest state) and Unity State (the nation's main oil-producing area), and in the Upper Nile a full-scale tank battle took place between opposing army factions. More than one thousand were killed and one hundred thousand displaced in the first week alone, and from the onset of the conflict government and opposition forces committed sexual atrocities, pursuing victims based on gender, ethnic, and perceived political identities.[54]

How could a civil war break out so soon after independence, and what were the real issues at stake for the two Sudanese factions? Øystein H. Rolandsen has argued that the war resulted from several factors, including a political crisis within the ruling Sudan People's Liberation Movement (a guerrilla body turned government army), a bellicose mentality, and lack of peaceful means for political contestation and transition.[55] Scholar Clement Sefa-Nyarko has noted that political differences between Kiir and Machar sparked the conflict and asserted that "lack [of] reform in the SPLM Party and the military (which were symbols of national unity and sovereignty), non-available and inefficient financial institutions, corruption, and nepotism also contributed to the outbreak of the conflict." Other factors prolonging the conflict, according to Sefa-Nyarko, included greed for oil, grievances by minority groups or groups excluded from governance, political and ethnic rivalry, and geographical proximity of crude oil to the center of governance.[56] While the root causes of the conflict may be subject for debate, what is undeniable is the hideous impact that the war wreaked on the people of South Sudan—a region that had already trudged through two of the twentieth century's most atrocious civil wars.[57]

When the December 2013 conflagration broke out, Ambassador Page went into action. "We made sure we called everybody back to the compound. Events had started late in the evening. We decided to make sure that none of the staff, including the local staff, came to work the next day unless they felt like it was safe. But we didn't think that was appropriate." Most stayed home, and there were occasions during the first days of the carnage when nearby shelling forced Page and others to go to their bulletproof safe havens on the residential compound. "There were a couple of us who couldn't quite make it to the safe haven, so we had to duck and cover in place where we were. . . . I was in my house with a bodyguard and we eventually made it once it was safe to get there." Page remembered that though they had their cellphones at the beginning of the fighting, the coverage was spotty, making it difficult to connect. After many late-night teleconferences with the State Department, national security advisor (Susan Rice), Defense Department, and Central Intelligence Agency, they (not Page) decided to order all nonessential staff to leave the US embassy and advised all American citizens to leave the country. "It was very difficult because we thought it was really important that we stay. . . . We did a massive evacuation."[58]

In the wake of the violence, President Obama issued a statement. He began by noting that millions of South Sudanese had voted in 2011 to create a new nation on the promise of a prosperous future for all of its people. Against odds, he continued, the nation had made progress toward breaking its long cycle of violence. "Today," he remarked, "that future is at risk. South Sudan stands at the precipice. Recent fighting threatens to plunge South Sudan back into the dark days of its past." However, he opined, it did not have to be that way: South Sudan's leaders could end the bloodshed and try to peacefully resolve tensions. Obama demanded that inflammatory rhetoric, targeted violence, and fighting to settle political scores or destabilize the government cease immediately. "Now is the time for South Sudan's leaders to show courage and leadership, to reaffirm their commitment to peace, to unity, and to a better future for their people." He concluded by affirming that the United States would remain a committed partner of the South Sudanese people as they pursued security and prosperity.[59]

Stateside, the Obama administration kept a keen eye on the situation. Secretary of State John Kerry spent hours on the phone trying to mediate between belligerents Kiir and Machar. Susan Rice recorded a message appealing to South Sudanese to unify and save their country. Though Rice maintains that she tried to reason with Kiir, she says, "They both [Kiir and Machar] were selfish and dismissive of the interests of their own people." With the US embassy threatened by violent groups on both sides, President Obama ordered forty-five US servicemen into Juba to reinforce the compound.[60] In order to rescue stranded Americans, Obama also ordered US military helicopters to fly north to Bor. The mission was aborted when an Osprey helicopter was hit as they descended, wounding four US personnel. Rice records that the threat to US personnel increased: "I had no choice but to convene the Principals [Committee] every day from December 21 through December 27, 2013, including remotely on Christmas Day. That holiday summons made me especially unpopular with my colleagues and staff, but the American president has no higher priority than the safety and security of American citizens. We could not and would not risk leaving Americans in proximate danger—especially barely a year after Benghazi [the September 2012 attack on US government facilities in Libya]."[61]

The reduction in diplomatic personnel meant that the US embassy in Juba would no longer provide consular assistance to US citizens. Instead, they would be redirected to the US embassy in Nairobi, in neighboring Kenya. On January 3, 2014, *Politico* reported that Ambassador Page would remain in Juba where, according to the State Department, she was in steady communication with the United Nations Mission in South Sudan (UNMISS), South Sudanese officials, and her foreign counterparts. By that date—less than a month after the tumult had begun—180,000 South Sudanese had already been displaced. In addition to the US embassy's decreased capacity, the State Department announced $49.8 million in humanitarian assistance to victims of the recent fighting. This amount came in addition to the more than $300 million given to aid South Sudanese refugees.[62]

Back in the States, two African American outlets covered the crisis emerging in South Sudan. On December 30, 2013, the African American newspaper *Washington Informer* published Bill Fletcher Jr.'s editorial on the looming civil war. Fletcher, an NNPA (National Newspaper Publishers Association) columnist and former president of the TransAfrica Forum, called on fellow African Americans to lend their voices to the world's calls for both sides to retreat from the edge. He went further, however, arguing, "We should also do a bit more in the future to ensure that we are not hoodwinked by simple answers to very complex questions." Besides, Fletcher continued, Black Americans had repeatedly showed that when they paid attention to foreign policy (whether the Vietnam War or apartheid), their position could impact American actions. "Perhaps, had we taken an alternative approach to the Sudan, events might be unfolding in a different manner."[63] Radio personality Joe Madison, who had earlier shined a light on slavery in southern Sudan, now brought attention to the new troubles facing South Sudan. In April 2014 Madison—who at the time was a host on the *Urban View* SiriusXM talk show—participated in a protest held at the UN's Dag Hammarskjold Plaza. The protest was aimed against human rights abuses in South Sudan. The group walked to the Ugandan Mission (where South Sudan's Mission is also located) and demanded reconciliation and an end to the violence. "Now is the time for the United States and the United Nations and the world to step up," Madison stated. "We are focused on the Ukraine, but right now there are more people dying in South Sudan." He was among three people arrested at the event.[64] If Fletcher's editorial in the *Washington Informer* showed the Black press's continued role in directing attention to Sudan, Madison's protest showed the enduring commitment that one African American activist had toward South Sudan long after the war with Khartoum had ended.

Susan Page's tenure as US ambassador to South Sudan ended in late August 2014. In an interview she provided to National Public Radio days before leaving the position, David Greene asked her how hard it was to leave an ambassadorship when a country was in worse shape than when she arrived. "Well, I hope that doesn't mean that I'm responsible for it being in worse shape," she replied. "It's painful to leave when things are not good. But I'm leaving. And I'm going back to work in the Office of the Special Envoy for Sudan and South Sudan. So that does make it a little bit easier to depart, knowing that I helped to build up the embassy as the first ambassador." Page added that knowing that she had helped make important operational changes (and aided in the evacuation, procuring a humanitarian assistance team, and getting the right people to return) also made it easier to depart. When Greene asked her about what gave her a sense of optimism, given the horrible state of things, she said:

> I believe in the people of South Sudan. . . . Yes, there are problems. But there are also a lot of success stories. . . .70 percent of the population is under 30. And that's where the future is. And so the more that we can do to prepare the next generation—and I'm not talking just about political power, but as educators, as business people, entrepreneurs—they should be empowered to have those options and to live their dreams.[65]

December 15, 2014, marked the one-year anniversary of South Sudan's hostilities. Nearly two million had been displaced from their homes while others were at risk of famine. That day, the *Washington Post* published a letter cosigned by Susan Rice and John Kerry. In it, two of the top US foreign policy leaders offered a scathing critique of South Sudan's leadership. "The tragedy is especially hard to accept because the violence was not imposed on South Sudan by outside forces; instead it was unleashed by a political dispute among the country's leaders." "Now," Rice and Kerry continued, "the responsibility is on their shoulders. . . . After months of delay and false pledges, both sides must return to negotiations, make necessary compromises and finally end this conflict without further delay. . . . It is past time for South Sudan's leaders to take responsibility and end the fighting." They stated that a transitional government mandated to create security agencies that protected all South Sudanese regardless of ethnicity or politics was imperative. That government furthermore needed to develop a transparent system for managing the nation's resources and agree on an inclusive constitutional drafting process focusing on improved governance. "Given the level of past violence, a reconciliation plan must also be established, accompanied by efforts to investigate atrocities and ensure that those involved are held accountable for their crimes." Rice and Kerry stated that the United States had helped organize a massive humanitarian effort, supported a UN peacekeeping force, and worked with local and regional partners to document abuses and support religious leaders working for reconciliation. "[But] none of it will be enough in the absence of effective leadership." They committed to increasing pressure on the warring parties until the violence ended and stated that those who chose more conflict would face harsher consequences.[66]

In February 2015 the National Security Service (NSS) Act became law, giving South Sudan's NSS officers great powers of arrest, search and seizure, and detention without evident judicial oversight. The following month, a downturn in fighting ended when the government launched one of the war's largest offensives. Government forces and allied militia killed hundreds of people and burned civilian property in opposition-held areas of Unity State. At least one hundred thousand were forced to flee, and food and scores of cattle were stolen, contributing to severe hunger. Rape was a common tactic employed in the offensive.[67] While the following incident did not occur during the aforementioned offensive (it happened the following year), it nevertheless illustrates the hellish experiences that some Sudanese civilians experienced. Poni, a forty-five-year-old woman from Bereka in Lainya, said that two or three government soldiers raped her behind a church after killing her husband and pastor:

> They were asking me questions and kicking me. One was saying "Let us kill her" and I said "I have five children, if you kill me who will take care of them now that my husband is gone?" The other said, "I will show her something." He grabbed me by the arms and dragged me around the church. . . . He forced himself on me. He spread my legs and raped me. He said "I will make it worse if you struggle." I was crying and begging but he did not stop. When he was done, the other soldier came and found me lying there. I begged him and he just kicked my private parts. He told me to turn around, saying that he did not want my diseases. He raped me in my anus. After he was finished, the two soldiers told me to go. And so I walked and it was painful and I was bleeding. They told me "Run or we will catch you again."[68]

While Obama-era sanctions and US economic inducements were certainly important, others also had their eye on the woeful situation in South Sudan. International opprobrium led to a slew of inducements from state and nonstate actors. In February 2014, UK Foreign Office minister for Africa Mark Simmonds met with South Sudan foreign minister Barnaba Benjamin. Simmonds urged Benjamin to make quick headway on investigation into human rights abuses, and France and the United States called on the UN Security Council to consider sanctions against the country. In July 2014, the European Union sanctioned individuals stymieing the nation's peace process and culpable for atrocities, and the following March the Security Council established a sanctions regime for South Sudan. On July 1, 2015, the Security Council imposed the first sanctions on six commanders in the country. These individuals—whose names were put forth by Britain, France, and the United States—were punished with a global travel ban and an assets freeze.[69]

Later that month, President Obama convened African leaders for discussions aimed at keeping South Sudan from collapse. The talks came during the Ethiopian portion of his tour through East Africa. Obama was joined by the Ethiopian prime minister, the presidents of Kenya and Uganda, Sudan's foreign minister, and the chair of the African Union. There were no plans for Obama or other US officials to meet with South Sudanese representatives. "The possibilities of renewed conflict in a region that has been torn by conflict for so long, and has resulted in so many deaths, [require] urgent attention from all of us," Obama stated.[70] The meeting focused on what had to happen between then and August 17 in the absence of an agreement (African leaders and the opposing contingents had agreed on that date as a deadline to decide on a path forward, with a peace proposal then under consideration).[71] In his comments before the African Union (AU) at Addis Ababa's Mandela Hall—the first time that a US president had ever addressed the AU—Obama noted that the joy of independence in South Sudan had devolved into a violent despair: "Neither Mr. Kiir, nor Mr. Machar have shown, so far, any interest in sparing their people from this suffering, or reaching a political solution. Yesterday, I met with leaders from this region. We agree that, given the current situation, Mr. Kiir and Mr. Machar must reach an agreement by August 17th—because if they do not, I believe the international community must raise the costs of intransigence." He added that the world waited the report of the AU's Commission of Inquiry because those responsible for committing atrocities had to be held accountable in order to achieve lasting peace in the country.[72]

In mid-August, President Kiir shocked US officials when he refused to sign a peace agreement with the rebels despite the internationally imposed deadline. His opponent Machar had signed the agreement. Following Kiir's failure to sign, Rice said that the United States had begun talks at the United Nations to sanction South Sudan if its government failed to sign a peace deal with rebels in fifteen days and if all sides didn't speedily execute a ceasefire. In a White House statement she said that Kiir had wasted a chance to bring peace and that the United States condemned that failure of leadership. The week after his refusal, Kiir agreed to peace with the rebels.[73] Speaking in Geneva, Rice stated that the United States welcomed his decision to accept the peace terms and sign the peace agreement. "However," she continued, "we do not recognize any reservations or addendums to that agreement.... Implementing this agreement will require commitment and resolve from all parties to the conflict as well as South Sudan's regional and international partners." After saying that the United States would support the South Sudanese as they began the implementation process, she added that it was imperative for the parties to stay committed to peace. Rice warned those who intended otherwise: "We will work with our international partners to sideline those who stand in the way of peace, drawing upon the full range of our multilateral and bilateral tools."[74]

That October, the White House canceled a meeting with senior South Sudanese officials because Kiir's government and Machar's opposition had not committed to the new IGAD-Plus peace deal. Susan Rice had invited Vice President James Wani Igga, Machar, and former detainee Pagan Amum to the White House for a discussion to push them to carry out the peace deal that the three parties had signed in August. However, according to NSC spokesman Ned Price, due to several factors—namely recent renewed fighting, Machar's reticence to compromise on security sector reform negotiations, and the South Sudanese government's decision to create twenty-eight new states—they decided not to receive the parties at the White House until they showed stronger resolve to promote peace. Machar was none too pleased with the cancelation and offered choice words for Rice: "She should listen to our challenges. She should listen to our concerns. She should listen to the challenges in the implementation of the peace agreement. Instead of hiding, she should come out and assist us."[75]

In March 2016—with less than a year remaining in Obama's presidency—Kelly McEvers interviewed Susan Rice on NPR's *All Things Considered*. The subject of their conversation was US policy on South Sudan and how the United States could support the peace process. McEvers noted that the situation was not good and that people were running out of food. If the situation further deteriorated into a larger conflict, McEvers asked, what would US options be? Rice responded that since South Sudan was now independent there was only so much that the United States or any other foreign power could do if the leaders refused to serve their people. "But what we will do," she continued, "is continue to be the largest donor of assistance to South Sudan. We have provided $1.5 billion in assistance in the last couple of years, and we'll continue to do our part. We'll use all of the weight of our diplomacy . . . in seeing a peaceful South Sudan." Rice added that the United States could remain engaged because it had a moral, humanitarian, and security stake in the South Sudanese people.[76]

In April 2016 Machar returned to Juba as the first step in ending the conflict, restored to his former position of vice president. Violence nevertheless erupted again between government and opposition forces. Thousands were displaced and, Machar, who himself fled, was eventually detained in South Africa.[77] One particularly macabre incident that summer sent shock waves through the aid community. Amid fighting that had broken out between troops loyal to Kiir and Machar, roughly two dozen aid workers took shelter inside Juba's Terrain Hotel grounds. Dozens of South Sudanese troops broke through the gates, and, despite frantic calls to the UN, the US embassy, and private security firms to send help, none came. Gang rapes occurred. According to one of the women in the hotel, "The soldiers just came to the bathroom where all the girls were hiding and they just picked us out of the bathroom one by one." In the aftermath of the violence, some relief agencies evacuated staff while others scaled back their operations. The Terrain Hotel incident was, to be sure, merely a microcosm of the appalling conditions on the ground. Insecurity for aid agencies in South Sudan came at a time when South Sudanese faced a cholera outbreak, rising malaria, and millions dependent on international food rations. By August 2016 two and a half million people had been displaced from their homes.[78]

The United Nations—the world's chief humanitarian agency—was not fully equipped to handle the refugee multitudes. In one incident early in the civil war, at least twenty civilians and two UNMISS peacekeepers were killed when an estimated two thousand armed youth, presumably Lou Nuer, surrounded the UN base in Akobo and opened fire on Dinka civilians seeking refuge inside. In 2014 peacekeepers were accused of standing by as the government attacked a UN base in Bor sheltering five thousand displaced people. More than fifty civilians were killed. In February 2016 government forces killed more than thirty civilians in an attack on a UN base in Malakal. Throughout the country, women often put themselves in harm's way (risking rape or other attack) by leaving UN Protection of Civilians (POC) sites in search for food.[79] According to Human Rights Watch, women and girls often had to walk outside the UNMISS base at Bentiu for hours at a time to collect firewood and charcoal. One displaced woman recounted that she was gathering firewood with another woman when a group of women ran in the opposite way, claiming that four members of their number had been taken by government soldiers. "They had left all their firewood behind and just ran. We ran as well. . . . I'm afraid to collect firewood now but what choice do I have? I don't have my house, my possessions, my cows, or any money. I can't buy firewood so I have to go back to collect it."[80]

In December 2016, with just weeks left in Obama's term in office, his administration tried to convince the United Nations to support an arms embargo against South Sudan. The United States, to be sure, had earlier considered an arms embargo to increase pressure on the belligerent parties against the backdrop of the July 2015 Ethiopian peace summit.[81] While Samantha Power (US permanent representative to the United Nations in 2013–2017) and John Kerry had earlier supported the idea of imposing an arms embargo, Susan Rice had not. "An arms embargo," she wrote, "which is always applied territorially, punishes one side disproportionately in a civil conflict (the government) and doesn't prevent rebels from acquiring weapons via neighboring countries when they take refuge." Rice also believed that if an arms embargo was imposed, the United States would forfeit its leverage on the South

Sudanese government—influence it could use to push the government to moderate its behavior and accept a negotiated settlement. "Perhaps out of personal history, unrealistic hopes for the people of South Sudan, and an overestimation of U.S. influence, I was too slow to conclude that neither side had the will to end the conflict [or] agree to a unity government."[82]

"It was not until 2016," Rice writes, "when the specter of genocide appeared on the horizon, that I finally concluded we had to drop the hammer on South Sudan's hopeless leaders." While she had hoped that the South Sudanese would enjoy the freedom and safety that had long evaded them, she identified South Sudan's leadership as the reason why the dream of self-determination wouldn't be realized. "That belated realization freed me to endorse the U.S. push in the Security Council for an arms embargo, which repeatedly failed to muster enough favorable votes [the Council failed to impose an embargo in December 2016 because Japan, Egypt, and some other members were opposed]. Only in July 2018 . . . did a U.S.-sponsored resolution to impose an arms embargo eventually gain the bare minimum number of votes to be adopted by the Security Council."[83]

Sudan figured into Barack Obama's journey to the White House and his foreign policy as president. Initially viewed in his youth as the off-putting, even embarrassing ancestral home for his father's Luo people, Sudan came to assume an important part of his foreign policy agenda during his brief senatorial career and subsequently during his eight years as president. While the earlier portion of his career focused heavily on the genocide in Darfur, his tenure in the White House focused much attention on South Sudan's leadup to the independence referendum, ensuring peace in the new nation, and pursuing peace amid a bloody civil war. Two African American women—Susan Rice and Susan Page—played pivotal roles in his administration's work of establishing firm relations with the world's newest nation. The work of these three African Americans came on the heels of earlier diplomatic labor performed by Black Americans in the 1950s–1970s, when the United States was then beginning its relationship with postcolonial Sudan. In each instance, African Americans played important roles in establishing the US relationship with new Sudanese states. Simply put, it is impossible to properly analyze the history of US-Sudan diplomatic relations without centering Black Americans.

However, despite the presence of Black Americans in some of most important US policy decisions regarding Sudan and South Sudan, their engagement appeared devoid of any sense of racial solidarity. For Obama and Rice, Lorenzo Morris has offered compelling explanations for this dynamic: their connections to typical Black communities are surprisingly marginal; their Democratic Party roots (among others) appear stronger than their connections to civil and human rights organizations like TransAfrica; and "the similarity of diverse American interest-group interests with that of the national government in peace-keeping [re: Darfur] has meant that the special interests of African American groups are not clearly special." Furthermore, Morris contends, Rice's affirmation as US representative in the United Nations looks less like a personal contribution and more like "standard American, liberal policy."[84] Given the history of systemic exclusion from leadership positions, one might point to these dynamics as a victory for liberalism—that African Americans like Obama and Rice can (or should) do their jobs freely and individually, without the externally imposed pressures placed on them by their own racial identity. On the other hand, one may wonder how those generations of African Americans who had earlier identified with the Sudanese on account of their race would respond to such an approach. Imbued with the power that comes with those high government positions and so long excluded from such agency, Obama and Rice might have been expected to deploy language of mutual aid, understanding, and interests based on race. Read against this grain, the absence of race in their public discourse concerning the Sudans appears like a missed opportunity for the administration to distinguish itself in the long history of Black American engagement with Sudan.

Since Obama left the Oval Office in early 2017, Sudan and South Sudan have continued to make US headlines. Sudan was included in President Donald Trump's infamous "Muslim ban"; longtime Sudanese leader Omar al-Bashir was forcibly removed from power in 2019 after thirty years in power; the South Sudanese civil war finally came to an end; and, in the twilight of his single term as president, Trump removed Sudan's designation as a state sponsor of terrorism. All these developments occurred in conjunction with social upheaval in the United States, typified by such events as the deadly 2017 demonstration in Charlottesville, Virginia; the deaths of Breonna Taylor and George Floyd at the hands of police; and the increasingly global Black Lives Matter movement. Within this convulsive environment, African Americans—has they had done for the past century—continued to keep an eye on the Nilotic Sudan thousands of miles away. The next (concluding) chapter clarifies this book's arguments, reexamines recent developments, and proposes some questions for the further study of Black America's relationship with Africa, the terms of Black identity politics as it pertains to the Arab world, and the global history of Sudan.

Conclusion

Black Lives Matter in Sudan

> I got t-shirts printed that said "South Sudan" in the front to educate and create dialogue. . . . In the next coming months I am adding "Black Lives Matter" at the back. . . . South Sudan is seen as so far away and distant by many who live in America. But what's happening in South Sudan, with unarmed black people being killed by authority figures, is actually very much the same issue as what we've seen happen in America.
> —Nykhor Paul, BBC interview

Nykhor Paul was born in 1989 in Akobo, Sudan (now South Sudan). In an interview posted by the BBC in July 2016, Paul described her childhood as "magical" and said that Akobo was a wonderful place to grow up. However, when the Second Sudanese Civil War inched closer to where she lived, she and her family fled in 1996 and moved "around the border of Ethiopia." Eventually settling in a refugee camp, Paul's parents sent her with her uncle to the United States in hopes that she would have a better life. Arriving in Nebraska, she was placed in foster care and was—as she frames it—"discovered" by a modeling agency. Paul embarked on a distinguished career, becoming the face of Louis Vuitton and participating in global fashion shows for the likes of Vivienne Westwood. "My life now is a whole world away from where I was born and where I come from," she said in 2016. Yet, despite the geographical, economic, and social chasms that might separate Paul from her family and other fellow South Sudanese, she has not forgotten where she came from. She obtained US citizenship so that she could more easily travel, and in 2014 she went back to the refugee camp where her family still resided and visited them for the first time since her arrival in the States eighteen years earlier. During the civil war that enveloped South Sudan shortly after its independence, Paul's social media posts concerning unrest generated thousands of likes.[1]

As a Black South Sudanese American, Nykhor Paul also followed the racial tension taking place in the United States. In 2013 activists Patrisse Cullors, Alicia Garza, and Opal Tometi launched Black Lives Matter (BLM) after George Zimmerman was acquitted on second-degree murder charges in his killing of an unarmed seventeen-year-old African American boy, Trayvon Martin. After the police shooting of unarmed Black teenager Michael Brown in Ferguson, Missouri, the following year, BLM grew into a nationwide protest movement.[2] When Paul's BBC interview was posted, the country was embroiled in a divisive presidential election in which one of the two major candidates—Republican Donald Trump—ran a campaign imbued with racist, nativist rhetoric. While the United States was not engaged in the type of literal civil war occurring in South Sudan, social cleavages were apparent, fierce, and polarizing. Against this backdrop, Paul said that she had "of course been following the recent racial tension here [in the United States closely." She credited that for including "Black Lives Matter" tags on her posts when she decided to increase social media awareness about South Sudan. After noting that the killing of unarmed Black people by authorities was an issue that linked the United States and South Sudan, Paul argued, "The way to help is to create a healthy peaceful dialogue between each other through education and care for our collective wellbeing. It is the 21st century. To reduce problems in Africa as being tribal is short-sighted but it's up to the African Diaspora to bring change."[3]

Bounds of Blackness provides an important foundation for those wishing to more deeply understand the historical relationship between African Americans and Sudan. While Sudanese-born figures like Nykhor Paul entered this history from the African perspective—and that history, to be sure, warrants its own book-length study—this book has focused on the African American side of the equation and the ways that Black Americans since the early twentieth century engaged Sudan through literary, cultural, and diplomatic endeavors. African Americans contributed to the constructions of newly independent Sudan and South Sudan, but Sudan also figured into Black American understandings of racial pride and consciousness through a sense of shared struggle not entirely dissimilar from what Nykhor Paul expressed (from a South Sudanese perspective) in 2016. As such, the modern connections that she has called for are rooted in over a century of Black American interactions with Sudan. Understanding this reality and Sudan's historical role in African American race consciousness is necessary for more properly placing into proper historical perspective African American engagement with (or, arguably, inattention to) Sudan and South Sudan during this Black Lives Matter moment. For Black Americans, Sudan is more than simply the land where the ancient civilizations of Nubia and Kush provided a counternarrative to Black degradation and inferiority. Black Americans engaged with colonial and postcolonial Sudan in ways that should complicate our understandings of race and racial solidarity in the African Diaspora.

Indeed, the guiding question undergirding this book is how modern Sudan informed African American understandings of Black definition, Black consciousness, and Black solidarity. Black America's interactions with Sudan show how Black racial solidarity can evolve within a single African diasporic relationship over the course of time. During Sudan's Anglo-Egyptian colonial period, African American newspapers framed Sudanese as Black racial kin under race-based state oppression. After independence and the eruption of civil wars between the Arab-run northern Sudanese government and non-Arab southern Sudanese rebels, Black Americans positioned northern Sudanese Arabs and southern Sudanese Blacks in an oppressor-oppressed binary. Some, however, resisted this polarizing framework. Against the backdrop of the Arab-Israeli conflict, some Black Americans—notably Louis Farrakhan and the Nation of Islam—deployed anti-Israeli, anti-Zionist language to express their support for Arab-run Sudanese governments even as Black Sudanese suffered under these governments. Simply put, the sociopolitical realities of colonialism and independence racialized different heroes and villains for Black Americans engaging Sudan. This evolving dynamic is not only important for understanding the paradoxical relationship African Americans have had with Sudan but should also invite us to interrogate Black America's broader relationship with Africa during the colonial and postcolonial eras. Racial solidarity is not bound to ancestral geography or physical appearance but is, instead, a fluid and capricious construction. What, then, are the bounds of Blackness? What circumstances determine who is included or excluded? What are the consequences of a racial solidarity that allows one to be racial kin in one moment and an antagonist in another?

Nowhere in this study have such questions been so evident than in the discursive approaches that Black Americans took when describing Arabs. While the Black-white dynamics of slavery and colonialism led to Black diasporic solidarities in narratives of Black oppressed and white oppressors, African Americans in this book showed their capacity to find, construct, and articulate racial solidarity in an oppressor-oppressed paradigm along Arab-Black lines. Thus, Black America's relationship with Sudan is not simply one piece in the larger puzzle of Black America's relationship with Africa. Rather, it is also fundamentally about its connection with the Arab world and, by extension, Pan-Africanism's relationship to Arabism. It is impossible to understand Black diasporic consciousness and politics without interrogating the African world's kaleidoscopic approach to Arabs. What sociopolitical factors determined when African Americans framed Sudanese as Black and/or Arab, and with what practical influence on solidarity practices? In what moments does Black racial solidarity partner with—or diminish—support for Arabs?

The significance of anti-Muslim sentiment in mainstream American politics necessitates an explicit mention of the interreligious auspices of such racially defined questions. According to the University of California's Haas Institute for a Fair and Inclusive Society, over 190 anti-Islamic bills were introduced between 2010 and 2016, with eighteen bills signed into law in twelve states. In addition to such legislative efforts, Sudanese trying to enter the United States were confronted with new barriers to entry. In 2015, in the wake of terrorist attacks in Paris and in San Bernardino, California, Congress modified the Visa Waiver Program that had previously allowed citizens of participating countries to travel to the United States without obtaining a visa. The modified program bars those who have visited Sudan, Iran, Iraq, or Syria since March 1, 2011, from entering the country (with few exceptions). The American Civil Liberties Union castigated the spending bill that includes the modified program, calling it discriminatory. Two years later, President Trump's infamous Executive Order 13769 barred foreigners from seven Muslim-majority countries—including Sudan—from entering the United States.[4] At this fraught moment in US history and amid such recent examples of state-sponsored Islamophobia, Black America's winding engagements with Sudan provide unique perspectives to offer conjecture on the current and future state of African American internationalism.

Implications for Black America and Beyond

To begin, *Bounds of Blackness* shows the impact that historically Black colleges and universities can have in African American relations with Africa moving forward. It is impossible to overstate the impacts that HBCUs and their graduates had in the historical narrative presented here, in a book that focused on Black interactions with just a single African country. Tuskegee's involvement in Leigh Hunt's cotton-cultivation scheme; William Leo Hansberry's pioneering courses on ancient African history at Howard; the editorial fervor of Hampton graduate Percival Prattis; the official foreign service work of Morehouse graduate Robert Kitchen—each of these examples illustrates the historical impact HBCUs had on African American consciousness, diplomacy, and activism concerning Sudan.[5] Due to state-sponsored Jim Crow and the legal (and extralegal) devices that white people employed to keep education segregated, it is on one hand not surprising that many of the actors in this history leading up to the 1970s had HBCU connections. However, with *Brown v. Board* and integration of university undergraduate and graduate education, those men and women who might have earlier matriculated at HBCUs and gone into some type of Africa-centered work have increasingly passed through the halls of predominantly white institutions.

Notwithstanding the demographic shifts that have occurred in American higher education in the last fifty years, it would be a mistake to presume that HBCUs no longer have a vital role to play in the centuries-old relationship linking African Americans with Africans. One need not look further than the ways Howard University has engaged with Sudan and Sudanese issues in recent years. Diane Ijoma, who as a Howard junior was named a 2019 David L. Boren Scholar, worked with US diplomats in Juba as an intern for the State Department. And, most prominently, Sudan's Makur Maker made headlines in 2020 when he became the first five-star basketball recruit to choose to play for an HBCU (Howard).[6] With these and a host of other examples, Howard University has had links with the Sudan long after desegregation in higher education. Apart from Howard, the historical connections between HBCUs and Africa are well-known and documented. HBCU alumni and officials attended independence celebrations of several African countries; three African presidents were educated at HBCUs (Nigeria's Nnamdi Azikiwe, Ghana's Kwame Nkrumah, and Malawi's Kamuzu Banda); and in the 1980s and early 1990s HBCU students participated in South Africa's anti-apartheid struggle.[7] Notwithstanding awareness of such important information, it would be worthwhile for scholarship to consider the role that HBCUs have more recently played in African American internationalism generally and with respect to Africa specifically in the twenty-first century. How have HBCUs, their students, and alumni responded to developments on the continent like the Arab Spring, the terrorist operations of Boko Haram and al-Shabab, and the migrant flight to Europe that has cost so many lives? While *Bounds of Blackness* and other books may offer insight into HBCU-Africa relations during the twentieth century, such studies should also compel us to consider that this history is not limited to the past but may continue in ways that reinforce and challenge established understandings.

The historical interactions that African Americans have had with Sudan should also lead us to consider the history, form, and implications of largely unexplored engagements that Black Americans have had with other African countries. While important books have been published concerning African American engagement with countries like South Africa, Liberia, Ghana, and the Congo, far fewer studies have been attempted that concentrate on North Africa or the Horn of Africa.[8] Because Black American decisions to liken themselves to or distinguish themselves from Sudanese allow us to further understand how we have made sense of their blackness, it stands to reason that our knowledge of Africa's importance to Black Americans' self-conceptions will be more complete when our historical relationships with more African countries are considered. This is not to say that research should no longer be done on how West, Central, and Southern Africa have figured in Black internationalism. The realities of the transatlantic slave trade and other violent systems of white structural state-based oppression in those regions have engendered particular relationships with those regions that should never be severed. But expanding our gaze beyond those regions and acknowledging that Black Americans have important—and perhaps hitherto unresearched—histories with other African regions will serve to diversify and deepen our understanding. We must not reinforce the Hegelian notion that "true" or "Black" Africa is bound to the areas south of the Sahara. To do so is to risk marginalizing—however unconsciously—the lives of certain Black peoples who are facing the same systemic oppression that compelled Cullors, Garza, and Tometi to launch Black Lives Matter.

A report from Algiers in July 2020 noted that the global wave of antiracism protests generated by the police killing of George Floyd had barely touched North Africa despite routine anti-Black discrimination in that region with a deep history of slavery. Indeed, observers agree that the Black Lives Matter movement has not spurred a major debate on racism or police violence against Black Africans in the Maghreb. Modern slave markets have been reported in Libya, where migrants are abused by human traffickers. Algeria and Tunisia bar foreign Africans from getting residency papers unless they are students.[9] Issues like residency or citizenship status, police surveillance and violence, and slavery would all be the types of issues BLM activists would openly denounce as oppressive. If Black Americans have always linked their struggle for rights to liberation movements in the Caribbean, Asia, Africa, and elsewhere, why should North Africa now be an exception?[10]

Bounds of Blackness has shown the foundational role that the creative and collective colossus that is the Black press played in the history of Black America's relationship with the Sudan. African American newspapers like the *Pittsburgh Courier*, *Chicago Defender*, and the *Final Call* have been rich arenas to explore Black opinion on the region. It was in the diversity of the Black press that African American writers on Sudan provided a particular definition of what it meant to be Black in the diaspora and, with it, a broader story about Black struggle, pride, and consciousness. The internet—with its news and culture sites, blogs, and social media platforms—could easily serve as the primary space for Black Americans to engage Sudan, other African countries, and the diaspora in the spirit of Black consciousness and solidarity. Reporting for the Pew Research Center, Brooke Auxier notes that Black Americans have long used such sites for political engagement and social activism, dating from years before the 2020 George Floyd protests demonstrated social media platforms' scope and power. According to Pew surveys, Black social media users are particularly likely to find such sites important for getting involved in issues they care about or locating like-minded people. African Americans are also likely to express positive views about the impact these platforms have for holding powerful people accountable and amplifying the voices of underrepresented groups. "The online community known as Black Twitter," writes Auxier, "has long been using these platforms to collectively organize, offer support and increase visibility online for Black people and issues that matter to them."[11]

While Nykhor Paul's online activism provides one template for the form such online activism can take, there are other examples testifying to the way people throughout the African diaspora have used the internet to publicize problems facing their communities. The hashtag #aboriginallivesmatter trended in Australia, where protests focused on the treatment of an indigenous population subjected to injustices from eviction to mass killings since the dawn of white settlement there. The phrase #AllPapuanLivesMatter went viral in Indonesia and called attention to the long secessionist movement in West Papua (which has created tension between minority Papuans and ethnic-majority Javanese). Finally, Black Lives Matter activists have used social media to create transnational alliances.[12] After Israeli settlers forced Palestinian families from their homes in the Sheikh Jarrah neighborhood in May 2021, Israelis and Palestinian witnessed some of the worst violence in a long time. BLM came out in support of the Palestinian fight for liberation and sent out the following tweet: "Black Lives Matter stands in solidarity with Palestinians. We are a movement committed to ending settler colonialism in all forms and will continue to advocate for Palestinian liberation. (always have. And always will be). #freepalestine."[13]

As provocative as that statement may be, it is a fact of history that African American support for Arabs or Israel has never been universal. For much of the twentieth century, African American writers invoked the history of slavery when describing Arabs in Sudan. This was done during Sudan's colonial period (when Egypt operated as a colonial master) and during the First Sudanese Civil War, as Black southerners warred against the Arab-ruled Sudanese government. However, as Arab-Israeli intrigue operated in the background of that conflict, some writers critiqued Israel's involvement in the Sudan and, in the process, added a layer to the issue of African American racial solidarity with Sudanese. What did it mean for an African American to support Black people (southern Sudanese) fighting Arabs (northern Sudanese) if other Arabs in the Middle East were struggling for liberation from a white Israeli state? The Arab-Israeli conflict's relationship to African American approaches to Sudan continued during the Second Sudanese Civil War, when Louis Farrakhan and the Nation of Islam accused Zionists of spreading misinformation about Omar al-Bashir's regime and slavery in Sudan. As Blacks suffered in western and southern Sudan, the Nation of Islam supported the government responsible for the violence using anti-Zionist rhetoric.

At the very least, the history and shifting solidarities presented in this book should spark reconsideration of Afro-Arab relations in their complexity and Black America's relationship with Israel and the Arab world. There are multiple ways one can make sense of BLM's expressed support for Palestinians. Given how Black and other nonwhite peoples the world over have been decimated by settler and extractive colonialism since the late fifteenth century, it is no wonder that BLM is "committed to ending settler colonialism in all forms." Its pledge to "continue to advocate for Palestinian liberation" makes sense, since liberation from slavery, colonialism, and all forms of oppression has long been an ideal of African Americans and others in the African diaspora. Finally, there is a white-brown racial dimension undergirding Palestinian-Israeli relations that may connect with BLM's support for Palestinians. However, complications arise if and when African American support for Palestine is conflated with Afro-Arab solidarity broadly. What made Farrakhan's accusations of Zionist conspiracy in his defense of Bashir's genocidal regime so troubling—among other reasons—is the fact that he indirectly pointed attention to the suffering of *nonwhite* people facing oppression from a *white* government (Palestinians and Israel) to support an African (northern Sudanese) government responsible for the oppression of *Black* people (southern Sudanese). What is to be gained from that posture?

To be sure, the question of solidarity politics in this racialized and ever-oppressive geopolitical landscape extends beyond Black American relationships with the Arab world to include such engagement with others around the world. The truth is that solidarity comes with thrilling benefits, weighty consequences, and, at times, serious contradictions. Consider, for example, the figure of longtime Cuban leader Fidel Castro. During his lifetime, Castro, who in 2016 died at the age of ninety, sought out Black leaders, met with Malcolm X in Harlem, and had a close relationship with Nelson Mandela. According to Sam Riddle, political director of the National Action Network's Michigan chapter, "It was Fidel who fought for the human rights for black Cubans." Noting that many Cubans "are as black as any black who worked the fields of Mississippi or lived in Harlem," Riddle said that Castro believed in medical care and education for all Cubans.[14]

Writing the same month as Castro's death, the *Miami Herald*'s Armando Salguero—who described himself as having been "born into Cuba's imprisonment"—painted the Cuban leader in an altogether different light. In an editorial describing Castro as "one of the 20th century's most enduring oppressors," he noted that Fidel Castro and his brother had stifled dissent in the country for more than half a century. Salguero vividly recounted a story from his youth when he and his parents were about to board a plane bound for the United States before a bearded guerrilla arbitrarily decided that only two of them could leave (he and his mother made the trip, and it would take another three years before his father could reunite with them). He also included a sobering indictment from Human Rights Watch, which described Cuban citizens as being systematically deprived of fundamental rights to free expression and subject to various tactics to enforce political conformity. These realities notwithstanding, none of them were new developments that warranted "breaking news" status in 2016. What, then, spurred Salguero to write about the Castros at that moment? It was San Francisco 49ers quarterback Colin Kaepernick, who during an NFL postgame news conference donned a T-shirt with photos from a 1960 meeting between Castro and Malcolm X.[15]

Salguero's disgust was palpable as he labeled Kaepernick an "unrepentant hypocrite." Why, he asked, would a man who protests oppression don a Castro shirt? "The tyrant is demonstrably a star on the world's All Oppressor Team," he asserted. Kaepernick immediately responded by saying that he had worn a Malcolm X shirt and that he believed in Malcolm X and his ideology. Kaepernick said that, for him, the fact that Malcolm met with Castro spoke to his willingness to hear different points of view. When Salguero asked the quarterback whether it is good to have an open mind about Castro and his oppression, Kaepernick responded, "I'm not talking about Fidel Castro and his oppression. I'm talking about Malcolm X and what he's done for people." Salguero was not satisfied and wrote:

> I hope Kaepernick is starting to realize how untenable his position is relative to the Castros. Even Malcolm X, who met with Castro in New York, for years afterward declined invitations to visit him in Cuba. I'm hoping Kaepernick understands one should not make broad statements about standing up for people's rights, then slip into a Fidel Castro shirt, suggesting approval for a man who has spent his days on the planet stifling people's rights.[16]

In a circuitous way, the hubbub concerning Kaepernick's T-shirt leads me back to BLM's tweet that it would always support Palestinian liberation. Rather than refer specifically to the Palestinian case, I am particularly concerned with the idea that any solidarity—racial, religious, or otherwise—be expressed as a permanent pledge of support irrespective of context or circumstance. Whether one finds oneself more in alignment with Salguero or Kaepernick, Salguero's question to Kaepernick is a fair one. In a world where one group's liberation hero is often another's oppressor, it is imperative that solidarities in the African diaspora be informed, nuanced, and malleable. It would behoove Africana scholarship to explore the possible tensions and contradictions that may arise when Black communities across national lines convey support for one another. But at a time when Black people the world over are still suffering from systemic racism, solidarity and activist efforts should be chiefly considered in light of whether or not they are effectual in advancing Black liberation.

Closing Thoughts: Beyond Nubia

The process of writing this book began over a decade ago, when I traveled to Egypt and England in the summer of 2011. Then a twenty-four-year-old, African American graduate student at the University of Michigan, I was slated to spend a few weeks in Cairo for an introductory Arabic course and proceed to Durham University to conduct preliminary dissertation research at its famed Sudan Archive. I had a mix of emotions as I embarked on the trip. Egypt was less than four months removed from the fall of longtime autocrat Hosni Mubarak in the Arab Spring. It was my first research trip, and I was desperate to find some valuable documents that I could use to write an exciting thesis.

Yet, despite the archival research and language instruction informing the trip, I—like so many Black Americans before me—found myself enamored with the ancient Egyptian past. When I looked at the Nile, I thought about that ancient river's role in the Book of Exodus. When I went to Coptic Cairo, I visited the cave commonly believed to have housed Jesus, Mary, and Joseph when they fled to Egypt to avoid Herod's persecution. I visited the ancient capital of Memphis, where I was blessed to visit the Step Pyramid in Saqqara and gaze upon a massive statue of Ramses the Great. And, of course, no trip to Cairo would have been complete without visiting the pyramid complex in Giza. Because my historically Black fraternity (Alpha Phi Alpha) has long prized Egyptian iconography, I packed a T-shirt emblazoned with "AΦA." As I stood in front of the pyramids and the Great Sphinx, I made sure to have my picture taken with the black and gold letters across my chest.

In the late 1990s, long before my graduate research took me to northeastern Africa, Harvard historian Henry Louis Gates Jr. visited Sudan as part of his six-hour, three-night televised documentary *Wonders of the African World*. "When you think of Africa," Gates said in an interview published in the *Baltimore Sun*, "what comes to mind for most Americans? Poverty and flies, famine, war and disease. How many of us know anything at all about the truly great ancient civilizations of Africa, which, in their day, were just as glorious and just as splendid as any on the face of the Earth?" He said that the experience of going to Nubia and filming pyramids where forty generations of Black royalty were buried was one of the great trips of his life.[17]

It is natural for one who is traveling to or otherwise learning about Sudan to venture into the ancient past. While the ancient civilizations of Egypt, Nubia, and Kush can conjure a sense of awe and wonder in any modern mind, they have held an especially strong grip on African Americans like myself, Gates, and so many others. For Black Americans living in a country that has experienced (and continues to perpetuate) all manners of systemic racism, one can derive much solace and pride in the reality that wealthy, sovereign, powerful Black civilizations existed on the Nile for centuries before the transatlantic age. Yet I leave this study of Black America's relationship to modern Sudan with a conviction that we do a disservice to ourselves as African Americans if our focus on the glorious Nilotic past is not coupled with strident, conscious attention to the realities facing contemporary Africa. While some African American intellectuals in the early twentieth century looked to redeem Africa's history in the face of pejorative images, they marginalized Africa's colonial present. Indeed, in the late nineteenth and early twentieth centuries, those Black Americans interested in Africa may have had strong sentiments concerning Africa's august history but believed that contemporary Africa lacked value and needed to be elevated.[18]

It is my deep and sincere hope that *Bounds of Blackness* can be used to discourage a similar ideological phenomenon today. We as Black people must not only look to African locales like Sudan as historical evidence that we *are* kings and queens because we *were* kings and queens. We must not confine Africa to our collective imagination, as merely representing the ancestral motherland from which our forebears were taken. While we must never forget the ancient African past, it is equally important that we not restrict our consciousness of Africa to Black history. Sudan and the rest of the continent are integral parts of our Black present.

As Black Americans engage with contemporary Africa, it is paramount that we interrogate the history of US power and imperialism in the continent. If a disservice is done by focusing on the African past at the expense of the present, similar disservice is done if one limits examination of US engagement with Africa to the eras of transatlantic slavery, colonialism, and the Cold War. Capitalism, power, and self-interest have governed US diplomacy with Africa in the past, and we must be mindful of the ways this is still true.

Notes

Introduction

1. "E. Frederick Morrow at the White House," White House Historical Association, accessed May 11, 2020, https://www.whitehousehistory.org/e-frederick-morrow-at-the-white-house; E. Frederic Morrow, *Black Man in the White House: A Diary of the Eisenhower Years by the Administrative Officer for Special Projects, the White House, 1955–1961* (New York: Conrad-McCann, 1963), 125–126, 142 (quote from 142).

2. Morrow, *Black Man in the White House*, 125–126 (quote from 125); Kevin Gaines, *American Africans in Ghana: Black Expatriates and the Civil Rights Era* (Chapel Hill: University of North Carolina Press, 2006), 85.

3. Morrow, *Black Man in the White House*, 131–135 (quote from 135).

4. Patrick Manning, *The African Diaspora: A History through Culture* (New York: Columbia University Press, 2009), 268.

5. Gaines, *American Africans in Ghana*, 2; James H. Meriwether, *Proudly We Can Be Africans: Black Americans and Africa, 1935–1961* (Chapel Hill: University of North Carolina Press, 2002), 163.

6. For more on Black America's attraction to Ghana upon its independence, see James T. Campbell, *Middle Passages: African American Journeys to Africa, 1787–2005* (New York: Penguin, 2006), 316; and Roger A. Davidson, Jr., "A Question of Freedom: African Americans and Ghanaian Independence," *Negro History Bulletin* 60, no. 3 (July–September 1997): 6.

7. Mahmood Mamdani, *When Victims Become Killers: Colonialism, Nativism, and the Genocide in Rwanda* (Princeton: Princeton University Press, 2001), 78. Steven Feierman explains how Fernand Braudel made a similar distinction between a "Black" and "White" Africa based on religious differences, and in his distinction between civilizations and cultures placed Black Africa under the "cultural" label. See Steven Feierman, "African Histories and the Dissolution of World History," in

Africa and the Disciplines: The Contributions of Research in Africa to the Social Sciences and Humanities, ed. Robert H. Bates, V. Y. Mudimbe, and J. O'Barr (Chicago: University of Chicago Press, 1993), 171–176.

8. Mamdani, *When Victims Become Killers*, 78.

9. W. E. B. Du Bois, *Black Folk, Then and Now: An Essay in the History and Sociology of the Negro Race* (New York: Henry Holt, 1939), 38.

10. "Middle East and North Africa," World Bank, accessed December 21, 2020, https://www.worldbank.org/en/region/mena; "Middle East/North Africa," Office of the United States Trade Representative, accessed December 21, 2020, https://ustr.gov/countries-regions/europe-middle-east/middle-east/north-africa; "Middle East and Northern Africa Region," United Nations Human Rights Office of the High Commissioner, accessed December 21, 2020, https://www.ohchr.org/en/countries/menaregion/pages/menaregionindex.aspx; "Sudan Fast Facts," CNN, updated December 17, 2020, https://www.cnn.com/2013/10/30/world/africa/sudan-fast-facts/index.html; Simon Tisdall, "Sudan and Algeria Have Ousted Leaders, but Revolutions Rarely End Happily," *Guardian*, April 13, 2019, https://www.theguardian.com/world/2019/apr/13/north-africa-sudan-algeria-revolutions-rarely-end-happily; Josef Federman and Samy Magdy, "Sudanese Officials: Diplomatic Deal with Israel Is Near," Associated Press, October 22, 2020, https://apnews.com/article/donald-trump-virus-outbreak-bahrain-africa-israel-c2a12e4a28ba5280c6e0d1fbbce030f0; Francis M. Deng, *War of Visions: Conflict of Identities in the Sudan* (Washington, DC: Brookings Institution, 1995), 2–4.

11. Deng, *War of Visions*, 4–5.

12. Krystal Strong, "Do African Lives Matter to Black Lives Matter? Youth Uprisings and the Borders of Solidarity," *Urban Education* 53, no. 2 (2018): 266; Alex Altman, "Black Lives Matter: A New Civil Rights Movement Is Turning a Protest Cry into a Political Force," *Time*, accessed January 6, 2021, http://time.com/time-person-of-the-year-2015-runner-up-black-lives-matter.

13. Definition taken from *AU Echo*, no. 5 (January 27, 2013), 1, as cited in Hakim Adi, *Pan-Africanism: A History* (London: Bloomsbury, 2018), 1.

14. Henry Louis Gates Jr., foreword to Charles Bonnet, *The Black Kingdom of the Nile* (Cambridge, MA: Harvard University Press, 2019), ix–x.

15. Meriwether, *Proudly We Can Be Africans*, 163, 285n18.

16. Manning, *The African Diaspora*, 268.

17. Meriwether, *Proudly We Can Be Africans*, 8.

18. See Carol Anderson, *Bourgeois Radicals: The NAACP and the Struggle for Colonial Liberation, 1941–1960* (New York: Cambridge University Press, 2014); and Jonathan Rosenberg, *How Far the Promised Land? World Affairs and the American Civil Rights Movement from the First World War to Vietnam* (Princeton: Princeton University Press, 2006), 7. Other examples of scholarship that has focused on the NAACP's global auspices include Jake Miller's "The NAACP and global human rights," *Western Journal of Black Studies* 26, no. 1 (Spring 2002): 22–31; Caroline Emmons, "Testing Boundaries: The NAACP and the Caribbean, 1910–1930," *Journal of Caribbean History* 52, no. 2 (2018): 198–216; and Kenneth R. Janken, "From Colonial Liberation to Cold War Liberalism: Walter White, the NAACP, and Foreign Affairs, 1941–1955," *Ethnic and racial studies* 21, no. 6 (1998): 1074–1095.

19. Eslanda Goode Robeson, *African Journey* (1945; repr., Westport, CT: Greenwood Press, 1972); Elton C. Fax, *Through Black Eyes: Journeys of a Black Artist to East Africa and Russia* (New York: Dodd, Mead, 1974); Keith B. Richburg, *Out of America: A Black Man Confronts Africa* (New York: Basic Books, 1997); James Leonard Mack, *My Life, My Country, My World* (Pittsburgh: Dorrance Publishing, 2008); Susan Rice, *Tough Love: My Story of the Things Worth Fighting For* (New York: Simon & Schuster, 2019).

20. Andrew Brimmer's papers can be found at Harvard University's Baker Library; Robert W. Kitchen's papers can be found at Howard University's Moorland-Spingarn Research Center; Arthur B. McCaw's papers can be found at Stanford University's Hoover Institution; and Joe Madison's papers can be found at Tulane University's Amistad Research Center.

21. Algernon Austin, *Achieving Blackness: Race, Black Nationalism, and Afrocentrism in the Twentieth Century* (New York: New York University Press, 2006), 12.

22. Austin, *Achieving Blackness*, 19; Michael Omi and Howard Winant, *Racial Formation in the United States*, 3rd ed. (New York: Routledge, 2015), 4.

23. Mark Ledwidge, *Race and US Foreign Policy: The African-American Foreign Affairs Network* (New York: Routledge, 2012), 1, 4.

24. Gerald Horne, *Mau Mau in Harlem? The U.S. and the Liberation of Kenya* (New York: Palgrave Macmillan, 2009), 3.

25. Rosenberg, *How Far the Promised Land?*, 2, 3, 11 (quote from 11).

26. Nico Slate, *Colored Cosmopolitanism: The Shared Struggle for Freedom in the United States and India* (Cambridge, MA: Harvard University Press, 2012), 2.

27. Gerald Horne, *The End of Empires: African Americans and India* (Philadelphia: Temple University Press, 2008), 2, 4 (quote from 4).

28. Slate, *Colored Cosmopolitanism*, 2; Horne, *The End of Empires*, 3–4.

29. Horne, *The End of Empires*, 4.

30. Vijay Prashad, *The Karma of Brown Folk* (Minneapolis: University of Minnesota Press, 2000), viii, x–xi (quotes from x–xi).

31. Alex Lubin, "Locating Palestine in Pre-1948 Black Internationalism," *Souls: A Critical Journal of Black Politics, Culture and Society* 9, no. 2 (2007): 97; Salim Yaqub, "Our Declaration of Independence': African Americans, Arab Americans, and the Arab-Israeli Conflict, 1967–1979," *Mashriq and Majhar* 3, no. 1 (2015): 12–14.

32. Michael R. Fischbach, *Black Power and Palestine: Transnational Countries of Color* (Stanford: Stanford University Press, 2019); Lenni Brenner and Matthew Quest, *Black Liberation and Palestine Solidarity* (Atlanta: On Our Own Authority, 2013); Elaine Mokhtefi, *Algiers, Third World Capital: Freedom Fighters, Revolutionaries, Black Panthers* (London: Verso Books, 2018); Melani McAlister, "One Black Allah: The Middle East in the Cultural Politics of African American Liberation, 1955–1970," *American Quarterly* 51, no. 3 (September 1999): 622–656.

33. Alex Lubin, *Geographies of Liberation: The Making of an Afro-Arab Political Imaginary* (Chapel Hill: University of North Carolina Press, 2014).

34. Paul Thomas Chamberlin, *The Global Offensive: The United States, the Palestine Liberation Organization, and the Making of the Post-Cold War Order* (New York: Oxford University Press, 2012), 15, 40; Penny M. Von Eschen, "Soul Call: The First World Festival of Negro Arts at a Pivot of Black Modernities," *Nka: Journal of Contemporary African Art*, no. 42–43 (2018): 126–127; David Murphy, "Introduction: The Performance of Pan-Africanism: Staging the African Renaissance at the First World Festival of Negro Arts," in *The First World Festival of Negro Arts, Dakar 1966: Contexts and Legacies* (Liverpool: Liverpool University Press, 2016), 1; Cédric Vincent, "'The Real Heart of the Festival': The Exhibition of L'Art nègre at the Musée Dynamique," in *The First World Festival of Negro Arts, Dakar 1966: Contexts and Legacies*, ed. David Murphy, 45–63 (Liverpool: Liverpool University Press, 2016), 53.

35. Paraska Tolan-Szkilnik, "'Collecting Bosoms': Sex, Race, and Masculinity at the Pan-African Festival of Algiers, 1969," *Arab Studies Journal* 29, no. 2 (2021): 98.

36. Andrew Apter, "Beyond Négritude: Black Cultural Citizenship and the Arab Question in FESTAC 77," *Journal of African Cultural Studies* 28, no. 3 (2016): 313 (abstract).

1. Negro Canaan

1. Louis R. Harlan, "Booker T. Washington and the White Man's Burden," *American Historical Review* 71, no. 2 (January 1966): 447 (see note 25 on same page); Sven Beckert, "From Tuskegee to Togo: The Problem of Freedom in the Empire of Cotton," *Journal of American History* 92, no. 2 (September 2005): 509; A. Zimmerman, *Alabama in Africa: Booker T. Washington, the German Empire, and the Globalization of the New South* (Princeton: Princeton University Press, 2010), 62.

2. Jonathan Robins also links emigration to Africa with Hunt's scheme. See Jonathan E. Robins, *Cotton and Race across the Atlantic: Britain, Africa, and America, 1900–1920* (Rochester: University of Rochester Press, 2016), 150 (and 186–187, where Black American emigration is spoken of more broadly).

3. See Pero Gaglo Dagbovie, "Exploring a Century of Historical Scholarship on Booker T. Washington," *Journal of African American History* 92, no. 2 (Spring 2007): 247–248, where he cites Harlan, "Booker T. Washington and the White Man's Burden," 441; Michael O. West, "The Tuskegee Model of Development in Africa: Another Dimension of the African/African-American Connection," *Diplomatic History: The Journal of the Society for Historians of American Foreign Relations* 16 (Summer 1992): 372; Mildred C. Fierce, *The Pan-African Idea in the United States, 1900–1910: African-American Interest in Africa and Interactions with West Africa* (New York: Garland, 1993), 176; and Edward O. Erhagbe, "African-Americans and the Defense of the African States against European Imperial Conquest: Booker T. Washington's Diplomatic Efforts to Guarantee Liberia's Independence, 1907–1911," *African Studies Review* 39 (April 1996): 56, 61 (quote from 61).

4. Kendahl L. Radcliffe, "The Tuskegee-Togo Cotton Scheme 1900–1909" (PhD diss., University of California, Los Angeles, 1998), ix–xi (quote from x).

5. Maya Peterson, "US to USSR: American Experts, Irrigation, and Cotton in Soviet Central Asia, 1929–32," *Environmental History* 21 (2016): 442, 450, 453–454.

6. Peterson, "US to USSR," 453–454.

7. See conclusion of this chapter, where I address this claim in the light of the US historian Sven Beckert's claim that Washington and his disciples worked to obtain freedom for both Black Americans and Africans by accommodating to powerful statesmen and capitalists.

8. *Sudan Times*, circa 1904 (from Sudan Archive, Durham University [hereafter SAD], 802/1/51).

9. Jessie Hunt, Leigh J. Hunt biography and reminiscences, 1947, folder #/title VF0451, p. 1, Acc. #4667–001, University of Washington Special Collections; Bob Gagen, "Etna Farm Boy Became Global Tycoon," *News-Sun and Evening Star* (Kendallville, IN), January 31, 2002, http://www.kpcnews.com/article_4463080f-be62-5631-bff1-a00dee3e25cd.html; *The Booker T. Washington Papers*, vol. 7, *1903–4*, ed. Louis R. Harlan and Raymond W. Smock (Urbana: University of Illinois Press, 1977), 403–404n1); Arthur Gaitskell, *Gezira: A Story of Development in the Sudan* (London: Faber and Faber, 1959), 51; "Leigh S. J. Hunt," *Annals of Iowa* 19, no. 4 (April 1934): 314; Laurance B. Rand, *High Stakes: the Life and Times of Leigh S. J. Hunt* (New York: Peter Lang, 1989), 177, 179.

10. Gaitskell, *Gezira*, 51; Andrew S. Natsios, *Sudan, South Sudan, and Darfur: What Everyone Needs to Know* (New York: Oxford University Press, 2012), xix, xxv, 24, 25–26; Robert O. Collins, "Sudan," in *Oxford Encyclopedia of the Modern World*, ed. Peter Stearns (Oxford University Press, 2008), Oxford Reference.

11. Natsios, *Sudan, South Sudan, and Darfur*, 26.

12. Iris Seri-Hersch, "Education in Colonial Sudan, 1900–1957," *Oxford Research Encyclopaedia of African History*, 2017, HAL Open Science, https://shs.hal.science/halshs-01514910/document;

Fatin Abbas, "Coming to Terms with Sudan's Legacy of Slavery," *African Arguments*, January 18, 2018, https://africanarguments.org/2016/01/coming-to-terms-with-sudans-legacy-of-slavery-2; Robert S. Kramer, Richard A. Lobban Jr., and Carolyn Fluehr-Lobban, *Historical Dictionary of the Sudan*, 4th ed. (Lanham, MD: Scarecrow Press, 2013), 389–390; Natsios, *Sudan, South Sudan, and Darfur*, 31.

13. Rand, *High Stakes*, 179, 184–185 (on 179 Rand cites letter from John G. Lang to David J. Hill, August 13, 1902, Consular Reports, National Archives).

14. Rand, *High Stakes*, 184–185; Harlan, "Booker T. Washington and the White Man's Burden," 447n26.

15. Hunt to Clarkson, April 19, 1903, Clarkson Papers, Library of Congress (hereafter LC), from Rand, *High Stakes*, 184.

16. Rand, *Stakes*, 185 [June 15, 1903, date inferred from June 18, 1903, letter from Clarkson to Jessie Hunt that Rand cites in *High Stakes*, 187].

17. Description and quotes from Rand, *High Stakes*, 187, which quotes Clarkson to Jessie Hunt, June 18, 1903, Hunt Papers.

18. James H. Meriwether, *Proudly We Can Be Africans: Black Americans and Africa, 1935–1961* (Chapel Hill: University of North Carolina Press, 2002), 6, 14; Michele Mitchell, "'The Black Man's Burden': African Americans, Imperialism, and Notions of Racial Manhood 1890–1910," *International Review of Social History* 4, supplement 7 (1999): 78, 90.

19. Nemata Blyden, *African Americans and Africa: A New History* (New Haven: Yale University Press, 2019), 128 (Blyden cites Jabez Ayo Langley, "Chief Sam's African Movement and Race Consciousness in West Africa," *Phylon* 32, no. 2 (1971): 165.

20. For more on Hawaii-Philippines plan, see Guy Emerson Mount, "The Last Reconstruction: Slavery, Emancipation, and Empire in the Black Pacific" (PhD diss., University of Chicago, 2018).

21. James T. Campbell, *Middle Passages: African American Journeys to Africa, 1787–2005* (New York: Penguin, 2006), 39–40, 45, 103, 113; Philippe R. Girard and Paul Finkelman, "Colonization," in *Encyclopedia of African American History, 1619–1895: From the Colonial Period to the Age of Frederick Douglass* (Oxford University Press, 2006), Oxford Reference.

22. Quoted in Campbell, *Middle Passages*, 113.

23. Rand, *High Stakes*, 189; J. A. Cannon, "Baring, Evelyn, 1st Earl of Cromer," in *The Oxford Companion to British History*, 2nd ed., ed. Robert Crowcroft and John Cannon (Oxford University Press, 2015), Oxford Reference; J. C. B. Richmond, *Egypt, 1798–1952: Her Advance towards a Modern Identity* (New York: Columbia University Press, 1977), 132.

24. Ransford W. Palmer, "Jamaica," in *The Oxford Encyclopedia of Economic History*, ed. Joel Mokyr (Oxford University Press, 2003), Oxford Reference.

25. Thomas C. Holt, *The Problem of Freedom: Race, Labor, and Politics in Jamaica and Britain, 1832–1938* (Baltimore: Johns Hopkins University Press, 1992), 76, 146 (quote from 146).

26. Holt, *The Problem of Freedom*, 42, 146–147, 167 (in note 16 on 147, Holt cites in his broader explanation William A. Green, *British Slavery Emancipation: The Sugar Colonies and the Great Experiment, 1830–1865* [Oxford: Clarendon, 1976], 188, 194; and Philip D. Curtin, *Two Jamaicas: The Role of Ideas in a Tropical Colony, 1830–1865* [Cambridge: Harvard University Press, 1975], 113, 121, 143, 156–57]). Quotes from 147 and 167.

27. Kramer, Lobban, and Fluehr-Lobban, *Historical Dictionary of the Sudan*, 4th ed., 389–392. For early Condominium efforts to stamp out slavery, see "Memorandum by Sir R. Wingate," in *Reports by His Majesty's Agent and Consul-General on the Finances, Administration, and Condition of Egypt and the Soudan in 1902* (London: Printed for His Majesty's Stationary Office, [1903]), 91–92; Earl of Cromer to the Marquess of Lansdowne, February 26, 1904 [no. 2] in *Reports by*

His Majesty's Agent and Consul-General on the Finances, Administration, and Condition of Egypt and the Soudan in 1903 (London: Printed for His Majesty's Stationary Office, [1904]), 89; and Earl of Cromer to the Marquess of Lansdowne, March 15, 1905 [no. 2] in *Reports by His Majesty's Agent and Consul-General on the Finances, Administration, and Condition of Egypt and the Soudan in 1904* (London: Printed for His Majesty's Stationary Office, [1905]), 133–134.

28. Earl of Cromer to the Marquess of Lansdowne, February 26, 1904 [no. 2] in Reports by His Majesty's Agent [published 1904], 78–80.

29. Hunt to Cromer, [1903] from Rand, *High Stakes*, 189–190. Same letter can be found in SAD 802/1/3–6; 1903 dating can be ascertained by the dating of Hunt's letter to Phillips, November 11, 1903, Barlow Rand Limited Archives, which is cited in Rand, *High Stakes*, 191n29.

30. Rand, *High Stakes*, 214; Sven Beckert, "From Tuskegee to Togo: The Problem of Freedom in the Empire of Cotto," *Journal of American History* 92, no. 2 (September 2005): 502, 504, 525.

31. Rand, *High Stakes*, 191 (citing Hunt to Phillips, November 11, 1903, Barlow Rand Limited Archives).

32. Earl of Cromer to the Marquess of Lansdowne, February 26, 1904 [No. 2] in *Reports by His Majesty's Agent* [published 1904], 80.

33. Rand, *High Stakes*, 191–192; Gaitskell, *Gezira*, 51.

34. Hunt to Roberts, November 20, 1903, from "Wants the American Negroes to Become Farm Owners in Africa: Colossal Scheme of Leigh Hunt," *Oregonian*, February 7, 1904, Readex.

35. Robert Trent Vinson, *The Americans Are Coming! Dreams of African American Liberation in Segregationist South Africa* (Athens: Ohio University Press, 2012), 37; Rand, *High Stakes*, 185; Beckert, "From Tuskegee to Togo," 509; West, "Tuskegee Model," 374; Edward H. Berman, "Tuskegee—in—Africa," *Journal of Negro Education* 41, no. 2 (Spring 1972): 99. With respect to the Black imaginary and its linkages to Africa and the Diaspora, see Nan Woodruff, *American Congo: The African-American Freedom Struggle in the Delta* (Cambridge, MA: Harvard University Press, 2003); and Brandon Byrd, "An Experiment in Self-Government: Haiti in the African-American Political Imagination, 1863–1915" (PhD diss., University of North Carolina, 2015).

36. Beckert, "Tuskegee to Togo," 508, 523; Zimmerman, *Alabama in Africa*, 13.

37. Harlan, "Booker T. Washington and the White Man's Burden," 447n26; Rand, *High Stakes*, 188.

38. Washington to Hunt, January 19, 1904, Washington Papers, LC.

39. Rand, *High Stakes*, 201 (which cites *Seattle Times*, September 27, 1903 in note 7).

40. "American Negroes Will Remove to Africa," *Trenton Evening Times*, September 29, 1903, Readex.

41. "To Teach the Black Races," *Worcester (MA) Daily Spy*, October 3, 1903, Readex.

42. Leigh Hunt to George Roberts, November 29, 1903, Clarkson Papers, State Historical Society of Iowa, from Rand, *High Stakes*, 201. See also Rand, *Stakes*, 201.

43. "The Angry Saxons," *Plaindealer* (Cleveland), May 13, 1904, Readex.

44. Hunt to Roberts, November 20, 1903, from "Wants the American Negroes."

45. "Wants the American Negroes."

46. "Booker Washington Dodged Newspaper Notoriety in France," *Montgomery (AL) Advertiser*, October 4, 1903, Readex.

47. See "Colonization of the Negro," *Daily Record-Miner* (Juneau, AK), October 5, 1903, Readex; and "Race Doings," *Cleveland Gazette*, October 17, 1903, Readex.

48. Kenneth C. Barnes, *Journey of Hope: The Back-to-Africa Movement in Arkansas in the Late 1800s* (Chapel Hill: University of North Carolina Press, 2004), 2, 9–10, 12 (quote from 2).

49. Barnes, *Journey of Hope*, 2.

50. "Adventures of Leigh S. J. Hunt," *Sunday Leader* (Port Townsend, WA), November 8, 1903, University of Washington Libraries.

51. J. S. R. Duncan, *The Sudan: A Record of Achievement* (London: William Blackwood & Sons, 1952), 123; Gilbert Falkingham Clayton, *An Arabian Diary*, ed. Robert O. Collins (Berkeley: University of California Press, 1969), 88n13; Rand, *High Stakes*, 217.

52. "Critical Period: The Growing Estrangement Between the Races," *Freeman* (Indianapolis), June 11, 1904, Readex.

53. "Cotton Growing in Sudan," *Grey River Argus* (Greymouth, New Zealand), June 6, 1904, Papers Past.

54. Gaitskell, *Gezira*, 51; Duncan, *The Sudan*, 123; Mohamed A. Dawoud and Ahmed Allam, "Effect of New Nag Hammadi Barrage on Groundwater and Drainage Conditions and Suggestion of Mitigation Measures," *Water Resources Management* 18 (2004): 321.

55. "Cotton Growing in Sudan."

56. [Untitled], *Freeman* (Indianapolis), June 11, 1904, Readex.

57. Booker T. Washington to Leigh Hunt, June 3, 1904, in *The Booker T. Washington Papers*, vol. 7, 520–521 (quote from 521).

58. *The Booker T. Washington Papers*, vol. 7, 425nn3–5); Rand, *High Stakes*, 218.

59. Harlan, "Booker T. Washington and the White Man's Burden," 447. For letter dating he cites Washington to Cain Triplett, Poindexter Smith, and John P. Powell, Dec. 12, 1904 (294), Washington Papers, LC.

60. Washington to Cain Triplett, Poindexter Smith, and John P. Powell, Dec. 12, 1904 (294), Washington Papers, from Harlan, "Booker T. Washington and the White Man's Burden," 447.

61. See Tunde Adeleke, *Un-African Americans: Nineteenth-Century Black Nationalists and the Civilizing Mission* (Lexington: University of Kentucky Press, 1998).

62. Ann Stoler, *Race and the Education of Desire: Foucault's History of Sexuality and the Colonial Order of Things* (Durham: Duke University Press, 1995), 10–11.

63. Rand, *High Stakes*, 230 (quoting Cain Triplett to Booker T. Washington, January 15, 1905, Washington Papers, LC).

64. John Perry Powell to Booker T. Washington, March 23, 1907, from *The Booker T. Washington Papers*, vol. 9, *1906–8*, ed. Louis R. Harlan and Raymond W. Smock (Urbana: University of Illinois Press, 1980), 231.

65. Hunt to Washington, February 3, 1905, in *The Booker T. Washington Papers*, vol. 7, 425. See also Harlan, "Booker T. Washington and the White Man's Burden," 447–448, where Harlan cites a portion of the same letter and frames Hunt's letter as enthusiastic. While *The Booker T. Washington Papers*, vol. 7, positions this letter as being written in 1904 (on 425), I used Harlan's 1905 dating of the aforementioned (in Harlan, "Booker T. Washington and the White Man's Burden," 448n28) to substantiate that these and subsequent letters that *The Booker T. Washington Papers*, vol. 7, dates as 1904 were actually written in 1905.

66. *The Booker T. Washington Papers*, vol. 7, 425nn1–2); Rand, *High Stakes*, 230–231; *The Booker T. Washington Papers*, vol. 8, *1904–6*, ed. Louis R. Harlan and Raymond W. Smock (Urbana: University of Illinois Press, 1979), first note 1 on 289.

67. Rand, *High Stakes*, 231.

68. Booker T. Washington to Cain Washington Triplett, John Perry Powell, Poindexter Smith, Ocie Romeo Burns, and John Brown Twitty, May 23, 1905, from *The Booker T. Washington Papers*, vol. 8, 288.

69. "Field for Educated Negroes: The Success of Four Tuskegee Graduates," *Freeman*, May 20, 1905, Readex.

70. Description of this encounter taken from Rand, *High Stakes*, 187, which cites Clarkson to Jessie Hunt, June 18, 1903, Hunt Papers.

71. Rand, *High Stakes*, 234–236. The November 1905 dating is inferred from the placement of the Eckstein to Hunt letter (January 6, 1906) on p. 235; M. W. Daly, *Empire on the Nile: The Anglo-Egyptian Sudan, 1898–1934* (Cambridge: Cambridge University Press, 1986, 221; Clayton, *An Arabian Diary*, 88n13; Gaitskell, *Gezira*, 51–52.

72. Rand, *High Stakes*, 241 (quoting John P. Powell to Booker T. Washington, March 23, 1907, Washington Papers, LC).

73. John Perry Powell to Booker T. Washington, March 23, 1907, from *The Booker T. Washington Papers*, vol. 9, 232.

74. Rand, *High Stakes*, 214 (which quotes from John P. Powell to Booker T. Washington, March 23, 1907, Washington Papers, LC).

75. Rand, *High Stakes*, 242 (which quotes from J. B. Twitty to Washington, April 17, 1907, Washington Papers, LC).

76. "Educational Etchings," *Freeman*, May 25, 1907, Readex.

77. Rand, *High Stakes*, 242.

78. Milfred C. Fierce, "Selected Black American Leaders and Organizations and South Africa, 1900–1977: Some Notes," *Journal of Black Studies* 17, no. 3 (March 1987): 311.

79. Vinson, *The Americans Are Coming!*, 30.

80. Clayton, *An Arabian Diary*, 88n13; Harlan, "Booker T. Washington and the White Man's Burden," 448; Kramer, Lobban, and Fluehr-Lobban, *Historical Dictionary*, 4th ed., 177, 440; Duncan, *The Sudan*, 124.

81. Alden Young, *Transforming Sudan: Decolonisation, Economic Development and State Formation* (Cambridge: Cambridge University Press, 2018), 35.

82. *The Booker T. Washington Papers*, vol. 7, 404n1; Gagen, "Etna Farm Boy Became Global Tycoon"; Leigh Hunt, January 19, 1931, SAD 802/1/42–43 (for dating see Hunt, SAD 802/1/41).

83. Hunt, January 19, 1931, SAD 802/1/42–43.

84. Beckert, "From Tuskegee to Togo," 526.

85. Robins, *Cotton and Race across the Atlantic*, 159.

86. Robins, *Cotton and Race across the Atlantic*, 158.

87. Harlan, "Booker T. Washington and the White Man's Burden," 467.

88. Erhagbe, "African-Americans and the Defense of the African States," 61 (from Dagbovie, "Exploring a Century of Historical Scholarship," 248).

89. Marybeth Gasman and Roger L. Geiger, introduction to *Higher Education for African Americans before the Civil Rights Era, 1900–1964* (New Brunswick: Transaction Publishers, 2012), 4; "Andrew Brimmer Retires as Tuskegee University Board Chairman" *Diverse Issues in Higher Education*, October 21, 2010, https://diverseeducation.com/article/14298; Helen R. Houston, "Brimmer, Andrew Felton (1926–2012)," in *Encyclopedia of African American Business*, vol. 1, A–L, updated and rev. ed., ed. Jessie Carney Smith (Santa Barbara: ABC-CLIO, 2018), 133.

90. Patrick S. Washburn, *The African American Newspaper: Voice of Freedom* (Evanston: Northwestern University Press, 2006), 134, 257; Meriwether, *Proudly We Can Be Africans*, 4, 19.

2. Plain Imperialism

1. "Horace Cayton Dies Abroad," *New York Amsterdam News*, January 31, 1970, ProQuest Historical Newspapers; Andrew Billingsley, "Horace R. Cayton 1903–1970," *American Sociologist*

5, no. 4 (November 1970): 380–381; Robert Washington, "Horace Cayton: Reflections on an Unfulfilled Sociological Career," *American Sociologist* 28, no. 1 (Spring 1997): 57; and Horace R. Cayton, *Long Old Road: Back to Black Metropolis* (New York: Routledge, 2017), 17 (for entire visit see 17–21).

2. Washington, "Horace Cayton," 65.

3. Horace Cayton, "Sudan Key to Africa's Freedom: UN Wonders Problem of Area Which Gave First Slaves to U.S.," *Courier*, October 27, 1951, ProQuest Historical Newspapers.

4. Cayton, "Sudan Key to Africa's Freedom."

5. Michael A. Gomez, *Reversing Sail: A History of the African Diaspora*, 2nd ed. (Cambridge: Cambridge University Press, 2020), 70.

6. Andrew S. Natsios, *Sudan, South Sudan, and Darfur: What Everyone Needs to Know* (New York: Oxford University Press, 2012), 28, 35.

7. James H. Meriwether, *Proudly We Can Be Africans: Black Americans and Africa, 1935–1961* (Chapel Hill: University of North Carolina Press, 2002), 8; Gerald Horne, *The Rise and Fall of the Associated Negro Press: Claude Barnett's Pan-African News and the Jim Crow Paradox* (Urbana: University of Illinois Press, 2017), 16.

8. Adam Lee Cilli, "Robert L. Vann and the *Pittsburgh Courier* in the 1932 Presidential Election: An Analysis of Black Reformism in Interwar America," *Pennsylvania Magazine of History and Biography* 143, no. 2 (April 2019): 141.

9. Kellie Hogue, "Garveyism," in *The Oxford Encyclopedia of the Modern World* (Oxford University Press, 2008), Oxford Reference; Abdel Malek Auda, "Duse Mohamad Ali (1867–1945): A Forerunner of Pan-Africanism," *Égypte Contemporaine* 58, no. 328 (1967): 63, 66–67; Michael Niblett, "African Times and Orient Review," in *The Oxford Companion to Black British History*, ed. David Dabydeen, John Gilmore, and Cecily Jones (Oxford University Press, 2007), Oxford Reference; Hakim Adi and Marika Sherwood, *Pan-African History: Political Figures from Africa and the Diaspora* (New York: Taylor & Francis, 2003), 4.

10. Hogue, "Garveyism"; Keisha N. Blain, *Set the World on Fire: Black Nationalist Women and the Global Struggle for Freedom* (Philadelphia: University of Pennsylvania Press, 2018), 12, 16–17.

11. Hollis R. Lynch, *Black American Radicals and the Liberation of Africa: The Council on African Affairs, 1937–1955* (Ithaca: Africana Studies and Research Center, Cornell University, 1978), 17; Kevin Shillington, *History of Africa*, 4th ed. (London: Red Globe Press, 2019), 408–410.

12. Meriwether, *Proudly We Can Be Africans*, 4; Brenda Gayle Plummer, *Rising Wind: Black Americans and U.S. Foreign Affairs, 1935–1960* (Chapel Hill: University of North Carolina Press, 1996), 6; Wendy Theodore, "The Declining Appeal of Diasporic Connections: African American Organising for South Africa, Haiti and Rwanda," *Global Society* 22, no. 2 (2008): 302; Michael L. Krenn, *Black Diplomacy: African Americans and the State Department, 1945–69* (Armonk, NY: M.E. Sharpe, 1999), 3.

13. Joseph Fronczak, "Local People's Global Politics," *Diplomatic History* 39, no. 2 (April 2015): 245, 271 (quote from 245).

14. Blain, *Set the World on Fire*, 120, citing Tony Martin, *Amy Ashwood Garvey: Pan Africanist, Feminist and Mrs. Garvey Number 1* (Dover, MA: Majority Press, 2008), 143.

15. For more on Black women's internationalism, see Blain, *Set the World on Fire*; Keshia Blain and Tiffany M. Gill, eds., *To Turn the Whole World Over: Black Women and Internationalism* (Urbana: University of Illinois Press, 2019); and Cheryl Higashida, *Black Internationalist Feminism: Women Writers of the Black Left, 1945–1995* (Urbana: University of Illinois Press, 2011).

16. Imaobong D. Umoren, *Race Women Internationalists: Activist-Intellectuals and Global Freedom Struggles* (Berkeley: University of California Press, 2018), 46n77; Eslanda Goode Robeson, *African Journey* (New York: John Day, 1945), 13; Maureen Mahon, "Eslanda Goode Robeson's

African Journey: The Politics of Identification and Representation in the African Diaspora," *Souls: A Critical Journal of Black Politics, Culture and Society* 8, no. 3 (2006): 102; Robert Shaffer, "Out of the Shadows: The Political Writings of Eslanda Goode Robeson," *Pennsylvania History: A Journal of Mid-Atlantic Studies* 66, no. 1 (Winter 1999): 47–48.

17. Umoren, *Race Women Internationalists*, 46; and, for the quote, "Our Closeness to Africa through the Negro American," lecture, March 19, 1944, p. 4, box 10, Eslanda Robeson Papers, Moorland-Spingarn Research Center [hereafter MSRC].

18. Eslanda Goode Robeson, *African Journey* (1945; repr., Westport, CT: Greenwood Press, 1972), 146–147 (quote from 147).

19. Lynch, *Black American Radicals*, 7, 17–18, 21; Umoren, *Race Women Internationalists*, 51.

20. Yosa Wawa, "Background to the Southern Sudan," in *Southern Sudanese Pursuits of Self-Determination: Documents in Political History*, ed. Yosa Wawa (Kampala: Marianum Press, 2005), 11; Anders Breidlid, ed., *A Concise History of South Sudan* (Kampala: Fountain Publishers, 2010), 143, 148–149; Gino Barsella and Miguel Ángel Ayuso Guixot, "A List of Major Dates in the Modern History of the Sudan," Nairobi, 2, 624 266.009 AAV Brack II, Comboni Mission Library, Rome, 2; Douglas H. Johnson, *South Sudan: A New History for a New Nation* (Athens: Ohio University Press, 2016), 118–119.

21. Rashed el-Barawy, "Egypt and the Sudan," *India Quarterly* 7, no. 4 (October–December 1951): 356.

22. Egypt-Sudan, Collection of Documents (published by the Ministry of Foreign Affairs, Cairo, 1947), p. 62, from Barawy, "Egypt and the Sudan," 357.

23. Breidlid, *Concise History*, 147, 156–159; M. W. Daly and Øystein H. Rolandsen, *A History of South Sudan: From Slavery to Independence* (Cambridge: Cambridge University Press, 2016), 66; Barsell and Guixot, "List of Major Dates," 3.

24. "Biographical Note," in *A Guide to the Rogers, Joel Augustus Collection, 1883–1966*, Fisk University Archives, accessed July 13, 2023, https://www.fisk.edu/wp-content/uploads/2020/06/rogers-joela.collection1930-1968.pdf; J. A. Rogers, *Nature Knows No Color-Line: Research into the Negro Ancestry in the White Race*, 3rd ed. (St. Petersburg, FL: Helga M. Rogers, 1952), 244; Patrick S. Washburn, *The African American Newspaper: Voice of Freedom* (Evanston: Northwestern University Press, 2006), 134, 257.

25. J. A. Rogers, "Ruling Abyssinians Consider Themselves Jews and Not Negroes, Says J. A. Rogers," *Philadelphia Tribune*, January 15, 1931, ProQuest Historical Newspapers.

26. J. A. Rogers, "Rogers Says: One Drop of Arab Blood Can Make a Non-Arab, White or Black, an Arab," *Pittsburgh Courier*, October 11, 1947, ProQuest Historical Newspapers.

27. "Guide to the Percival L. Prattis Papers, 1916–1980 AIS.2007.01," University of Pittsburgh ULS Archives & Special Collections, accessed March 31, 2020, https://digital.library.pitt.edu/islandora/object/pitt%3AUS-PPiU-ais200701/viewer.

28. Percival L. Prattis, "The Horizon: Sudanese Are the People in Egypt Who Are Most Like American Negroes," *Pittsburgh Courier*, August 6, 1949, ProQuest Historical Newspapers.

29. Percival L. Prattis, "Horizon: Sudanese Are Foxy," *Pittsburgh Courier*, January 1, 1955, ProQuest Historical Newspapers.

30. Prattis, "Sudanese Are the People in Egypt."

31. Prattis, "Sudanese Are the People in Egypt."

32. Percival L. Prattis, "The Horizon: Egyptian Grab for Sudan Is Plain Imperialism of the White Ruling Class," *Courier*, October 27, 1951, ProQuest Historical Newspapers.

33. Percival L. Prattis, "The Horizon: American Negroes Should Be Concerned about What Is Happening in Egypt," *Courier*, November 17, 1951, ProQuest Historical Newspapers.

34. Nael Shama, "Egypt's Foreign Policy from Faruq to Mubarak," in *Routledge Handbook on Contemporary Egypt*, eds. Robert Springborg, Amr Adly, Anthony Gorman, Tamir Moustafa, Aisha

Saad, Naomi Sakr, and Sarah Smierciak (London: Routledge/Taylor & Francis Group, 2021), 43; Arthur Goldschmidt Jr., *Historical Dictionary of Egypt*, 4th ed. (Lanham, MD: Scarecrow Press, 2013), xv, 41; Soheir A. Morsy, "Beyond the Honorary 'White' Classification of Egyptians: Societal Identity in Historical Context," in *Race*, ed. Roger Sanjek and Steven Gregory (New Brunswick, NJ: Rutgers University Press, 1994), 177–178.

35. Shama, "Egypt's Foreign Policy," 45–46; Morsy, "Beyond the Honorary," 180; "The Rise and Fall of Pan-Arabism" (interview with Mohammad-Mahmoud Ould Mohamedou), Geneva Graduate Institute, January 31, 2019, https://www.graduateinstitute.ch/communications/news/rise-and-fall-pan-arabism.

36. Robert S. Kramer, Richard A. Lobban Jr., and Carolyn Fluehr-Lobban, *Historical Dictionary of the Sudan*, 4th ed. (Lanham, MD: Scarecrow Press, 2013), 66; Heather J. Sharkey, "Arab Identity and Ideology in Sudan: The Politics of Language, Ethnicity, and Race," *African Affairs* 107, no. 226 (Jan. 2008): 21–23.

37. Sharkey, "Arab Identity and Ideology," 21.

38. Amir H. Idris, *Conflict and Politics of Identity in Sudan* (Houndmills, Basingstoke, UK: Palgrave Macmillan, 2005), 48.

39. Sharkey, "Arab Identity and Ideology," 21; and Abdel Rahman Ali Taha [minister of education], "Introduction of the Teaching of Arabic into the Curriculum of Schools in the Southern Provinces," ca. late 1940s, p. 1, box ZD 29, folder ZD.17.3 [Summer 2012], South Sudan National Archives (hereafter SSNA).

40. Mohamed Omer Beshir, *Educational Development in the Sudan, 1898–1956* (Oxford: Clarendon Press, 1969), 152, from Oluwadare Aguda, "Arabism and Pan-Arabism in Sudanese Politics," *Journal of Modern African Studies* 11, no. 2 (June 1973): 184.

41. Philip Abbas, "Growth of Black Political Consciousness in Northern Sudan," *Africa Today* 20, no. 3 (1973): 32–33 ("the only true Sudanese" quote is from 32). Adam's name is at one point spelled "Ahdam" in Abbas's article but elsewhere "Adam" (32).

42. Jacob Rama Berman, *American Arabesque: Arabs and Islam in the 19th-Century Imaginary* (New York: New York University Press, 2012), 1.

43. Randa Kayyali, "US Census Classifications and Arab Americans: Contestations and Definitions of Identity Markers," *Journal of Ethnic and Migration Studies* 39, no. 8 (2013): 1301.

44. Hind Makki, "Why Are Some Black Africans Considered White Americans?," *Al Jazeera*, February 16, 2017, https://www.aljazeera.com/indepth/opinion/2017/02/black-africans-considered-white-americans-170215073123425.html; Khaled A. Beydoun, "Are Arabs White?," *Al Jazeera*, July 16, 2015, https://www.aljazeera.com/indepth/opinion/2015/07/arabs-white-150716110921150.html.

45. Michael Woods and Mary B. Woods, *The Tomb of Tutankhamen: Unearthing Ancient Worlds* (Minneapolis: Twenty-First Century Books, 2008), 9.

46. "King Tut-Ankh-Amen Was Part Negro, Declares Leader of the Colored Race, ca. 1922," W. E. B. Du Bois Papers (MS 312), Special Collections and University Archives, University of Massachusetts Amherst Libraries, http://credo.library.umass.edu/view/full/mums312-b167-i138.

47. Thabiti Asukile, "The Admiration and Complementary Africana Historical Scholarship of W. E. B. Du Bois and Joel Augustus Rogers," *Africology: The Journal of Pan African Studies* 11, no. 8 (June 2018): 195. Asukile cites W. E. B. Du Bois, *The World and Africa: An Inquiry into the Part Which Africa Has Played in World History* (New York: Viking Press, 1947), 99.

48. J. A. Rogers, *100 Amazing Facts about the Negro with Complete Proof: A Short Cut to the World History of the Negro* (Lebanon, NH: Wesleyan University Press, 1995), 12.

49. Wilson J. Moses, *Afrotopia: The Roots of African American Popular History* (Cambridge: Cambridge University Press, 1998), 24; Margaret Malamud, "Black Minerva: Antiquity

in Antebellum African American History," in *African Athena: African Agendas*, eds. Daniel Orrells, Gurminder K. Bhambra, and Tessa Roynon (New York: Oxford University Press, 2011), 88.

50. Prattis, "The Horizon: Egyptian Grab for Sudan."

51. George Padmore, "World Views: Sudanese Leaders," *Chicago Defender*, national ed., November 1, 1947, ProQuest Historical Newspapers.

52. George F. McCray, "Negroes to Gain Self Government," *Atlanta Daily World*, January 3, 1952, ProQuest Historical Newspapers.

53. Prattis, "Sudanese Are the People in Egypt."

54. Hugh Weston, "'Color Line Exists in Egypt, but It Is Very Thin'—Weston," *Pittsburgh Courier*, August 10, 1946, ProQuest Historical Newspapers.

55. Hugh Weston, "Hollywood's Racialism Portraying Negro in Bad Light before Eyes of the World," *Pittsburgh Courier*, June 22, 1946, ProQuest Historical Newspapers.

56. George S. Schuyler, "The World Today," *Pittsburgh Courier*; September 20, 1947, ProQuest Historical Newspapers.

57. "Egypt Seeks Rule of Sudan Riches," *Chicago Defender*, national ed., February 22, 1947, ProQuest Historical Newspapers.

58. W. E. B. Du Bois, "The Black Mahdi," ca. June 1947, 1, 4, W. E. B. Du Bois Papers, MS 312, Special Collections and University Archives, University of Massachusetts Amherst Libraries, http://credo.library.umass.edu/view/pageturn/mums312-b209-i083/#page/1/mode/1up.

59. Gabriel Warburg, *Islam, Sectarianism, and Politics in Sudan Since the Mahdiyya* (Madison: University of Wisconsin Press, 2003), 81, 83; M. W. Daly, *Imperial Sudan: The Anglo-Egyptian Condominium, 1934–1956* (Cambridge: Cambridge University Press, 1991), 6; Gabriel Warburg, *Islam, Nationalism and Communism in a Traditional Society: The Case of Sudan* (Totowa, NJ: Frank Cass, 1978), 38.

60. "Egypt-Arab Rule Threatens Sudan," *Chicago Defender*, national ed., February 15, 1947, ProQuest Historical Newspapers.

61. Padmore, "World Views."

62. Prattis, "The Horizon: Egyptian Grab for Sudan."

63. Shillington, *History of Africa*, 463.

64. Nicholas Grant, *Winning Our Freedoms Together: African Americans and Apartheid, 1945–1960* (Chapel Hill: University of North Carolina Press, 2017), 5–8.

65. Prattis, "The Horizon: American Negroes Should Be Concerned."

66. "Guide to the Percival L. Prattis Papers."

67. Weston, "Hollywood's Racialism."

68. Prattis, "Sudanese Are the People in Egypt."

69. Schuyler, "The World Today"; Prattis, "The Horizon: Egyptian Grab for Sudan"; "Another Nation Wants Independence," *Courier*, January 6, 1951, ProQuest Historical Newspapers.

70. Prattis, "The Horizon: Egyptian Grab for Sudan."

71. James T. Campbell, *Middle Passages: African American Journeys to Africa, 1787–2005* (New York: Penguin, 2006), 316.

72. Meriwether, *Proudly We Can Be Africans*, 162–163 (for direct quotes, in note 5 Meriwether cites "Hail Ghana!" editorial, *New York Amsterdam News*, March 9, 1957).

73. Patrick Manning, *The African Diaspora: A History through Culture* (New York: Columbia University Press, 2009), 268; Meriwether, *Proudly We Can Be Africans*, 285.

74. "U.S. Relations with Sudan," Bureau of African Affairs Bilateral Relations Fact Sheet, October 24, 2022, https://www.state.gov/u-s-relations-with-sudan.

3. An Atmosphere of Good Relations

1. Louis E. Martin, "Dope and Data," *Chicago Defender* (national ed.), January 14, 1956, ProQuest Historical Newspapers; Neil A. Lewis, "Louis E. Martin, 84, Aide to 3 Democratic Presidents," *New York Times*, January 30, 1997.

2. Martin, "Dope and Data."

3. For scholarship on Black American engagements with these countries in the mid-twentieth century, see Kevin K. Gaines, *American Africans in Ghana: Black Expatriates and the Civil Rights Era* (Chapel Hill: University of North Carolina Press, 2006); Ira Dworkin, *Congo Love Song: African American Culture and the Crisis of the Colonial State* (Chapel Hill: University of North Carolina Press, 2017); Nicholas Grant, *Winning Our Freedoms Together: African Americans and Apartheid, 1945–1960* (Chapel Hill: University of North Carolina Press, 2017).

4. Emily Jane O'Dell, "X Marks the Spot: Mapping Malcolm X's Encounters with Sudan," *Journal of Africana Religions* 3, no. 1 (2015): 96–115; "U.S. Congressman Diggs Visits Sudan," *Nile Mirror*, January 20, 1972, Center for Research Libraries; "Shirley Graham Du Bois," Harvard University Schlesinger Library, accessed May 11, 2020, https://www.radcliffe.harvard.edu/schlesinger-library/collection/shirley-graham-du-bois; Gerald Horne, *Race Woman: The Lives of Shirley Graham Du Bois* (New York: New York University Press, 2000), 155–156 (citing Shirley Graham Du Bois to Cedric Belfrage, December 22, 1958, box 2, Cedric Belfrage Papers; *Baltimore Afro-American*, February 3, 1959); Elton C. Fax, *Through Black Eyes: Journeys of a Black Artist to East Africa and Russia* (New York: Dodd, Mead, 1974), book jacket; Lisa E. Davenport, *Jazz Diplomacy: Promoting America in the Cold War Era* (Jackson: University Press of Mississippi, 2009), 57–58; "Lois Jones Pierre-Noel Art Professor Returns from Africa," *Chicago Daily Defender*, January 4, 1971, ProQuest Historical Newspapers; "Sets Precedent in Her Position with the AID," *New Journal and Guide*, June 20, 1964, ProQuest Historical Newspapers. In addition to this group was Edgar Draper (dean of New York City's Borough of Manhattan Community College), who served as deputy chief for the UN Institute of Public Administration in Khartoum. See "Dr. Draper Heads Manhattan College," *New York Amsterdam News*, June 6, 1970, ProQuest Historical Newspapers.

5. Veronica Nmoma, "The Shift in United States-Sudan Relations: A Troubled Relationship and the Need for Mutual Cooperation," *Journal of Conflict Studies* (Winter 2006): 49 (citing Donald Petterson, *Inside Sudan: Political Islam, Conflict and Catastrophe* (Boulder, CO: Westview, 1999), 9); Robert S. Kramer, Richard A. Lobban Jr., and Carolyn Fluehr-Lobban, *Historical Dictionary of the Sudan*, 4th ed. (Lanham, MD: Scarecrow Press, 2013), 440.

6. See "U.S. Agency for International Development," USA.gov, accessed May 11, 2020, https://www.usa.gov/federal-agencies/u-s-agency-for-international-development; and James Leonard Mack, *My Life, My Country, My World* (Pittsburgh: Dorrance Publishing, 2008), 58 (quote).

7. Kramer, Lobban, and Fluehr-Lobban, *Historical Dictionary of the Sudan*, 4th ed., 440; Anders Breidlid, Avelino Androga Said, and Astrid Kristine Breidlid, eds., *A Concise History of South Sudan*, rev. ed. (Kampala: Fountain Publishers, 2014), 200.

8. Deng D. Akol Ruay, *The Politics of Two Sudans: The South and the North, 1821–1969* (Uppsala: Nordic Africa Institute, 1994), 35.

9. Muddathir 'Abd Al-Rahim, "Arabism, Africanism, and Self-Identification in the Sudan," *Journal of Modern African Studies* 8, no. 2 (July 1970): 242n1 (citing his "The Development of British Policy in the Southern Sudan," in *Middle Eastern Studies* (London) 2, no. 3 [April 1966]).

10. Iris Seri-Hersch, "Sudan and the British Empire in the Era of Colonial Dismantlement (1946–1956): History Teaching in Comparative Perspective," in *The Road to the Two Sudans*, eds.

Souad T. Ali, Stephanie Beswick, Richard Lobban and Jay Spaulding (New Castle upon Tyne: Cambridge Scholars Publishing, 2014), 177.

11. Breidlid, Said, and Breidlid, *A Concise History of South Sudan*, rev. ed., 200.

12. Nmoma, "The Shift in United States-Sudan Relations," 50; Kramer, Lobban, and Fluehr-Lobban, *Historical Dictionary of the Sudan*, 4th ed., 441; Øystein H. Rolandsen, "A False Start: Between War and Peace in the Southern Sudan, 1956–62," *Journal of African History* 52, no. 1 (2011): 105; Mack, *My Life, My Country*, 58.

13. Nmoma, "The Shift in United States-Sudan Relations," 50.

14. Nmoma, "The Shift in United States-Sudan Relations," 50; Kramer, Lobban, and Fluehr-Lobban, *Historical Dictionary of the Sudan*, 4th ed., 441.

15. "Being Black in a 'Lily White' State Department," Terence Todman, Association for Diplomatic Studies and Training, interviewed by Michael Krenn, accessed December 8, 2022, Association for Diplomatic Studies and Training, https://adst.org/oral-history/fascinating-figures/being-black-in-a-lily-white-state-department.

16. Michael L. Krenn, *Black Diplomacy: African Americans and the State Department, 1945–69* (Armonk, NY: M. E. Sharpe, 1999), 7.

17. "Memorandum from the Deputy Under Secretary of State for Administration (Crockett) to the Assistant Secretary of State for African Affairs (Palmer)," May 9, 1966, document 72, Office of the Historian, Foreign Service Institute, US Department of State, https://history.state.gov/historicaldocuments/frus1964-68v33/d72.

18. Stephanie Storm, "Andrew Brimmer, 86, First Black on Fed," *New York Times*, October 12, 2012; "Biography of Andrew F. Brimmer" in "Description of Andrew Brimmer Papers," box 172, folder 12, Baker Library, Harvard [hereafter BL]); Helen R. Houston, "Brimmer, Andrew Felton (1926–2012)," in *Encyclopedia of African American Business*, vol. 1, A–L, updated and rev. ed., ed. Jessie Carney Smith (Santa Barbara: ABC-CLIO, 2018), 133; "Federal Reserve Bank Appointee Busy Scholar," *Jet*, March 24, 1966, 26.

19. Houston, "Brimmer, Andrew Felton (1926–2012)," 133; Storm, "Andrew Brimmer, 86."

20. Alan Holmes and Andrew Brimmer to Mr. Hayes, "Central Bank Mission to the Sudan," March 20, 1957, box 40, folder 2, Andrew Brimmer Papers, BL.

21. Magda Ismail Abdel Mohsin, "The Practice of Islamic Banking System in Sudan," *Journal of Economic Cooperation* 26, no. 4 (2005): 28; Alden Young, *Transforming Sudan: Decolonisation, Economic Development and State Formation* (Cambridge: Cambridge University Press, 2018), 141.

22. For more on the role the economic auspices of Sudan's early independence era, see Young, *Transforming Sudan*, and my review of that book, "Fragile States: Nation-Building in Sudan," *Books and Ideas*, October 25, 2018, https://booksandideas.net/Fragile-States-Nation-building-in-Sudan.html.

23. Storm, "Andrew Brimmer, 86."; "Biography of Andrew F. Brimmer."

24. "Robert Kitchens Addresses Morehouse Founders' Day," *Atlanta Daily World*, February 24, 1962, ProQuest Historical Newspapers; "Negro Heading U.S. Mission to Sudan," *Los Angeles Tribune*, April 18, 1958, Readex; "Sudan to Receive U. S. Financial Aid," *Atlanta Daily World*, April 17, 1958, ProQuest Historical Newspapers; "Name Robert Kitchen to Head Sudan Mission," *Jet*, April 17, 1958, 3.

25. "Negro Heading U.S. Mission to Sudan"; "Sudan to Receive U.S. Financial Aid."

26. "Name Robert Kitchen," 3.

27. "Robert Kitchens Addresses Morehouse Founders' Day"; "Martha Kitchen," *East Bay Times*, accessed May 13, 2020, https://www.legacy.com/obituaries/eastbaytimes/obituary.aspx?n=martha-kitchen&pid=142393844.

28. François M. Dickman, interview by Stanley Brooks, February 9, 2001, Foreign Affairs Oral History Collection, Association for Diplomatic Studies and Training (hereafter ADST), https://www.adst.org/OH%20TOCs/Dickman,%20Francois%20M.toc.pdf?_ga=2.174856737.283742220.1621951167-1474005595.1621951167, pp. 3, 5 (quote from 5).

29. Robert W. Kitchen Jr. to John W. Davis, April 26, 1958, box 168–8, folder 1, John W. Davis Papers, MSRC.

30. Madison Broadnax, interview by W. Haven North, September 18, 1998, ADST, https://adst.org/OH%20TOCs/Broadnax-Madison.pdf, pp. 1, 6 (quote from 6); "Says Americans Can Aid Newly Developed Nations," *Atlanta Daily World*, July 12, 1961, ProQuest Historical Newspapers.

31. Broadnax interview, 7; El Subki Mohamed El Gizouli, "Higher Education in the Sudan from Its Origins to 1966, with Special Reference to University Education" (PhD diss., Durham University, 1968), 206.

32. El Gizouli, "Higher Education," 125–126.

33. El Gizouli, "Higher Education," 206; Heather J. Sharkey, "Colonialism, Character, Building and the Culture of Nationalism in the Sudan, 1898," in *The Decolonization Reader*, ed. James D. Le Sueur (New York: Routledge, 2003), 218.

34. Broadnax interview, 8, 10.

35. Broadnax interview, 9.

36. Broadnax interview, 7, 12, 14 (first quote from 7, second from 14).

37. F. Dennis Conroy, "United States Economic Aid to Africa: 2. Aid Program in the Sudan," *African Studies Bulletin* 7, no. 1 (March 1964): 7–8; L. Berry and S. Geistfeld, *Eastern African Country Profiles: Sudan*, rev. ed. (Worcester, MA: Clark University International Development Program, 1983), 80.

38. Berry and Geistfeld, *Eastern African Country Profiles*, 80.

39. Robert W. Kitchen Jr. to John Davis, December 23, 1958, box 168–8, folder 1, John W. Davis Papers, MSRC.

40. Robert W. Kitchen Jr. to John Davis, May 11, 1959, box 168–8, folder 1, John W. Davis Papers, MSRC.

41. Robert W. Kitchen, Jr. to John Davis, July 1, 1959, box 168–8, folder 1, John W. Davis Papers, MSRC.

42. Simeon Booker, "Tape U.S.A.," *Jet*, September 3, 1959, 11; "Robert Kitchens Addresses Morehouse Founders' Day"; "Kitchen, Kuykendall May Be Ambassadors," *Jet*, March 10, 1960, 3; "Robert Kitchen Named to $18,900 U.S. Post," *New Journal and Guide*, November 16, 1963, ProQuest Historical Newspapers.

43. Vita Bite, *African-American Participation at the United Nations* (Congressional Research Service, Library of Congress, 1995), p. CRS-10, https://www.everycrsreport.com/files/19951020_95-1095_e85094c7801edf426015d7e5a4a296a386b7d269.pdf; "U.S. Relations with Sudan," U.S. Department of State, accessed January 27, 2023, https://www.state.gov/u-s-relations-with-sudan.

44. "To Sudan," *Courier*, July 15, 1961, African American Communities database, Atlanta History Center; "College Roundup," *New York Amsterdam News*, May 5, 1962, ProQuest Historical Newspapers; "A&T Prof. Back from Sudan Stay," *Pittsburgh Courier*, July 14, 1962, ProQuest Historical Newspapers.

45. "Printer Gets Post with State Dept," *New Journal and Guide*, June 29, 1963, ProQuest Historical Newspapers.

46. "Prominent Harlemites Equip African School," *New York Amsterdam News*, February 3, 1962, ProQuest Historical Newspapers.

47. For her being a Delta, see Jeanne L. Noble, national president to Arthur B. McCaw, October 9, 1962, box 1, Arthur B. McCaw Papers, Hoover Institution Archives (hereafter HIA). For other biographical material, see "Valaria Sarah Lee McCaw," Find A Grave, accessed April 25, 2020, https://www.findagrave.com/memorial/190442966/valaria-sarah-mccaw; "Arthur McCaw, 79, Who Served 2 Presidents," *Orlando Sentinel*, March 14, 1985, https://www.orlandosentinel.com/news/os-xpm-1985-05-14-0300080275-story.html.

48. "Blind Sudanese Remember Wife of Aid Official," *New Journal and Guide*, March 19, 1966, ProQuest Historical Newspapers.

49. "Blind See Beauty by Sculpting: Diplomat's Wife Starts Ceramics Class for Blind," *Pittsburgh Courier*, March 26, 1966, ProQuest Historical Newspapers.

50. Damion Thomas, "Goodwill Ambassadors: African American Athletes and U.S. Cultural Diplomacy, 1947–1968," in *African Americans in U.S. Foreign Policy: From the Era of Frederick Douglass to the Age of Obama*, ed. Linda Heywood, Allison Blakely, Charles Stith, and Joshua C. Yesnowitz (Urbana: University of Illinois Press, 2015), 129; Davenport, *Jazz Diplomacy*, 57–58 (in note 110, Davenport cites, in her broader explanation of Wilbur de Paris, G. Lewis Johns, ambassador, Tunis, to DOS [Department of State], FSD [Foreign Service Dispatch]-465, "Tunisian Tour of WDP Orchestra," May 9, 1957, 10). See also Kones, Tunis, to SOS, DOS Incom. [Department of State Incoming Telegram] 615, May 7, 1957, box 100, folder Wilbur De Paris, DF 032, 1955–1959. (DF stands for National Archives and Records Administration, Records of the Department of State, College Park, Maryland, RG-59, Decimal File 032, 1955–1959.)

51. John W. Davis to Robert Kitchen, June 2, 1958, box 168–8, folder 1, John W. Davis Papers, MSRC.

52. "Fla. Guild off on Tour of Africa," *New York Amsterdam News*, October 4, 1958, ProQuest Historical Newspapers.

53. See Anthony Tommasini, "Leonard de Paur Dies at 83; Lincoln Center Administrator," *New York Times*, November 11, 1998; and Mack, *My Life*, 64 (quote from Mack).

54. Mack, *My Life*, 1–2, 5–6 (quote from 5).

55. Mack, *My Life*, 45–46.

56. Mack, *My Life*, 53–54, 74 (quote from 54).

57. Mack, *My Life*, 62.

58. Mack, *My Life*, 63.

59. "L[angston] H[ughes] with others, Sudan," Beinecke Rare Book and Manuscript Library Digital Collections, accessed May 14, 2020, https://brbl-dl.library.yale.edu/vufind/Record/3724708; Mack, *My Life*, 63; and "Langston Hughes," American Academy of Poets, accessed May 14, 2020, https://poets.org/poet/langston-hughes; "The Morning News," Library of Congress, accessed November 3, 2022, https://www.loc.gov/item/sn95021307; "American Negro Poet Visits Khartoum," *Morning News*, May 1, 1966.

60. "American Negro Poet Visits Khartoum."

61. Mack, *My Life*, 63–64.

62. Mack, *My Life*, 64.

63. James T. Campbell, *Middle Passages: African American Journeys to Africa, 1787–2005* (New York: Penguin, 2006), xix.

64. Langston Hughes, "The Negro Speaks of Rivers," Poetry Foundation, accessed May 14, 2020, https://www.poetryfoundation.org/poems/44428/the-negro-speaks-of-rivers.

65. Mack, *My Life*, 64.

66. Elias Nyamell Wakson, "Islamism and Militarism in Sudanese Politics: Its Impact on Nation-Building," *Northeast African Studies*, New Series, 5, no. 2: 58–59 (quote from 59), 78.

67. Mack, *My Life*, 63–64 (quote from 64).

68. Mack, *My Life*, 64.

69. Scott Wilson, *Resting Places: The Burial Sites of More than 14,000 Famous Persons*, 3rd ed. (Jefferson, NC: McFarland, 2016), 359.

70. Paula Giddings, *In Search of Sisterhood: Delta Sigma Theta and the Challenge of the Black Sorority Movement* (New York: Perennial, 2002), 15.

71. "Tour of 45 members of Delta Sigma Theta Sorority to Africa and Europe," Department of State Airgram, No: CA-303, to Accra, Addis Ababa, Athens, Cairo, Dakar, Khartoum, Lagos, London, Monrovia, Nairobi, Rome (7/5/62), box, 1, Arthur B. McCaw Papers, HIA; "Deltas Tour of Africa," *New York Amsterdam News*, January 27, 1962, ProQuest Historical Newspapers; "Deltas' African Tour," *New York Amsterdam News*, May 5, 1962, ProQuest Historical Newspapers.

72. "African Tour with Deltas Begins July 26," *Pittsburgh Courier*, May 5, 1962, ProQuest Historical Newspapers.

73. Freddye Henderson to Arthur B. McCaw, July 18, 1962, box 1, Arthur B. McCaw Papers, HIA (quote is from this correspondence). For the biographical information on Henderson, see Tiffany M Gill, "How a Black Female Fashion Designer Laid the Groundwork for Ghana's 'Year of Return,'" *Washington Post*, January 10, 2020. For the information on Arthur McCaw, see "Biographical Data" and untitled document with biographical information (p. 3), box 1, Arthur B. McCaw Papers, HIA.

74. "Tour of 45 members of Delta Sigma Theta Sorority to Africa and Europe."

75. Arthur B. McCaw to Robert Johnson, box 1, Arthur B. McCaw Papers, HIA.

76. Arthur B. McCaw to Robert Johnson, box 1, Arthur B. McCaw Papers, HIA.

77. "World: Delta Tour," *Jet*, September 6, 1962, 39.

78. Jeanne L. Noble to Arthur B. McCaw, October 9, 1962, box 1, Arthur B. McCaw Papers, HIA.

79. "Christmas Greetings 1963—Happy New Year 1964—From the McCaw's" box 1, Arthur B. McCaw Papers, HIA.

80. See "Africans to Here [sic] What U.S. Women Think of Them through Tapes," *Chicago Daily Defender*, November 1, 1962, ProQuest; and "World: Delta Tour" *Jet*, September 6, 1962, 39.

4. The Great Divergence

1. Andrew Brimmer, January 1, 1957, correspondence in box 41, folder, 7, Andrew Brimmer Papers, BL.

2. Brimmer, March 3, 1957, box 41, folder, 7, p. 140, Andrew Brimmer Papers, BL.

3. Brimmer, "Dear Frank (copy of letter to Mr. Coombs, Mrs Karius, [Eoreign (*sic*) and Domestic Research Div.)," January 5, 1957, box 41, folder 7, Andrew Brimmer Papers, BL.

4. Tom W. Smith, "Changing Racial Labels: From 'Colored' to 'Negro' to 'Black' to 'African American,'" *Public Opinion Quarterly* 56, no. 4 (1992): 499; Jeffrey O. G. Ogbar, *Black Power: Radical Politics and African American Identity*, updated ed. (Baltimore: Johns Hopkins University Press, 2019), 1; Randolph Hohle, introduction to *Black Citizenship and Authenticity in the Civil Rights Movement* (New York: Routledge, 2013), 1–2 (quote from 2).

5. Sharon E. Hutchinson, *Nuer Dilemmas: Coping with Money, War, and the State* (Berkeley: University of California Press, 1996), 312.

6. Edward O. Erhagbe, "The Congressional Black Caucus and United States Policy toward Africa: 1971–1990," *Transafrican Journal of History* 24 (1995): 85; Shelly Leanne, "The Clinton Administration and Africa: Perspective of the Congressional Black Caucus and TransAfrica,"

Issue: A Journal of Opinion 26, no. 2 (1998): 17; Edward O. Erhagbe, "The American Negro Leadership Conference on Africa: A New African-American Voice for Africa in the United States, 1962–1970," Boston University African Studies Center Working Papers, 1991, 3; Wendy Theodore, "The Declining Appeal of Diasporic Connections: African American Organising for South Africa, Haiti and Rwanda," *Global Society* 22, no. 2 (2008): 304; Theodore E. Brown [American Negro Leadership Conference on Africa letterhead with Dorothy Height's name listed] letter, October 10, 1962, box 270, folder 15, Walter P. Reuther Papers, Wayne State University Archives of Labor & Urban Affairs.

7. Seth M. Markle, *A Motorcycle on the Run: Tanzania, Black Power, and the Uncertain Future of Pan-Africanism, 1964–1974* (East Lansing: Michigan State University Press, 2017), 6.

8. George M. Houser, "Meeting Africa's Challenge: The Story of the American Committee on Africa," *Issue: A Journal of Opinion* 6, no. 2/3 (Summer/Autumn 1976): 21 (quotes), 26.

9. Mitch Lerner, "Climbing off the Back Burner: Lyndon Johnson's Soft Power Approach to Africa," *Diplomacy and Statecraft* 22 (2011): 582; Hollis R. Lynch, *Black American Radicals and the Liberation of Africa: The Council on African Affairs, 1937–1955* (Ithaca: Africana Studies and Research Center, Cornell University, 1978), 11.

10. Theodore Brown, interview by Robert Martin, August 20, [1968?], Ralph Bunche Oral History Collection (#294), MSRC, 1, 5, 7 (quotes from 5 and 7).

11. Lerner, "Climbing off the Back Burner," 582.

12. James H. Meriwether, *Proudly We Can Be Africans: Black Americans and Africa, 1935–1961* (Chapel Hill: University of North Carolina Press, 2002), 5.

13. "End of the Affair," *Pittsburgh Courier*, January 7, 1956, ProQuest Historical Newspapers.

14. "'Sanafrica' to Bring out Negro's Place in History," *Daily Defender*, July 1, 1957, ProQuest Historical Newspapers. Other instances of Black newspapers framing early independent Sudan as Black: "Let's Get Acquainted," *Pittsburgh Courier*, March 10, 1956, ProQuest Historical Newspapers; and George S. Schuyler, "World Today," *Pittsburgh Courier*, August 2, 1958, ProQuest Historical Newspapers.

15. "New Republic of Sudan Offers Full Equality for All the Races," *New Journal and Guide*, February 16, 1957, ProQuest Historical Newspapers.

16. "Arab League Fast Facts," CNN, last modified March 31, 2023, https://www.cnn.com/2013/07/30/world/meast/arab-league-fast-facts/index.html.

17. Marguerite Cartwright, "World Backdrop: Sudan," *Pittsburgh Courier*, October 5, 1957, ProQuest Historical Newspapers.

18. Anders Breidlid, Avelino Androga Said, and Astrid Kristine Breidlid, eds., *A Concise History of South Sudan*, rev. ed. (Kampala: Fountain Publishers, 2014), 104–105; Andrew S. Natsios, *Sudan, South Sudan, and Darfur: What Everyone Needs to Know* (New York: Oxford University Press, 2012), 31; Robert O. Collins, "Slavery in the Sudan in History," *Slavery and Abolition* 20, no. 3 (1999): 76; UNESCO World Heritage Convention, "Deim Zubeir—Slave Route Site," accessed October 7, 2022, https://whc.unesco.org/en/tentativelists/6275.

19. "Slavery in the Sudan. Lazy and Happy Slaves—Cruelty of the Captors," *New York Globe*, June 2, 1883 [from *London News*], Readex.

20. "Making a World," *African Repository*, January 1, 1885, Readex.

21. "The Soudan: General Kitchener's Great Task Successfully Accomplished," *Colored American*, September 24, 1898, Readex.

22. "The Coming Mahdi: A More Notable Figure in Africa than Paul Kruger," *Wisconsin Weekly Advocate*, July 9, 1900 [reprinted from *New York News*], Readex.

23. Gabriel Warburg, "Ideological and Practical Considerations Regarding Slavery in the Mahdist State and the Anglo-Egyptian Sudan, 1881–1918," in *The Ideology of Slavery in Africa*, edited by Paul E. Lovejoy (Beverly Hills: Sage, 1981), 258.

24. Steven Serels, *Starvation and the State: Famine, Slavery, and Power in Sudan, 1883–1956* (New York: Palgrave Macmillan, 2013), xx; Collins, "Slavery in the Sudan in History," 81.

25. J. A. Rogers, "Rambling Ruminations: Slavery Still Exists," *New York Amsterdam News*, July 9, 1930, ProQuest Historical Newspapers.

26. J. A. Rogers, "Abyssinians Charged with Slave Raids," *Philadelphia Tribune*, September 29, 1932, ProQuest Historical Newspapers.

27. "Slave Traffic Rampant in Africa," *Pittsburgh Courier*, January 11, 1930, ProQuest Historical Newspapers.

28. Collins, "Slavery in the Sudan in History," 81.

29. "Sudan Revolts Parallels Civil War," *Atlanta Daily World*, September 16, 1955, ProQuest Historical Newspapers.

30. George S. Schuyler, "Views and Reviews," *Pittsburgh Courier*, December 12, 1959, ProQuest.

31. Chimamanda Adichie, "The Danger of a Single Story," TedTalk (2009), https://www.classacthr73.org/resources/Documents/Event%20Materials/Chimamanda%20Adichie%20The%20Danger%20of%20a%20Single%20Story.pdf.; and "The Danger of a Single Story," TED, accessed January 27, 2023, https://www.ted.com/talks/chimamanda_ngozi_adichie_the_danger_of_a_single_story?language=en.

32. Natsios, *Sudan, South Sudan, and Darfur*, 44–45 (quote from 45).

33. Natsios, *Sudan, South Sudan, and Darfur*, 45; William K. DuVal to editor of the *New York Times*, August 25, 1965, box 1, folder 10, United Presbyterian Church in the U.S.A. Commission on Ecumenical Mission and Relations Office of the General Secretary Records, Presbyterian Historical Society Archives (hereafter PHS).

34. "Sudan Is Battleground in Negro-Arab Dispute," *Chicago Daily Defender*, December 8, 1964, ProQuest Historical Newspapers.

35. "Negroes, Arabs Clash in Sudan," *Chicago Daily Defender*, December 9, 1964, ProQuest Historical Newspapers.

36. "Trouble in Sudan," *Chicago Daily Defender*, December 10, 1964, ProQuest Historical Newspapers.

37. "Claims Sudanese Neither Arab or Negro, but Fusion of Both," *Chicago Defender*, national ed., December 26, 1964, ProQuest Historical Newspapers. That it was a Negro Press International piece is inferred from Chatwood Hall, "Behind the Headlines," *Chicago Daily Defender*, December 28, 1964, ProQuest Historical Newspapers.

38. University of Chicago Library, finding aid for Homer Smith papers, accessed July 21, 2023, https://bmrc.lib.uchicago.edu/portal/view/?id=BMRC.HARSH.SMITH_HOMER.xml.

39. Hall, "Behind the Headlines."

40. Edward E. Curtis IV and Sylvester A. Johnson, "Bayyinah Sharrieff: African American Traveler, University of Khartoum Student, National of Islam Leader," *Journal of Africana Religions* 5, no. 1 (2017): 72; "An Open Letter to Tuskegee Students: Use Education to Help Your Own People," *Muhammad Speaks*, February 23, 1968, 20–21 (from Curtis and Johnson, "Sharrieff," 131); "Reappraisal of Old Habits Follows Musical Party at Sundanese University," *Muhammad Speaks*, June 10, 1967, 11 (from Curtis and Johnson, "Sharrieff," 80); "How Muslims in Sudan View Christians," *Muhammad Speaks*, June 2, 1967, 11, 19 (from Curtis and Johnson, "Sharrieff," 78; quote taken from here); and "Life in Girls Hostel at University of Khartoum," *Muhammad Speaks*, December 5, 1967, 19–20 (from Curtis and Johnson, "Sharrieff," 114).

41. "Life in Girls Hostel at University of Khartoum."

42. See Curtis and Johnson, "Sharrieff," 73; and "Life in Girls Hostel at University of Khartoum" (second quote is from Curtis and Johnson, "Sharrieff," 115).

43. "How Muslims in Sudan View Christians," *Muhammad Speaks*, June 2, 1967, 11, 19 (from Curtis and Johnson, "Sharrieff," 79 [first quote]); and "An Open Letter to Tuskegee Students: Use Education to Help Your Own People," *Muhammad Speaks*, February 23, 1968, 20–21 (from Curtis and Johnson, "Sharrieff," 132).

44. "Elton C. Fax Papers, 1930–1974," New York Public Library Archives and Manuscripts, accessed June 10, 2020, http://archives.nypl.org/scm/20719; Elton C. Fax, *Through Black Eyes: Journeys of a Black Artist to East Africa and Russia* (New York: Dodd, Mead, 1974), inside book jacket.

45. "Negro American [sic] Artist to Visit Sudan," *Morning News* (Khartoum), March 17, 1964, 3.

46. Fax, *Through Black Eyes*, 35–36 (quotes from 36).

47. Fax, *Through Black Eyes*, 36.

48. "National Security Council Report," NSC 5719/1, Office of the Historian, Foreign Relations of the United States, 1955–1957, Africa, vol. 18, accessed December 16, 2022, https://history.state.gov/historicaldocuments/frus1955-57v18/d24.

49. "Memorandum from the Secretary of State's Special Assistant (Holmes) to Secretary of State Dulles," February 6, 1958, Office of the Historian, Foreign Relations of the United States, 1958–1960, Africa, vol. 14, accessed December 16, 2022, https://history.state.gov/historicaldocuments/frus1958-60v14/d1.

50. See, for example, "Second Draft: For Presentation to Africa Cttee, July 25th, 1944. Proposed Developments of C.M.S. Work in the Gordon Memorial Mission of the Southern Sudan," 664/9/11, SAD; "From the Right Revered Oliver C. Allison: As from C.M.S. Juba, 23rd January, 1949," *Southern Sudan Mail Bag*, no. 10 (February 1949), 15; and N. E. Ainley and M.C. Warburton, "Education of Women and Girls in the Area Occupied by the Church Missionary Society in the Southern Sudan: Report of the Commission Appointed by the Sudan Government and the Church Missionary Society, March 1939" (April 15, 1939), CMS/G/Y/S2 (1–114/4), Church Missionary Society Archives, Birmingham University (hereafter CMS).

51. Fax, *Through Black Eyes*, 37.

52. Fax, *Through Black Eyes*, 37. Omar's USIS connection is gleaned from letter by James H. Robinson to Ismail El Azahry, December 13, 1965, box 63, folder "ALP-Sudan-Correspondence, etc., 1965–1967, 1978 Miscellaneous Item 63/28," Operation Crossroads Africa collection, Amistad Research Center (hereafter ARC), Tulane University, New Orleans.

53. Fax, *Through Black Eyes*, 42.

54. Fax, *Through Black Eyes*, 42, 45–46.

55. Fax, *Through Black Eyes*, 46.

56. Vijay Prashad, *The Darker Nations: A Biography of the Short-Lived Third World* (New Delhi: LeftWord Books, 2007), 49; Nic Cheeseman, Eloïse Bertrand, and Sa'eed Husaini, "Bandung Conference," in *A Dictionary of African Politics* (Oxford University Press, 2019), Oxford Reference.

57. Jalāl Hāshim, *To Be or Not to Be: Sudan at Crossroads, A Pan-African Perspective* (Dar es Salaam: Mkuki Na Nyota, 2019), 85.

58. Hāshim, *To Be or Not to Be*, 86, 87.

59. Joseph Lagu, *Sudan: Odyssey through a State: From Hope to Ruin* (Omdurman: MOB Center for Sudanese Studies, Omdurman Ahlia University, 2006), 74.

60. "The Church in the World," *Tablet* (London), September 18, 1965, 1045, A/96/8/47, Comboni Mission Archive (hereafter ACR).

61. For the information on the 1967 summit, see Richard A. Lobban Jr., Robert S. Kramer, and Carolyn Fluehr-Lobban, *Historical Dictionary of the Sudan*, 3rd ed. (Lanham, MD: Scarecrow Press, 2002), 157; and David W. Lesch, *The Arab-Israeli Conflict: A History* (New York: Oxford University Press, 2008), 215.

62. "Brief Report on the Life of the S. Refugees Bordering North-East Congo and North-West Uganda, 1971, p. 1, ACR.A/98/4/11, ACR; Natsios, *Sudan South Sudan, and Darfur*, 47; Hāshim, *To Be or Not to Be*, 87.

63. "Feed South Sudan Victims of Hostile Arab Majority," *Pittsburgh Courier*, July 30, 1966, ProQuest Historical Newspapers.

64. "Arabs," *New York Amsterdam News*, November 2, 1968, ProQuest Historical Newspapers.

65. "Black Americans Picket for Southern Sudanese," *New York Amsterdam News*, January 22, 1972, ProQuest Historical Newspapers.

66. "Sudan v. Christians," *Time*, February 1, 1963, https://content.time.com/time/subscriber/article/0,33009,829787,00.html.

67. Lawrence Fellows, "The Unknown War in the Sudan," *New York Times*, September 22, 1968, ProQuest Historical Newspapers; C. C. Miniclier, "Death Toll Placed at 500,000 in Sudan's Little-Noticed War," *Washington Post*, August 7, 1969, ProQuest Historical Newspapers; "Sudan Trying to Surmount Poverty, War," *Los Angeles Times*, January 11, 1970, ProQuest.

68. "Gaza: Why Are Israel and the Palestinians Fighting over Gaza?" BBC, February 20, 2015, https://www.bbc.co.uk/newsround/20436092; "The Arab-Israeli War of 1948," Office of the Historian, US Department of State, accessed June 16, 2020, https://history.state.gov/milestones/1945-1952/arab-israeli-war; Joel Beinin and Lisa Hajjar, *Palestine, Israel, and the Arab-Israeli Conflict: A Primer* (Washington, DC: Middle East Research and Information Project, 2014), https://mcrip.org/palestine-israel-primer; "Israel Profile—Timeline," BBC, April 9, 2019, https://www.bbc.com/news/world-middle-east-29123668.

69. Beinin and Hajjar, "Palestine, Israel, and the Arab-Israeli Conflict"; "Israel Profile—Timeline"; "Gaza: Why Are Israel and the Palestinians Fighting over Gaza?"

70. Yossi Alpher, *Periphery: Israel's Search for Middle East Allies* (Lanham, MD: Rowman and Littlefield, 2015), 30; Lobban, Kramer, and Fluehr-Lobban, *Historical Dictionary of the Sudan*, 3rd ed., xlvi, 27–28, 157; Lesch, *The Arab-Israeli Conflict*, 215.

71. Alpher, *Periphery*, 35–36 (and 34 for further information on Israeli motivations); Joel Peters, *Israel and Africa: The Problematic Relationship* (London: British Academic Press, 1992), 9.

72. Alex Lubin, "Locating Palestine in pre-1948 Black Internationalism," *Souls: A Critical Journal of Black Politics, Culture and Society* 9, no. 2 (2007): 97; Brenda Gayle Plummer, *In Search of Power: African Americans in the Age of Decolonization, 1956–1974* (New York: Cambridge University Press, 2013), 45, 297; Salim Yaqub, "'Our Declaration of Independence': African Americans, Arab Americans, and the Arab-Israeli Conflict, 1967–1979," *Mashriq and Majhar* 3, no. 1 (2015): 12–14.

73. "Whitney M. Young, Jr.," National Park Service, accessed June 11, 2020, https://www.nps.gov/people/whitney-young-jr.htm.

74. Whitney M. Young Jr., "To Be Equal," *Milwaukee Star*, September 21, 1968, Readex.

75. "Get Israeli Arms," *Philadelphia Tribune*, June 30, 1970, ProQuest Historical Newspapers.

76. Veronica Johnson, "Sudan," *New York Amsterdam News*, March 14, 1970, ProQuest Historical Newspapers.

77. S. Norman Grouse, "Arabs, Jews, Us," *New York Amsterdam News*, March 14, 1970, ProQuest Historical Newspapers.

78. Stephen E. Appell, "Arabs-Israeli," *New York Amsterdam News*, August 22, 1970, ProQuest Historical Newspapers.

79. Richard Levinson, "Pulse of New York's Public: Palestinians and Blacks," *New York Amsterdam News*, October 3, 1970, ProQuest Historical Newspapers.

80. James R. Lawson, "Planes to Israel?," *New York Amsterdam News*, July 11, 1970, ProQuest Historical Newspapers.

81. Harold S. Rogers, "Imperialism in Africa," *Black Scholar* 3, no. 5 (January 1972): 42.

82. Rogers, "Imperialism in Africa," 41.
83. "Race War in the Sudan: Big White Lie," *SOBU Newsletter*, May 1, 1971, African American Periodicals; and Ibram H. Rogers, "From Black to African: Identity Shifts and Pan-African Activism in the Black Campus Movement, 1965–1972," in *Historical and Contemporary Pan-Africanism and the Quest for African Renaissance*, edited by Njoki Wane and Francis Adyanga Akena (Newcastle upon Tyne: Cambridge Scholars Press, 2019), 32–33.
84. "Race War in the Sudan"; and Robert S. Kramer, Richard A. Lobban Jr., and Carolyn Fluehr-Lobban, *Historical Dictionary of the Sudan*, 4th ed. (Lanham, MD: Scarecrow Press, 2013), 78.
85. "Race War in the Sudan."
86. "Race War in the Sudan."
87. Harold D. Nelson, Margarita Dobert, Gordon C. McDonald, James McLaughlin, Barbara J. Marvin, and Philip W. Moeller, *Area Handbook for the Democratic Republic of Sudan* (Washington, DC: US Government Printing Office, 1973), 214; Kwame Essien and Toyin Falola, *Culture and Customs of Sudan* (Westport, CT: Greenwood Press, 2009), 95; William A. Rugh, *Arab Mass Media: Newspapers, Radio, and Television in Arab Politics* (Westport, CT: Praeger, 2004), 53.
88. "From the Arabic Press," *Morning News* (Khartoum), July 27, 1967.

5. Call to Brotherhood

1. Fiza Pirani, "Who Is Louis Farrakhan? 10 Things to Know about the Nation of Islam Leader, Black Activist," *Atlanta Journal Constitution*, October 18, 2018, https://www.ajc.com/news/national/who-louis-farrakhan-things-know-about-the-nation-islam-leader-black-activist/1zUaxjihBLiqOKso5h262H; Louis Farrakhan and Henry Louis Gates Jr., "Farrakhan Speaks," *Transition* 70 (1996): 140, 142; "What's Next for the Nation of Islam?," National Public Radio, February 26, 2007, https://www.npr.org/templates/story/story.php?storyId=7601345; "Louis Farrakhan Fast Facts," CNN, June 19, 2020, https://www.cnn.com/2013/05/24/us/louis-farrakhan-fast-facts/index.html.
2. S. Craig Watkins, "Framing Protest: News Media Frames of the Million Man March," *Critical Studies in Media Communication* 18, no. 1 (2001): 85; Tim J. Brown and Rita L. Rahoi-Gilchrest, "Postmodern Personas in Combat: The NAACP and the Reverend Benjamin Chavis," *Howard Journal of Communication* 10, no. 1 (1999): 30.
3. Maize Woodford, "A Chronology: Farrakhan's 'World Friendship Tour' to Africa and the Middle East: January–February 1996," *Black Scholar* 26, nos. 3–4 (1996): 35, 37; Steven A. Holmes, "Farrakhan's Angry World Tour Brings Harsh Criticism at Home," *New York Times*, February 22, 1996, ProQuest.
4. Noah Salomon, "Religion after the State: Secular Soteriologies at the Birth of South Sudan," *Journal of Law and Religion* 29, no. 3 (2014): 450–452, 457; Allen D. Hertzke, *Freeing God's Children: The Unlikely Global Alliance for Global Human Rights* (Lanham, MD: Rowman & Littlefield, 2004), 239, 242; John Ashworth and Maura Ryan, "'One Nation from Every Tribe, Tongue, and People': The Church and Strategic Peacebuilding in South Sudan," *Journal of Catholic Social Thought* 10 (2013): 48.
5. Steven A. Holmes, "Slavery Is an Issue Again as U.S. Looks to Sudan," *New York Times*, March 24, 1996, ProQuest.
6. Amal Hassan Fadlalla, *Branding Humanity: Competing Narratives of Rights, Violence, and Global Citizenship* (Stanford: Stanford University Press, 2018), 35.

7. Fadlalla, *Branding Humanity*; Hertzke, *Freeing God's Children*; Melani McAlister, *The Kingdom of God Has No Borders: A Global History of American Evangelicals* (New York: Oxford University Press, 2018).

8. "About Us," *Final Call*, 2019, http://www.finalcall.com/artman/publish/aboutus/aboutus.shtml; Farrakhan and Gates, "Farrakhan Speaks," 142; Lawrence H. Mamiya, "From Black Muslim to Bilalian: The Evolution of a Movement," *Journal for the Scientific Study of Religion* 21, no. 2 (June 1982): 141; Martha F. Lee, *The Nation of Islam: An American Millenarian Movement* (Syracuse: Syracuse University Press, 1996), 78.

9. Dawn-Marie Gibson, *A History of the Nation of Islam: Race, Islam, and the Quest for Freedom* (Santa Barbara: Praeger, 2012), 1, 2, 11; Edward E. Curtis IV, *Muslims in America: A Short History* (New York: Oxford University Press, 2009), 119; Zafar Ishaq Ansari, "Islam among African-Americans," in *Muslims' Place in the American Public Square: Hope, Fears, and Aspirations*, edited by Zahid H. Bukhari, Sulayman S. Nyang, Mumtaz Ahmad, and John L. Esposito (Walnut Creek, CA: AltaMira Press, 2004), 235.

10. Patrick D. Bowen, "Satti Majid: A Sudanese Founder of American Islam," *Journal of Africana Religions* 1, no. 2 (2013): 194–195, 200–201; Sally Howell, *Old Islam in Detroit: Rediscovering the Muslim American Past* (New York: Oxford University Press, 2014), 37; Rogaia Mustafa Abusharif, *Wanderings: Sudanese Migrants and Exiles in North America* (Ithaca: Cornell University Press, 2002), 3, 22–23.

11. Howell, *Old Islam in Detroit*, 83; José Vittorio Pimienta-Bey, "Some 'Myths' of the Moorish Science Temple: An Afrocentric Historical Analysis" (PhD diss., Temple University, 1995), iv; Herbert Berg, "Mythmaking in the African American Muslim Context: The Moorish Science Temple, the Nation of Islam, and the American Society of Muslims," *Journal of the American Academy of Religion* 73, no. 3 (September 2005): 686, 689–690 (quote from 686).

12. Howell, *Old Islam in Detroit*, 83–84 ("errors" from 83); Bowen, "Satti Majid," 197.

13. Michael A. Gomez, *Reversing Sail: A History of the African Diaspora* (New York: Cambridge University Press, 2005), 174–175; Ansari, "Islam among African-Americans," 237; E. U. Essian-Udom, *Black Nationalism: A Search for an Identity in America* (Chicago: University of Chicago Press, 1962), 125–126.

14. Ansari, "Islam among African-Americans," 243; C. Riches and J. Palmowski, "Civil Rights Movement," in *A Dictionary of Contemporary World History*, 4th ed. (Oxford University Press, 2016), Oxford Reference; Essian-Udom, *Black Nationalism*, 321–322 (quote).

15. Robin D. G. Kelley, "Malcolm X," in *The Oxford Companion to United States History*, ed. Paul S. Boyer (Oxford University Press, 2001), Oxford Reference; Dennis Wainstock, *Malcolm X, African American Revolutionary* (Jefferson, NC: McFarland, 2009), 49–50; Emily O'Dell, "Following in the Footsteps of Malcolm X," *HuffPost*, last updated December 6, 2017, https://www.huffingtonpost.com/emily-odell/following-in-the-footstep_3_b_6434534.html; Emily Jane O'Dell, "X Marks the Spot: Mapping Malcolm X's Encounters with Sudan," *Journal of Africana Religions* 3, no. 1 (2015): 96–97 (quotes from 97).

16. O'Dell, "X Marks the Spot," 102, 104, 107.

17. Gutbi Mahdi Ahmed, "Muslim Organizations in the United States," in *The Muslims of America*, ed. Yvonne Yazbeck Haddad (New York: Oxford University Press, 1991), 21; Mattias Gardell, *In the Name of Elijah Muhammad: Louis Farrakhan and The Nation of Islam* (Durham: Duke University Press, 1996), 226; Ansari, "Islam among African-Americans," 250; Wilson J. Moses, *Black Messiahs and Uncle Toms: Social and Literary Manipulations of a Religious Myth*, rev. ed. (University Park: Pennsylvania State University Press, 1994), x, 191 (quotes from 191).

18. Martina Könighofer, *The New Ship of Zion: Dynamic Diaspora Dimensions of the African Hebrew Israelites of Jerusalem* (Piscataway, NJ: Transaction, 2008), 117; Michael Muhammad

Knight, *Metaphysical Africa: Truth and Blackness in the Ansaru Allah Community* (University Park: Pennsylvania State University Press, 2020), 29.

19. Knight, *Metaphysical Africa*, 60.

20. Allen D. Hertzke, "African American Churches and U.S. Policy in Sudan," *Review of Faith and International Affairs* 6, no. 1 (2008): 19; Robert O. Collins, "Civil Wars in the Sudan," *History Compass* 5, no. 6 (2007): 1783–1784; Carolyn Fluehr-Lobban, "Islamization in Sudan: A Critical Assessment," *Middle East Journal* 44, no. 4 (1990): 619–620; John O. Voll, "The Sudan after Nimeiry," *Current History* 85, no. 511 (1986): 214.

21. Andrew S. Natsios, *Sudan, South Sudan, and Darfur: What Everyone Needs to Know* (New York: Oxford University Press, 2012), xxvi.

22. Amir Idris, "Slavery, Colonialism, and Political Violence: The Case of South Sudan," in *Sudan's Killing Fields: Political Violence and Fragmentation*, ed. Laura N. Beny and Sondra Hale (Trenton, NJ: Red Sea Press, 2015), 71; Robert S. Kramer, Richard A. Lobban Jr., and Carolyn Fluehr-Lobban, *Historical Dictionary of the Sudan*, 4th ed. (Lanham, MD: Scarecrow Press, 2013), 392.

23. Clarence Page, "How Can We Still Ignore Slavery in the Sudan?," *Chicago Tribune*, June 23, 1996, https://www.chicagotribune.com/news/ct-xpm-1996-06-23-9606230177-story.html.

24. Holmes, "Slavery Is an Issue Again."

25. Hertzke, *Freeing God's Children*, 242.

26. Collins, "Civil Wars in the Sudan," 1778, 1791; Natsios, *Sudan, South Sudan, and Darfur*, xxvii; Kramer, Lobban, and Fluehr-Lobban, *Historical Dictionary of the Sudan*, 4th ed., liii–lv, lxiii; Hertzke, "African American Churches," 19–20.

27. Fadlalla, *Branding Humanity*, 3, 17.

28. Hertzke, "African American Churches," 21; Fadlalla, *Branding Humanity*, 32.

29. Hertzke, "African American Churches," 21; Fadlalla, *Branding Humanity*, 30 (quote).

30. "The Abolitionist Black Clergy," *Washington Times*, July 3, 2000, https://www.washingtontimes.com/news/2000/jul/3/20000703-011710-8248r.

31. Kim Lawton, "Black Churches Taking Lead on Pressing Sudan Issue," Religion News Service, August 23, 2005, https://religionnews.com/2005/08/23/black-churches-taking-lead-on-pressing-sudan-issue; Hertzke, "African American Churches," 22–23; Peter Brown, "Joe Madison Witnesses the Horror of Slavery in Sudan," *Crisis*, November–December 2000, 27; Richard Crockett, *Sudan: The Failure and Division of an African State*, 2nd ed. (New Haven: Yale University Press, 2016), 152, 154; Kimberly Davis, "The Truth about Slavery in Sudan," *Ebony*, August 2001, 37; Fadlalla, *Branding Humanity*, 33; "2 Goats Can Free a Slave in Sudan," *New York Times*), June 29, 2001, ProQuest.

32. Crockett, *Sudan*, 153.

33. Fadlalla, *Branding Humanity*, 33.

34. Alice Bullard, "De la colonisation à la mondialisation. Les vicissitudes de l'esclavage en Mauritanie," in "Esclavage moderne ou modernité de l'esclavage?," special issue, *Cahiers d'Études Africaines* 45 (2005): 756; Walid Phares, *The Coming Revolution: Struggle for Freedom in the Middle East* (New York: Threshold Editions, 2010), 251; Charles Jacobs, "Farrakhan's Secret Relationship," *Daily Californian*, March 16, 2012, https://www.dailycal.org/2012/03/16/farrakhans-secret-relationship; Samuel Cotton, *Silent Terror: A Journey into Contemporary Slavery* (New York: Harlem River Press), vii, 2.

35. Bullard, "De la colonisation à la mondialisation," 756; Cotton, *Silent Terror*, 61–62.

36. Cotton, *Silent Terror*, 62–63 (the press release Cotton reproduces is titled "One More Big Lie: America Accuses Libya of Enslaving Black People," March 24, 1995).

37. Cotton, *Silent Terror*, 71.

38. Cotton, *Silent Terror*, 63.

39. Clarence Page, "Black on Black Crime," *Chicago Tribune*, May 3, 1995, https://www.chicagotribune.com/news/ct-xpm-1995-05-03-9505030387-story.html.

40. McAlister, *The Kingdom of God Has No Borders*, 184 (quote); Judy Rakowsky, "Lawsuits Dropped, but Battles over Boston Mosque Continue," *Forward*, June 27, 2007, https://forward.com/news/11052/lawsuits-dropped-but-battles-over-boston-mosque-c-00063. McAlister, *The Kingdom of God Has No Borders*, 184n38, cites Sam Dillon, "Columbia to Check Reports of Anti-Jewish Harassment," *New York Times*, October 29, 2004, N. R. Kleinfield, "Mideast Tensions Are Getting Personal on Campus at Columbia," *New York Times*, January 18, 2005, and Karen Arenson, "Panel's Report on Faculty at Columbia Spurs Debate," *New York Times*, April 1, 2005.

41. Rakowski, "Lawsuits Dropped"; and "About," *Forward*, accessed September 20, 2022, https://forward.com/about-us.

42. JTA, "Once 'Combative' Pro-Israel Group Joins Hillel International," *Times of Israel*, August 25, 2017, https://www.timesofisrael.com/once-combative-pro-israel-group-joins-hillel-international.

43. Saeed Shabazz, "In Harlem, a Discussion on the Sudan," *Final Call*, last updated November 23, 2004, http://www.finalcall.com/artman/publish/National_News_2/In_Harlem_a_discussion_on_the_Sudan_1636.shtml.

44. Shabazz, "In Harlem."

45. Page, "How Can We Still Ignore Slavery in the Sudan?"; Tony Norman, "The Rev. Al Sharpton Has Begun Opening His Mind," *Pittsburgh Post-Gazette*, April 13, 2001, http://old.post-gazette.com/columnists/20010413tony.asp; Holmes, "Slavery Is an Issue Again."

46. Gilbert A. Lewthwaite, "'Verify' Sudan Slave reports, Farrakhan Urges; Nation of Islam Leader Condemns Slavery," *Baltimore Sun*, July 17, 1996, https://www.baltimoresun.com/news/bs-xpm-1996-07-17-1996199064-story.html (quoting *Final Call*).

47. Louis Farrakhan, "Reconnecting the International Struggles of Black people," *Final Call*, excerpts from *Open Line* broadcast of May 7, 2006, last updated July 26, 2006, http://www.finalcall.com/artman/publish/Minister_Louis_Farrakhan_9/Reconnecting_the_international_struggles_of_Black__2793.shtml.

48. Page, "How Can We Still Ignore Slavery in the Sudan?" See also Jacobs, "Farrakhan's Secret Relationship" (for information on the press conference and Farrakhan's comments there).

49. Page, "How Can We Still Ignore Slavery in the Sudan?"; Donald Altschiller, "American Anti-Slavery Group (AASG)," in *Slavery in the Modern World: A History of Political, Social, and Economic Oppression*, vol. 1: *A–N*, ed. Junius P. Rodriguez (Santa Barbara, CA: ABC-CLIO, 2011), 106; Jacobs, "Farrakhan's Secret Relationship."; Lewthwaite, "Verify Sudan Slave Reports."

50. Lewthwaite, "Verify Sudan Slave Reports."

51. "Minister Farrakhan's Q&A with the Sudan Media," *Final Call*, last updated September 30, 2004, http://www.finalcall.com/artman/publish/Minister_Louis_Farrakhan_9/Minister_Farrakhan_s_Q_amp_A_with_the_Sudan_Media_1589.shtml.

52. Farrakhan, "Reconnecting the International Struggles."

53. Askia Muhammad, "Sudanese President Answers Questions on Darfur," *Final Call*, last updated May 14, 2007, http://www.finalcall.com/artman/publish/World_News_3/Sudanese_president_answers_questions_on_Darfur_3474.shtml [coverage reprinted from *Final Call* 26, no. 22] (quotes); "Sudanese President Addresses Nation of Islam Members in US," *Sudan Tribune*, February 23, 2007, https://sudantribune.com/spip.php?article20411.

54. Muhammad, "Sudanese President Answers Questions on Darfur."

55. Page, "Black on Black Crime"; for Page's African American identity, see Eric Asher, "Clarence Page Credits ADHD with Making Him a Better Journalist," Respect Ability, February 11,

2018, https://www.respectability.org/2018/02/clarence-page-credits-adhd-with-making-him-a-better-journalist.

56. Cotton, *Silent Terror*, 151.

57. Holmes, "Slavery Is an Issue Again"; "TransAfrica Forum," Linktank, accessed August 17, 2023, https://linktank.com/organization/transafrica-forum/about (from which information on TransAfrica Forum was used). The "40 million" number, to be sure, was certainly exaggerated; one estimate puts the US Muslim population to have been around six million people in 2001. See Houssain Kettani, "Muslim Population in the Americas: 1950–2020," *International Journal of Environmental Science and Development* 1, no. 2 (June 2010): 129.

58. "South Sudan: Rebel with a Cause," *Embassy*, accessed September 23, 2020, https://embassymagazine.com/south-sudan.

59. Sabit Abbe Alley, "Genocide and Slavery in the Sudan: The Farrakhan Connection," *City Sun* (Brooklyn), June 6–11, 1996, in *Abolish* (American Anti-Slavery Group), https://www.iabolish.org/genocide-and-slavery-in-the-sudan-the-farrakhan-connection.

60. Alley, "Genocide and Slavery in the Sudan."

61. Alley, "Genocide and Slavery in the Sudan."

62. Alley, "Genocide and Slavery in the Sudan."

63. Kuyok Abol Kuyok, *South Sudan: The Notable Firsts* (Bloomington, IN: AuthorHouse, 2015), 481–482, 484.

64. "The Annual Bayard Rustin Lecture," *Sudan Democratic Gazette* 10, no. 113 (October 1999): 14; "Our History," A. Philip Randolph Institute, accessed September 25, 2020, http://www.apri.org/our-history.html.

65. "The Annual Bayard Rustin Lecture," 14.

66. "The Annual Bayard Rustin Lecture," 14–15.

67. Natsios, *Sudan, South Sudan, and Darfur*, xxvi–xxvii; "Origins of the Darfur Crisis," *PBS News Hour*, July 3, 2008, https://www.pbs.org/newshour/politics/africa-july-dec08-origins_07-03; Abdullah Osman El-Tom, "Darfur People: Too Black for the Arab-Islamic Project of Sudan," in *Darfur and the Crisis of Governance in Sudan: A Critical Reader*, ed. Salah Hassan and Carina Ray (Ithaca: Cornell University Press, 2009), 85, 90; Scott Baldauf, "Sudan 101: Is the Darfur Conflict a Fight between Arabs and Africans?," *Christian Science Monitor*, April 26, 2010, https://www.csmonitor.com/World/Africa/2010/0426/Sudan-101-Is-the-Darfur-conflict-a-fight-between-Arabs-and-Africans; Mohanad Hashim, "A Step Towards Peace?" BBC, February 11, 2020, https://www.bbc.com/news/world-africa-51462613.

68. Phares, *The Coming Revolution*, 261. Farrakhan's pointing to oil occurs in Louis Farrakhan, "Reconnecting the International Struggles of Black People," *Final Call*, last updated July 26, 2006, http://www.finalcall.com/artman/publish/Minister_Louis_Farrakhan_9/Reconnecting_the_international_struggles_of_Black__2793.shtml. For information on the protest and Lantos, see Matthew O'Rourke, "5 Lawmakers Arrested Protesting Darfur Violence," *Los Angeles Times*, April 29, 2006, https://www.latimes.com/archives/la-xpm-2006-apr-29-na-darfur29-story.html; "Tom Lantos," Lantos Foundation for Human Rights & Justice, accessed September 23, 2020, https://www.lantosfoundation.org/about-tom-lantos.

69. Farrakhan, "Reconnecting the International Struggles."

70. Farrakhan, "Reconnecting the International Struggles." For another instance in which Farrakhan alluded to the role of oil in America's interest in Sudan, see Louis Farrakhan, "Is Oil the Motive for War?," *Final Call*, September 13, 2002, http://www.finalcall.com/columns/mlf/mlf_iraq09-17-2002.html.

71. Farrakhan, "Reconnecting the International Struggles."

72. Natsios, *Sudan, South Sudan, and Darfur*, 56; Areig Elhag, "Sudan-Israel Relations: Ensuring Civilian Buy-In during a Democratic Transition," Washington Institute Fikra Forum, August 26, 2020, https://www.washingtoninstitute.org/fikraforum/view/sudan-israel-relations-democratic-transition-normalization.

73. Louis Farrakhan, "The War of Armageddon—Part 3," *Final Call*, last updated May 6, 2007, http://www.finalcall.com/artman/publish/Minister_Louis_Farrakhan_9/The_War_of_Armageddon_-Part_3_3451.shtml.

74. William Reed, "Take Another Look at the 'Save Darfur' Crowd," *Final Call*, last updated January 4, 2008, http://www.finalcall.com/artman/publish/Perspectives_1/Take_another_look_at_the_Save_Darfur_crowd_4231.shtml.

75. Jehron Muhammad, "Black Media Delegation Returns from Darfur," *Final Call*, last updated May 15, 2007, http://www.finalcall.com/artman/publish/World_News_3/Black_media_delegation_returns_from_Darfur_3486.shtml.

76. Cotton, *Silent Terror*, 151.

6. A Worthy Cause

1. "Barack Obama," White House, accessed June 1, 2021, https://www.whitehouse.gov/about-the-white-house/presidents/barack-obama; "President Barack Obama," Barack Obama Presidential Library, accessed June 1, 2021, https://www.obamalibrary.gov/obamas/president-barack-obama; Barack Obama, *Dreams from My Father: A Story of Race and Inheritance* (New York: Crown Publishers, 1995), 5, 62–63.

2. Obama, *Dreams from My Father*, 63–64.

3. "Barack Obama: The 44th President of the United States," White House, accessed January 28, 2023, https://www.whitehouse.gov/about-the-white-house/presidents/barack-obama.

4. Mike Brand, "Obama's Upsetting Decision to Lift Sanctions on Sudan," *The Hill*, January 13, 2017, https://thehill.com/blogs/congress-blog/foreign-policy/314191-obamas-upsetting-decision-to-lift-sanctions-on-sudan; "Genocide in Darfur," C-Span, April 30, 2006, https://www.c-span.org/video/?192217-1/genocide-darfur; Richard Williamson, "How Obama Betrayed Sudan," *Foreign Policy*, November 11, 2010, https://foreignpolicy.com/2010/11/11/how-obama-betrayed-sudan; "Transcript: Obama Addresses U.N. General Assembly," CNN, accessed January 20, 2023, https://www.cnn.com/2009/POLITICS/09/23/obama.transcript/index.html; #teamEBONY, "Read President Obama's Full Speech at DNC," *Ebony*, September 7, 2012, https://www.ebony.com/news/full-text-president-obama-addresses-dnc.

5. Jesse Moore, "President Obama Marks the 50th Anniversary of the Marches from Selma to Montgomery," White House–President Barack Obama, March 8, 2015, https://obamawhitehouse.archives.gov/blog/2015/03/08/president-obama-marks-50th-anniversary-marches-selma-montgomery; #teamEBONY, "[WATCH]President Obama's Moving #Selma50 Speech," *Ebony*, March 9, 2015, https://www.ebony.com/news/watch-president-obamas-moving-selma50-speech-403.

6. "Susan Rice," American University, accessed June 1, 2021, https://www.american.edu/sis/faculty/srice.cfm; Christine Houle, "An Interview with Susan D. Page, U.S. Ambassador to South Sudan," *The Politic*, August 13, 2013, https://thepolitic.org/article/an-interview-with-susan-d-page-u-s-ambassador-to-south-sudan.

7. Ibrahim Sundiata, "Obama, African Americans, and Africans: The Double Vision," in *African Americans in U.S. Foreign Policy: From the Era of Frederick Douglass to the Age of Obama*, ed. Linda Heywood, Allison Blakely, Charles Stith, and Joshua C. Yesnowitz (Urbana: University of Illinois Press, 2015), 209–210 (quote from 210).

8. Andrew S. Natsios, *Sudan, South Sudan, and Darfur: What Everyone Needs to Know* (New York: Oxford University Press, 2012), 171.

9. Herman J. Cohen, "Sudan: American Policy towards the Land of Endless Conflict," *American Foreign Policy Interests* 34, no. 6 (2012): 325.

10. Cohen, "Sudan," 326; "U.S.-Sudan Relations," U.S. Embassy in Sudan, accessed June 1, 2021, https://sd.usembassy.gov/our-relationship/policy-history/us-sudan-relations; Benjamin Talton, *In This Land of Plenty: Mickey Leland and Africa in American Politics* (Philadelphia: University of Pennsylvania Press, 2019), 210–211.

11. "Susan Rice"; Rebecca Hamilton, "Special Report: The Wonks Who Sold Washington on South Sudan," Reuters, July 11, 2012, https://www.reuters.com/article/us-south-sudan-midwives/special-report-the-wonks-who-sold-washington-on-south-sudan-idUSBRE86A0GC20120711; Lorenzo Morris, "African American Representatives in the United Nations: From Ralph Bunche to Susan Rice," in *African Americans in U.S. Foreign Policy: From the Era of Frederick Douglass to the Age of Obama*, ed. Linda Heywood, Allison Blakely, Charles Stith, and Joshua C. Yesnowitz (Urbana: University of Illinois Press, 2015), 190.

12. Toyin Falola and Raphael Chijioke Njoku, *United States and Africa Relations, 1400s to the Present* (New Haven: Yale University Press, 2020), 299; Brand, "Obama's Upsetting Decision"; "Genocide in Darfur"; untitled image of Kwesi Mfume, Barack Obama, Joe Madison, and Al Sharpton at a Save Darfur rally on the National Mall, April 30, 2006, box 3, Joe Madison Papers, 2008 addendum to the papers, ARC; Kevin Rector, "A Secret Vote Pushed Kweisi Mfume Out as NAACP Leader Amid 'Growing Dissatisfaction' with His Performance, Records Show," *Baltimore Sun*, January 17, 2020, https://www.baltimoresun.com/politics/bs-md-pol-mfume-naacp-tenure-20200117-lqspcf54e5hfnp4z3weqw44un4-story.html; Joe Madison's nametag: "Save Darfur Now: Rally to Stop Genocide (April 30, 2006)," program schedule, box 8, Joe Madison Papers.

13. Brand, "Obama's Upsetting Decision."

14. "Thousands Rally at Capitol for Immediate Aid to Darfur," *Jet*, May 15, 2006, 8.

15. Stacy Gilliam, "Where Are the Black Voices in the Sudan Crisis?," *Crisis* (July–August 2006), 8; "Aid and Action Urged for Darfur," *Jet*, May 15, 2006, 12 (quote).

16. "Sen. Obama Visits Darfur Refugees in Chad," National Public Radio, September 3, 2006, https://www.npr.org/templates/story/story.php?storyId=5760323.

17. Falola and Njoku, *United States and Africa Relations*, 299; "Summary: H.R.3127—109th Congress (2005–2006)," Congress.gov, accessed June 1, 2021, https://www.congress.gov/bill/109th-congress/house-bill/3127.

18. "Obama Launches Presidential Bid," BBC News, February 10, 2007, http://news.bbc.co.uk/2/hi/americas/6349081.stm.

19. "Obama and Darfur," *Wall Street Journal*, October 22, 2009, ProQuest.

20. Williamson, "How Obama Betrayed Sudan."

21. Elise Labott, "Obama Is Asked to Focus on Darfur," CNN, November 12, 2008, https://www.cnn.com/2008/WORLD/africa/11/12/obama.darfur/index.html.

22. Amie Parnes, "Move Over Oprah? Obama Sells books," *Politico*, May 30, 2009, https://www.politico.com/story/2009/05/move-over-oprah-obama-sells-books-023114; Jesse A. Zink, *Christianity and Catastrophe in South Sudan: Civil War, Migration, and the Rise of Dinka Anglicanism* (Waco, TX: Baylor University Press, 2017), 114 (citing Mark Bixler, *The Lost Boys of Sudan: An American Story of the Refugee Experience*. Atlanta: University of Georgia Press, 2005); Dave Eggers,

"What Is the What Reader's Guide," Penguin Random House, accessed June 1, 2021, https://www.penguinrandomhouse.com/books/45422/what-is-the-what-by-dave-eggers/9780307385901/readers-guide.

23. Parnes, "Move Over Oprah?"

24. Ayelet Golz, "Former UN Ambassador Susan Rice to Highlight Founders Day," Colorado State University, December 18, 2019, https://source.colostate.edu/former-un-ambassador-susan-rice-to-highlight-founders-day; Morris, "African American Representatives," 190.

25. Susan Rice, *Tough Love: My Story of the Things Worth Fighting For* (New York: Simon & Schuster, 2019), 272–273.

26. "Transcript: Obama Addresses U.N. General Assembly."

27. Rice, *Tough Love*, 273.

28. Hamilton, "Special Report"; Rice, *Tough Love*, 273; Williamson, "How Obama Betrayed Sudan."

29. "U.S. President Obama UN Speech on Sudan," Chr. Michelsen Institute, October 6, 2010, https://www.cmi.no/news/718-u-s-president-obama-un-speech-on-sudan.

30. Rice, *Tough Love*, 273–274 (quote from 274).

31. Williamson, "How Obama Betrayed Sudan"; Hamilton, "Special Report"; "Obama Reaffirms US Support for South Sudan Referendum Vote," *Voice of America*, December 22, 2010, https://www.voanews.com/africa/obama-reaffirms-us-support-south-sudan-referendum-vote.

32. Natsios, *Sudan, South Sudan, and Darfur*, 213.

33. Zachariah Mampilly, "Witnessing the Birth of a Nation in Southern Sudan" *The Root*, January 10, 2011, https://www.theroot.com/witnessing-the-birth-of-a-nation-in-southern-sudan-1790862340. For information on *The Root*, see Shannon Bond, "Univision Buys African-American Focused Website; Media," *Financial Times*, May 22, 2015, Nexis Uni.

34. Natsios, *Sudan, South Sudan, and Darfur*, 213; Hamilton, "Special Report."

35. "Statement on the Southern Sudan Independence Referendum," January 16, 2011, American Presidency Project, https://www.presidency.ucsb.edu/documents/statement-the-southern-sudan-independence-referendum.

36. "Remarks by the President in State of Union Address," White House Office of the Press Secretary, January 25, 2011, https://obamawhitehouse.archives.gov/the-press-office/2011/01/25/remarks-president-state-union-address.

37. "Statement of President Barack Obama Recognition of the Republic of South Sudan," White House Office of the Press Secretary, July 9, 2011, https://obamawhitehouse.archives.gov/the-press-office/2011/07/09/statement-president-barack-obama-recognition-republic-south-sudan.

38. Martin Luther King Jr. to "Mr. Taban," undated letter, King Center Digital Archive, accessed April 27, 2016, http://www.thekingcenter.org/archive/document/letter-mlk-mr-taban.

39. Ashley Makar, "Triumph of Liberation Repeats Itself," *Huntsville (AL) Times*, July 17, 2011, NewsBank; Ashley Makar, "My Take: Why Egypt's Christians Are Hopeful but Nervous," *CNN Belief Blog*, accessed November 25, 2022, https://religion.blogs.cnn.com/2011/02/10/my-take-why-egypts-christians-are-excited-but-nervous.

40. "Statement of President Barack Obama."

41. Houle, "An Interview with Susan D. Page"; "Exit Interview: Page Steps Down as U.S. Ambassador to South Sudan," National Public Radio, August 22, 2014, https://www.npr.org/2014/08/22/342354105/exit-interview-page-steps-down-as-u-s-ambassador-to-south-sudan.

42. "Exit Interview."

43. Susan Page, "Capital Download: Hopes, Then Civil War in South Sudan," *USA Today*, September 2, 2014, https://www.usatoday.com/story/news/world/2014/09/02/capital-download-susan-page-ambassador-south-sudan/14970159; Hamilton, "Special Report."

44. Page, "Capital Download."
45. Houle, "An Interview with Susan D. Page."
46. Doug Palmer, "U.S. Extends Trade Benefit Program to South Sudan," Reuters, March 26, 2012, https://www.reuters.com/article/uk-usa-southsudan-trade-idUKBRE82P14620120326; Denis Scopas, "Bound by Oil: How Petroleum Is Bringing Sudan and South Sudan Closer Together," *Middle East Eye*, October 26, 2019, https://www.middleeasteye.net/news/bound-oil-how-petroleum-bringing-sudan-and-south-sudan-closer-together; *The Situation in South Sudan: Hearing before the Committee on Foreign Relations* (Washington, DC: U.S. Government Publishing Office, 2015), 28, https://www.govinfo.gov/content/pkg/CHRG-113shrg93484/pdf/CHRG-113shrg93484.pdf.
47. Houle, "An Interview with Susan D. Page."
48. James Copnall and David Smith, "Sudan and South Sudan Close to War," *Guardian*, April 23, 2012, https://www.theguardian.com/world/2012/apr/23/sudan-south-sudan-war-close; Clement Sefa-Nyarko, "Civil War in South Sudan: Is It a Reflection of Historical Secessionist and Natural Resource Wars in 'Greater Sudan'?," *African Security* 9, no. 3 (2016): 209n63.
49. "Obama Urges Talks between Rival Sudans," *Al Jazeera*, April 21, 2012, https://www.aljazeera.com/news/2012/4/21/obama-urges-talks-between-rival-sudans.
50. Ulf Laessing, "Sudan, South Sudan Sign Deals to Restart Oil, Secure Border," Reuters, September 27, 2012, https://www.reuters.com/article/us-sudan-south-talks/sudan-south-sudan-sign-deals-to-restart-oil-secure-border-idUSBRE88Q1R820120927.
51. "Statement on the Agreement between Sudan and South Sudan," Administration of Barack Obama, 2012, https://www.govinfo.gov/content/pkg/DCPD-201200754/pdf/DCPD-201200754.pdf.
52. Dan Roberts, "Obama Appoints 'Pragmatic' Susan Rice as US National Security Adviser," *Guardian*, June 5, 2013, https://www.theguardian.com/world/2013/jun/05/obama-susan-rice-national-security-adviser.
53. Rice, *Tough Love*, 395.
54. Jennifer Williams, "The Conflict in South Sudan, Explained," *Vox*, updated January 9, 2017, https://www.vox.com/world/2016/12/8/13817072/south-sudan-crisis-explained-ethnic-cleansing-genocide; "South Sudan Profile—Timeline," BBC, August 6, 2018, https://www.bbc.com/news/world-africa-14019202; and Daniel Howden, "South Sudan: The State That Fell Apart in a Week," *Guardian*, December 23, 2013, https://www.theguardian.com/world/2013/dec/23/south-sudan-state-that-fell-apart-in-a-week; and "Untold Suffering in South Sudan as Conflict Enters Fifth Year," Amnesty International, accessed September 6, 2022, https://www.amnesty.org/en/latest/campaigns/2017/12/end-the-suffering-of-south-sudanese-people-now.
55. Øystein H. Rolandsen, "Another Civil War in South Sudan: The Failure of Guerrilla Government?," *Journal of Eastern African Studies*, 9, no. 1 (2015): 164–165.
56. Sefa-Nyarko, "Civil War in South Sudan," 189, 194 (quote from 194).
57. For a deep dive into the causes of the civil war, see Alex De Waal's "When Kleptocracy Becomes Insolvent: Brute Causes of the Civil War in South Sudan," *African Affairs* 113, no. 452 (2014): 347–369.
58. Page, "Capital Download."
59. "Statement by President Barack Obama on South Sudan (December 20, 2013)," U.S. Embassy and Consulate in Nigeria, accessed July 25, 2023, https://web.archive.org/web/20210413113018/https://ng.usembassy.gov/statement-president-barack-obama-south-sudan-december-20-2013.
60. Rice, *Tough Love*, 395.
61. Rice, *Tough Love*, 396.

62. Jose Delreal and Philip Ewing, "State Calls Back South Sudan Staff," *Politico*, January 3, 2014, https://www.politico.com/story/2014/01/south-sudan-embassy-staff-exit-101722.

63. Bill Fletcher Jr., "A Civil War Looming in South Sudan," *Washington Informer*, December 30, 2013, https://www.washingtoninformer.com/a-civil-war-looming-in-south-sudan. For information on the *Washington Informer*, see Sherrie Flynt Wallington, Bridget Oppong, Marquita Iddirisu, and Lucile L. Adams-Campbell, "Developing a Mass Media Campaign to Promote Mammography Awareness in African American Women in the Nation's Capital," *Journal of Community Health* 43, no. 4 (2018): 634.

64. Breanna Edwards, "Joe Madison Arrested in NY Protest against Injustice in South Sudan," *The Root*, April 14, 2014, https://www.theroot.com/joe-madison-arrested-in-ny-protest-against-injustice-in-1790875331.

65. "Exit Interview."

66. John F. Kerry and Susan E. Rice, "John Kerry and Susan Rice: South Sudan's Leaders Need to Set Aside their Dispute: Officials in South Sudan Must Finally Take Responsibility and End the Fighting there," *Washington Post*, December 15, 2014, ProQuest.

67. "South Sudan Events of 2015," Human Rights Watch, accessed November 20, 2020, https://www.hrw.org/world-report/2016/country-chapters/south-sudan.

68. "'Help Has Not Reached Me Here': Donors Must Step Up Support for South Sudanese Refugees in Uganda," Amnesty International, June 18, 2017, https://www.amnesty.org/en/documents/afr59/6422/2017/en.

69. "Timeline of International Response to the Conflict in South Sudan," Global Centre for the Responsibility to Protect, accessed July 26, 2023, https://web.archive.org/web/20221003080404/https://s156658.gridserver.com/media/files/timeline-of-international-response-to-the-situation-in-south-sudan.pdf ; "US and France Press UN for S Sudan Sanctions," *Al Jazeera*, April 24, 2014, https://www.aljazeera.com/news/2014/4/24/us-and-france-press-un-for-s-sudan-sanctions; "South Sudan Events of 2015"; Carole Landry, "UN Imposes First Sanctions on Six South Sudan Commanders," *Times of Israel*, July 2, 2015, https://www.timesofisrael.com/un-imposes-first-sanctions-on-six-south-sudan-commanders.

70. "Obama Pushes for Peace in Sudan," *Jet*, July 27, 2015, https://www.jetmag.com/news/obama-pushes-for-peace-in-sudan.

71. "Obama Pushes for Peace in Sudan"; Michelle Kosinski, "Obama, African leaders Meet to End South Sudan's Civil War," *CNN*, July 27, 2015, https://www.cnn.com/2015/07/27/politics/south-sudan-obama-ethiopia-meeting/index.html.

72. "Remarks by President Obama to the People of Africa," White House Office of the Press Secretary, July 28, 2015, https://obamawhitehouse.archives.gov/the-press-office/2015/07/28/remarks-president-obama-people-africa.

73. "South Sudan President Salva Kiir Signs Peace Deal," BBC News, August 26, 2015, https://www.bbc.com/news/world-africa-34066511; "U.S. Pushes U.N. to Level Sanctions on South Sudan Unless It Signs Peace Deal," *Japan Times*, August 19, 2015, https://www.japantimes.co.jp/news/2015/08/19/world/politics-diplomacy-world/u-s-pushes-u-n-level-sanctions-south-sudan-unless-signs-peace-deal/#.XeaAMy2ZOqA.

74. "Security Advisor Susan Rice: Together, We Must Help South Sudan Implement the Peace Agreement," U.S. Mission to International Organizations in Geneva, August 27, 2015, https://geneva.usmission.gov/2015/08/27/security-advisor-susan-rice-together-we-must-help-south-sudan-implement-the-peace-agreement.

75. Karin Zeitvogel, "US Cancels Meeting with South Sudan Officials," Voice of America, October 7, 2015, https://www.voanews.com/archive/us-cancels-meeting-south-sudan-officials.

76. "'Both Sides Are at Fault': Susan Rice on South Sudan's Civil War," National Public Radio, March 8, 2016, https://www.npr.org/2016/03/08/469692236/both-sides-are-at-fault-susan-rice-on-south-sudans-civil-war.

77. "Civil War in South Sudan," Council on Foreign Relations, last modified November 19, 2020, https://www.cfr.org/global-conflict-tracker/conflict/civil-war-south-sudan.

78. Jason Beaubien, "U.N. Report Addresses Gang Rape of Aid Workers in South Sudan," National Public Radio, August 23, 2016, https://www.npr.org/sections/goatsandsoda/2016/08/23/491057541/gang-rape-of-aid-workers-in-south-sudan-is-a-turning-point.

79. UN News, "South Sudan: Security Council Condemns Killing of Civilians, Peacekeepers at UN Compound," *Africa Renewal*, accessed September 6, 2022, https://www.un.org/africarenewal/news/south-sudan-security-council-condemns-killing-civilians-peacekeepers-un-compound; Akshaya Jumar, "UN Peacekeepers Turn Blind Eye To Rape in South Sudan," Human Rights Watch, November 3, 2016, https://www.hrw.org/news/2016/11/03/un-peacekeepers-turn-blind-eye-rape-south-sudan; "Untold Suffering in South Sudan."

80. "'They Burned It All': Destruction of Villages, Killings, and Sexual Violence in Unity State South Sudan," Human Rights Watch, July 22, 2015, https://www.hrw.org/report/2015/07/22/they-burned-it-all/destruction-villages-killings-and-sexual-violence-unity-state#_ftn63.

81. Lesley Wroughton, "Exclusive: U.S. to Impose Arms Embargo on South Sudan to End Conflict—Sources," Reuters, February 2, 2018, https://www.reuters.com/article/us-usa-southsudan-arms-exclusive/exclusive-u-s-to-impose-arms-embargo-on-south-sudan-to-end-conflict-sources-idUSKBN1FM0ZE; "Obama Pushes for Peace in Sudan."

82. Rice, *Tough Love*, 397; "Samantha Power," Harvard Kennedy School, accessed July 3, 2023, https://web.archive.org/web/20210228220923/https://www.hks.harvard.edu/faculty/samantha-power.

83. Rice, *Tough Love*, 397; Jonathan Pedneault, "Starving under the Bullets in South Sudan," Human Rights Watch, April 11, 2017, https://www.hrw.org/news/2017/04/11/starving-under-bullets-south-sudan#.

84. Lorenzo Morris, "The United Nations and the African American Presence: From Ralph Bunche to Susan Rice," in *Charting the Range of Black Politics: National Political Science Review*, vol. 14, ed. Michael Mitchell and David Covin (New Brunswick, NJ: Transaction Publishers, 2012), 52, 54, 55 (quotes from 55).

Conclusion

1. "Black Lives Should Matter in South Sudan Too" (Nykhor Paul interview), BBC, July 27, 2016, https://www.bbc.com/news/blogs-trending-36893134.

2. "Black Lives Should Matter in South Sudan Too"; Keshia N. Blain, "Civil Rights International: The Fight against Racism Has Always Been Global," *Foreign Affairs* 99, no. 5 (September/October 2020), https://www.foreignaffairs.com/articles/united-states/2020-08-11/racism-civil-rights-international.

3. "Black lives Should Matter in South Sudan Too."

4. Patrick Strickland, "US: Are 'Anti-Sharia' Bills Legalising Islamophobia?" *Al Jazeera*, October 1, 2017, https://www.aljazeera.com/news/2017/10/1/us-are-anti-sharia-bills-legalising-islamophobia; Elsadig Elsheikh, Basima Sisemore, Natalia Ramirez Lee, "Legalizing Othering: The United States of Islamophobia," University of Berkeley Haas Institute for a Fair and Inclusive Society, September 2017, https://belonging.berkeley.edu/sites/default/files/haas_institute_legalizing_othering_the_united_states_of_islamophobia.pdf.

5. For more on Hansberry at Howard, see "Editorial: A New Course in History at Howard University," *Howard University Record* 17, no. 5 (March 1923): 237–239.

6. Misha Cornelius, "Two Howard University Students Named 2019 Boren Scholar and Fellow," Howard University Office of University Communications, June 5, 2019, https://newsroom.howard.edu/newsroom/static/10666/two-howard-university-students-named-2019-boren-scholar-and-fellow; Adrian Wojnarowski, "Sources: Howard Star Freshman Makur Maker Entering NBA Draft," ESPN, May 28, 2021, https://www.espn.com/nba/story/_/id/31528054/sources-howard-star-freshman-makur-maker-entering-nba-draft.

7. Lekan Oguntoyinbo, "Forging Leaders: HBCUs Produce Leaders Not Only Domestically, but Also Abroad," *Diverse: Issues in Higher Education*, February 28, 2013, 16; Steve D. Mobley Jr. and Jennifer M. Johnson, "The Role of HBCUs in Addressing the Unique Needs of LGBT Students," *New Directions for Higher Education*, no. 170 (2015): 79.

8. Robert Trent Vinson, *The Americans Are Coming! Dreams of African American Liberation in Segregationist South Africa* (Athens: Ohio University Press, 2012); Brian G. Shellum, *African American Officers in Liberia: A Pestiferous Rotation, 1910–1942* (Lincoln: University of Nebraska Press, 2018); Ira Dworkin, *Congo Love Song: African American Culture and the Crisis of the Colonial State* (Chapel Hill: University of North Carolina Press, 2017).

9. "Black Lives Matter Skirts North Africa Despite Everyday Racism," France 24, July 20, 2020, https://www.aol.com/news/black-lives-matter-skirts-north-africa-despite-everyday-021102728.html.

10. Blain, "Civil Rights International."

11. Brooke Auxier, "Social Media Continue to Be Important Political Outlets for Black Americans," Pew Research Center, December 11, 2020, https://www.pewresearch.org/fact-tank/2020/12/11/social-media-continue-to-be-important-political-outlets-for-black-americans.

12. David Pilling, "All Eyes on America," *Financial Times*, June 22, 2020, Nexis Uni; "In 2020, Protests Spread Across the Globe with a Similar Message: Black Lives Matter," National Public Radio, December 30, 2020, https://www.npr.org/2020/12/30/950053607/in-2020-protests-spread-across-the-globe-with-a-similar-message-black-lives-matt; Blain, "Civil Rights International."

13. Erum Salam, "Black Lives Matter Protesters Make Palestinian Struggle Their Own," *Guardian*, June 16, 2021, https://www.theguardian.com/world/2021/jun/16/black-lives-matter-palestinian-struggle-us-left.

14. Corey Williams, "Some Blacks Applaud Castro Legacy of Racial Equality," Associated Press, November 28, 2016, https://apnews.com/article/4ad817d973a742dfbe69bfabedae0916.

15. Armando Salguero, "Unrepentant Hypocrite Colin Kaepernick Defends Fidel Castro," *Miami Herald*, November 25, 2016, https://www.miamiherald.com/sports/spt-columns-blogs/armando-salguero/article117033883.html.

16. Salguero, "Unrepentant Hypocrite."

17. David Zurawik, "Rewriting History; Harvard Professor Henry Louis Gates Jr. Is Determined to Unearth the 'Wonders of the African World' and Bury the Lies of Colonizers. His Efforts Make for Fascinating TV," *Baltimore Sun*, October 25, 1999, https://www.baltimoresun.com/news/bs-xpm-1999-10-25-9910250195-story.html.

18. James H. Meriwether, *Proudly We Can Be Africans: Black Americans and Africa, 1935–1961* (Chapel Hill: University of North Carolina Press, 2002), 19.

Bibliography

Archives

England

Church Missionary Society (CMS) Archives, University of Birmingham
Sudan Archive, Durham University (SAD)

United States

Amistad Research Center (ARC), Tulane University, New Orleans
Baker Library (BL), Harvard University, Cambridge, Massachusetts
Hoover Institution Archives (HIA), Stanford University, Stanford, California
Library of Congress (LC), Washington, DC
Moorland-Spingarn Research Center (MSRC), Howard University, Washington, DC
New York Public Library Archives and Manuscripts
Presbyterian Historical Society (PHS), Philadelphia
University of Massachusetts Amherst Libraries, Robert S. Cox Special Collections and University Archives, Amherst

University of Washington Libraries, Special Collections, Seattle
Walter P. Reuther Library Archives of Labor and Urban Affairs, Wayne State University, Detroit

Italy

Comboni Mission Archive, Rome (ACR)
Comboni Mission Library, Rome

South Sudan

South Sudan National Archive (SSNA), Juba

Sources

A. Philip Randolph Institute. "Our History." Accessed September 25, 2020. http://www.apri.org/our-history.html.
'Abd Al-Rahim, Muddathir. "Arabism, Africanism, and Self-Identification in the Sudan." *Journal of Modern African Studies* 8, no. 2 (July 1970): 233–249.
Abbas, Fatin. "Coming to Terms with Sudan's Legacy of Slavery." *African Arguments*, January 18, 2018. https://africanarguments.org/2016/01/coming-to-terms-with-sudans-legacy-of-slavery-2.
Abbas, Philip. "Growth of Black Political Consciousness in Northern Sudan." *Africa Today* 20, no. 3 (1973): 29–43.
Abusharif, Rogaia Mustafa. *Wanderings: Sudanese Migrants and Exiles in North America*. Ithaca: Cornell University Press, 2002.
Adi, Hakim. *Pan-Africanism: A History*. London: Bloomsbury, 2018.
Adi, Hakim, and Marika Sherwood. *Pan-African History: Political Figures from Africa and the Diaspora*. New York: Taylor & Francis, 2003.
Adichie, Chimamanda. "The Danger of a Single Story." TED talk transcript, 2009. https://www.classacthr73.org/resources/Documents/Event%20Materials/Chimamanda%20Adichie%20The%20Danger%20of%20a%20Single%20Story.pdf.
Adeleke, Tunde. *Un-African Americans: Nineteenth-Century Black Nationalists and the Civilizing Mission*. Lexington: University of Kentucky Press, 1998.
Administration of Barack Obama. "Statement on the Agreement between Sudan and South Sudan." US Government Publishing Office, September 27, 2012. https://www.govinfo.gov/content/pkg/DCPD-201200754/pdf/DCPD-201200754.pdf.
Aguda, Oluwadare. "Arabism and Pan-Arabism in Sudanese Politics." *Journal of Modern African Studies* 11, no. 2 (June 1973): 177–200.
Ahmed, Gutbi Mahdi. "Muslim Organizations in the United States." In *The Muslims of America*, edited by Yvonne Yazbeck Haddad, 11–24. New York: Oxford University Press, 1991.

"Aid and Action Urged for Darfur." *Jet*, May 15, 2006, 12.
Alley, Sabit Abbe. "Genocide and Slavery in the Sudan: The Farrakhan Connection." *City Sun* (Brooklyn), June 6–11, 1996. https://www.iabolish.org/genocide-and-slavery-in-the-sudan-the-farrakhan-connection.
Alpher, Yossi. *Periphery: Israel's Search for Middle East Allies*. Lanham, MD: Rowman and Littlefield, 2015.
Altman, Alex. "Black Lives Matter: Person of the Year, the Short List, No. 4." *Time*, December 21, 2015. http://time.com/time-person-of-the-year-2015-runner-up-black-lives-matter/.
Altschiller, Donald. "American Anti-Slavery Group (AASG)." In *Slavery in the Modern World: A History of Political, Social, and Economic Oppression*, vol. 1, A–N, edited by Junius P. Rodriguez, 105–107. Santa Barbara: ABC-CLIO, 2011.
American Academy of Poets. "Langston Hughes." Accessed May 14, 2020. https://poets.org/poet/langston-hughes.
American University. "Susan Rice." Accessed June 1, 2021. https://www.american.edu/sis/faculty/srice.cfm.
Amnesty International. "'Help Has Not Reached Me Here': Donors Must Step Up Support for South Sudanese Refugees in Uganda." June 18, 2017. https://www.amnesty.org/en/documents/afr59/6422/2017/en.
———. "Untold Suffering in South Sudan as Conflict Enters Fifth Year." Accessed September 6, 2022. https://www.amnesty.org/en/latest/campaigns/2017/12/end-the-suffering-of-south-sudanese-people-now.
Anderson, Carol. *Bourgeois Radicals: The NAACP and the Struggle for Colonial Liberation, 1941–1960*. New York: Cambridge University Press, 2014.
"Andrew Brimmer Retires as Tuskegee University Board Chairman." *Diverse Issues in Higher Education*, October 21, 2010. https://diverseeducation.com/article/14298.
"The Annual Bayard Rustin Lecture." *Sudan Democratic Gazette* 10, no. 113 (October 1999): 14–15.
Ansari, Zafar Ishaq. "Islam among African-Americans: An Overview." In *Muslims' Place in the American Public Square: Hope, Fears, and Aspirations*, edited by Zahid H. Bukhari, Sulayman S. Nyang, Mumtaz Ahmad, and John L. Esposito, 222–267. Walnut Creek, CA: AltaMira Press, 2004.
Apter, Andrew. "Beyond Négritude: Black Cultural Citizenship and the Arab Question in FESTAC 77." *Journal of African Cultural Studies* 28, no. 3 (2016): 313–326.
"Arab League Fast Facts." CNN. Last modified March 31, 2023. https://www.cnn.com/2013/07/30/world/meast/arab-league-fast-facts/index.html.
Asher, Eric. "Clarence Page Credits ADHD with Making Him a Better Journalist." RespectAbility, February 11, 2018. https://www.respectability.org/2018/02/clarence-page-credits-adhd-with-making-him-a-better-journalist.
Ashworth, John, and Maura Ryan. "'One Nation from Every Tribe, Tongue, and People': The Church and Strategic Peacebuilding in South Sudan." *Journal of Catholic Social Thought* 10, no. 1 (2013): 47–67.
Association for Diplomatic Studies and Training. "Being Black in a 'Lily White' State Department." Accessed December 8, 2022. https://adst.org/oral-history/fascinating-figures/being-black-in-a-lily-white-state-department.

Asukile, Thabiti. "The Admiration and Complementary Africana Historical Scholarship of W. E. B. Du Bois and Joel Augustus Rogers." *Africology: The Journal of Pan African Studies* 11, no. 8 (June 2018): 182–221.

Auda, Abdel Malek. "Duse Mohamad Ali (1867–1945): A Forerunner of Pan-Africanism." *Égypte Contemporaine* 58, no. 328 (1967): 63–72.

Austin, Algernon. *Achieving Blackness: Race, Black Nationalism, and Afrocentrism in the Twentieth Century.* New York: New York University Press, 2006.

Auxier, Brooke. "Social Media Continue to Be Important Political Outlets for Black Americans." Pew Research Center, December 11, 2020. https://www.pewresearch.org/fact-tank/2020/12/11/social-media-continue-to-be-important-political-outlets-for-black-americans.

Barack Obama Presidential Library. "President Barack Obama." Accessed June 1, 2021. https://www.obamalibrary.gov/obamas/president-barack-obama.

Barawy, Rashed el-. "Egypt and the Sudan." *India Quarterly* 7, no. 4 (October–December 1951): 351–363.

Barnes, Kenneth C. *Journey of Hope: The Back-to-Africa Movement in Arkansas in the Late 1800s.* Chapel Hill: University of North Carolina Press, 2004.

Beaubien, Jason. "U.N. Report Addresses Gang Rape of Aid Workers in South Sudan." *National Public Radio*, August 23, 2016. https://www.npr.org/sections/goatsandsoda/2016/08/23/491057541/gang-rape-of-aid-workers-in-south-sudan-is-a-turning-point.

Beckert, Sven. "From Tuskegee to Togo: The Problem of Freedom in the Empire of Cotton." *Journal of American History* 92, no. 2 (September 2005): 498–526.

Beinin, Joel, and Lisa Hajjar. *Palestine, Israel, and the Arab-Israeli Conflict: A Primer.* Washington, DC: Middle East Research and Information Project, 2014. https://merip.org/palestine-israel-primer.

Berg, Herbert. "Mythmaking in the African American Muslim Context: The Moorish Science Temple, the Nation of Islam, and the American Society of Muslims." *Journal of the American Academy of Religion* 73, no. 3 (2005): 685–703.

Berman, Edward H. "Tuskegee—in—Africa." *Journal of Negro Education* 41, no. 2 (Spring 1972): 99–112.

Berman, Jacob Rama. *American Arabesque: Arabs and Islam in the 19th-Century Imaginary.* New York: New York University Press, 2012.

Berry, L., and S. Geistfeld. *Eastern African Country Profiles: Sudan.* Rev. ed. Worcester, MA: Clark University International Development Program, 1983.

Beydoun, Khaled A. "Are Arabs White?" *Al Jazeera*, July 16, 2015. https://www.aljazeera.com/indepth/opinion/2015/07/arabs-white-150716110921150.html.

Billingsley, Andrew. "Horace R. Cayton 1903–1970." *American Sociologist* 5, no. 4 (November 1970): 380–381.

"Black Lives Matter Skirts North Africa Despite Everyday Racism." *AFP*, July 19, 2020. https://www.france24.com/en/20200720-black-lives-matter-skirts-north-africa-despite-everyday-racism.

"Black Lives Should Matter in South Sudan Too." *BBC*, July 27, 2016. https://www.bbc.com/news/blogs-trending-36893134.

Blain, Keshia N. "Civil Rights International: The Fight against Racism Has Always Been Global." *Foreign Affairs* 99, no. 5 (September/October 2020). https://www.foreignaffairs.com/articles/united-states/2020-08-11/racism-civil-rights-international.

———. *Set the World on Fire: Black Nationalist Women and the Global Struggle for Freedom*. Philadelphia: University of Pennsylvania Press, 2018.

Blain, Keshia, and Tiffany M. Gill, eds. *To Turn the Whole World Over: Black Women and Internationalism*. Urbana: University of Illinois Press, 2019.

Blyden, Nemata. *African Americans and Africa: A New History*. New Haven: Yale University Press, 2019.

Booker, Simeon. "Tape U.S.A." *Jet*, September 3, 1959.

The Booker T. Washington Papers, vol. 7, *1903–4*. Edited by Louis R. Harlan and Raymond W. Smock. Urbana: University of Illinois Press, 1977.

The Booker T. Washington Papers, vol. 8, *1904–6*. Edited by Louis R. Harlan and Raymond W. Smock. Urbana: University of Illinois Press, 1979.

The Booker T. Washington Papers, vol. 9, *1906–8*. Edited by Louis R. Harlan and Raymond W. Smock. Urbana: University of Illinois Press, 1980.

"'Both Sides Are at Fault': Susan Rice on South Sudan's Civil War." National Public Radio, March 8, 2016. https://www.npr.org/2016/03/08/469692236/both-sides-are-at-fault-susan-rice-on-south-sudans-civil-war.

Bowen, Patrick D. "Satti Majid: A Sudanese Founder of American Islam." *Journal of Africana Religions* 1, no. 2 (2013): 194–209.

Brand, Mike. "Obama's Upsetting Decision to Lift Sanctions on Sudan." *The Hill*, January 13, 2017. https://thehill.com/blogs/congress-blog/foreign-policy/314191-obamas-upsetting-decision-to-lift-sanctions-on-sudan.

Breidlid, Anders, ed. *A Concise History of South Sudan*. Kampala: Fountain Publishers, 2010.

Breidlid, Anders, Avelino Androga Said, and Astrid Kristine Breidlid, eds. *A Concise History of South Sudan*. Rev ed. Kampala: Fountain Publishers, 2014.

Brenner, Lenni, and Matthew Quest. *Black Liberation and Palestine Solidarity*. Atlanta: On Our Own Authority, 2013.

Brown, Peter. "Joe Madison Witnesses the Horror of Slavery in Sudan." *The Crisis*, November-December 2000, 26–28.

Brown, Tim J., and Rita L. Rahoi-Gilchrest. "Postmodern Personas in Combat: The NAACP and the Reverend Benjamin Chavis." *Howard Journal of Communication* 10, no. 1 (1999): 29–45.

Bullard, Alice. "De la colonisation à la mondialisation. Les vicissitudes de l'esclavage en Mauritanie)." In "Esclavage moderne ou modernité de l'esclavage?," special issue, *Cahiers d'Études Africaines* 45 (2005): 751–769.

Bureau of African Affairs, U.S. Department of State. "U.S. Relations with Sudan." October 24, 2022. https://www.state.gov/u-s-relations-with-sudan.

Byrd, Brandon. "An Experiment in Self-Government: Haiti in the African-American Political Imagination, 1863–1915." PhD diss., University of North Carolina, 2015.

Campbell, James T. *Middle Passages: African American Journeys to Africa, 1787–2005*. New York: Penguin, 2006.

Cannon, J. A. "Baring, Evelyn, 1st Earl of Cromer." In *The Oxford Companion to British History*, 2nd ed., edited by Robert Crowcroft and John Cannon. Oxford University Press, 2015. Oxford Reference.

Cayton, Horace R. *Long Old Road: Back to Black Metropolis*. New York: Routledge, 2017.

Chamberlin, Paul Thomas. *The Global Offensive: The United States, the Palestine Liberation Organization, and the Making of the Post-Cold War Order*. New York: Oxford University Press, 2012.

Cheeseman, Nic, Eloïse Bertrand, and Sa'eed Husaini. "Bandung Conference." In *A Dictionary of African Politics*. Oxford University Press, 2019. Oxford Reference.

Chr. Michelsen Institute. "U.S. President Obama UN Speech on Sudan." October 6, 2010. https://www.cmi.no/news/718-u-s-president-obama-un-speech-on-sudan.

Cilli, Adam Lee. "Robert L. Vann and the *Pittsburgh Courier* in the 1932 Presidential Election: An Analysis of Black Reformism in Interwar America." *Pennsylvania Magazine of History and Biography* 143, no. 2 (April 2019): 141–176.

"Civil War in South Sudan." Council on Foreign Relations. Accessed July 2, 2023. https://www.cfr.org/global-conflict-tracker/conflict/civil-war-south-sudan.

Clayton, Gilbert Falkingham. *An Arabian Diary*. Edited by Robert O. Collins. Berkeley: University of California Press, 1969.

Cohen, Herman J. "Sudan: American Policy towards the Land of Endless Conflict." *American Foreign Policy Interests* 34, no. 6 (2012): 322–328.

Collins, Robert O. "Civil Wars in the Sudan." *History Compass* 5, no. 6 (2007): 1778–1805.

———. "Slavery in the Sudan in History." *Slavery and Abolition* 20, no. 3 (1999): 69–95.

———. "Sudan." In *Oxford Encyclopedia of the Modern World*, edited by Peter Stearns. Oxford University Press, 2008. Oxford Reference.

Congress.gov. "Summary: H.R.3127—Darfur Peace and Accountability Act of 2006." 109th Congress (2005–2006). Accessed June 1, 2021. https://www.congress.gov/bill/109th-congress/house-bill/3127.

Conroy, F. Dennis. "United States Economic Aid to Africa: 2. Aid Program in the Sudan." *African Studies Bulletin* 7, no. 1 (March 1964): 6–11.

Cornelius, Misha. "Two Howard University Students Named 2019 Boren Scholar and Fellow." Howard University Office of University Communications, June 5, 2019. https://newsroom.howard.edu/newsroom/static/10666/two-howard-university-students-named-2019-boren-scholar-and-fellow.

Cotton, Samuel. *Silent Terror: A Journey into Contemporary Slavery*. New York: Harlem River Press, 1998.

Crockett, Richard. *Sudan: The Failure and Division of an African State*. 2nd ed. New Haven: Yale University Press, 2016.

Curtis, Edward E., IV. *Muslims in America: A Short History*. New York: Oxford University Press, 2009.

Curtis, Edward E., IV, and Sylvester A. Johnson. "Bayyinah Sharrieff: African American Traveler, University of Khartoum Student, National of Islam Leader." *Journal of Africana Religions* 5, no. 1 (2017): 71–153.

Dagbovie, Pero Gaglo. "Exploring a Century of Historical Scholarship on Booker T. Washington." *Journal of African American History* 92, no. 2 (Spring 2007): 239–264.

Daly, M. W. *Empire on the Nile: The Anglo-Egyptian Sudan, 1898–1934*. Cambridge: Cambridge University Press, 1986.

———. *Imperial Sudan: The Anglo-Egyptian Condominium, 1934–1956*. Cambridge: Cambridge University Press, 1991.

Daly, M. W. and Øystein H. Rolandsen. *A History of South Sudan: From Slavery to Independence*. Cambridge: Cambridge University Press, 2016.

Davenport, Lisa E. *Jazz Diplomacy: Promoting America in the Cold War Era*. Jackson: University Press of Mississippi, 2009.

Davidson, Roger A, Jr. "A Question of Freedom: African Americans and Ghanaian Independence." *Negro History Bulletin* 60, No. 3 (July–September 1997): 6–12.

Davis, Kimberly. "The Truth about Slavery in Sudan." *Ebony*, August 2001, 37–40.

Dawoud, Mohamed A., and Ahmed Allam. "Effect of New Nag Hammadi Barrage on Groundwater and Drainage Conditions and Suggestion of Mitigation Measures." *Water Resources Management* 18 (2004): 321–337.

De Waal, Alex. "When Kleptocracy Becomes Insolvent: Brute Causes of the Civil War in South Sudan." *African Affairs* 113, no. 452 (2014): 347–369.

Delreal, Jose, and Philip Ewing, "State Calls Back South Sudan Staff." *Politico*, January 3, 2014. https://www.politico.com/story/2014/01/south-sudan-embassy-staff-exit-101722.

Deng, Francis M. *War of Visions: Conflict of Identities in the Sudan*. Washington, DC: Brookings Institution, 1995.

Du Bois, W. E. B. *Black Folk, Then and Now: An Essay in the History and Sociology of the Negro Race*. New York: Henry Holt, 1939.

Duncan, J. S. R. *The Sudan: A Record of Achievement*. London: William Blackwood & Sons, 1952.

Dworkin, Ira. *Congo Love Song: African American Culture and the Crisis of the Colonial State*. Chapel Hill: University of North Carolina Press, 2017.

"Editorial: A New Course in History at Howard University." *Howard University Record* 17, no. 5 (March 1923): 237–239.

Edwards, Breanna. "Joe Madison Arrested in NY Protest Against Injustice in South Sudan." *The Root*, April 14, 2014. https://www.theroot.com/joe-madison-arrested-in-ny-protest-against-injustice-in-1790875331.

El Gizouli, El Subki Mohamed. "Higher Education in the Sudan from Its Origins to 1966, with Special Reference to University Education." PhD diss., Durham University, 1968.

El-Tom, Abdullah Osman. "Darfur People: Too Black for the Arab-Islamic Project of Sudan." In *Darfur and the Crisis of Governance in Sudan: A Critical Reader*, edited by Salah Hassan and Carina Ray, 84–102. Ithaca: Cornell University Press, 2009.

Elhag, Areig. "Sudan-Israel Relations: Ensuring Civilian Buy-In during a Democratic Transition." Washington Institute Fikra Forum, August 26, 2020. https://www.washingtoninstitute.org/fikraforum/view/sudan-israel-relations-democratic-transition-normalization.

Elsheikh, Elsadig, Basima Sisemore, and Natalia Ramirez Lee. *Legalizing Othering: The United States of Islamophobia*. Berkeley: Haas Institute for a Fair and Inclusive Society, 2017. https://belonging.berkeley.edu/sites/default/files/haas_institute_legalizing_othering_the_united_states_of_islamophobia.pdf.

Emmons, Caroline. "Testing Boundaries: The NAACP and the Caribbean, 1910–1930." *Journal of Caribbean History* 52, no. 2 (2018): 198–216.

Erhagbe, Edward O. "African-Americans and the Defense of the African States against European Imperial Conquest: Booker T. Washington's Diplomatic Efforts to Guarantee Liberia's Independence, 1907–1911." *African Studies Review* 39 (April 1996): 55–65.

———. "The American Negro Leadership Conference on Africa: A New African-American Voice for Africa in the United States, 1962–1970." Boston University African Studies Center Working Papers, 1991.

———. "The Congressional Black Caucus and United States Policy toward Africa: 1971–1990." *Transafrican Journal of History* 24 (1995): 84–96.

Essian-Udom, E. U. *Black Nationalism: A Search for an Identity in America*. Chicago: University of Chicago Press, 1962.

Essien, Kwame, and Toyin Falola, *Culture and Customs of Sudan*. Westport, CT: Greenwood Press, 2009.

"Exit Interview: Page Steps Down as U.S. Ambassador to South Sudan." National Public Radio, August 22, 2014. https://www.npr.org/2014/08/22/342354105/exit-interview-page-steps-down-as-u-s-ambassador-to-south-sudan.

Fadlalla, Amal Hassan. *Branding Humanity: Competing Narratives of Rights, Violence, and Global Citizenship*. Stanford: Stanford University Press, 2018.

Falola, Toyin, and Raphael Chijioke Njoku. *United States and Africa Relations, 1400s to the Present*. New Haven: Yale University Press, 2020.

Farrakhan, Louis, and Henry Louis Gates Jr. "Farrakhan Speaks." *Transition* 70 (1996): 140–167.

Fax, Elton C. *Through Black Eyes: Journeys of a Black Artist to East Africa and Russia*. New York: Dodd, Mead, 1974.

"Federal Reserve Bank Appointee Busy Scholar." *Jet*, March 24, 1966, 26.

Federman, Josef, and Samy Magdy. "Sudanese Officials: Diplomatic Deal with Israel Is Near." Associated Press, October 22, 2020. https://apnews.com/article/donald-trump-virus-outbreak-bahrain-africa-israel-c2a12e4a28ba5280c6e0d1fbbce030f0.

Feierman, Steven. "African Histories and the Dissolution of World History." In *Africa and the Disciplines: The Contributions of Research in Africa to the Social Sciences and Humanities*, edited by Robert H. Bates, V. Y. Mudimbe and Jean O'Barr, 167–212. Chicago: University of Chicago Press, 1993.

Fierce, Milfred C. *The Pan-African Idea in the United States, 1900–1910: African-American Interest in Africa and Interactions with West Africa*. New York: Garland, 1993.

———. "Selected Black American Leaders and Organizations and South Africa, 1900–1977: Some Notes." *Journal of Black Studies* 17, no. 3 (March 1987): 305–326.

Final Call. "About Us." Accessed July 1, 2023. http://www.finalcall.com/artman/publish/aboutus/aboutus.shtml.

Fischbach, Michael R. *Black Power and Palestine: Transnational Countries of Color.* Stanford: Stanford University Press, 2019.
Fluehr-Lobban, Carolyn. "Islamization in Sudan: A Critical Assessment." *Middle East Journal* 44, no. 4 (1990): 610–623.
Forward. "About." Accessed September 20, 2022. https://forward.com/about-us.
"From the Right Revered Oliver C. Allison. As from C.M.S. Juba, 23rd January, 1949." *Southern Sudan Mail Bag*, no. 10 (February 1949): 14–17.
Fronczak, Joseph. "Local People's Global Politics." *Diplomatic History* 39, no. 2 (April 2015): 245–274.
Gaines, Kevin K. *American Africans in Ghana: Black Expatriates and the Civil Rights Era.* Chapel Hill: University of North Carolina Press, 2006.
Gaitskell, Arthur. *Gezira: A Story of Development in the Sudan.* London: Faber and Faber, 1959.
Gardell, Mattias. *In the Name of Elijah Muhammad: Louis Farrakhan and the Nation of Islam.* Durham: Duke University Press, 1996.
Gasman, Marybeth, and Roger L. Geiger. Introduction to *Higher Education for African Americans before the Civil Rights Era, 1900–1964*, 1–16. New Brunswick: Transaction Publishers, 2012.
Gates, Henry Louis, Jr. Foreword to *The Black Kingdom of the Nile*, Charles Bonnet, vii–xi. Cambridge, MA: Harvard University Press, 2019.
"Genocide in Darfur." C-Span, April 30, 2006. https://www.c-span.org/video/?192217-1/genocide-darfur.
Gibson, Dawn-Marie. *A History of the Nation of Islam: Race, Islam, and the Quest for Freedom.* Santa Barbara: Praeger, 2012.
Giddings, Paula. *In Search of Sisterhood: Delta Sigma Theta and the Challenge of the Black Sorority Movement.* New York: HarperCollins, 2002.
Gilliam, Stacy. "Where Are the Black Voices in the Sudan Crisis?" *Crisis*, July/August 2006, 8.
Girard, Philippe R., and Paul Finkelman. "Colonization." In *Encyclopedia of African American History, 1619–1895: From the Colonial Period to the Age of Frederick Douglass.* Oxford University Press, 2006. Oxford Reference.
Global Centre for the Responsibility to Protect. "Timeline of International Response to the Conflict in South Sudan." Accessed October 21, 2022. https://docplayer.net/31355340-Timeline-of-international-response-to-the-conflict-in-south-sudan.html.
Goldschmidt, Arthur, Jr. *Historical Dictionary of Egypt.* 4th ed. Lanham, MD: Scarecrow Press, 2013.
Golz, Ayelet. "Former UN Ambassador Susan Rice to Highlight Founders Day." Colorado State University, December 18, 2019. https://source.colostate.edu/former-un-ambassador-susan-rice-to-highlight-founders-day.
Gomez, Michael A. *Reversing Sail: A History of the African* Diaspora. New York: Cambridge University Press, 2005.
———. *Reversing Sail: A History of the African Diaspora.* 2nd ed. Cambridge, UK: Cambridge University Press, 2020.

Grant, Nicholas. *Winning Our Freedoms Together: African Americans and Apartheid, 1945–1960*. Chapel Hill: University of North Carolina Press, 2017.

"Guide: Why Are Israel and the Palestinians Fighting over Gaza?" BBC, February 20, 2015. https://www.bbc.co.uk/newsround/20436092.

Hamilton, Rebecca. "Special Report: The Wonks Who Sold Washington on South Sudan." Reuters, July 11, 2012. https://www.reuters.com/article/us-south-sudan-midwives/special-report-the-wonks-who-sold-washington-on-south-sudan-idUSBRE86A0GC20120711.

Harlan, Louis R. "Booker T. Washington and the White Man's Burden." *American Historical Review* 71, no. 2 (January 1966): 441–467.

Harvard Kennedy School. "Samantha Power." Accessed July 3, 2023. https://web.archive.org/web/20210228220923/https://www.hks.harvard.edu/faculty/samantha-power.

Harvard University, Radcliffe Institute for Advanced Study, Schlesinger Library. "Shirley Graham Du Bois." Accessed July 3, 2023. https://www.radcliffe.harvard.edu/schlesinger-library/collection/shirley-graham-du-bois.

Hāshim, M. Jalāl. *To Be or Not to Be: Sudan at Crossroads, a Pan-African Perspective*. Dar es Salaam: Mkuki Na Nyota, 2019.

Hashim, Mohanad. "A Step towards Peace?" BBC, February 11, 2020, https://www.bbc.com/news/world-africa-51462613.

Hertzke, Allen D. "African American Churches and U.S. Policy in Sudan." *Review of Faith and International Affairs* 6, no. 1 (2008): 19–26.

———. *Freeing God's Children: The Unlikely Global Alliance for Global Human Rights*. Lanham, MD: Rowman & Littlefield, 2004.

Higashida, Cheryl. *Black Internationalist Feminism: Women Writers of the Black Left, 1945–1995*. Urbana: University of Illinois Press, 2011.

Hogue, Kellie. "Garveyism." In *The Oxford Encyclopedia of the Modern World*. Oxford University Press, 2008. Oxford Reference.

Hohle, Randolph. Introduction to *Black Citizenship and Authenticity in the Civil Rights Movement*, 1–39. New York: Routledge, 2013.

Holt, Thomas C. *The Problem of Freedom: Race, Labor, and Politics in Jamaica and Britain, 1832–1938*. Baltimore: Johns Hopkins University Press, 1992.

Horne, Gerald. *The End of Empires: African Americans and India*. Philadelphia: Temple University Press, 2008.

———. *Mau Mau in Harlem? The U.S. and the Liberation of Kenya*. New York: Palgrave Macmillan, 2009.

———. *Race Woman: The Lives of Shirley Graham Du Bois*. New York: New York University Press, 2000.

———. *The Rise and Fall of the Associated Negro Press: Claude Barnett's Pan-African News and the Jim Crow Paradox*. Urbana: University of Illinois Press, 2017.

Houle, Christine. "An Interview with Susan D. Page, U.S. Ambassador to South Sudan." *The Politic*, August 13, 2013. https://thepolitic.org/an-interview-with-susan-d-page-u-s-ambassador-to-south-sudan.

Houser, George M. "Meeting Africa's Challenge: The Story of the American Committee on Africa." *Issue: A Journal of Opinion* 6, no. 2/3 (Summer/Autumn 1976): 16–26.

Houston, Helen R. "Brimmer, Andrew Felton (1926–2012)." In *Encyclopedia of African American Business*, vol. 1, A–L, updated and rev. ed., edited by Jessie Carney Smith, 133–135. Santa Barbara: ABC-CLIO, 2018.

Howell, Sally. *Old Islam in Detroit: Rediscovering the Muslim American Past*. New York: Oxford University Press, 2014.

Hughes, Langston. "The Negro Speaks of Rivers." Poetry Foundation. Accessed May 14, 2020. https://www.poetryfoundation.org/poems/44428/the-negro-speaks-of-rivers.

Human Rights Watch. "South Sudan Events of 2015." Accessed November 20, 2020. https://www.hrw.org/world-report/2016/country-chapters/south-sudan.

———. "'They Burned it All': Destruction of Villages, Killings, and Sexual Violence in Unity State South Sudan." July 22, 2015. https://www.hrw.org/report/2015/07/22/they-burned-it-all/destruction-villages-killings-and-sexual-violence-unity-state#_ftn63.

Hutchinson, Sharon E. *Nuer Dilemmas: Coping with Money, War, and the State*. Berkeley: University of California Press, 1996.

Idris, Amir H. *Conflict and Politics of Identity in Sudan*. Houndmills, Basingstoke, UK: Palgrave Macmillan, 2005.

———. "Slavery, Colonialism, and Political Violence: The Case of South Sudan." In *Sudan's Killing Fields: Political Violence and Fragmentation*, edited by Laura N. Beny and Sondra Hale, 59–75. Trenton, NJ: Red Sea Press, 2015.

"In 2020, Protests Spread across the Globe with a Similar Message: Black Lives Matter." National Public Radio, December 30, 2020. https://www.npr.org/2020/12/30/950053607/in-2020-protests-spread-across-the-globe-with-a-similar-message-black-lives-matt.

"Israel Profile—Timeline." BBC, April 9, 2019. https://www.bbc.com/news/world-middle-east-29123668.

Janken, Kenneth R. "From Colonial Liberation to Cold War Liberalism: Walter White, the NAACP, and Foreign Affairs, 1941–1955." *Ethnic and Racial Studies* 21, no. 6 (1998): 1074–1095.

Johnson, Douglas H. *South Sudan: A New History for a New Nation*. Athens: Ohio University Press, 2016.

Jumar, Akshaya. "UN Peacekeepers Turn Blind Eye to Rape in South Sudan." Human Rights Watch, November 3, 2016. https://www.hrw.org/news/2016/11/03/un-peacekeepers-turn-blind-eye-rape-south-sudan.

Kayyali, Randa. "US Census Classifications and Arab Americans: Contestations and Definitions of Identity Markers." *Journal of Ethnic and Migration Studies* 39, no. 8 (2013): 1299–1318.

Kelley, Robin D. G. "Malcolm X." In *The Oxford Companion to United States History*, edited by Paul S. Boyer. Oxford University Press, 2001. Oxford Reference.

Kettani, Houssain. "Muslim Population in the Americas: 1950–2020." *International Journal of Environmental Science and Development* 1, no. 2 (June 2010): 127.

"Kitchen, Kuykendall May Be Ambassadors." *Jet*, March 10, 1960, 3.

Knight, Michael Muhammad. *Metaphysical Africa: Truth and Blackness in the Ansaru Allah Community*. University Park: Pennsylvania State University Press, 2020.

Königshofer, Martina. *The New Ship of Zion: Dynamic Diaspora Dimensions of the African Hebrew Israelites of Jerusalem*. Piscataway, NJ: Transaction, 2008.

Kosinski, Michelle. "Obama, African Leaders Meet to End South Sudan's Civil War." CNN, July 27, 2015. https://www.cnn.com/2015/07/27/politics/south-sudan-obama-ethiopia-meeting/index.html.

Kramer, Robert S., Richard A. Lobban Jr., and Carolyn Fluehr-Lobban. *Historical Dictionary of the Sudan*. 3rd ed. Lanham, MD: Scarecrow Press, 2002.

———. *Historical Dictionary of the Sudan*. 4th ed. Lanham, MD: Scarecrow Press, 2013.

Krenn, Michael L. *Black Diplomacy: African Americans and the State Department, 1945–69*. Armonk, NY: M.E. Sharpe, 1999.

Kuyok, Kuyok Abol. *South Sudan: The Notable Firsts*. Bloomington, IN: AuthorHouse, 2015.

Labott, Elise. "Obama Is Asked to Focus on Darfur." CNN, November 12, 2008, https://www.cnn.com/2008/WORLD/africa/11/12/obama.darfur/index.html.

Lagu, Joseph. *Sudan: Odyssey through a State: From Hope to Ruin*. Omdurman: MOB Center for Sudanese Studies, Omdurman Ahlia University, 2006.

Lantos Foundation for Human Rights and Justice. "Tom Lantos." Accessed September 23, 2020. https://www.lantosfoundation.org/about-tom-lantos.

Lawton, Kim. "Black Churches Taking Lead on Pressing Sudan Issue." Religion News Service, August 23, 2005. https://religionnews.com/2005/08/23/black-churches-taking-lead-on-pressing-sudan-issue.

Leanne, Shelly. "The Clinton Administration and Africa: Perspective of the Congressional Black Caucus and TransAfrica." *Issue: A Journal of Opinion* 26, no. 2 (1998), 17–22.

Ledwidge, Mark. *Race and US Foreign Policy: The African-American Foreign Affairs Network*. New York: Routledge, 2012.

Lee, Martha F. *The Nation of Islam: An American Millenarian Movement*. Syracuse: Syracuse University Press, 1996.

"Leigh S. J. Hunt," *Annals of Iowa* 19, no. 4 (April 1934): 314–315.

Lerner, Mitch. "Climbing off the Back Burner: Lyndon Johnson's Soft Power Approach to Africa." *Diplomacy and Statecraft* 22 (2011): 578–607.

Lesch, David W. *The Arab-Israeli Conflict: A History*. New York: Oxford University Press, 2008.

"Louis Farrakhan Fast Facts." CNN, June 19, 2020. https://www.cnn.com/2013/05/24/us/louis-farrakhan-fast-facts/index.html.

Lubin, Alex. *Geographies of Liberation: The Making of an Afro-Arab Political Imaginary*. Chapel Hill: University of North Carolina Press, 2014.

———. "Locating Palestine in pre-1948 Black Internationalism." *Souls: A Critical Journal of Black Politics, Culture and Society* 9, no. 2 (2007): 95–108.

Lynch, Hollis R. *Black American Radicals and the Liberation of Africa: The Council on African Affairs, 1937–1955*. Ithaca: Africana Studies and Research Center, Cornell University, 1978.

Mack, James Leonard. *My Life, My Country, My World*. Pittsburgh: Dorrance Publishing, 2008.

Mahon, Maureen. "Eslanda Goode Robeson's *African Journey*: The Politics of Identification and Representation in the African Diaspora." *Souls: A Critical Journal of Black Politics, Culture and Society* 8, no. 3 (2006): 101–118.

Makar, Ashley. "My Take: Why Egypt's Christians Are Hopeful but Nervous." *CNN Belief Blog*. Accessed November 25, 2022. https://religion.blogs.cnn.com/2011/02/10/my-take-why-egypts-christians-are-excited-but-nervous.

"Making a World." *African Repository*, January 1, 1885.

Makki, Hind. "Why Are Some Black Africans Considered White Americans?" *Al Jazeera*, February 16, 2017. https://www.aljazeera.com/indepth/opinion/2017/02/black-africans-considered-white-americans-170215073123425.html.

Malamud, Margaret. "Black Minerva: Antiquity in Antebellum African American History." In *African Athena: African Agendas*, edited by Daniel Orrells, Gurminder K. Bhambra, and Tessa Roynon, 71–89. New York: Oxford University Press, 2011.

Mamdani, Mahmood. *When Victims Become Killers: Colonialism, Nativism, and the Genocide in Rwanda*. Princeton: Princeton University Press, 2001.

Mamiya, Lawrence H. "From Black Muslim to Bilalian: The Evolution of a Movement." *Journal for the Scientific Study of Religion* (1982): 138–152.

Mampilly, Zachariah. "Witnessing the Birth of a Nation in Southern Sudan." *The Root*, January 10, 2011. https://www.theroot.com/witnessing-the-birth-of-a-nation-in-southern-sudan-1790862340.

Manning, Patrick. *The African Diaspora: A History through Culture*. New York: Columbia University Press, 2009.

Markle, Seth M. *A Motorcycle on the Run: Tanzania, Black Power, and the Uncertain Future of Pan-Africanism, 1964–1974*. East Lansing: Michigan State University Press, 2017.

McAlister, Melani. *The Kingdom of God Has No Borders: A Global History of American Evangelicals*. New York: Oxford University Press, 2018.

———. "One Black Allah: The Middle East in the Cultural Politics of African American Liberation, 1955–1970." *American Quarterly* 51, no. 3 (September 1999): 622–656.

Meriwether, James H. *Proudly We Can Be Africans: Black Americans and Africa, 1935–1961*. Chapel Hill: University of North Carolina Press, 2002.

Miller, Jake. "The NAACP and Global Human Rights." *Western Journal of Black Studies* 26, no. 1 (Spring 2002): 22–31.

Mitchell, Michele. "'The Black Man's Burden': African Americans, Imperialism, and Notions of Racial Manhood 1890–1910." *International Review of Social History* 4, supplement 7 (1999): 77–99.

Mobley, Steve D., Jr., and Jennifer M. Johnson. "The Role of HBCUs in Addressing the Unique Needs of LGBT Students." *New Directions for Higher Education*, no. 170 (2015): 79–89.

Mohsin, Magda Ismail Abdel. "The Practice of Islamic Banking System in Sudan." *Journal of Economic Cooperation* 26, no. 4 (2005): 27–50.

Mokhtefi, Elaine. *Algiers, Third World Capital: Freedom Fighters, Revolutionaries, Black Panthers*. London: Verso Books, 2018.

Moore, Jesse. "President Obama Marks the 50th Anniversary of the Marches from Selma to Montgomery." President Barack Obama White House archives, March 8, 2015. https://obamawhitehouse.archives.gov/blog/2015/03/08/president-obama-marks-50th-anniversary-marches-selma-montgomery.

Morris, Lorenzo. "African American Representatives in the United Nations: From Ralph Bunche to Susan Rice." In *African Americans in U.S. Foreign Policy: From the Era of Frederick Douglass to the Age of Obama*, edited by Linda Heywood, Allison Blakely, Charles Stith, and Joshua C. Yesnowitz, 177–199. Urbana: University of Illinois Press, 2015.

———. "The United Nations and the African American Presence: From Ralph Bunche to Susan Rice." In *Charting the Range of Black Politics: National Political Science Review*, edited by Michael Mitchell and David Covin, 41–56. New Brunswick, NJ: Transaction Publishers, 2012.

Morsy, Soheir A. "Beyond the Honorary 'White' Classification of Egyptians: Societal Identity in Historical Context." In *Race*, edited by Roger Sanjek and Steven Gregory, 175–198. New Brunswick, NJ: Rutgers University Press, 1994.

Moses, Wilson J. *Afrotopia: The Roots of African American Popular History*. Cambridge: Cambridge University Press, 1998.

———. *Black Messiahs and Uncle Toms: Social and Literary Manipulations of a Religious Myth*. Revised edition. University Park: Pennsylvania State University Press, 1994.

Mount, Guy Emerson. "The Last Reconstruction: Slavery, Emancipation, and Empire in the Black Pacific." PhD diss., University of Chicago, 2018.

Murphy, David. "Introduction: The Performance of Pan-Africanism: Staging the African Renaissance at the First World Festival of Negro Arts." In *The First World Festival of Negro Arts, Dakar 1966: Contexts and Legacies*, edited by David Murphy, 1–52. Liverpool: Liverpool University Press, 2016.

"Name Robert Kitchen to Head Sudan Mission." *Jet*, April 17, 1958, 3.

National Park Service. "Whitney M. Young, Jr." Accessed June 11, 2020. https://www.nps.gov/people/whitney-young-jr.htm.

Natsios, Andrew S. *Sudan, South Sudan, and Darfur: What Everyone Needs to Know*. New York: Oxford University Press, 2012.

Nelson, Harold D., Margarita Dobert, Gordon C. McDonald, James McLaughlin, Barbara J. Marvin, and Philip W. Moeller. *Area Handbook for the Democratic Republic of Sudan*. Washington, DC: US Government Printing Office, 1973.

Niblett, Michael. "African Times and Orient Review." In *The Oxford Companion to Black British History*, edited by David Dabydeen, John Gilmore, and Cecily Jones. Oxford University Press, 2007. Oxford Reference.

Nmoma, Veronica. "The Shift in United States-Sudan Relations: A Troubled Relationship and the Need for Mutual Cooperation." *Journal of Conflict Studies* (Winter 2006): 44–70.

O'Dell, Emily Jane. "Following in the Footsteps of Malcolm X." *HuffPost*, January 13, 2015. https://www.huffingtonpost.com/emily-odell/following-in-the-footstep_3_b_6434534.html.

———. "X Marks the Spot: Mapping Malcolm X's Encounters with Sudan." *Journal of Africana Religions* 3, no. 1 (2015): 96–115.

Obama, Barack. *Dreams from My Father: A Story of Race and Inheritance*. New York: Crown Publishers, 1995.

———. "Statement on the Southern Sudan Independence Referendum." January 16, 2011. American Presidency Project. Accessed June 1, 2021. https://www.presidency.ucsb.edu/documents/statement-the-southern-sudan-independence-referendum.

"Obama Launches Presidential Bid." BBC News, February 10, 2007. http://news.bbc.co.uk/2/hi/americas/6349081.stm.

"Obama Pushes for Peace in Sudan." *Jet*, July 27, 2015. https://www.jetmag.com/news/obama-pushes-for-peace-in-sudan.

"Obama Reaffirms US Support for South Sudan Referendum Vote." Voice of America, December 22, 2010. https://www.voanews.com/africa/obama-reaffirms-us-support-south-sudan-referendum-vote.

"Obama Urges Talks between Rival Sudans." *Al Jazeera*, April 21, 2012. https://www.aljazeera.com/news/2012/4/21/obama-urges-talks-between-rival-sudans.

Office of the Historian, US Department of State. "The Arab-Israeli War of 1948." Accessed June 16, 2020. https://history.state.gov/milestones/1945-1952/arab-israeli-war.

Office of the United States Trade Representative. "Middle East/North Africa." Accessed December 21, 2020. https://ustr.gov/countries-regions/europe-middle-east/middle-east/north-africa.

Ogbar, Jeffrey O. G. *Black Power: Radical Politics and African American Identity*. Updated ed. Baltimore: Johns Hopkins University Press, 2019.

Oguntoyinbo, Lekan. "Forging Leaders: HBCUs Produce Leaders Not Only Domestically, but Also Abroad." *Diverse: Issues in Higher Education*, February 28, 2013, 16–17.

Omi, Michael, and Howard Winant. *Racial Formation in the United States*. 3rd ed. New York: Routledge, 2015.

"Origins of the Darfur Crisis." *PBS News Hour*, July 3, 2008. https://www.pbs.org/newshour/politics/africa-july-dec08-origins_07-03.

Palmer, Doug. "U.S. extends trade benefit program to South Sudan." *Reuters*, March 26, 2012. https://www.reuters.com/article/uk-usa-southsudan-trade-idUKBRE82P14620120326.

Palmer, Ransford W. "Jamaica." In *The Oxford Encyclopedia of Economic History*, edited by Joel Mokyr. Oxford University Press, 2003. Oxford Reference.

Parnes, Amie. "Move Over Oprah? Obama Sells Books." *Politico*, May 30, 2009. https://www.politico.com/story/2009/05/move-over-oprah-obama-sells-books-023114.

Pedneault, Jonathan. "Starving under the Bullets in South Sudan." Human Rights Watch, April 11, 2017. https://www.hrw.org/news/2017/04/11/starving-under-bullets-south-sudan.

Peters, Joel. *Israel and Africa: The Problematic Relationship*. London: British Academic Press, 1992.

Peterson, Maya. "US to USSR: American Experts, Irrigation, and Cotton in Soviet Central Asia, 1929–32." *Environmental History* 21 (2016): 442–466.

Phares, Walid. *The Coming Revolution: Struggle for Freedom in the Middle East*. New York: Threshold Editions, 2010.

Pimienta-Bey, José Vittorio. "Some 'Myths' of the Moorish Science Temple: An Afrocentric Historical Analysis." PhD diss., Temple University, 1995.

Plummer, Brenda Gayle. *In Search of Power: African Americans in the Age of Decolonization, 1956–1974*. New York: Cambridge University Press, 2013.

———. *Rising Wind: Black Americans and U.S. Foreign Affairs, 1935–1960*. Chapel Hill: University of North Carolina Press, 1996.

Prashad, Vijay. *The Darker Nations: A Biography of the Short-Lived Third World*. New Delhi: LeftWord Books, 2007.

———. *The Karma of Brown Folk*. Minneapolis: University of Minnesota Press, 2000.

"Race War in the Sudan: Big White Lie." *SOBU Newsletter* (Student Organization for Black Unity, Greensboro, NC), May 1, 1971.

Radcliffe, Kendahl L. "The Tuskegee-Togo Cotton Scheme 1900–1909." PhD diss., University of California, Los Angeles, 1998.

Rand, Laurance B. *High Stakes: The Life and Times of Leigh S. J. Hunt*. New York: Peter Lang, 1989.

"Read President Obama's Full Speech at DNC." *Ebony*, September 7, 2012. https://www.ebony.com/news/full-text-president-obama-addresses-dnc.

Rakowsky, Judy. "Lawsuits Dropped, but Battles over Boston Mosque Continue." *Forward*, June 27, 2007. https://forward.com/news/11052/lawsuits-dropped-but-battles-over-boston-mosque-c-00063.

Reports by His Majesty's Agent and Consul-General on the Finances, Administration, and Condition of Egypt and the Soudan, 1902–1904. London: His Majesty's Stationary Office, 1903–1905.

Rice, Susan. *Tough Love: My Story of the Things Worth Fighting For*. New York: Simon & Schuster, 2019.

Richburg, Keith B. *Out of America: A Black Man Confronts Africa*. New York: Basic Books, 1997.

Riches, C., and J. Palmowski. "Civil Rights Movement." In *A Dictionary of Contemporary World History*, 4th edition. Oxford University Press, 2016. Oxford Reference.

Richmond, J. C. B. *Egypt, 1798–1952: Her Advance towards a Modern Identity*. New York: Columbia University Press, 1977.

"The Rise and Fall of Pan-Arabism." Geneva Graduate Institute, January 31, 2019. https://www.graduateinstitute.ch/communications/news/rise-and-fall-pan-arabism.

Robeson, Eslanda Goode. *African Journey*. Westport, CT: Greenwood Press, 1972. Originally published 1945 by John Day (New York).

Robins, Jonathan E. *Cotton and Race across the Atlantic: Britain, Africa, and America, 1900–1920*. Rochester, NY: University of Rochester Press, 2016.

Rogers, Harold S. "Imperialism in Africa." *Black Scholar* 3, no. 5 (January 1972): 36–48.

Rogers, Ibrahm H. "From Black to African: Identity Shifts and Pan-African Activism in the Black Campus Movement, 1965–1972." In *Historical and Contemporary Pan-Africanism and the Quest for African Renaissance*, edited by Njoki Wane and Francis Adyanga Akena, 29–45. Newcastle upon Tyne: Cambridge Scholars Press, 2019.

Rogers, J. A. *Nature Knows No Color-Line: Research into the Negro Ancestry in the White Race*. 3rd ed. St. Petersburg, FL: Helga M. Rogers, 1980.

———. *100 Amazing Facts about the Negro with Complete Proof: A Short Cut to the World History of the Negro*. Lebanon, NH: Wesleyan University Press, 1995.

Rolandsen, Øystein H. "Another Civil War in South Sudan: The Failure of Guerrilla Government?" *Journal of Eastern African Studies*, 9, no. 1 (2015): 163–174.

———. "A False Start: Between War and Peace in the Southern Sudan, 1956–62." *Journal of African History* 52, no. 1 (2011): 105–123.

Rosenberg, Jonathan. *How Far the Promised Land? World Affairs and the American Civil Rights Movement from the First World War to Vietnam*. Princeton: Princeton University Press, 2006.

Ruay, Deng D. Akol. *The Politics of Two Sudans: The South and the North, 1821–1969*. Uppsala: Nordic Africa Institute, 1994.

Rugh, William A. *Arab Mass Media: Newspapers, Radio, and Television in Arab Politics*. Westport, CT: Praeger, 2004.

Salomon, Noah. "Religion after the State: Secular Soteriologies at the Birth of South Sudan." *Journal of Law and Religion* 29 (2014): 447–469.

Scopas, Denis. "Bound by Oil: How Petroleum Is Bringing Sudan and South Sudan Closer Together." *Middle East Eye*, October 26, 2019. https://www.middleeasteye.net/news/bound-oil-how-petroleum-bringing-sudan-and-south-sudan-closer-together.

"Security Advisor Susan Rice: Together, We Must Help South Sudan Implement the Peace Agreement." U.S. Mission to International Organizations in Geneva, August 27, 2015. https://geneva.usmission.gov/2015/08/27/security-advisor-susan-rice-together-we-must-help-south-sudan-implement-the-peace-agreement.

Sefa-Nyarko, Clement. "Civil War in South Sudan: Is It a Reflection of Historical Secessionist and Natural Resource Wars in 'Greater Sudan'?" *African Security* 9, no. 3 (2016): 188–210.

"Sen. Obama Visits Darfur Refugees in Chad." National Public Radio, September 3, 2006. https://www.npr.org/templates/story/story.php?storyId=5760323.

Serels, Steven. *Starvation and the State: Famine, Slavery, and Power in Sudan, 1883–1956*. New York: Palgrave Macmillan, 2013.

Seri-Hersch, Iris. "Education in Colonial Sudan, 1900–1957." *Oxford Research Encyclopaedia of African History*, 2017. HAL Open Science, https://shs.hal.science/halshs-01514910/document.

———. "Sudan and the British Empire in the Era of Colonial Dismantlement (1946–1956): History Teaching in Comparative Perspective." In *The Road to the Two Sudans*, edited by Souad T. Ali, Stephanie Beswick, Richard Lobban and Jay Spaulding, 177–219. Newcastle upon Tyne: Cambridge Scholars Publishing, 2014.

Shaffer, Robert. "Out of the Shadows: The Political Writings of Eslanda Goode Robeson." *Pennsylvania History* 66, no. 1 (Winter 1999): 47–64.

Shama, Nael. "Egypt's Foreign Policy from Faruq to Mubarak." In *Routledge Handbook on Contemporary Egypt*, edited by Robert Springborg, Amr Adly, Anthony Gorman, Tamir Moustafa, Aisha Saad, Naomi Sakr, and Sarah Smierciak, 43–54. London: Routledge/Taylor & Francis Group, 2021.

Sharkey, Heather J. "Arab Identity and Ideology in Sudan: The Politics of Language, Ethnicity, and Race." *African Affairs* 107, no. 226 (January 2008): 21–43.

———. "Colonialism, Character, Building and the Culture of Nationalism in the Sudan, 1898." In *The Decolonization Reader*, edited by James D. Le Sueur, 218–237. New York: Routledge, 2003.

Shellum, Brian G. *African American Officers in Liberia: A Pestiferous Rotation, 1910–1942*. Lincoln: University of Nebraska Press, 2018.

Shillington, Kevin. *History of Africa*. 4th ed. London: Red Globe Press, 2019.

The Situation in South Sudan: Hearing before the Committee on Foreign Relations. Washington, DC: US Government Publishing Office, 2015. https://www.govinfo.gov/content/pkg/CHRG-113shrg93484/pdf/CHRG-113shrg93484.pdf.

Slate, Nico. *Colored Cosmopolitanism: The Shared Struggle for Freedom in the United States and India*. Cambridge, MA: Harvard University Press, 2012.

Smith, Tom W. "Changing Racial Labels: From 'Colored' to 'Negro' to 'Black' to 'African American.'" *Public Opinion Quarterly* 56, no. 4 (1992): 496–514.

"South Sudan President Salva Kiir Signs Peace Deal." BBC News, August 26, 2015. https://www.bbc.com/news/world-africa-34066511.

"South Sudan Profile—Timeline." BBC, August 6, 2018. https://www.bbc.com/news/world-africa-14019202

"South Sudan: Rebel with a cause." *Embassy*. Accessed September 23, 2020. https://embassymagazine.com/south-sudan.

Stoler, Ann. *Race and the Education of Desire: Foucault's History of Sexuality and the Colonial Order of Things*. Durham: Duke University Press, 1995.

Strickland, Patrick. "US: Are 'Anti-Sharia' Bills Legalising Islamophobia?" *Al Jazeera*, October 1, 2017. https://www.aljazeera.com/news/2017/10/1/us-are-anti-sharia-bills-legalising-islamophobia.

Strong, Krystal. "Do African Lives Matter to Black Lives Matter? Youth Uprisings and the Borders of Solidarity." *Urban Education* 53, no. 2 (2018): 265–285.

"Sudan Fast Facts." CNN, updated December 17, 2020. https://web.archive.org/web/20201217164003/https://www.cnn.com/2013/10/30/world/africa/sudan-fast-facts/index.html.

"Sudan v. Christians." *Time Magazine*, February 1, 1963. https://content.time.com/time/subscriber/article/0,33009,829787,00.html.

Sundiata, Ibrahim. "Obama, African Americans, and Africans: The Double Vision." In *African Americans in U.S. Foreign Policy: From the Era of Frederick Douglass to the Age of Obama*, edited by Linda Heywood, Allison Blakely, Charles Stith, and Joshua C. Yesnowitz, 200–212. Urbana: University of Illinois Press, 2015.

Talton, Benjamin. *In This Land of Plenty: Mickey Leland and Africa in American Politics.* Philadelphia: University of Pennsylvania Press, 2019.

Theodore, Wendy. "The Declining Appeal of Diasporic Connections: African American Organising for South Africa, Haiti and Rwanda." *Global Society* 22, no. 2 (2008): 297–318.

Thomas, Damion. "Goodwill Ambassadors: African American Athletes and U.S. Cultural Diplomacy, 1947–1968." In *African Americans in U.S. Foreign Policy: From the Era of Frederick Douglass to the Age of Obama,* edited by Linda Heywood, Allison Blakely, Charles Stith, and Joshua C. Yesnowitz, 129–140. Urbana: University of Illinois Press, 2015.

"Thousands Rally at Capitol for Immediate Aid to Darfur." *Jet*, May 15, 2006, 6–8.

Tolan-Szkilnik, Paraska. "Collecting Bosoms:" Sex, Race, and Masculinity at the Pan-African Festival of Algiers, 1969." *Arab Studies Journal* 29, no. 2 (2021): 96–117.

Tounsel, Christopher. "Fragile States: Nation-Building in Sudan." *Books and Ideas*, October 25, 2018. https://booksandideas.net/Fragile-States-Nation-building-in-Sudan.html.

"TransAfrica Forum." Linktank. Accessed August 17, 2023. https://linktank.com/organization/transafrica-forum/about.

"Transcript: Obama Addresses U.N. General Assembly." CNN. Accessed January 20, 2023. https://www.cnn.com/2009/POLITICS/09/23/obama.transcript/index.html.

Umoren, Imaobong D. *Race Women Internationalists: Activist-Intellectuals and Global Freedom Struggles.* Berkeley: University of California Press, 2018.

UNESCO World Heritage Convention. "Deim Zubeir—Slave Route Site." Accessed October 7, 2022. https://whc.unesco.org/en/tentativelists/6275.

United Nations Human Rights Office of the High Commissioner. "Middle East and Northern Africa Region." Accessed December 21, 2020. https://www.ohchr.org/en/countries/menaregion/pages/menaregionindex.aspx.

UN News, "South Sudan: Security Council Condemns Killing of Civilians, Peacekeepers at UN Compound." *Africa Renewal*. Accessed September 6, 2022. https://www.un.org/africarenewal/news/south-sudan-security-council-condemns-killing-civilians-peacekeepers-un-compound.

"US and France Press UN for S Sudan Sanctions." *Al Jazeera*, April 24, 2014. https://www.aljazeera.com/news/2014/4/24/us-and-france-press-un-for-s-sudan-sanctions.

U.S. Department of State. "U.S. Relations with Sudan." October 24, 2022. https://www.state.gov/u-s-relations-with-sudan.

U.S. Embassy in Sudan. "U.S.-Sudan Relations." Accessed June 1, 2021. https://sd.usembassy.gov/our-relationship/policy-history/us-sudan-relations.

USA.gov. "U.S. Agency for International Development." Accessed May 11, 2020. https://www.usa.gov/federal-agencies/u-s-agency-for-international-development.

Vincent, Cédric. "'The Real Heart of the Festival': The Exhibition of *L'Art nègre* at the Musée Dynamique." In *The First World Festival of Negro Arts, Dakar 1966: Contexts and Legacies*, edited by David Murphy, 45–63. Liverpool: Liverpool University Press, 2016.

Vinson, Robert Trent. *The Americans Are Coming! Dreams of African American Liberation in Segregationist South Africa*. Athens: Ohio University Press, 2012.

Voll, John O. "The Sudan after Nimeiry." *Current History* 85, no. 511 (1986): 213–216, 231–232.

Von Eschen, Penny M. "Soul Call: The First World Festival of Negro Arts at a Pivot of Black Modernities." *Nka: Journal of Contemporary African Art*, no. 42–43 (2018): 124–135.

Wainstock, Dennis. *Malcolm X, African American Revolutionary*. Jefferson, NC: McFarland, 2009.

Wakson, Elias Nyamell. "Islamism and Militarism in Sudanese Politics: Its Impact on Nation-Building." *Northeast African Studies*, New Series, 5, no. 2: 47–94.

Wallington, Sherrie Flynt, Bridget Oppong, Marquita Iddirisu, and Lucile L. Adams-Campbell. "Developing a Mass Media Campaign to Promote Mammography Awareness in African American Women in the Nation's Capital." *Journal of Community Health* 43, no. 4 (2018): 633–638.

Warburg, Gabriel. "Ideological and Practical Considerations Regarding Slavery in the Mahdist State and the Anglo-Egyptian Sudan, 1881–1918." In *The Ideology of Slavery in Africa*, edited by Paul E. Lovejoy, 245–270. Beverly Hills: Sage, 1981.

———. *Islam, Nationalism and Communism in a Traditional Society: The Case of Sudan*. Totowa, NJ: Frank Cass, 1978.

———. *Islam, Sectarianism, and Politics in Sudan since the Mahdiyya*. Madison: University of Wisconsin Press, 2003.

Washburn, Patrick S. *The African American Newspaper: Voice of Freedom*. Evanston, Ill.: Northwestern University Press, 2006.

Washington, Robert. "Horace Cayton: Reflections on an Unfulfilled Sociological Career." *American Sociologist* 28, no. 1 (Spring 1997): 55–74.

"[WATCH] President Obama's Moving #Selma50 Speech." *Ebony*, March 9, 2015, https://www.ebony.com/news/watch-president-obamas-moving-selma50-speech-403.

Watkins, S. Craig. "Framing Protest: News Media Frames of the Million Man March." *Critical Studies in Media Communication* 18, no. 1 (2001): 83–101.

Wawa, Yosa. "Background to the Southern Sudan." In *Southern Sudanese Pursuits of Self-Determination: Documents in Political History*, edited by Yosa Wawa, 1–21. Kampala: Marianum Press, 2005.

West, Michael O. "The Tuskegee Model of Development in Africa: Another Dimension of the African/African-American Connection." *Diplomatic History: The Journal of the Society for Historians of American Foreign Relations* 16 (Summer 1992): 371–387.

"*What Is the What* Reader's Guide." Focus: Dave Eggers's novel *What Is the What*. Penguin Random House. Accessed June 1, 2021. https://www.penguinrandomhouse.com/books/45422/what-is-the-what-by-dave-eggers/9780307385901/readers-guide.

"What's Next for the Nation of Islam?" National Public Radio, February 26, 2007. https://www.npr.org/templates/story/story.php?storyId=7601345.

The White House. "Barack Obama." Accessed June 1, 2021. https://www.whitehouse.gov/about-the-white-house/presidents/barack-obama.

The White House. "Barack Obama: The 44th President of the United States." Accessed January 28, 2023. https://www.whitehouse.gov/about-the-white-house/presidents/barack-obama.

White House. President Barack Obama. "Statement by President Barack Obama on South Sudan." December 19, 2013. https://obamawhitehouse.archives.gov/the-press-office/2013/12/19/statement-president-south-sudan.

White House Historical Association. "E. Frederick Morrow at the White House." Accessed May 11, 2020. https://www.whitehousehistory.org/e-frederick-morrow-at-the-white-house.

White House Office of the Press Secretary. "Remarks by President Obama to the People of Africa." Accessed June 1, 2021. https://obamawhitehouse.archives.gov/the-press-office/2015/07/28/remarks-president-obama-people-africa.

———. "Remarks by the President in State of Union Address," January 25, 2011. https://obamawhitehouse.archives.gov/the-press-office/2011/01/25/remarks-president-state-union-address.

———. "Statement of President Barack Obama Recognition of the Republic of South Sudan." July 9, 2011. https://obamawhitehouse.archives.gov/the-press-office/2011/07/09/statement-president-barack-obama-recognition-republic-south-sudan.

Williams, Corey. "Some Blacks Applaud Castro Legacy of Racial Equality." Associated Press, November 28, 2016. https://apnews.com/article/4ad817d973a742dfbe69bfabedae0916.

Williams, Jennifer. "The Conflict in South Sudan, Explained." *Vox*, updated January 9, 2017. https://www.vox.com/world/2016/12/8/13817072/south-sudan-crisis-explained-ethnic-cleansing-genocide.

Williamson, Richard. "How Obama Betrayed Sudan." *Foreign Policy*, November 11, 2010. https://foreignpolicy.com/2010/11/11/how-obama-betrayed-sudan.

Wilson, Scott. *Resting Places: The Burial Sites of More than 14,000 Famous Persons*. 3rd ed. Jefferson, NC: McFarland, 2016.

Wojnarowski, Adrian. "Sources: Howard Star Freshman Makur Maker Entering NBA Draft." ESPN, May 28, 2021. https://www.espn.com/nba/story/_/id/31528054/sources-howard-star-freshman-makur-maker-entering-nba-draft.

Woodford, Maize. "A Chronology: Farrakhan's 'World Friendship Tour' to Africa and the Middle East: January–February 1996." *Black Scholar* 26, no. 3–4 (1996): 35–40.

Woodruff, Nan. *American Congo: The African-American Freedom Struggle in the Delta*. Cambridge, MA: Harvard University Press, 2003.

Woods, Michael, and Mary B. Woods. *The Tomb of Tutankhamen: Unearthing Ancient Worlds*. Minneapolis: Twenty-First Century Books, 2008.

"World: Delta Tour." *Jet*, September 6, 1962, 39.

The World Bank. "Middle East and North Africa." Accessed December 21, 2020. https://www.worldbank.org/en/region/mena.

Wroughton, Lesley. "Exclusive: U.S. to Impose Arms Embargo on South Sudan to End Conflict—Sources." Reuters, February 2, 2018. https://www.reuters.com/article/us-usa-southsudan-arms-exclusive/exclusive-u-s-to-impose-arms-embargo-on-south-sudan-to-end-conflict-sources-idUSKBN1FM0ZE.

Yaqub, Salim. "'Our Declaration of Independence': African Americans, Arab Americans, and the Arab-Israeli Conflict, 1967–1979." *Mashriq and Majhar* 3, no. 1 (2015): 12–29.

Young, Alden. *Transforming Sudan: Decolonisation, Economic Development and State Formation.* Cambridge: Cambridge University Press, 2018.

Zeitvogel, Karin. "US Cancels Meeting with South Sudan Officials." Voice of America, October 7, 2015. https://www.voanews.com/archive/us-cancels-meeting-south-sudan-officials.

Zimmerman, A. *Alabama in Africa: Booker T. Washington, the German Empire, and the Globalization of the New South.* Princeton: Princeton University Press, 2010.

Zink, Jesse A. *Christianity and Catastrophe in South Sudan: Civil War, Migration, and the Rise of Dinka Anglicanism.* Waco, TX: Baylor University Press, 2017.

Index

Note: Page numbers in *italics* refer to illustrations.

Abboud, Ibrahim, 69, 99, 101, 109
'Abd al-Rahim, Muddathir, 69
Adam, Adam, 56–57
Addis Ababa Agreement (1972), 118
Adichie, Chimamanda, 99
African Americans: African liberation and, 92–95; Black Lives Matter, 172–173, 176–180; on goodwill tours, 81; Historically Black Colleges and Universities, 78–79, 175–176; politics of post-emancipation labor, 26–29. *See also* blackness; Hunt-Washington cotton project; internationalism, Black; press, Black; women, African American
African Nationalist Activist Movements, 94
African Repository, 96
African Times and Orient Review (*ATOR*), 47–48
African Union: Bashir and, 141; Darfur crisis and, 149; Obama and, 159, 166; South Sudan independence and, 153
Afro-Asian Conference (Bandung summit), 55, 105
agricultural development, 75–77

aid work: economic, 72–79; social and cultural, 81–90. *See also* Hunt-Washington cotton project
Al-Azhar University, 121
al-Da'in (Darfur) massacre, 124
Algeria, 177
Ali, Dusé Mohamed, 47–48
Ali, Muhammad, 95–96
Ali, Noble Drew, 120–121
Alley, Sabit Abbe, 134–135, 138
Alor, Deng, 160
Alpher, Yossi, 110
Al Sahafa (Sudan), 114–115
American Anti-Slavery Group (AASG), 127–128
American Colonization Society (ACS), 25, 33
American Committee on Africa (ACOA), 93–94
"American Negro Fiction" (Hughes; lecture), 83–85
American Negro Leadership Conference on Africa (ANLCA), 93–94
Amum, Pagan, 166–167
Anglo-Egyptian Agreement (1953), 52

Anglo-Egyptian Condominium: agreement to terminate, 52; Arabness and, 56; banking system, 73; cotton and, 41; educated elite and, 51; North-South division and Southern Policy, 69–70; rule of, 6, 22–23, 46; slavery and, 26, 96–98. *See also* Hunt-Washington cotton project
Anglo-Egyptian Treaty (1899), 46
Ansarulla, 122–123
Anyanya separatists, 112, 123
A. Philip Randolph Institute (APRI), 136–137
Appell, Stephen, 112
Arab-Black dichotomy: in American public imagination, 108; Black Lives Matter and, 178–179; Black press and, 94–95, 98–103; exclusion of Arabs from African art festival, 13–14; Farrakhan and, 135, 137; First Sudanese Civil War and, 99–108; Israel and, 12–13; multiculturalism and, 105; Nation of Islam and, 131–132; oppressor as Northern Arabs vs. Egypt, 92; Second Sudanese Civil War and, 125; Sudan's dual heritage, 3–4
Arabic language, 56
Arab-Israeli conflict: African Americans and, 13; Arab League Summit and, 106; Black Lives Matter and, 178–179; Camp David Accords, 139; enduring proximity of, 140; events of, 108–110
Arab League, 46, 55, 95
Arab League Summit (Khartoum, 1967), 106
Arabness: American conception of, 57; Egypt and, 54–55; Nation of Islam on anti-Arab agenda, 130; Nimeiri and, 71; Pan-Arabism, 55, 71, 105–106; Sudan, Arabism, and, 55–57; Sudan as Arab state, 105–106. *See also* Arab-Black dichotomy
Ashigga (Ashiqqa) Party, 51, 57
Athie, Mohammed, 127
Atlanta Daily World, 59, 98
Atlantic Charter, 51
Austin, Algernon, 9
Azania Liberation Front, 113–114
Azikiwe, Nnamdi, 175

Badri, Malik, 121–122
Bakhita, Josephine, 126–127
Baltimore Sun, 131
Banda, Kamuzu, 175
Bandung summit (Afro-Asian Conference), 55, 105
Ban Ki-Moon, 151
banking system, 73
Barnes, Kenneth C., 33–34
Bashir, Omar al-, 118, 124, 132–134, *133*, 138, 140–141, 159, 170

Benjamin, Barnaba, 165
Ben-Uziel, David, 110
bin Laden, Osama, 139–140
Black Lives Matter (BLM), 172–173, 176–180
blackness: American system of racial categorization, 9–10; bounds of, 8–9; comparison of Sudanese to African Americans, 53, 102, 133; Egyptians and, 57–60; Farrakhan and, 135, 137; Hegel's "true" or "Black" Africa and, 3, 176; international politics and, 10–11; Nation of Islam and, 132–134; race vs., 9–10; shifting US meanings of, 91; Sudanese and, 45–46, 53–54; Sudan recognized as Black, 95; US government and, 103–105. *See also* Arab-Black dichotomy; solidarity, racial
Black Scholar, 112–113
Black-white dynamics, 12
blind education, 80
Bradshaw, Gordon L., 79
Brimmer, Andrew, 44, 72–73, 90–91
British Cotton Growing Association, 28
British Sudan. *See* Anglo-Egyptian Condominium
Broadnax, Madison, 74–79
Broadsky, Phillip, 128
Brown, Michael, 172
Brown, Theodore, 94
Brownback, Sam, 126, 149
Burns, Ocie Romeo, 37, 39–40
Bush, George W., 146, 149

Camp David Accords, 139
Carson, Johnnie, *157*
Carter, Howard, 58
Castro, Fidel, 179–180
Cayton, Horace R., Jr., 45–47, 122–123
Central African Republic, 140
Central Bank of Sudan, 73
Chad, 148–149
Chicago Defender, 53, 59–62, 67, 95, 99–102
Christian Solidarity International (CSI), 125–127, 131
Chukudum Agreement, 136
City Sun (New York), 127–128, 134
civil wars. *See* First Sudanese Civil War; Second Sudanese Civil War; South Sudan
Clarkson, James S., 23–24
Cleveland Gazette, 33–34
Clinton, Bill, 125–126, 146
Clinton, Hillary, 144, 151
Clyburn, James, 125–126
Cohen, Herman J., 146
College of Agriculture, 75–76
Collier's Weekly, 34

colonization schemes, 24–25
Colored American, 96
Communist Party of Sudan, 84
Comprehensive Peace Agreement (CPA), 118, 125, 149–153
Congo, 107, 113
Congo, Democratic Republic of, 139, 140
Congressional Black Caucus, 93, 125–126
Congress on Racial Equality (CORE), 94, 107
Conkey, Frank, 39
Cotton, Samuel, 127–129, 134, 137–138, 141–142
cotton project. *See* Hunt-Washington cotton project
Council on African Affairs (CAA), 50, 93. *See also* International Committee on Africa
Crisis, The, 8, 148
Crockett, William J., 72
Cromer, Evelyn Baring, first Earl of, 26–28, 42–43
Cubans, 179–180
Cullors, Patrisse, 172

Daily Record-Miner (Juneau), 33
Darfur crisis and genocide, 131–133, 138–141, 147–151
Darfur Peace and Accountability Act (US, 2006), 149
Darfur Rebellions, 138
David Project, 128
Davis, Henrietta Vinton, 48
Davis, John Warren, 75, 78, 81
Defalla, Nezeer El, 84–85
Delta Sigma Theta Sorority, 80, 85–88
De Mena, Maymie, 48
Deng, Francis, 3–4
Deng, Valentino Achak, 149–150
dentistry education, 79–80
de Paris, Wilbur, 81
De Paur Chorus, 81–82
Dickman, François M., 74–75
Diggs, Charles, 68
Dinka, 59, 124, 131, 160, 168
Douglass, Frederick, 24–25, 58, 126–127
Du Bois, Shirley Graham, 68
Du Bois, W. E. B., 3, 58, 60, 110

economic aid work, 72–79
Edgard, Mildred, 87
Edmonds, Randolph, 81
education aid, 79–80
Eggers, Dave, 149–150
Egypt: ancient, 58, 144, 181–182; Arab imperialism and, 60–64; Arabness and, 54–55; Bandung summit and, 105; blackness and, 57–60; Israel and, 139–140; Soviet alliance, 69, 71; Sudanese in, 54; union with Sudan, question of, 51
Eibner, John, 125–126
emigration movement: about, 24–25; in Arkansas, 33–34; Garvey and, 48; Hunt, Roosevelt, and, 38; media on, 31–32. *See also* Hunt-Washington cotton project
Essian-Udom, E. U., 121
Ethiopia, 44, 48–49, 105
European Union, 165

famines in Sudan, 124
Farrakhan, Louis Abdul, 117–119, 129–131, 134–142
Fauntroy, Walter, 126
Fax, Elton, 68, 102–105, 106–107
Federal Reserve Central Banking mission, 73
Federation of Pan-African Nationalist Organizations, 94
Fellows, Lawrence, 108
Final Call, 119, 140–141
First Sudanese Civil War (1955–1972): Addis Ababa Agreement (1972), 118; agricultural production disrupted by, 77; Arab-Black binary and, 99–108; Israeli involvement in, 111–115; refugees from, 107; slavery, race, and, 98–99; Sudanese newspapers on Israel and, 114–115; Torit mutiny, 98
Fischbach, Michael R., 13
Fletcher, Bill, Jr., 162–163
Florida A&M University Playmakers Guild, 81
Floyd, George, 176–177
Fortune, T. Thomas, 24–25
Frazer, Jandayi, 146
Freeman (Indianapolis), 35, 37–38, 40
Fur tribe, 138

Garang, John, 118, 123, 125, 130, 146
Garang, Rebecca, 130
Garvey, Amy Ashwood, 48–49
Garvey, Amy Jacques, 48
Garvey, Marcus, 47–48
Garza, Alicia, 172
Gates, Henry Louis, Jr., 5, 181
genocide in Darfur, 131–133, 138–141
Gezira Scheme, 41–42
Ghana, 1–3, 65–66, 105
Ghandour, Ibrahim, 140
Gold Coast, 25
Golden, Oliver, 20–21
goodwill tours, 81
Graduates' General Congress, 51, 56
Grant, Anna Harvin, 86–87
Gration, Scott, 150

Greene, David, 163
Grey River Argus (New Zealand), 35
Grouse, S. Norman, 111–112

Halim, Ahmed Abdul, 84–85
Hall, Bill, 72
Hall, Chatwood (pseud. for Homer Smith), 101–102
Hammond, Ray, 126
Hampton Institute, 53, 74, 79, 175
Hansberry, William Leo, 82–83, 175
Hassoun, Sheikh, 122
Hegel, G. W. F., 3, 176
Height, Dorothy, 93
Helms, Jesse, 126
Henderson, Freddye, 86
Hill, Norman, 136
Historically Black Colleges and Universities (HBCUs), 78–79, 175–176. *See also* Hunt-Washington cotton project
Holmes, Alan, 73
Holmes, Julius C., 104
Houser, George, 93
Howard University, 80–83, 85, 175
Hughes, Langston, 83–85
Hunt, Leigh S. J., 19, 21–22, 41–42, 175. *See also* Hunt-Washington cotton project
Hunter, Charlayne, 86
Huntsville Times, 155
Hunt-Washington cotton project: background, 19–23; Cromer's report, 26–28; emigration schemes, colonization movement, and, 24–25; Hunt's arrival in Sudan, 28–29; Hunt's early planning and Roosevelt, 23–24; implications, 42–44; malaria and returns to US, 39–42; media coverage, 30–35, 37–38; Sudan Experimental Plantations Syndicate, 34–41; Sudan Plantations Syndicate, 41–42; Washington enlisted, 29–30

Idris, Amir, 56
Igga, James Wani, 166–167
Ijoma, Diane, 175
India: African Americans and, 10–11
Innis, Roy, 107
International Committee on Africa (ICA), 50, 74, 78–79
International Criminal Court (ICC), 138
internationalism, Black: Italian invasion of Ethiopia and, 44, 64; rise of, 47–50, 52; Washington and, 20
internet, 177–178
Isa, Imam, 122–123
Islam, African American, 120–123. *See also* Nation of Islam

Israel: African Americans and, 13–14; Du Bois and Prattis in, 110; formation of modern state, 108–109; positive and negative views in Black press, 111–114; Sudan ties with, 109, 139–140. *See also* Arab-Israeli conflict
Italy, 44, 48–49

Jabir, Jabir al-Ahmad al-, 106
Jacobs, Charles, 127–128
Jamaica, 26
Jet, 74, 78, 87–88, 148
Johnson, Lyndon, 71
Johnson, Veronica, 111

Kaepernick, Colin, 180
Kane, Gregory, 131
Kennedy, John F., 71
Kerry, John, 161–162, 164, 168
Kessel, Joseph, 97
Khalifa, al-Sirr al-, 71
Kiir, Salva, 146, 152, 159–162, 166–167
King, Martin Luther, Jr., 2, 93, 110–111, 114, 121, 154–155
Kirk, Ron, 157
Kitchen, Martha, 74, 78
Kitchen, Robert, 74–75, 77–79, 175
Kitchener, Herbert, 96
Kush, 5, 173, 181–182
Kutla as-Suda (the Black Bloc), 57
Kuwait, 106

Lang, John, 23
Lantos, Tom, 139
Lawson, James R., 112
Levinson, Richard, 112
Lewthwaite, Gilbert A., 131
Liberia, 24, 33–34, 105
Libya, 95, 105–106, 131, 162, 177
London News, 96
Los Angeles Times, 108
Lubin, Alex, 13
Luo, 6, 143–144, 169
Lwoki, Benjamin, 90–91
Lyman, Princeton, 152

Machar, Riek, 160–162, 166–167
Mack, James, 82–85, 88
Mack, Marjorie, 82–83
Madison, Joe, 126, 147–148, 163
Mahdi, Abdul Rahman Mohammed Ahmed el, 60–62, 61, 133
Mahdi, Al-Hadi al-, 122
Mahdi, Ishag el, 84–85
Mahdi, Muhammad Ahmad ("the Madhi"), 22, 96, 98–99, 122–123
Mahdi, Sadiq al-, 71, 124

Mahdism, 22, 60–61, 96
Mahgoub, Muhammad, 106
Mahjub, Muhammad Ahmad, 71
Majid, Satti, 120–121
Major, Gerri, 87
Makar, Ashley, 155–156
Maker, Makur, 175
malaria, 39–42
Malcolm X, 68, 117, 121–123, 179–180
Malwal, Bona, 135–138
Mamphilly, Zachariah, 152–153, 155
Mandela, Nelson, 179
Manibe, Kosti, 160
Manning, Patrick, 3, 6
Mardenborough, John, 33
Martin, Louis, 67
Martin, Trayvon, 172
Masaslit tribe, 138
Matin, Le, 97
Mboro, Clement, 99
McCaw, Arthur, 80, 86–88
McCaw, Valaria, 80, 86–88
McCray, George F., 59
McDonough, Denis, 151–152
McEvers, Kelly, 167
Mfume, Kweisi, 147–148
Miami Herald, 179–180
Miniclier, C. C., 108
Ministry of Agriculture, 75–77
Montgomery (AL) Advertiser, 33
Moorish Science Temple (MST), 120–121
Morehouse College, 74, 82, 175
Morning News (Sudan), 103
Morris, Lorenzo, 170
Morrow, E. Frederic, 1–3
Muhammad, Abdul Akbar, 141
Muhammad, Akbar, 127–129, 131–132, 139
Muhammad, Askia, 132–133
Muhammad, Elijah, 117–118, 121
Muhammad, Jehron, 140–141
Muhammad, W. D. Fard, 121
Muhammad Speaks, 102
Muslim Brotherhood, 71, 84, 140
Mutume, James, 130
My Sister's Keeper, 126

Namibia, 62–63
Nasser, Gamal Abdel, 55, 71, 105–106
National Association for the Advancement of Colored People (NAACP), 8, 148
nationalism: African, 76, 79; Black, 47, 93, 117, 121–122; Egyptian, 55; pan-Arab, 110; Sudanese, 51, 56
National Newspaper Publishers Association, 130
National Urban League, 111

Nation of Islam (NOI): about, 117–118, 121; anti-Zionism of, 127–129, 139; Farrakhan and, 117–119, 129–131, 134–142; *Final Call*, 119, 130–133, 140–141; Muhammad's defense against Jacobs, 127–129; *Muhammad Speaks*, 102; strategy and rhetorical approach to Sudan, 119, 142
N'djamena Humanitarian Ceasefire Agreement (2004), 138
"Negro Speaks of Rivers, The" (Hughes), 84
Negro World, 48, 52
New Journal and Guide, 79, 95
newspapers, Black. *See* press, Black
New York Amsterdam News, 79–81, 85–86, 97, 107, 111–112
New York Globe, 96
New York Times, 107–108, 127, 134
New York World, 38
Nimeiri, Jaafar, 71, 106, 139–140
Nixon, Richard, 1–2
Nkrumah, Kwame, 1–2, 65–66, 175
Noble, Jeanne L., 86–87
North Africa, 3, 13–14, 176–177
Nubia, ancient, 5–6, 12, 101, 173, 181–182
Nuer, 59, 124, 160

Obama, Barack, *148*; Darfur crisis and, 147–151; East Africa tour and African Union address (2015), 165–166; first term, 150–159; life and family background, 6, 143–144; Susan Page as ambassador to South Sudan, 145, 156–158, 161–163; presidential campaign (2008), 149–150; recognition of South Sudan, 153–155; second term, 159; in Selma, AL, 144; as Senator, 147–149; silence on race, 145, 169–170; South Sudanese Civil War and, 159–169; South Sudan nation-building and, 156–159; South Sudan referendum and, 151–153; UN arms embargo on South Sudan and, 168–169. *See also* Rice, Susan
October Revolution (1964), 99
oil, 129, 139, 157
Omar, Ahmed, 104
Oregonian, 32–33
Our Families Protection Association, 94

Padmore, George, 59, 61–62, 133
Page, Clarence, 134, 137–138
Page, Susan, 145, 156–158, *158*, 161–163
Palestinian National Liberation Movement, 13
Palestinians, 106, 139–140, 178–179. *See also* Arab-Israeli conflict
Palmer, Joseph, II, 72
Pan-African Congress, 30
Pan-African festival, 13–14

Pan-Africanism, 5, 11–12, 145, 174
Pan-Africanist Student Organization for Black Unity (SOBU), 113–114
Pan-Arabism, 55, 71, 105–106
Parks, Rosa, 121
Paul, Nykhor, 171–173
Payne, Donald, 126
Pharaohs, Black, 5
Philadelphia Tribune, 52–53, 97, 111
Philippines, 24–25
Pittsburgh Courier: on Arab-Black dichotomy, 95; Cayton in, 45–47; on Delta Sigma Theta tour, 86; on First Sudanese Civil War, 107; McCaw in, 80; Prattis in, 62–64, 133; on slave traffic, 97; on Sudanese blackness, 52–54; Weston in, 59–60
Plaindealer (Topeka), 31
Powell, Adam Clayton, Jr., 72, 93
Powell, Colin, 146, *157*
Powell, John P., 35–37, 39–40
Power, Samantha, 168
Prashad, Vijay, 11
Prattis, Percival, 53–54, 58–59, 62–64, 110, 133, 135, 175
President's Special International Program for Cultural Presentations, 81
press, Black: about, 7–8; Arab-Black racial dichotomy in, 94–95; Arab-Israeli conflict and, 108, 111–115; boom of, 47; on Egyptian rule of Sudan as Arab imperialism, 60–64; on Egyptian-Sudanese relationship as racial, 57–60; First Sudanese Civil War and, 107; on Hunt-Washington cotton project, 31–34; on Sudanese blackness, 45–46, 52–54; on US diplomacy and aid activity, 78–79. *See also specific writers and newspapers by name*
Price, Ned, 167
pump irrigation system, 41

Quashee syndrome stereotype, 26

Radcliffe, Kendahl, 20
Rakowsky, Jan, 128
Randolph, A. Philip, 93, 136
Reed, William, 140
refugees, 107, 171–172
Rice, Condoleeza, 146
Rice, Susan, *147*, *157*; on arms embargo, 168–169; career of, 145–147, 159; Darfur crisis and, 150–151; NPR interview, 167; silence on race, 169–170; South Sudanese Civil War and, 159, 161–162, 164, 166–168; South Sudan referendum and, 151–152; *Tough Love*, 159–160
Riddle, Sam, 179

Roberts, George, 35
Robeson, Eslanda Goode, 49–50
Robeson, Paul, 49–50
Robinson, Eloise, 49
Robinson, Randall, 134, 138
Rogers, Harold S., 112–113
Rogers, J. A. (Joel Augustus), 52–53, 58, 97
Rolandsen, Øystein H., 160
Rone, Jemera, 124
Roosevelt, Theodore, 23–26, 38, 42–43
Root, The, 152–153
Rosenberg, Jonathan, 8, 10
Rustin, Bayard, 136

Sadat, Anwar, 139–140
Salguero, Armando, 179–180
sanctions: on South Sudan, 165, 168–169; on Sudan, 146, 150–151
Save Darfur: Rally to Stop Genocide (2006), 147–148
Schuyler, George, 60, 64, 98
Seattle Times, 30–31
Second Sudanese Civil War (1983–2005): Arab-Black binary and, 132–134; beginnings of, 118; Black Christian solidarity with southern Sudan, 125–128; Black Sudanese responses to Farrakhan, 134–138; Darfur genocide, 131–133, 138–141; Darfur Rebellions, 138; end of, 145–146; events of, 123–125; Farrakhan's support for the government, 118, 129–131; Islamization and sharia, 123; jihad, 118, 124; Nation of Islam's anti-Zionism and, 127–129; slavery during, 124–138, 141–142
Sefa-Nyarko, Clement, 160
Selassie, Haile, 48, 82–83
Self-Government Statute, 51–52
Senghor, Leopold, 13–14
Shambat Institute of Agriculture, 75–77
Sharpton, Al, 126, 147–148
Sharrieff, Bayyinah (Christine Wilson), 102
Simmonds, Mark, 165
Slate, Nico, 11
slavery: First Civil War and racial view of, 98–99; Muslims on trans-Atlantic slave ships, 120; Second Sudanese Civil War and Nation of Islam denials of, 124–138, 141–142; in Sudan, 23, 26, 95–98; US-Sudan connection, claimed, 46, 54
Smith, Homer (pen name Chatwood Hall), 101–102
Smith, Poindexter, 35–37, 39–40
social and cultural aid work, 81–90
social media, Black, 172, 177–178
solidarity, racial: Arabs and, 107, 115–116; Black internationalism and, 47–50, 52; as

fluid and capricious construction, 173; forms of, 12–13; geopolitical landscape and politics of, 179; Hunt and, 32; Israel and, 92; al-Mahdi and, 61–62; Nation of Islam and, 130, 133, 138, 140; Obama's silence on, 145, 169–170; Pan-Africanism and, 5, 13–14; print media and, 141–142; problematic of, 180; religion and, 125–127; Washington's silence on, 40–41, 43–44. *See also* Nation of Islam; press, Black
South Africa: apartheid and African Americans, 62–63, 93; apartheid and Sudanese, 115; Makar on, 155; Namibia, occupation of, 62–63; Washington and, 40–41
Southern Christian Leadership Conference, 154–155
Southern Union Party, 70
South Sudan: civil war, 159–169; independence and US recognition, 153–156; map, *154*; National Security Service Act, 164; nation-building, 156–158; Page as US ambassador to, 145, 156–158, *158*, 161–163; referendum, 151–153; sanctions on, 165, 168–169; US aid to, 156–157; US embassy in, *157*, 161–162
Soviet Union, 69, 71
Spurlock, Lewis Nathaniel, 37
State Department, US: Black people in, 71–72; embassy in South Sudan, *157*, 161–162; Farrakhan on, 131; goodwill tours, 81; Page as US ambassador to South Sudan, 145, 156–158, *158*, 161–163; understanding of Sudan, 102–105
St. Louis Globe-Democrat, 31–32
Student Nonviolent Coordinating Committee, 13, 111, 113
Sudan: dual Arab and African heritage, 3–4; history of, 5–6, 22–23; independence of, 6, 46, 51–52; map at independence, *70*; multiculturalism in, 105; sanctions on, 146, 150–151. *See also* Anglo-Egyptian Condominium
Sudan Democratic Gazette, 136
Sudan Experimental Plantations Syndicate. *See* Hunt-Washington cotton project
Sudan People's Armed Forces, 123
Sudan People's Liberation Movement/Army (SPLM/A), 118, 123–124, 134, 136, 145–146, 152, 160
Sudan Plantations Syndicate, Ltd. (SPS), 41–42. *See also* Hunt-Washington cotton project
Sudan Times, 136
Suez Canal, 46, 109–110
Sunday Leader (Port Townsend), 34

Through Black Eyes (Fax), 103
Time, 108
Todman, Terence, 71
Togoland, 20, 30
Tometi, Opal, 172
Torit mutiny, 98
Toynbee, Arnold, 58
Trenton Evening Times, 31
Triplett, Cain, 35–37, 39–40
Trump, Donald, 170, 172, 174
Tunisia, 177
Turabi, Hassan al-, 140
Turco-Egyptian Sudan, 22
Turner, Henry McNeal, 24
Tuskegee Institute, 29, 44, 175. *See also* Hunt-Washington cotton project
Tuskegee Student, 37
Tutankhamen, 58
Twitty, J. Brown, 37, 39–40

Uganda, 113, 139, 140
Umma Party, 51, 57, 136
United Nations: Obama's first General Assembly speech, 151; peacekeepers in South Sudan, 168; protests at, 107, 163; resolutions, 109, 149; Rice as ambassador to, 145; sanctions on South Sudan, 165, 168–169; Security Council delegation to Sudan, 152
United States: anti-Islamic legislative efforts, 174; Bush (G. W.) administration, 146; Congressional Black Caucus, 93, 125–126; Darfur Peace and Accountability Act (2006), 149; early Sudan-US relations, 69–72; embassy in South Sudan, *157*, 161–162; power, US, 7; understanding of Sudan, 103–105. *See also* Obama, Barack; Rice, Susan; State Department, US
Universal Negro Improvement Association (UNIA), 48
University of Khartoum, 79–80, 83–85
US Agency for International Development (USAID), 69, 72, 74–79
US Information Agency (USIA), 69, 72, 82
US Information Service (USIS), 104

Vigilant (Khartoum), 136

Walkley, R. Barrie, *157*
Ward, Samuel Ringgold, 58
Washington, Booker T., *29*; African affairs, involvement in, 30; Black internationalism and, 20; Cayton and, 45; Hunt-Washington cotton project and, 29–31, 34–43; Pan-Africanist views of, 19; silence on Sudan and the Sudanese, 40–41, 43–44

Washington Informer, 162–163
Washington Post, 108, 164
Wells, William, 58
Weston, Hugh, 59–60, 64
What Is the What (Eggers and Deng), 149–150
Wheeler, Oliver, 73
White-Hammond, Gloria, 126
whiteness and Arabness, 54–55, 57
Wiesel, Eli, 139
Williams, F. A., 79
Williams, W. Kenneth, 80
Wilson, Christine (Bayyinah Sharrieff), 102
Wingate, Reginald, 28, 42–43
Wisconsin Weekly Advocate, 96

women, African American, 48–49. *See also specific women by name*
Worcester (MA) Daily Spy, 31
World Black and African Festival of Arts and Culture (FESTAC), 14
World Festival of Negro Arts, 13–14

Yergan, Max, 50
Young, Whitney, Jr., 111
Youth for Africa Foundation, 141

Zaghawa tribe, 138
Zamir, Zvi, 110
Zanders, Roosevelt, 80
Zionist movement, 13–14, 127–129, 139

Printed in the USA
CPSIA information can be obtained
at www.ICGtesting.com
CBHW021508240524
9058CB00017B/68/J